William Henry Thomes

Lewey and I or Sailor boys wanderings

William Henry Thomes

Lewey and I or Sailor boys wanderings

ISBN/EAN: 9783743339163

Manufactured in Europe, USA, Canada, Australia, Japa

Cover: Foto ©ninafisch / pixelio.de

Manufactured and distributed by brebook publishing software (www.brebook.com)

William Henry Thomes

Lewey and I or Sailor boys wanderings

LEWEY AND I

OR

SAILOR BOYS' WANDERINGS

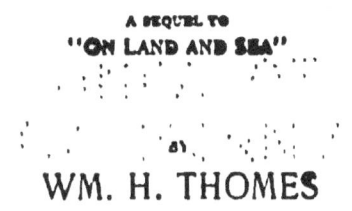

A SEQUEL TO
"ON LAND AND SEA"

BY

WM. H. THOMES

Author of "The Ocean Rovers," "The Bushrangers," "Running the Blockade," "On Land and Sea," "The Belle of Australia," "A Manila Romance," "A Slaver's Adventures," "A Goldhunter's Adventures," "A Whaleman's Adventures," "The Goldhunters in Europe and "Daring Deeds."

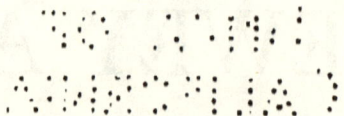

Copyright, MDCCCLXXXIV, by WM. H. THOMES

Copyright, 1892, by LAIRD & LEE

(LEWIS AND L.)

To Worshipful Brother

CAPTAIN ALBERT A. FOLSOM,

SUPERINTENDENT OF THE BOSTON AND PROVIDENCE RAILROAD,

THIS BOOK OF ADVENTURES IN CALIFORNIA, DURING THE MEXICAN

WAR, IS RESPECTFULLY DEDICATED, WITH FRATERNAL

GREETING, BY THE AUTHOR,

WM. H. THOMES.

OPIE READ'S
GREAT
Character Novels

25c — RETAIL PRICE — 25c

"TURKEY EGG" GRIFFIN
A striking romance of love and chivalry. A masterpiece in character delineation.

THE HARKRIDERS
Opie Read's masterpiece. A most fascinating romance, bubbling over with the author's quaint humor. Among the scenes is a fox hunt graphically described.

THE STARBUCKS
A charming love story. Rich in unconscious drollery, with tender touches of pathos. Its characters true to life. One of the most delightful romances of modern times.

THE JUCKLINS
One of Mr. Read's very brightest and most humorous stories.

THE CARPETBAGGER
By OPIE READ and FRANK PIXLEY. Dramatized and played with great success.

OLD EBENEZER
"Mr. Read's new story is fully as capable of successful dramatization as was 'The Jucklins.'" — *Chicago Tribune.*

MY YOUNG MASTER
"We fancy this book will become recognized as his masterpiece, as a classic of the ante-bellum period." — *Commercial Traveler's Home Magazine.*

A KENTUCKY COLONEL
This is one of the most beautifully written and the most striking in character, as well as the most thrilling and chaste, pieces of fiction ever written.

A TENNESSEE JUDGE
This is a thorough delineation of certain phases of public life. It is a supreme character sketch and an unusually interesting story.

ON THE SUWANEE RIVER
The characters in this story are strongly drawn and full of interest.

THE COLOSSUS
Pronounced by an eminent literary critic to be "the most delightful romance of modern production."

EMMETT BONLORE
The story combines the strong qualities of Opie Read's style, and is full of action, incident and humor.

LEN GANSETT
"No one can read the book without being bettered." — *American Commercial Traveler.*

THE TEAR IN THE CUP and Other Stories
Many of these are world wide in fame, and every one has some startling denouement. They are typical American stories.

THE WIVES OF THE PROPHET
The theme, the plot, and the style of this remarkable story have no counterpart in American literature.

For sale everywhere, or sent postpaid, on receipt of price, by

LAIRD & LEE, PUBLISHERS, 263-265 WABASH AVENUE, **CHICAGO**

CONTENTS.

CHAPTER I.

SAN DIEGO IN 1846. — AN OLD SEAMAN'S PROTEST. — DON ANTONIO SANCHOS, OF SAN FRANCISCO, AND HIS SCARRED HAND. — A FORENOON'S SPORT. — OUR DOG JACK AND THE TURTLE. — CAPTAIN FITCH EXPRESSES HIS OPINION IN FORCIBLE TERMS — A MYSTERIOUS SHOT. — THE EXHIBITION, AND HOW IT WAS INTERRUPTED.

CHAPTER II.

DON ANTONIO SANCHOS CREATES A SENSATION. — HE CHARGES ME WITH BEING A SPY, AND AN ENEMY OF CALIFORNIA. — AN APPEAL TO THE ALCALDA. — SCOTCH JACK IS FULL OF FIGHT AND AGUARDIENTE. — THE CALABOZO. — A LITTLE LOVE-MAKING. — AN OATH OF ALLEGIANCE. — THE BLOW, AND SANCHOS THREATS. — A PLAN FOR ESCAPE.

CHAPTER III.

LEWEY MAKES LOVE, AND QUITE SUCCESSFULLY. — DON SANCHOS PAYS US A VISIT, AND IS CAUGHT IN A TRAP. — A GALLANT FIGHT IN WHICH OUR DOG TAKES PART. — ESCAPE FROM THE CALABOZO. — A VISIT TO THE HIDE-HOUSE BY THE MEXICANS. — AN ATTACK, AND A DEFEAT. — THE SOIREE WHICH JACK GAVE. — INDIGNANT SAILORS AND KANAKAS. — THE FIRE. — A RETROSPECTION.

CHAPTER IV.

PREPARATIONS FOR A LONG JOURNEY. — FAREWELL TO SAN DIEGO. — EN ROUTE TO RANCHE REFUGIO. — A VAQUERO AND BULL. — THE LONELY ADOBE HOUSE, AND A PRAIRIE-FLOWER. — THE MOUNTAIN LION. — LEWEY IS AGAIN IN LOVE. — AN INTERRUPTION TO A MIDNIGHT COURTSHIP. — THE THREAT. — WILD INDIANS ON THE TRAIL.

CHAPTER V.

THE APACHE ATTACK. — PAINTED WARRIORS, AND THEIR CHARGE. — DEATH TO THE INDIANS. — RETURN TO THE RANCHE. — THE GOVERNMENT COURIER. — A HORSE TRADE. — OUR JOURNEY RESUMED. — THE FEAST OF THE BUZZARDS AND COYOTES. — TROUT FISHING — RANCHE VALLECITO. — A PROPOSITION. — THE NIGHT CAMP, AND A STARTLING APPARITION.

CHAPTER VI.

A SURPRISED GREETING. — A MIDNIGHT VISITOR. — AN ANGRY BEAR. — AN OWL'S HOOT. — A BAND OF WARRIORS. — THE CHIEF'S COMMANDS. — ESCAPING WITH OUR SCALPS. — THE SULPHUR SPRING AND PATH. — THE RANCHERO'S FEARS. — THE NIGHT CAMP AT THE FOOT OF THE MOUNTAINS. — THE PROWLING LION. — HOMESICKNESS. — A STRANGE MEETING. — THE LONELY CANYON. — LOS ANGELES. — DON SANCHOS APPEARS.

Contents.

CHAPTER VII.

DON ANTONIO SANCHOS MAKES IT UNPLEASANT, AND ACCUSES US OF MURDERING THE GOVERNMENT COURIER. — TO THE CALABOZO. — AN EXAMINATION, AND SURPRISE. — HEROES OF THE DAY. — WANTED FOR THE ARMY. — OFF FOR SANTA BARBARA, AND INCIDENTS ON THE WAY. — THE CAVALRY, AND ITS HURRIED MARCH. — SANTA BARBARA, AND SOME OLD ACQUAINTANCES. — RANCHE REFUGIO, AND OUR RECEPTION BY A STRONG-MINDED WOMAN.

CHAPTER VIII.

A MUTUAL AGREEMENT. — AN OLD ACQUAINTANCE. — THE RANCHE. — A FANDANGO, AND AN UNEXPECTED MEETING. — A GRAND SURPRISE TO ALL. — DON ANTONIO SANCHOS PUTS IN AN APPEARANCE. — A STRUGGLE FOR LIFE. — A DISAPPOINTED GREASER. — ON THE MARCH. — A SWIFT EXECUTION. — A LADY'S GRATITUDE. — A NEW PROGRAMME. — THE ESCORT AND ENCAMPMENT.

CHAPTER IX.

A BRUSH WITH LADRONES. — A YOUNG LADY'S MODE OF EXPRESSING THANKS. — THE PEON'S MURDER. — A LONG CONFESSION. — ON THE MOUNTAIN SIDE. — THE TRAPPERS. — MONTEREY ONCE MORE. — DON SANCHOS RECEIVES A BLOW. — THE AMERICAN CONSUL EXPRESSES AN OPINION. — AGREEABLE QUARTERS. — AN EARTHQUAKE, AND A TUMULT. — AN INTERVIEW WITH GENERAL CASTRO. — ANTONIO AND CARLOS SANCHOS ARE SNUBBED. — A DANGEROUS MISSION TO CAPTAIN FREMONT.

CHAPTER X.

CAPTAIN FREMONT'S CAMP. — THE MESSAGES AND DESPATCHES. — A NIGHT SCENE AROUND A FIRE. — THE COYOTES' CALL. — THE LETTERS FOR GENERAL CASTRO AND MR. LARKIN. — INSTRUCTIONS. — ON THE TRAIL. — THE INDIAN WOMAN. — THE CAVALRY SQUAD. — THE SEARCH FOR LETTERS. — GENERAL CASTRO IS SURPRISED. — LEWEY TELLS SOME STORIES. — STORMING THE CAMP. — FISHING IN A FOG. — THE AMERICAN FRIGATE. — SPIES ON ALL SIDES. — A FRIENDLY WARNING.

CHAPTER XI.

THE ATTACK ON THE HOUSE AND ITS REPULSE. — EDWARDO SANCHOS MEETS A JUST FATE. — THE RESCUING PARTY FROM THE FRIGATE CUMBERLAND. — A WINDFALL OF GOLD. — THE BREAKFAST. — A PREDICTION. — HOISTING THE AMERICAN FLAG AT MONTEREY. — A LAST VIEW OF THE TOWN. — ON THE MARCH. — TERRIBLE DEATH OF TWO WOMEN AND A SPEEDY EXECUTION. — A NIGHT SCENE ON THE BEACH.

CHAPTER XII.

I BID SENORA COSTELLO FAREWELL, AND HAVE NO COMMENTS TO MAKE. — THE MARCH TO LOS ANGELES. — THE BATTLE AND ITS RESULTS. — ON THE ROUTE TO SAN DIEGO. — A LUCKY FIND OF GOLD. — A DISAPPOINTMENT ALL ROUND. — SAN DIEGO. — SCOTCH JACK GIVES US A RECEPTION. — A UNITED STATES FLEET. — OFF FOR MAZATLAND. — HOME AT LAST. — LEWEY'S BEAUTIFUL SISTER. — A HAPPY LIFE AND A DARK CLOUD. — THE END.

LEWEY AND I;

OR,

SAILOR BOYS' WANDERINGS.

CHAPTER I.

SAN DIEGO IN 1846. — AN OLD SEAMAN'S PROTEST. — DON ANTONIO SANCHOS, OF SAN FRANCISCO, AND HIS SCARRED HAND. — A FORENOON'S SPORT. — OUR DOG JACK AND THE TURTLE. — CAPTAIN FITCH EXPRESSES HIS OPINION IN FORCIBLE TERMS — A MYSTERIOUS SHOT. — THE EXHIBITION, AND HOW IT WAS INTERRUPTED.

IT will be remembered that the ship Admittance had sailed from San Diego, California, for Boston, in January, 1846, and left the French lad, Lewey, and myself at the hide-house, on the beach, having been discharged, and paid off, by Captain Peterson, at our own request. We had simulated severe sickness, in the shape of smallpox, so successfully, that even the quack doctor of the town had been deceived, as well as the officers of the vessel. In my previous work, "ON LAND AND SEA," I have fully pictured Lewey's unhappiness, as well as my own, when we saw the old ship leave the harbor, and pile on studding-sails, alow and aloft, as she passed Point Loma, and shaped her course — about south by west — for Cape Horn and home. For a long time I refused to be comforted, and even Lewey's sunny nature, encouraging words, cheerful smiles, and glowing pictures of the happy lives we should lead as free, roving rancheros, husbands of Engracia and Anita, could not lift the weight of sorrow from my heart, as I thought of home, relatives, and what a fool I had made of myself in remaining at San Diego, with strangers for friends, and no one to care for our future welfare except an old shipmate, — Scotch Jack, — who had charge of the hide-house, and Captain Fitch, a merchant of the town, our treasurer and guardian for the time being, a very clever man, but who had cares enough of his own to attend to without bestowing much thought on two comparatively unknown sailor boys, who were not supposed to have position or influence at home, and were classed with the usual run of beach-combers, we supposed, for I did not know at the time that my old master had made a very pronounced report to Mr. Fitch in my behalf, and, perhaps, gave me a better reputation than I had reason to expect, or deserved. Of Lewey he knew nothing, and so had merely stated that the French boy was smart, active, and impudent, at times, and likely to lead a good lad, like myself, into trouble, unless a little advice was given me at stated periods, when it was supposed I should need it most.

Had I been Lewey's brother he could not have treated me more tenderly, or done more to make me forget the unfortunate position in which I was placed, through his skillful inducements and persuasions to remain in California, and link our fortunes with those of two dark-haired, dark eyed young females, who were not even on a level with the sailor boys, which we chanced to be, as neither of the girls had the slightest claims to an education, and could not read nor write even a word of the musical language which they spoke so rapidly, if not grammatically. But they were handsome, and had the most willowy and graceful forms of any girls of their class on the coast, and we loved them with all of a boy's ardor and passionate nature, and were willing to forsake homes and relatives for the sake of enjoying their companionship, to be with them, and pass our days in idleness, riding horseback over ranches, and rounding in our cattle, in imagination, when we wanted a little pleasant excitement, aside from fandangos and cock-fighting.

Lewey saw that he had made a mistake, but he did not let it appear, either on his face or in his conversation. To me he represented everything as rose colored, and that there was no occasion for anxiety, or care for the future. There were brilliant prospects before us, he said, love, happiness, and wealth, and what more could we wish on our part? We were now our own masters, and could do as we pleased, go where we desired, and need care for no one, as long as we remained honest, and treated all with respect, and consideration befitting their rank.

Notwithstanding all of Lewey's eagerness to make my position a pleasant one, I could not prevent tears from flowing every time I was alone, or after I had turned into my bunk for the night, and many a hearty crying spell did I indulge in during the long and dreary hours of the rainy season, when the floods descended upon the roof of the hide-house, and the wind swept in mournful cadence over the solitary bay, as there was no vessel at anchor in the harbor, all having left the port for the northern part of the coast, in search of hides and tallow.

More than a dozen times did I find Lewey on the beach, all alone, smoking his short black pipe, and looking toward the ocean, as though watching for the old ship, hoping that something had happened to her, and thus cause her return for repairs. But the French lad, as soon as he saw that I noted his dejection, would brighten up, and let a smile pass over his handsome face, as though he were the happiest boy in the country, and cared nothing for home or friends. He would fling at me a gay jeu d'esprit, or witty saying, and ask me what I thought Engracia or Anita might do when they saw us at their home, with our pockets full of dollars, and love and admiration in our hearts. But I knew that Lewey suffered in his mind as well as myself, only he concealed his emotions better than I could, and was not so faint-hearted under adverse circumstances. He strove to cheer me when he needed words of encouragement himself, poor fellow, and I have no doubt but that his pillow was wet with tears as often as my own, only he was too manly to confess his weakness, or make me a confidant of his anxiety.

One forenoon, about a week after the Admittance had sailed for home, and when we had exhausted the resources of the hide-houses, by borrowing all the books, and reading them, to be found on the beach, time hung heavily on our hands, as we did not want to start on our long journey by land for Ranche Refugio, on account of the severe rains at that season of the year, rendering travel extremely unpleasant, Lewey and I sat down to breakfast, in company with Scotch Jack and a kanaka, the others having been discharged when the ship sailed, as there was no work for them, only about one thousand hides being in the house, and two men could cure them in time for shipment, during the spells of sunshine, which did come once in a while in the wet season.

"Boys," said Jack, as he helped himself to a bountiful supply of beefsteak, and then to a pot of coffee, " what plans have you made for the future? You don't mean to remain anchored in this bloody hole all your lives, do you? "

"Are you tired of our company, Jack? " and, with a faint suspicion that such might be the case, I asked the question a little eagerly.

" No, boys," was the ready answer. " I don't tire of good company so easily. Besides, the old man left orders to keep you just as long as you desired to remain. But you had some object in leaving the ship, and I wants to know what it is."

" We mean to get married, and settle down on a ranche," I answered, and then a sniff of deep contempt passed over the weather-beaten, rugged face of the old salt, and he uttered a strong expletive, and said, —

'Well, of all the young greenhorns and fools that I ever seed, you is the wusser!"

" Vy?" asked Lewey, as he filled his pipe, preparatory for a smoke, and glanced at my face, to see how the announcement affected me.

" 'Cos, how does you think your people would like it if you married a bloody greaser?" and the master of the hide-house uttered a deep sniff of disgust as he looked at us and a half-caste Indian woman, who was wandering along the beach, seeking to attract the notice of some kanakas who were at work on hides in the premises adjoining our own. " They is all alike," Jack continued, when he noticed that the female had retraced her steps toward the town, followed by the hooting yells of the natives of the Sandwich Islands. " Would I marry a greaser?" he asked, quite severely.

As we did not know we remained discreetly silent.

" Look at me," Jack said. " I 'm an old, battered sailor-man, but there 's Scotch blood in my veins, and a true son of old Scotland never disgraces his name."

Considering that Jack got drunk as often as he had a chance, we thought this boasting a little premature, although the man was as honest a person as there was in California at the time.

" Look at my face," the old sailor said, "and tell me what for should I want a wife?"

It was a hard-looking face, all seamed and blackened by exposure to hot suns and heavy gales, and we did not imagine for a moment that a woman would be likely to fall in love with it, unless there was wealth to back it, and Jack was not rich in worldly goods, as he was dependent upon his fifteen dollars per month for support, and a shot in the locker for old age.

" No," the sailor continued, as soon as he had got his pipe well under way, " a man is best off without a wife, for what could I do with one if I was disposed to marry? Take my advice, and keep single, like me, and when you come to my years and wisdom, splice a white woman, and one of your kind, and see to it that she has a little property to fall back upon, when you takes a short vige for the sake of peace and quietness, which you can't always have at home if you is married. But no greaser for me, boys, and none for you, if my advice is followed."

"But ve loves de girls," pleaded Lewey. "Dey is sich nice ones, and dey loves us so much dat dey vould die for us if ve vanted dem to."

"Bah!" was the contemptuous expression. "Don't you believe yerself. They all say that, and then sell you out at the first chance they gets. Think of your friends, and of your future, and let the women alone, if you knows what is good for yerself."

This was kind advice, and worthy of a man of better position than Scotch Jack, and we should have done well to have heeded it, but boys in love never think that their advisers and elders know anything, so of course we did not change our opinion on the subject that was nearest our hearts.

"If I supposed for a moment that you lads was goin' to make fools of yerselves, blank me if I would n't clap you in irons, and keep you on bread and water till I 'd starved the nonsense all out of you, that 's what I 'd do."

We laughed at the words, for Jack did not possess the power to carry his threat into execution, as there were no irons on the beach, and I doubt if there were handcuffs at San Diego, as lashings of rawhide were employed to bind refractory Indians, or thieving Mexicans of the lower class, if one should be arrested accidentally, and held for trial.

As Jack uttered the last ominous words, our dog, the lively little fellow we had bought and trained a year or two before, and kept on board the Admittance until we were removed to the shore, with pretended symptoms of the smallpox, uttered several ominous growls, got up from under the table, and walked toward the door, sniffing and barking.

"Some greaser is near the house," said the Scotchman. "You can always tell by Jack's movements. He do so hate a Mexican; one of the thieving class."

Our dog Jack, ever since the noted fight with the vaquero's mastiff, had a great antipathy to the poorer class of Mexicans, and never allowed one to venture near the hide-house until he had uttered a protest.

As we drew back from the table, for the purpose of going to the door, and seeing who approached our premises, a tall, lank, swarthy Mexican, with serape around his shoulders, and broad-brimmed sombrero on his head, covering a shock of thick black hair that had never known brush or comb, darkened the entrance of our house, and stood for a moment at the threshhold, gazing at us and the dog, as though he did not know which was the most dangerous, for Jack was sniffing at his heels, and had not quite made up his mind from what part of the greaser's body he should take a mouthful, and the Mexican seemed disposed to kick the dog, or else assail him with the long knife that he carried in a sheath in his leggings.

"Come here, Jack," I said in a stern tone, and the little bull dog obeyed, but did so reluctantly, and, while retreating to his quarters, under the table, uttered indignant protests, in the shape of savage growls.

"Buenos dias, caballeros," the new-comer said, doffing his heavy hat, with a stately grace that even the poorest Mexican beggar can assume, when it suits his purpose to be polite and courteous to those whom he meets, even if he hates them with an undying hatred, and the fellow who stood at the door had occasion to dislike Lewey and myself, as we afterward discovered, to our sorrow.

"Buenos dias, senor," Lewey responded, in a careless manner. "Be pleased to enter, and take a seat."

The Mexican did not respond to the invitation for some reason, but stood in the doorway, and looked at Lewey and myself as though he was endeavoring to recall our faces to his mind.

"You do not remember me," the Mexican said, in a pleasant tone. "I have met you two young caballeros quite often in San Francisco. Do you know me, senors?"

Yes, we recollected him quite well, now that he spoke, and smiled on us in such a friendly manner. It was Antonio Sanchos, of Yerba Buena, one of three brothers, and greater scoundrels, and more cruel, blood thirsty monsters never existed in the country, previous to its annexation. They were named respectively Antonio, Carlos, and Edwardo, and were ugly and treacherous in the order mentioned, the first being the eldest, and considered the leader of the gang. They would steal and murder all who were thrown in their way, unless the intended victim was well armed, and then they were too crafty to make an open attack.

"We remember you," said Lewey, speaking in Spanish. "You are Don Antonio Sanchos," giving the fellow his full title as a compliment, knowing it would please him.

The Mexican bowed, and a smile passed over his dark, hairy face, as he liked the designation of don, — to which he was not entitled, — the same as some people like to be called "honorable," or "general," in this part of the world, under the impression that no one will discover the deception, and that they will be elevated in a social scale by the aid of a handle to their names.

"Come and have a drop of coffee," I said, for the fellow did not move from his position, but still stood near the door, smiling, and rubbing his hands.

"Ah. senor, a thousand thanks for your kind offer," the Mexican re plied. "In your invitation I see the generous hospitality of los Americanos. They never refuse a hungry man a bite or a drink."

He moved toward the table, and the dog growled ominously, as though to warn us that there was danger in the smiling, sneaking scoundrel who was about to partake of our breakfast.

"Will the dog bite, senors?" the fellow asked, drawing back a little from the vicinity of Jack's teeth.

"Not unless he is told to do so," I said. "Be quiet, Jack. The Mexican is our guest."

Even this did not seem to assure Jack that all was right, for he walked across the room, still growling, and showing his teeth, laid down in a corner, and watched the greaser with his fierce, wicked-looking eyes, as though longing for an encouraging word, so that he could spring, and bite one whom he considered an enemy to us and our surroundings.

"Thanks, caballeros," Don Sanchos said, as he raised a pot of coffee to his lips. "I'm glad to meet my American friends once more. It is a great pleasure, I assure you."

"I 'm no American," Lewey cried, in his usual thoughtless manner. "I 'm a Frenchman, and would not change my flag for all the nations of the world. Wherever you see fun and frolic, there you will find one of my countrymen. Where the fight is the thickest, there you will meet my people leading the van. Yes, I 'm French, and next to the belle nation comes the Americano."

Luckily Scotch Jack did not understand half a dozen words that Lewey uttered, as he was speaking in Spanish, so there was no occasion for a quarrel, as the old sailor, although he had sailed for years in the American merchant marine, was a little tenacious on the subject of Scottish rights, and great deeds, as he had reason to be from the records of his country.

"This caballero is also French?" asked the Mexican, pointing to me, and smiling, as he sipped his coffee.

"No," said Lewey, "he boasts of being a full-blooded American, and thinks that his people can lick all the world with one hand tied, and a foot thrown out of gear. He is Yankee all over, as any one can see; but he is good enough for a Frenchman though."

"Ah, yes, he one nice Americano," and the greaser looked for a moment as though he did not like me, and then set his pot of hot coffee on the table, and slowly rubbed his right hand over his left, where a livid scar was to be seen, an inch and a half long.

I knew that scar, and how he had received it, and the sight made me feel a little uncomfortable for a moment, as I thought of all the circumstances of the past, and why the fellow had been injured. Then I looked up, and saw that Lewey's eyes had followed my own, and we exchanged glances that were full of significant meaning, and once more we began to think that we had made a deep mistake in remaining in California instead of going home on the Admittance.

The greaser noted the expression that was on both of our faces, and I thought I detected a flash of his sinister eyes that did not speak of good intentions, but he betrayed no further irritation, even if he did continue to rub the scar that showed so vividly on his dark, dirty hand.

There was something fascinating in the Mexican's movements, and I sat and looked at him and the old wound, and recalled all the circumstances of how it was given, nearly a year before.

We were at Yerba Buena, and one day Antonio Sanchos had been on board the ship to do a little trading, or stealing, just as the occasion served. He did not buy much, and when we set him on shore, in company with three ladies, he had crowded one of them so much, in a rude and vulgar manner, in the stern-sheets of the boat, that she complained to me about the incivility of the greaser. I asked him to give the ladies more room, and to take a seat on a vacant thwart, but, instead of doing so, consigned me and the women to a place much warmer than San Diego in the summer-time. As I knew the greaser was cowardly at heart, and more cowardly than ever on the water, for fear that he would get wet, I dropped the yoke-lines, by which I was steering the boat, told the boys to stop rowing, caught the fellow by the long hair of his head, gave him a sudden jerk, and threw him under a thwart, and then Lewey put his foot on the man's neck, and held him captive until we beached the boat, when the ladies anded, and thanked me for the protection which I had granted them.

The Mexican did not dare vent his spite on the women, as they were members of influential families, with fathers and husbands, brothers and cousins, who would have revenged a premeditated insult with instant death, or have set a hundred wild Indians on the whole race of Sanchos, and exterminated them from the face of the earth, consequently Antonio, as soon as Lewey removed his foot from the prostrate neck, sprang to his feet, drew a long knife from his legging, and made a lunge at the French lad that would have ended his adventurous career then and there, and the Gaulic nation might have lost a good and brave admiral, who is now serving his country with honor, in great hopes of sometime making it as grand and warlike as before the disasters in front of the German hosts.

At this time I happened to have the boat-hook in my hand, for the purpose of pushing the boat further on the beach, and, as I noted the greaser's threatened move, struck at the weapon, and Lewey was saved. Then, as Sanchos stooped to pick up the knife, with deep curses on his lips, I saw that he meant more mischief, so just jabbed his hand with the point of the boat hook, and the result was a yell, more imprecations, and a bad wound that caused him to carry his hand in a sling for many a day, and to forego all thoughts of killing any one on the beach. The wound had healed, but the scar remained, and so did the memory of the injury, as I could tell by the man's face, for this was the first time I had seen him since the fracas. The incidents had almost passed from my mind, as I did not consider them of sufficient consequence to remember, we had so many adventures while hide droghing, and Lewey was constantly in hot water, on some account or other.

"Do you know," said Lewey, speaking in French, "I really believe this thief of the world recollects that punch of the boat-hook, which you gave him at San Francisco. at the time he cut at me with his knife, and you saved my life"

"If such is the case, what brings him here? He seems friendly enough at the present time," I answered.

The greaser listened attentively, but he could not comprehend a word that we uttered, neither did he know anything of the English tongue, but we feared he might.

"This fellow is like a woman," the irrepressible Lewey said. "He is smiling and rubbing his wound at the same time. No one does that but a female who desires revenge for some fancied injuries, and so abides her time before she is ready to show her claws, and scratch. Thom. we must watch this man, and be on our guard. He means mischief, I believe."

"Nonsense! Do you think he would come to us, when it might be just as easy to keep at a distance, and remain unknown? I think he has forgiven and forgotten all about the jab of the boat-hook."

"Don't you believe it. A greaser's memory is long, and his revenge is a family trait, born in the blood, and never eradicated until death. I have a great mind to shoot the cur as he sits here at the table, and so end his career, and ensure our safety at the same time," Lewey said.

"Bosh! don't talk like a bravo. You are incapable of killing one of the numerous geese that is flying over the bay, without shedding tears and delivering a funeral oration over the remains. You have not got down to a level with a murderer just yet, and talk to keep your tongue going."

Lewey smiled, as though he could not deny the charge, and then Scotch Jack and the kanaka left the room to look after some hides in the vats, as they did not find the French or Spanish languages particularly pleasant, not being able to understand them.

Sanchos, while we were conversing, looked from Lewey's face to my own, as if to read our thoughts, as he could not comprehend our words. Then he quietly rubbed his old wound, as if to quicken his ideas and remembrances of the past.

"Is the master of the house an American?" asked Sanchos, as the old sailor disappeared.

"No; he is a Scotchman, and a good fellow in the bargain," I said.

"Bueno," was the response.

"What is good?" asked the French lad, in an abrupt tone.

"The man. The maestre de casa. He is a Scotchman. We like the Scotch."

"And the French?" asked Lewey.

"Oh, we adore the French," was the answer, in a sneering tone.

"And the Americanos?" I said.

"Ah, what friends we are! No one can adore the Yankees as the Mexicans do. They come here and trade, and marry our women, get rich, and lead such lazy lives. We envy them for their enterprise and desire to make money. Oh, yes, we all love the gringoes. They are so good."

Here he rubbed his scar, and smiled on us, but it was not a pleasant smile.

"We think of marrying in a few weeks," Lewey said, in a careless tone, as though it was an every day occurrence on our part.

"May I ask the names of the fortunate senoritas?" demanded the Mexican, with a grin that did not become his dark, dirty face.

"Oh, yes. They are called Anita and Engracia, and reside at Ranche Refugio. We have been acquainted with them for many months," said the impulsive and frank-spoken Lewey, who always made a confidant of every one about his love affairs.

"Anita and Engracia," repeated the greaser, and once more rubbed his scar. "I shall remember those names for a long time, and hope to wish you joy on your bridal day. It will be very pleasant."

Here the dog uttered an ominous growl, and walked toward the Mexican, and sniffed at his feet, as though anxious for a bite of his flesh.

"You left the ship for the sake of the senoritas?" demanded the greaser, as soon as we had called off the brute.

"Oh, yes, we like California, the people, and the filles," Lewey remarked. "Especially the latter."

"Then you have applied for matriculador papers?" the greaser inquired, as he finished his coffee.

"What are matriculador papers?" I asked, for I had never before heard of such documents. In fact, matriculador was a new Spanish word, and we were anxious to learn its meaning.

"Matricula for," responded the greaser, "means to register before the alcalda of a town that you intend to take up your residence in the country, and in time become a citizen of California, after being naturalized, and taking an oath of allegiance to Mexico. It is an important step toward securing the protection and good will of the people."

"Then it is necessary that we should be reg'stered?" we asked, a little dismayed, for we had never before heard of the regulation, and there was no reason why we should, as it was a matter that did not seem to concern us. We supposed that California was a free country, where one could come and go at pleasure, but we were mistaken.

"Certainly it is important," the Mexican remarked, as he arose from the table. "But if you ship on board some American vessel there will be no occasion for papers. I suppose that you know your own minds, and what you intend to do."

"Certainly. We mean to marry, and purchase a ranche," Lewey and I responded.

"Ah, well, there is no hurry. Take your time about it. You have treated me so well that perhaps I may be able to help you in a way that is quite unexpected," and then the Mexican smiled, and rubbed the livid scar on his right hand, and, to speak frankly, we did not like his grin, or the way in which he constantly irritated the old wound, inflicted when we little thought that the greaser would become involved in our insignificant fortunes.

"Muchos gracious," we both exclaimed, and we thought the fellow was not as bad as we supposed him to be when we first met him at Yerba Buena. He spoke fairly enough.

Sanchos grinned, and walked toward the door, followed by Lewey and myself, and Jack, the dog. The brute did not seem to lose any of his animosity by the departure of the greaser, for he continued to growl, and show signs of a desire to fasten on one of the Mexican's legs, and we had to speak sharply to induce the animal to keep at a distance.

"A nice dog," the Mexican said, but there was an evil look in his dark, flashing eyes as he uttered the words. "He is not like his masters, for he does not know a friend from an enemy. Well, adios. I must return to San Diego, as I have business there."

We thought it singular that a greaser should have business of any kind, except stealing cattle, but said nothing, as we did not care to detain him, being rather glad to get rid of the man for the time being.

"By the way," asked Lewey, as the fellow was about to mount his horse, "when did you leave the bay of San Francisco?"

"Three weeks since," was the reply, as the man swung his lithe form into the saddle, and headed his horse for the town.

"Was there much news of importance?" we questioned. Not that we thought there could be any of moment.

"There are great events happening up North," was the response. "An American named Fremont is on the Sacramento River, with a band of ladrones, and General Castro has left Monterey to drive him over the mountains to his wretched home, or kill all who oppose him."

We laughed at the idea of Castro putting Fremont and his Rocky-Mountain trappers to flight, and the Mexican seemed to resent it, for he said, —

"There is more news of an important nature. The United States has annexed Texas, and war has been declared between the two countries. There will be bloody battles and hot work before long."

"And why did you leave San Francisco if fighting was to take place so soon?" Lewey asked, in a sneering tone.

"I am the bearer of despatches, and the courier and agent of General Castro," was the prompt answer. "I have left orders at every town on the coast, and am now on my way to San Diego."

"It is lucky we have you as a friend," I said. "Without some one to speak for us, and protect us, we fear that we should never be able to establish a ranche, and marry the girls we love."

"Yes," grinned the greaser, as he gathered up his reins, "it is very lucky that we met at the bay some months ago, so that I can vouch for you as two bueno machachos, who would harm no one. Oh, yes, you are all right. Adios, senors," and, striking the horse with his long, heavy spurs, he dashed over the road that led along the bay toward San Diego.

Lewey and I looked at each other's faces when the greaser had disappeared from sight. We did not see much to encourage either of us in our respective countenances.

"Well," I said at length, "I wish that I was on board of the old Admittance once more. We are in a confounded mess, and no mistake."

"So do I," responded Lewey, "but ve is here on de beach, and ne amount of vishin' can put us on de ship. Ve must make de best of it. Ve vill be what you call neutral, and let de udders do de fightin'. Dat vill suit us better den hard knocks."

"But what do you think of the greaser, Sanchos?" I asked. "Is he honest? Does he mean what he says? Will he be a friend or enemy?"

"Did you ebber know a half-caste Mexican to forget one injury?" demanded the French lad, with a touch of scorn, which he made no effort to conceal. "He rubs 'um hand to keep alive de thought of de punch you gib him vid de boat-hook. I no trust a greaser fudder den I can throw a tail by de bull."

Lewey had rather mixed the familiar quotation, but I was too troubled in mind to set him right. War between the United States and Mexico might be a serious business for us, and unsettle all of our plans. To be sure, we could ship on board some vessel, and thus escape all serious trouble, but we did not want any more surf experiences, or to pull and haul ropes, furl sails, and brace yards. We had anticipated a more pleasant life, and could not imagine one that suited our ideas better than living with the girls we loved. There was no use to borrow trouble just at present, we thought, but resolved to see Captain Fitch, our treasurer and guardian, and consult him at the first convenient opportunity, and abide by his advice. He was a man of influence in the country, and the Mexicans had great confidence in his judgment. Besides, they always borrowed his money when they were hard up, and paid him good interest for the same, and the principal when God was willing, and not before.

"Jack," we said, as we wandered down to the vats where the Scotchman and the kanaka were stirring up some hides, "that greaser says the United States and Mexico have gone to war."

"What bloody fools," was the response of the old sailor, as he stopped work to light his pipe, and listen to our communication. "Well," he continued, after a moment's pause, "may the best man win," having an idea that it was something after the fashion of a prize-fight, involving bottle-holders and a ring.

"But we fear the trouble will injure our prospects," I suggested.

"No one is goin' to injure you two chicks while you is on the beach, and ander my protection," responded the sturdy old Scotchman. "If the bloody greasers come foolin' around here I 'll blow 'em out of the water, now you jist believe me."

"But dey von't come by de vater," remarked Lewey who could not remain serious for any length of time.

"Never you mind where they comes from, they 'll get their heads broke just the same if they puts a hand on any old shipmate of mine, now I tells you."

"How could you defend us and the hide house at the same time?" I asked.

"With the two old ship-muskets the skipper left me when he sailed. They is over my bunk, and lots of powder and shot stowed away in my chest. I could hold out agin a hundred greasers for a week," and Jack sucked away at his pipe in perfect contentment, and I have no doubt really believed what he uttered.

He was about to renew his work when the current of his thoughts was changed by an enormous flock of wild geese that flew along the shore, and honked to each other, as they looked out for a place to alight and feed, on the shoals and muddy banks of the bay, and all along Spanish Bight. The tide was half ebb, and the ducks and other fowl were coming in from all directions to feast on the insects and fiddler-crabs that had been left by the receding waters.

"Tell you what it is, shipmates," Jack said, "I have n't had a goose or duck this season. I feel a longing for something different from fresh meat. Come, you boys has nothin' to do. Take the two old guns, and the skiff, and see if you can't shoot a little game. The trip will do you good, and occupy your time. I don't like to have boys mope. 'T a'n't a good sign. Now if you drank aguardiente we could go to town and have a mighty good spree, but there a'n't no sense getting drunk all alone. Besides, the old man told me to set you a good example, and I s'pose I must."

"Do you think there is any danger of the guns bursting?" I asked, for I had had some experience with the weapons up North.

"Not if you is careful, and don't put in too much of a load. Good Lord, any one can kill geese and ducks here in the bay. They is never hunted, and you can get close on 'em. Come, go along with you, and be back by supper time. I 've got my work to do, and don't want to stand here spinnin' yarns all day, and that kanaka settin' on the sand, and never carin' if I don't turn him too. Be careful, and not shoot each other, and bring back some geese and ducks."

As we needed a little recreation, to keep our thoughts from dwelling on the possibilities of the future, we jumped at the proposal to go after ducks and geese. We hunted up the old muskets, — flint-locks and enormous bores, heavy and clumsy, — cleaned them from rust and dirt, took enough powder and shot for a dozen or twenty discharges, whistled for Jack, the dog, entered the small skiff that belonged to our hide-house, pushed off, and drifted over to Spanish Bight, where the shore was alive with fowl.

There was no need of approaching them with caution, for they merely looked up from feeding, honked a few times, and then paid us no further attention.

Lewey, who was inclined to be a little selfish when sport was on the tapis, thought that I had better scull the boat toward the geese an ducks, and let him do the shooting, as he claimed that he was the better marksman. I had no particular objection, although I cautioned the French lad against loading the gun with too heavy a charge, but he sniffed at me for the advice, and intimated that he had handled fire-arms before I was born, which was not true, and he knew it, as he was only eighteen months older than myself, but much more experienced in the affairs of the world.

"You vill seed me knock 'em ober," Lewey remarked, as he loaded up, and was not over-particular how much powder and shot he put in. "I vas alvays a great gunner in mine own country. Ah, many is de sparrow vot I has killed, and made in de nice pie."

Right before us was a mob of black brant, a bird that must be rather scarce at this time on the shores of San Diego bay, as the flesh is so good that the hunters of modern days would not give it much rest, but in 1846 there were thousands to be seen at every low tide, unsuspicious of guns and death-traps, killed only by the Indians when they were hungry, and could get nothing better to eat than game. Beside the brant there were white geese, curlews, waders, willets, dowitchers, and snipe, a variety that would, at the present time, make an Eastern sportsman crazy with delight at the prospect before him.

We were within ten fathoms of the fowl when the brant and geese looked up, suspending their feeding operations for the purpose of inspecting us, and seeing what we were like, and desired.

"Now, Lewey," I whispered, "give it to them. There is a good chance."

The lad steadied his elbow on one of the thwarts, knelt down on his right knee, turned a little pale, and uttered a short prayer to his patron saint, as he thought of the danger he was wilfully incurring. I never knew the name of his patron saint, and should not have supposed that he had one, if he had n't stated that such was the fact more than a dozen times during his adventures in company with myself. Of course I had to believe him, as he appeared to be sincere in his assertion that he was religious.

"Why don't you fire?" I asked, holding the boat in place with one hand, and the lively little Jack with the other, for the dog seemed possessed with the idea that the expedition was gotten up on his own account, and that he was privileged to make as much noise as he pleased, jump overboard, swim to the game, and attack it single-handed.

"My dear ami," said the French lad, removing the gun from his shoulder, and looking at me, as though doubtful how the confession would be reeelved, "I is afraid of dis old musket. You fires him if you vill. I is just and ginerous."

"Give me the gun," I cried, in a firm tone. "I will show you how to kill game."

This boasting irritated my friend, for he said, —

"Niver. I takes de risk all on mineself. I can shoot 'em as well as you. Now seed me."

Once again he raised the musket, took a good aim at the unsuspecting game, shut both eyes, and then there was a roar, a flash, and a sheet of flame issued from the old musket, and the next moment Lewey was lying under one of the thwarts, and the gun went overboard, in two feet of water.

There was a flutter among the geese and fowl, feathers flew in all directions, and a dozen dead and wounded brant and ducks were lying on the sand and mud, while the uninjured, with cackles and honks of astonishment, flew to other feeding grounds, where they could fill up undisturbed.

Jack, with loud barks of astonishment and delight, bounded out of the boat into the water, and made for the shore, to finish the work of destruction, biting the fluttering ducks, and fighting the hissing geese as if fearful that he would not do his share unless an immense amount of activity was displayed on his part.

I dropped the oar, by which I was sculling the skiff, and went to the aid of my friend.

"Lewey," I said, as I pulled him out from under the thwart, "are you dead, or only injured?"

"I is not dead," was the answer, "but I is most killed vid my shoulder. Did you seed how I hits 'em? Ah, vot one could beat dat shot? I slays cousands of 'em.'

He sat up, rubbed his head, and looked around in a dazed sort of way, as if not realizing where he was, or what had knocked him over.

I feared that he had dislocated his shoulder-blade, but, as he could move his arm quite freely, knew that he would soon be all right, although he might suffer from a bad bruise for a day or two.

"De next time you fires him yourself," the French boy said. "I has killed mine share for one day. Ah, vot a shot vos dat, and how much it reminds me of dear old France."

"Do all the guns in France kick like this?" I asked.

"Ah, by gar, much vusser! Dese guns is nothin' like mine country's," and, if such was the case, I mentally pitied the hunters and sportsmen of la belle nation. But I think he was boasting, or lying.

Finding that the boy's injuries were not so serious as I supposed, we paddled the skiff back to the place where the old musket was quietly reposing on the bottom of the bay, managed to secure it, and then landed on the beach, where Jack was impatiently awaiting us, all the wounded ducks and brant killed, and piled up in a heap, awaiting inspection and approval.

There were seven brant, two gray geese, six ducks, and three snipe. Not a bad shot, but then the old musket was overcharged, and scattered fearfully at long range.

Lewey was delighted at his success, and declared that no one could excel him as a marksman, and I have no doubt but that his gunning experience still furnishes him a fruitful theme for conversation when he has company at his dinners on shore and sea. How his listeners must quietly wink at each other, as he talks, and wonder that a man should always manage to lie when talking about hunting and fishing. The last time I saw my friend he appealed to me to corroberate his statement, and, when I did so, noted certain expressions on the faces of those present that showed how polite the gentlemen were, for, although they did not doubt our words, it was evident they had never seen wild fowl as plentiful as we had on the shores of San Diego bay, near Ballast Point, Point Loma, and Spanish Bight.

We gathered up the spoil, and once more paddled around the bay, in search of game. We saw large numbers of geese and ducks near Ballast Point, and headed for them, the boat moving along quietly so as not to disturb the fowl. This time Lewey thought that I should have a shot, and, although I was not enthusiastic, after his experience, I did not show the white feather, for fear of exciting his ridicule. But I loaded the gun with a small quantity of powder and shot, and hoped for the best.

When we were in shoal water, and within ten fathoms of the game, the ducks and geese raised their heads and looked at us, but did not offer to move from their feeding grounds.

"Now you gib dem fits," whispered Lewey, and just then Jack, who thought that it was a command for him to show his usefulness, jumped out of the boat, and made for the shore.

The ducks and geese were alarmed at the plunge, took to their wings with noisy honks and quackings, and, just as they arose, I aimed at the thickest flock, my gun went off, and down tumbled a dozen geese, brant, and ducks, some killed outright, and others with broken wings and legs.

"Vell done! I could n't mineself have improved on dat! I vould n't hab believed dat you could do so vell!" shouted Lewey, who wanted to give me as much praise as he could, consistent with his own ideas of what was just and proper, and not detract from his accidental yet lucky shot, of which he was so proud.

I did feel a little elated, and appreciated my friend's praise, and, when we landed, and gather d up the spoils, by the exertions of Jack, who did not allow a single bird to escape, we found that we had enough game for one day, and it seemed wicked to slaughter wild fowl unless we could make use of them. We began to like the sport, and agreed to do a little gunning every week.

We now turned our attention to crawfish, secured a dozen or more, and, while we were searching for them among the rocks, Lewey gave a yell, and shouted, —

"Oh, by gar! do come here, and see de valkin' snuffbox! Ah, now ve shall hab de fun!"

I ran to where he was, on a piece of sandy beach, and found the boy jumping up and down, dancing around a hundred-pound turtle, and screaming in French and broken English as though he had found a prize of a thousand dollars, and did not know how he should spend it.

"See de old valkin' snuffbox! I finds him all by mineself! Oh, de nice soup he vill make! Ah, vould you?" as the turtle showed a disposition to seek the water, and then Lewey showered down stones on the animal's protruding head.

"We must turn it over on its back," I said, and the impulsive Lewey rushed forward to accomplish the job, but, as he approached, the turtle commenced using its flippers, and threw clouds of sand and gravel in the air, striking the face of the boy, and for a moment blinding him, so that he had to cover his eyes to save them from the fury of the storm.

I ran ahead of the turtle, and, when the sand cloud was less dense, turned the prize on its back, and thus had it secure, and at our mercy.

"Nebber seed anyding like dat afore," Lewey remarked, as he brushed the gravel-stones from his eyes and hair. "He fight all behind like de sting-ray. But now ve has him, and de good soup at de same time. Ah, vot fortunate boys ve is. Ve alvays comes on our feet ven dere is much danger."

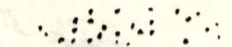

That was all true, but how were we to get the turtle in the boat, and escape some serious bites from the ponderous jaws, that seemed powerful enough to crush a piece of iron? We could not cut off its head, for, whenever we made the attempt, it would draw it in beneath the shell. After all other expedients had failed we obtained some spun-yarn from the boat, made a slip-noose, dropped it over the turtle's neck, and, with the aid of an oar, prepared to carry the prize to the skiff. It was n't pleasant for the turtle, and neither would it have been agreeable to us had the powerful jaws closed on one of our limbs.

Jack wanted to take a hand in the entertainment, and once or twice sniffed around the turtle as though wondering if there was any fight in it, for he had never seen such an animal before, and seemed inclined to the opinion that he could lick it in a fair combat, and, when he turned to ask our advice on the matter, allowed his tail to get within biting distance of the prize. There was a snap, a yell, and the most surprised dog in the bay of San Diego. With a shrill " Ki-yi!" Jack turned to run, but he could not draw a load of a hundred pounds, so pawed sand and gravel until the air was full of small particles of dirt, resembling the shower which the turtle had thrown at Lewey.

"Did you ebber seed sich a fool in all your born days?" asked the French lad. "Vot de debil vill ve do now? Cut de dog's tail off, or de head of de tur'le? By gar! dis beats eberyding dat I has seen in my long and eventful life."

But, while Lewey was talking, the dog was suffering, and yelping like a wild Indian making an attack on a defenceless party of emigrants. We out with our claspknives, and hacked away at the turtle's neck, but for a long while did not seem to make any impression, or cause the jaws to let go their terrible grip. But blood commenced to flow, and our stabs grew fiercer as we thought of Jack's sufferings. At last the jaws were relaxed, the tail was free, and then if that plucky little bulldog did n't turn around, and make a grab at one of his enemy's flippers, and bite as though to be avenged for what he had suffered. It was a long time before we could get the brute to relax his hold, for he was as tenacious as his antagonist when he fastened his grip on an opponent.

Jack's tail was lacerated a little, but it soon got well, as we put some warm tar on it, thus protecting the wound from the flies and fleas which were very abundant on the beach, and at the hide-house.

We rowed back to our quarters, or, rather, drifted, for the tide was flood, and, when we struck the beach, Scotch Jack and the kanaka came down to meet us, and see what luck we had had. Their amazement and commendations were great when they saw the result of our forenoon's work. The turtle they were a little suspicious of, and Jack said that it was no good for humans to eat, but, after Lewey had eulogized the beautiful soup that it would produce, although he frankly acknowledged that he did not know how to make it, the old sailor said that we had better land the turtle, and stow it away in the hide-house until such time as he could study up on the subject, and see how it would be proper to prepare the soup.

The game found welcome customers among the people on the beach, but after we had supplied all who wanted a goose or duck, found that we had half a dozen brant and geese left for our own consumption.

But the Scotchman mourned for the wet, rusty musket, and refused to be comforted until we had taken the gun all to pieces, and oiled it in a thorough manner. Then he was satisfied, and said that we could go gunning again the next morning, or as often as we wished, but we never had another day's sport on the shores of the bay of San Diego, having other and more important business to attend to. We often thought of Jack, the hide house, and the ducks and geese of Spanish Bight, and I sometimes wonder, o late years, if sportsmen of Southern California take the trouble to indulge in hunting, and for a time forget the cares of business life. For those fond of the gun and rod there never was a place like San Diego, and its vicinity, many years ago. Then no skill or tact was required to fill a boat with fish or fowl in a short time.

We took a swim, dined, had the usual afternoon's siesta, and roused up, lighted our pipes, and wondered what we should do for an evening's entertainment, as new books were very scarce, when who should enter the hide-house but our friend and guardian, Captain Fitch, of San Diego.

"Well, lads," he asked, "are you all right? No more smallpox, hey? Symptoms all gone? Did you play a prank on Peterson, or, honest and true, were you ill?"

"We were very sick," stammered I, and Lewey re-echoed my words with a deep sigh, as though he felt that he had met with a hard line of luck in being left on shore.

"All right then. I'll allow you were sick. Now, what do you mean to do with yourselves? You don't intend to stay here, do you?"

"No, sir. We think of buying a ranche, and getting married," I made bold to answer, knowing that the ice had got to be broken at some time, and the quicker the better.

"What?" howled the old gentleman, in a regular quarter-deck tone of voice, and he jumped from his chair, and came toward us, as though about to lay hands on our sacred persons.

"Ve is in love vid two booful young ladies," Lewey said, thinking to smooth the matter over in a speedy manner.

"In fiddlestick!" the captain cried. "Look ahere, if you go to make fools of yourselves, by the Lord Harry I'll spank both of you until your noses bleed. I never heard of such ridiculous foolishness in all my life. Good Lord, how I wish that I could get word to Peterson. Would n't he take the nonsense out of you with a rope's-end."

"Can't a man get married in this country if he is in love?" I asked.

"A man, yes. A boy, no. Don't talk to me. I'll clap you both in irons if you say another word," and then, as he paced the room in which the conversation was held, suddenly stopped, and asked, " Who are the females? Black or white? Where do they live? Lord! don't I wish Peterson was here. How he would pound you if such a proposition was broached to him. I'm too easy, too good-natured with boys. Why the devil don't you tell me what the girls are like?"

"Dey is booful," said Lewey, with a smack of his lips.

"Bah! I never heard of such nonsense," was the fierce rejoinder. "White or black?"

"A little dark, — off-colored," I ventured to remark.

"Greasers! by the Lord Harry," was the contemptuous exclamation. "To think that boys who have been well brought up, and have a little education, should lower their record by taking half-caste girls for wives. I never heard of such greenness."

"A voman is a voman, no matter vot is de color ob de face," remarked Lewey.

"I know better," cried the frank Captain. "A greaser woman is no mate for a nice white man. Do you stop to think what you are doing? Do you consider for a moment what a dark colored Mexican mother-in-law is like?"

"She vould help keep de house in order, and vip all de shildrens," the frank-spoken Lewey said, with a far-away look in his eyes, as though his thoughts were of the future, and he could picture an elderly lady bossing the infants, and making life pleasant for the husband.

"You don't know what you are talking about," snarled Captain Fitch. "She would scold your heads off, she would yarn you blind in less than a month, and give all no peace unless you went to confession once a week."

"You seem to know something of California married life," I suggested, and, at the words, the captain turned on me to see if there was any hidden meaning in my words, but, seeing that I was not inclined to be sarcastic, for his matrimonial existence was said to be a very happy one, he only answered, —

"I know what I know, and you don't. But let us drop the subject, for I have more important duties to attend to. There is a rumor in town that war has been declared between Mexico and the United States. At any rate the latter country has annexed Texas, and, if there is no war now there soon will be. This will make the positions of unnaturalized citizens in California a little precarious, for the greasers may be terribly excited against the gringos, and perhaps resort to acts of violence which we cannot prevent, do the best we can to shield our countrymen. I have some power in this part of the State, and will do what I can for you, providing you give up this idea of marrying, settle on a ranche, and raise cattle, instead of children. But, to do all this you must take out a matriculador, and then declare your intention of becoming a naturalized citizen. I hold four hundred dollars of your money, left in trust by Captain Peterson, and with that you can do much in the way of a start. Will you think of what I have said, and let me know your decision in the course of a few days?"

"Yes, sir, but our minds are all made up on the subject of getting married. We have pledged our words, and they should be sacred," I said, and Lewey nodded an acquiescence of my sentiments.

"My boys," the captain remarked, in a low tone, "there is nothing sacred here in California, when one's interest runs counter to his anticipations. You be guided by me, and all will come out right, and I may see you rich and prosperous rancheros before many years. But keep away from the girls, and by and by, when the proper time comes along, I'll see if I can't find you two decent young women as companions for life. Leave all to me, and don't be blanked fools."

We did not desire to argue the point any more, and so held our tongues, but perhaps it would have been as well if we had taken his advice, for he meant well by us, and really desired to better our fortunes, and the course he pointed out was the proper one to take. But we were infatuated, and, when such is the case, reason and prudence are thrown aside by beardless boys.

We told the captain of our gunning expedition, the capture o. the turtle, and killing of the geese and ducks, and the old gentleman rubbed his hands, as he said, —

"I 'm going to have some swell Mexicans at my house tomorrow evening, and I will give them a bit of supper, and a little entertainment. I'll buy the turtle and some of the game. They are just what I want. How much shall I pay you for all? Say two geese, a pair of brant, and the turtle."

We assured the captain that he was welcome to all he wanted, and that we could not think of taking a medio from him.

"Nonsense! I don't want your property without paying for it. Here's five dollars. Is that enough?" and the captain threw on the table five Mexican dollars, and refused to return them to his pocket, even after we had disclaimed all intention of selling the products of our excursion on the shores of the bay.

"It is all right, boys," the captain said, in a cheery tone. "I'll send a peon and cart down tonight, after I return home, for the turtle and geese, and tomorrow night they shall grace my table." Then he hesitated a moment, as though there was something on his mind, and finally said, "By the way, Peterson told me that you two lads once gave an entertainment before some of the best people of Monterey, and that there were lots of fun connected with it. I have forgotten now just what it was, but would you like to oblige me by repeating it at my house tomorrow evening? Of course I can't ask you to sit down with my guests, for they are as proud as Lucifer, and might not like it, but I will give you a good supper, a fair bed, a bottle of wine, and a dollar each for your trouble."

"If you will withdraw the offer of money, and let us volunteer our services, we should be pleased to oblige you," and Lewey nodded an acquiescence, and smiled, as he thought of the exhibition at Monterey, the firey serpent, the yells of the old women, squeals of the young girls, and the hoarse blanks of the aged caballeros.

"Well, just as you please. I won't offer you money, but you shan't lose by it if you will come, and amuse my guests. They never saw any sleight-of-hand, and it will surprise them. I'll send some horses down to the boat-house at dark, and you can ride up to town, and remain all night."

"Yes, but what's to become of me?" Scotch Jack asked, having entered the room, and heard the last part of the conversation. "It's blanked lonesome nights without the boys. I've got used to their company, and don't want them to bunk outside of the house. Can't I come up and look on, and see the fun?"

Captain Fitch hesitated for a moment, and then said, —

"Where can I stow you, Jack?"

"Oh, just where you pleases, sir. I a'n't quarter deck company, I know. Put me on the forecastle, and let me tend the head sheets, and I'll be all right."

"A gentleman's parlor is not like a ship's deck, Jack," the captain remarked.

"I know all that, sir, but I'm one of the kind what can do duty anywhere. I can help the cook, pass the grub, or turn my hand to anything," Jack said.

"Even to drinking more than your share of aguardiente, Jack?" the captain hinted, in a bantering tone.

"Well, sir, I never yet had my full share, and don't think that I ever shall. But, all the same, I'd like to see the lads give their great exhibition."

"Will you promise to keep sober, Jack?" demanded Captain Fitch, and now he was speaking seriously, for the Scotchman was a terror when he got full of native rum, and wil'ing to fight half a dozen greasers at the same time, or any one who defied him.

"Lord, sir, a judge could n't keep more sober than me, when I gives my word for it. I'll only drink when you axes me to, and I hope it will be as often as you thinks is all right and proper. Say about one tot to each bell all the evening. That won't be much, sir, for an able seaman, what knows his duty, alow and aloft, on land and water."

As Jack could be relied on, when he pledged his word, the captain smiled, and said that he might come, but he must keep in the background, and pretend to be one of the mass of helpers, for the grandees who were to partake of his hospitality would not tolerate a sailorman in their company, unless he was an officer, and master of a ship, at that.

So it was all settled quite satisfactorily to every one, and during supper, in the evening, Jack was enthusiastic over the good time he was to have, and how Providence seemed to have interfered in his behalf, when such nice boys were left to console him in his solitude, and to share his quarters.

The next day we got out the wooden balls and sticks, and practiced for two hours, or until Lewey could spin the plates without letting them fall, and all the time we were thus occupied Jack and the kanaka watched our movements with the most absorbing interest, praising and criticising very freely when things did not go to suit us, or them. At last the son of the Sandwich Islands could no longer repress his admiration, and he exclaimed, —

"Me like much. Me want to go too, and see de fun."

" Don't you know it is a place for gentlemen?" demanded Scotch Jack, in an indignant tone. "The likes of you is not admitted where we is goin'. Keep your place, and not try to force yourself into good company. It's white men what mixes with white men, and not with blacks. You can't go, so there's no more to be said on the subject. What would the greasers think?"

The kanaka uttered a doleful sigh, as he thought of the great gulf that separated him from the sailor, and boss, but made no further efforts to force his presence upon us. He was a meek little fellow, and looked up to Jack as a being who could pass muster most anywhere. First, as an able seaman, and second, as the master of the hide-house, a position of great responsibility and trust, in those days, when much valuable property was left on shore by the ships belonging to our owners.

We had too much to look after for a gunning expedition that day, but took our usual afternoon siesta, and then dressed in our neat sailor costumes, nice stockings, low shoes, and silk handkerchiefs. Jack did not look so bad when he had shaved, and changed his clothes, but persisted in wearing a white duck jumper over his shirt, as he thought it gave tone and rather an aristocratic appearance to his tout ensemble, or general make up. This, in connection with a tarpaulin hat, that was so heavy and hard it seemed capable of crushing the man's skull, caused the Scotchman to assume rather a jaunty expression, and to glance at his little shaving-glass several times with peculiar satisfaction, as though he had found something new to admire in his weather-beaten face. Once I asked him if he expected to make a conquest of some woman in the course of the evening. To this he answered that the female did not live to whom he would give his hand, and when I inquired what he would say to her if she was backed with lots of money and cattle, with a distillery for making native rum, he wisely shook his head, and said he would wait until such a paragon made her appearance, and showed her good sense by wanting him very much. He was in no hurry.

At six o'clock the horses were brought to the door by a peon, and then we almost broke our dog's heart by tying him up so that he could not follow us. He howled his disgust as we mounted, but we had not gone more than a mile, at a gentle lope, when we were overtaken by our pet, and he capered around the feet of our horses as he barked his delight at being free. Jack had slipped the rope from around his neck, or else the kanaka had let him loose, and he followed us as fast as his active, muscular little legs could carry him.

We did not care to send Jack back, so spoke a few words of kindness to him, and that satisfied the brute he was all right, and could go with us.

We had to ride slowly, on account of Scotch Jack, who was not much of a cavalier, but, just as twilight was closing in around us, rendering objects a little indistinct, we were surprised to hear the report of a rifle in a thick copse of willows, or bushes, on the left of the road, and then the old sailor's stiff tarpaulin fell into the mud, and Jack was swearing with all the energy of his rugged nature at the disaster.

For a moment we could not realize what had happened, but the Scotchman dismounted, saying as he did so, —

"That was a narrow squeak, boys. An inch or two nearer, and old Jack would have been laid away forever."

"Do you mean to tell us that a ball struck your hat?" Lewey and I demanded, both speaking at once.

"That 's what I intended to convey," the sailor said. "See here," and he thrust one of his fingers through a hole near the rim of the hat.

"Go for him, Jack!" I shouted to the dog, who was looking at us in wonderment, and waiting for orders.

The animal gave an angry growl, and dashed toward the copse of bushes. The next instant Lewey and I were heading our horses in the same direction, heedless of the Scotchman's cries to come back, as it was no use to give chase, for a stern one is a long one, and we did not know the country any too well.

We plunged through the green bush, and then heard the clatter of horse's feet in the distance, and saw a vaquero, mounted on a powerful mustang, fleeing toward the open country, and turning in his saddle to see if he was pursued.

Jack was racing after the fellow, but we saw at a glance that the latter had a long start, and owned a faster horse than the ones we were riding.

"It vas no use to go arter him," Lewey said. "He vill get avay from us. Call back de dog."

We whistled to Jack to return, and the plucky little animal gave up the pursuit, but, when he joined us, we could see disgust on his expressive face, because he had not been more successful in the chase.

We returned to the old sailor, and wondered what the shot meant, and if the rifle bullet was an accident, or the result of a deliberate plan to rid the Scotchman of the cares of the world, or to show contempt for his hat, in which he took so much pride.

"Well, old man," we said, "what do you make of this?"

"I don't make much of it," he answered, "except that I nearly lost the number of my mess. The cuss came pretty near the old man's head. An inch lower and he would have had me."

"Have you an enemy in San Diego?" I inquired.

"Not that I knows of. To be sure, a fellow can't get drunk, and clean out a town of greasers, without some person getting hurted, but I did n't think any one held a grudge agin me since I allers healed all the wounds with a drink at my expense."

"You has not to some voman made de love, and den vhat you call deserted her, has you?" asked Lewey.

"No," was the prompt reply. "I don't bothers with female greasers like some people."

As there was no solution to the problem, we rode on toward the captain's house, and arrived there just at dark, when we met peons ready to look after our horses, and then Mr. Fitch came out, and made us welcome, and led us to a small room that overlooked the garden, where we found some fruit, and were told to make ourselves as comfortable as possible until the proper time for our appearance before the company.

The house was lighted in every part, and we could smell the odor of cooked viands, and hear the shrill voices of the servants, as they called to each other to perform certain duties. We could note the company as it arrived, and the cheery tones of the captain, as he welcomed his guests. Then there was the usual strumming of harps, and the twanging of guitars, and an occasional song from some sweet-voiced doncellita, who sang of love and romance. At last there was a hush, and Captain Fitch, his face flushed with hospitality and wine, came to the room, and said that the audience was all ready for us.

"Do the best you can, boys," our host remarked. "The alcalda, and all the great people of the town are present, and count on much amusement at your hands."

We took our dishes, balls, and sticks, and followed the captain to the principal room of the house, where we found a hundred ladies and gentlemen assembled, and, as we entered the apartment, there was a low murmur of applause, and the girls smiled on us, and waved their fans in token of recognition, for all of them had seen us many times when we were members of the crew of the Admittance, and the little beauties came to the ship for the purpose of buying their usual stock of finery, in the shape of silks and buttons, laces and shoes. Most of the people present did not know that we had been left on shore when the ship sailed, so there was a hum of astonishment from the men, and loud whispers on the part of the elderly ladies.

Captain Fitch introduced us to the audience in a little speech, that was rather embarrassing to us, even if it was frank and truthful, and, while he was making his address, Lewey and I were compelled to listen in modest silence.

"Ladies and gentlemen," said the candid captain, "these two lads have chosen to remain on shore, to be discharged from the ship, for a certain purpose. Now I do not believe that there is a person present who can guess what their motive is in staying here, instead of returning to their friends."

The girls giggled and whispered to each other, while the old women looked as though they did not care about the matter at all. The men lighted cigarettes, and seemed to wonder when the eating would begin.

"These lads," continued the captain, after a pause, "prefer to remain in California because they want to get married, and are in love with two dark-eyed girls of Ranche Refugio."

There was a sensation among the girls. They smiled on us, showed their white teeth, and looked as though they did not consider it a crime to be in love, or to want to marry. They rather approved of the plan, if we could judge by their eyes, while the men groaned, and muttered that we were locos, or crazy. Lewey and I blushed, and thought that this was more embarrassing than the night at Monterey, when we electrified the audience with our wonderful serpent.

"I have tried to talk this nonsense out of their heads," continued the captain, "as it is not for their good."

Here there were some hisses on the part of the young girls, and looks of indignation directed toward the captain. The married men applauded, as a matter of course, and, when I glanced at their wives, I did not blame them.

"However," continued Mr. Fitch, "the question now is for our entertainment, and not for that of the lads. As they grow older they will know better, I have no doubt."

Cries of "shame" from the senoritas, and grins of approval from the men.

"Without further delay," the captain went on, "I have the pleasure of presenting to you the young lads who are anxious to give an exhibition of legerdemain for your amusement. Step this way, boys."

It was rather embarrassing to go forward under such a battery of bright eyes, for all the girls were looking at us, and our neat clothes, and more than one remarked that the French lad was quite handsome, which rather encouraged Lewey, for he was apt to be conceited where women were concerned, and I felt a little envious on account of the attention which his good-looking face inspired.

We took our places at the extreme end of the room, where the lights were the most powerful, and then Lewey balanced a plate on a stick, whirled it around, let the support rest on his chin, head, and face, and, when he had three plates, all moving at once, the applause was liberal, and the girls said that it was the most wonderful thing they had ever seen, and no doubt they were correct, for many of them had never been beyond the confines of San Diego in their short and uneventful lives.

Scotch Jack, who was standing in the doorway, in company with the servants, shouted for "three cheers." Some one had given him a drink of aguardiente, and it was having its usual effect on a susceptible disposition. A look from the captain, however, silenced the sailor, but Jack, our dog, showed that he appreciated the call by uttering several energetic barks, and then came to the place where we stood, and laid down, facing the audience, and examined each person present, as though he had but little respect for any one except those to whom he owed allegiance.

As soon as the plate trick was exhausted, I handed Lewey the balls, and he kept them in motion around his head, all in a circle, and that delighted the audience, for they uttered murmurs of surprise, and Lewey's heart swelled with pride, as he thought of the impression he was making, and, as I watched the pretty girls before me, I wondered if we had not better wait a little while before marrying, and see if we could n't get a few cattle and hides as well as brides?

The next incident was batting the sticks, and this was also approved, and then we gave them the handkerchief trick, as we had saved the remnants of the two pannelos which we used in Monterey. While we were employed in putting the pieces in a hat, we noticed a stir at the door, and heard a few loud words, and then Jack, the dog, started to his feet, and would have made a rush to the entrance had I not caught him by the collar, and stifled his barks, by pressing his jaws together so that he could not utter a sound.

The ladies looked toward the door in surprise, as if debating in their minds what the noise was all about, and then I saw Scotch Jack, with his white jumper on, pushing some one, as if to prevent him from entering the apartment.

"What is the meaning of the noise at the door?" demanded Captain Fitch, in a stern tone, for he thought that some of his servants had been drinking a little more of the country wine than was good for their faithful attention to household duties. He spoke in Spanish, but the old Scotchman knew enough of the language to understand the question, and he answered, —

" A lot of blanked greasers want to come in, and mix with the ladies and gentlemen, and I 'm keepin' 'em out."

" But we are coming in at all hazard," a familiar voice said, and then Don Antonio Sanchos, of San Francisco, followed by half a dozen villainous-looking Mexicans, pushed aside the servants, and entered the room.

" Sorry to disturb the company," Sanchos said, in a sneering tone, "but I want that American boy. I arrest him as a suspect, — a sospechoso, — an enemy to the State and to Mexico. He is my prisoner, in the name of the law.'

CHAPTER II.

DON ANTONIO SANCHOS CREATES A SENSATION. — HE CHARGES ME WITH BEING A SPY, AND AN ENEMY OF CALIFORNIA. — AN APPEAL TO THE ALCALDA. — SCOTCH JACK IS FULL OF FIGHT AND AGUARDIENTE. — THE CALABOZO. — A LITTLE LOVE-MAKING. — AN OATH OF ALLEGIANCE. — THE BLOW, AND SANCHOS THREATS. — A PLAN FOR ESCAPE.

FOR a moment there was a death-like silence, even Captain Fitch seeming to be too much surprised to speak, and the ladies and gentlemen mutely gazed at each other, at Sanchos, and myself. I had been pronounced a sospechoso by the biggest scoundrel in California, and for what reason was beyond my comprehension, although I knew enough to be aware that such an accusation, by an unscrupulous man, was not intended to do me any good at that particular time, when national feeling was raging quite lively, and Americans were not in great favor with the people of the State.

Captain Fitch, as master of the house, was the first to recover speech, and he showed the anger that was raging within him by his red face and flashing eyes.

"You blanked scoundrel," the captain asked, "what do you mean by entering the house without an invitation, and disturbing my company in this way?"

"Gently, senor," the Mexican said, as he rubb d the scar on the back of his right hand, and glanced around the room. "Let us have no harsh words here, for I am one to command tonight, and not to be commanded. I am here to arrest that American boy, and shall take him into custody, and land him in the calabozo. Let no man stand in my way at his peril."

"Dog of a greaser" shouted Captain Fitch. "If you lay a hand on that

American lad I'll have you flogged through the town at the tail of a cart. The alcalda is here in the room, and will give the order. Get you gone, and the cut-throats that you have brought with you. This is no place for you and your companions. Depart, or I'll command my servants to punish you."

"Have a moment's patience, O renegade of a Yankee," Don Sanchos said, in a sneering tone, but, before he could utter another word, Scotch Jack, who had in some mysterious manner put out of sight two glasses of aguardiente, and was fast getting into a fighting mood, when he would stop at nothing that stood before him, raised one of his hardened, ponderous fists, and struck the foul-mouthed greaser under the ear, and he tumbled to the floor as though felled by the axe of an abattoir butcher, and then our dog, thinking that he saw a good chance to put in a little work on his own account, made a spring for the fallen man, and would have seized him by the throat, if Lewey had not run up, and dragged him away just in time to prevent serious injuries to the prostrate fellow's windpipe.

The ladies were a little excited, and arose from their seats, perhaps the better to see the battle, while the men regarded the whole thing as something gotten up for their especial benefit, and would not have cared if there had been more fighting, only with the proviso that knives should be drawn, and blood shed, for the sake of variety. A Mexican can endure a large amount of cruelty if there is a liberal flow of blood thrown in, to give it spice, although, as a general thing, he don't care to spill his own vital fluid nearly as well as his neighbors'.

The several Mexicans who had accompanied Don Sanchos to the house seemed a little disconcerted at the fall of their leader, and two of them laid their hands on the hilts of large cuchillos, as if with the intention of using them, and, had they carried out their intention, the Scotchman would have been cut to pieces, as he was unarmed, before his friends could go to his assistance.

"Is there another greaser what wants to stand afore me?" demanded the old sailor, the native rum beginning to work. "If there is, just set him foul of me. I can lick a dozen of 'em, and not half try."

"Be quiet, Jack," commanded Captain Fitch. "You will make a bad matter worse by your hasty action. This is something that can't be settled by a rough-and-tumble fight. The law will reach the fellow who came here and insulted us as he has done. The alcalda must attend to him."

"Yes," said the chief magistrate of the town, "I will look after him to-morrow. No one can be arrested in San Diego without my warrant. The

American lad shall not be disturbed. He is a good boy, and has done nothing that makes him a sospechoso."

The young girls murmured their approval of this edict, but, while they were thus expressing their satisfaction at the alcalda's assurances, Don Sanchos slowly arose from the floor, shook his head, as if to be assured that it was on his shoulders, rubbed the scar on his hand, scowled at Lewey and myself, at Captain Fitch and Scotch Jack, and, when he could collect his scattered senses, thus addressed the company: —

"I have been struck by a gringo, but a brave Mexican gentleman knows how to avenge his honor without the aid of law. I will look after the marinaro some time when he will not expect a visit from me. Now I have other work. Senor Alcalda, I demand the arrest of the Americano muchacho as a sospechoso and spy."

"Bosh!" returned the official, or something equivalent to it. "Of what do you suspect the boy?"

"Of being a spy, left here to note the actions of the brave Californians."

There was a little sensation at these words, for Sanchos had hit the weak side of the Mexican character, — suspicion of all foreigners, and readiness to believe evil of them.

"The boy was left on shore with his companion because they had the smallpox, and it was thought they would die if taken to sea. I am their guardian, and will be security for their good behaviour," the captain said, addressing the alcalda, and the gentlemen present.

"That is good! That is enough," was the muttered exclamation, for Captain Fitch had lived many years in San Diego, and was well liked by all parties.

"It is not enough," cried the Mexican greaser, with a savage growl. "I demand the arrest of the Americano."

"You may demand until you are tired and thirsty," the alcalda said in a stern tone. "The boy shall not be arrested or molested. I have said it, and a Mexican gentleman never violates his word."

This so amused Lewey that he actually turned and winked at me, and then smiled in a subdued manner at the eager-looking senoritas who were before him.

"Then see what effect this will have on you," Don Sanchos cried, as he took from his bosom a paper, sealed with sealing wax, held it over his head, waved it in triumph, and continued, "The United States and Mexico are now at war. That is the report at San Francisco. Our land is already invaded by a horde of robbers, under one Fremont, who refuses to leave our borders. Every one who is not for us is against us. Senor Alcalda, read this document, and see if I have authority to act as I do," and Don Sanchos handed the paper to the town official, and then gave me a glance that showed some of the hate burning in his breast, and which had been smothered for a time, when he supposed there was no opportunity to revenge his fancied wrongs.

He touched the scar on his hand as he looked at me, and I saw that he was likely to prove a bitter enemy if he could have his own way in regard to my treatment.

The alcalda took the document, and, as he slowly opened it, Sanchos said, —

"You will see that General Castro, the commander-in-chief of the Mexican forces in this State, has appointed me as his courier and secret agent, with power to arrest all sospechosos in California. That document is also endorsed by the governor, and by Pio Pico, and his brother, Andreus Pico, the second in command. Let no one interfere with me, or cross me in my line of duty. I am supreme."

"But not in my house," cried the hot-headed Captain Fitch. "You and Castro may be blanked for all that I care, but you can't enter my premises, and arrest a boy on your absurd suspicions. Leave the place, or I'll kick you and your gang of thieves out of the room."

There was a murmur of assent to this threat from the gentlemen present, and the impulsive Lewey called out for three cheers for the host, but no one responded except Scotch Jack, who gave a yell that made even Sanchos turn toward the door, in the expectation of seeing a rescuing party near at hand.

The alcalda was a very cautious man, and rather conservative. He knew the power that devolved upon him as a law officer, and would take no risks. He did not propose to butt his head against the military and civic officers of the State, when the only question was a boy, a beach-comber, who was of no account in the affairs of California. Therefore the magistrate did not hasten his movements as he read the official document before him. The young girls were in an agony of impatience as usual, and asked him to hurry up, so that they could learn the final decision. The announcement which Captain Fitch had made early in the evening, that we were in love and wanted to get married, had great influence in swaying their judgment, and, to a girl, they were with us, as far as sympathy was concerned.

"The poor boy," one young creature said, looking at me with tearful eyes. "Only think what a misfortune it would be for him if he should not obtain a wife after all."

I tried to maintain my composure during the whole of the tumult, but did not feel any too comfortable when I thought of my future, or what was to become of me in case the villain Sanchos once had it in his power to do as he pleased, and to pay off old scores for the unfortunate blow of the boat-hook. Lewey gave me an encouraging glance once in a while, as if to assure me that he would stand by my side in adversity, and Jack, the dog, crouched at my feet, and showed his white, sharp-pointed teeth every time the San Francisco ruffian spoke.

"The document," said the alcalda at last, "is perfectly correct. Don Antonio Sanchos claims nothing that this paper does not impower him to do. He can arrest any sospechoso that he pleases, and I must lend him my aid if he requires it. But there is no one here tonight who believes that the boy is a spy, or a suspicious person, and he can prove that very easily. He is a native of the United States, but that does not make him an enemy at the present time. Until we have received from Mexico an official notice that war is declared, we are bound to protect him, and shall do so until further orders."

"Three cheers for de alcalda of San Diego," cried Lewey in English, and Scotch Jack joined in the howl with much spirit, for he had got hold of another glass of aguardiente, in some mysterious manner, and it was telling on him by actions and words. He already began to weary of standing idle, and wanted to fight some one for the love of it. He had already forgotten his promises.

"Keep quiet, my lad," Captain Fitch said, in a mild tone. "You make too much noise for a small boy," addressing Lewey.

"But jist dink of de occasion, sir," was the French lad's response. "It is not de often time dat one friend of mine is nabbed by a willain as a sospechoso. He is good. He is noble. For him I die."

"Well, you won't have to do that just at present," the captain said. "I will stand by him and you as long as I have a shot in the locker, and it will go hard unless we get the boy out of this scrape."

The alcalda waited until the conversation ceased. He was not a man to do anything in a hurry. He even lighted a cigarette,—one that his wife rolled for him, and had all ready by the time he finished reading Sanchos' document.

"Now," said the chief official of the town, as he took a whiff, and let the smoke escape from his nostrils in two streams, like the spout of a right whale, "the boy is an American. That he admits. He does not belong to any ship. That also is admitted," turning to Captain Fitch.

The old gentleman bowed an acquiescence to the statement.

"Very well. He probably has a full discharge in regular form," the alcalda continued.

"I demand to see it," Don Sanchos cried in an impatient tone, for matters did not move along as fast as he thought they should.

"Wait until the proper time arrives," the official said quite calmly.

"I have the discharge of both boys locked up in my safe, with their scanty hoard of dollars," the captain interrupted.

"We will come to that presently," the alcalda remarked. "As far as I am concerned your word is sufficient."

"But not for me," Sanchos growled, like a beast, hungry for its prey.

"Oh, may the saints have me in their keeping, but at what time are we going to have supper?" yawned an elderly lady, who cared nothing for law, or any pleasures, except those of the table. She had come for a feast, and feared that it would be cold before the tables were spread, and the company called in.

"Peace, amigo," the alcalda remarked to the Mexican half-caste, and paying no attention to the female's moans. "There is but one thing to be decided upon at the present time, and that we can arrive at very quickly."

The old fellow beamed on us boys, and then said, as he folded up the official document, —

"Now let the lads produce their protections, and all will be well. They can rely on them to show that the American government has spread its arms over the sailors, and is able to take care of all who can boast of United States birth. The protections will prove that, even if the boys are enemies of the great and glorious Republic of Mexico, they can be held as prisoners of war only, and are thus entitled to that kind and humane treatment which our country always bestows upon those who fall into its power."

Lewey looked at me in consternation. Our protections were on board the Admittance. Mine in my own name, and Lewey's under some alias, picked up by an unscrupulous shipping-master, and sent to the Boston custom house a few days before we sailed, to prove that two-thirds of the crew were natives of America, as the laws of Congress required, but which every ship-captain and owner violated week after week, because not enough United-States residents could be induced to turn their attention to the sea, starve, and be ill-treated on ship-board. Alas, the Admittance was more than a thousand miles from San Diego, on her passage home. Captain Peterson had gone away and left us without giving our protections a single thought. We had not seen the documents from the time we gave them in charge of the captain, some three years before, in Boston.

"Now, lads," cried Captain Fitch, "just tell me where the protections are, and when they can be seen, and then we will have a bit of supper, and turn these vagabonds out of the house."

We made no reply, and could not. We saw that we were in a disagreeable predicament, and did not feel like crushing the captain by our confession that we had no protections to show the alcalda.

"Why do the boys hesitate?" sneered Sanchos, and held the vivid scar up to view, striking it gently with his left hand.

The scoundrel, quick-witted and unscrupulous, suspected the true state of the case, and there was a fierce light in his black, evil eyes, as he continued, —

"The French lad will go unharmed, even if he has no protection. I owe him no ill-will, if he did insult me one day at Yerba Buena. He is a native of a friendly country, at the present time, so let him pass. It is the Yankee gringo whom I want to settle with. He once struck me with a boat hook, and here is the wound," holding up the black and dirty hand on which the scar was deeply imprinted.

"You needed the blow," I said, as I saw the audience disposed to sympathize with the fellow. "You insulted a relative of General M. G. Vallejo. She complained to me, and I punished you as you deserved. I would have done the same thing had one of these young ladies or their mothers been forced to blush at the rudeness of an impolite man like you."

There was a ripple of applause, and the ladies seemed to change sides once more, to range themselves among my friends. Sanchos saw this, and quickly endeavored to counteract it.

"We have talked enough for one evening," he said. "The point is not what I or the muchachos did, for those are old accounts. The question now is, has the boy a protection, or is he a matriculador? The records have been searched, and he has not applied for registry. Now let him furnish the alcalda with his protection."

"That is just," some of the men said, looking at each other.

"The saints defend us, but will the men never cease talking so that we can have some supper," cried two or three of the old women.

"Yes, tell us of your protection," the alcalda cried, turning to me.

"Lie a little about it," whispered Lewey. "Anyding for a delay of a few hours, so ve can hire some von to knock de greaser in de head, and put hin out of de vay. Lie, if you never did afore such a ding do."

But I disliked to take the advice, for I thought the question might as well be met one time as another. I did not believe that the Mexicans would dare to injure a good boy, one who had never made himself conspicuous except in ducking the old ladies and men in the surf at the other ports. But the people of San Diego could never have heard of such misfortunes, and would not have paid much attention to them if they had, supposing they were accidents of the ordinary nature.

"No, Lewey," I said, turning to the boy, and speaking in English, "I will not lie to shield myself from harm."

"More de fool yous be," he stuttered in his eagerness. "I lie for any one, and to save mine friend, much more den vot is good for me. Do not much de truth speak now."

"Senor Alcalda," I said, "I throw myself upon your generosity. I had a protection, but it is now on board the ship Admittance. I forgot that I should need any on shore. I am an American, but not a dangerous one."

"No, I 'll swear to that," Captain Fitch remarked. "You are one of the nicest boys I ever saw," which was complimentary, if not exactly true.

"Then you admit, Mr. Alcalda, that I have the power to arrest the gringo as a sospechoso?" asked Sanchos.

"I do not deny that you are authorized to imprison him if you see proper. I shall not assist in the act, nor prevent you. But I should advise you to let him alone, and become a matriculado in proper form."

"Never," was the surly answer. "He is my prey, and the pain and humiliation of this wound shall be repaid by his punishment."

"I will go security for the lad's appearance at any place, at any time, and before any court," said Captain Fitch. "Name the sum desired, and I 'll be responsible for it to the last peso."

"It is in vain you plead," was the defiant answer. "There are no longer any courts in California," shouted Sanchos, with a devilish leer of triumph on his black, hairy face.

"What do you mean?" asked half a dozen of the most prominent men, among them the alcalda.

"This is what I mean," cried the vindictive scamp, as he pulled a second paper from his bosom. "All the civil and criminal courts of California are closed by the order of General Castro and Pio Pico. Martial law has been proclaimed from the north to the south. Here is the pronunciamento signed by the gentlemen named. War is now raging, and the soldier steps to the front."

The alcalda read the paper in his usual calm manner, while the Mexicans in the room looked at each other in mute surprise. They saw forced loans, seizure of cattle and horses, and no law but a tyrant's will, or the caprice of some pompous officer placed over them.

"Dios gracios, will the feast never be served?" muttered the hungry o'd ladies. "It is talk, talk, talk, and the food is spoiling, we know."

"I must bow to the will of the general and his advisers," the alcalda said, rather reluctantly, as I imagined, after a moment's thought. "The lad is in the custody of the agent of the government, and he can do with him as he pleases, but I shall immediately write to General Castro, stating all the facts of the case, and offering to be personally responsible for the boy as long as he remains under my jurisdiction. I will send the letter by a special courier, with orders to ride day and night until the general is found. He is probably in Monterey, so I can hope to get an answer in ten or fifteen days at most. And in the mean time the lad shall have good treatment, but he must remain in the custody of Don Sanchos, and I hope that he will be considerate and careful of his welfare."

"Oh, I will be very tender with the boy," sneered the Mexican scoundrel. "But, to prevent all mistakes, shall lodge him in the calabozo until I receive further instructions."

"You will not dare to commit him to prison!" cried Captain Fitch, speaking English in his excitement.

"Send one of my shipmates to the calabozo!" roared Scotch Jack. "Blank me if I stands that, you know. Here's one who will make a fight over it, no matter what you white-livered Mexicans may do about the matter."

He raised his ponderous right fist, and let it fall upon the face of the nearest follower of Don Sanchos, and the fellow dropped to the floor, with blood gushing from his nose.

Half a dozen knives were drawn, and flashed in the lamp-light, and Jack's days would have been numbered had not the mayordomo of Captain Fitch's establishment struck up the arms of the nearest ladrones, gave Jack a violent push, that sent him reeling from the room, and then hastily closed the door, and prevented the angry men from wreaking their vengeance on the sailor. We heard a loud altercation in the entry, and then all was hushed. Scotch Jack had been hustled out of the way, and perhaps pacified with a glass of grog, or the promise of one.

In the mean time Lewey and I had remained passive spectators of the scene, for we knew that we could not hope for success in a contest with men who would have liked the job of cutting us to pieces at the bidding of their leader. Had we been armed with rifles and pistols we could have driven the crowd of robbers out of the house in confusion, for they were not the men to stand before cold lead and good marksmen. But we had only our pocket-knives, and they were useless in the presence of half-breeds, who knew how to handle long and keen cuchillos from their childhood.

Under these circumstances we concluded that it was best to submit to the inevitable, although it cost Lewey a groan as he ranged alongside of me, and whispered, —

"We can't fight much now, and you go must, but don't fear. I stick you by, and nebber leave mine dear ami," and Mr. Fitch also took occasion to say, in a low tone, —

"Make no resistance, Thom. The scamps have got us in their pow' and can do as they please, but no one shall harm you at present. I am well acquainted with General Castro, and will write to him all the facts of the case, and secure your liberation. He will soon want some money, and not a dollar shall he get from me unless he complies with my request."

"Senor Alcalda," asked Sanchos, during a moment's pause, "is the boy my prisoner?"

"Yes, if you choose to take him," was the answer. "But I had much rather you let him go. I assure that you that he is harmless. He is known to all of us."

"Of that I am the best judge," was the sullen reply, and then the fellow rubbed the scar on his hand, and motioned for his followers to approach. "Seize that boy, and tie his hands so that he can't use them," was the order given.

The ruffians were only too glad to obey. They approached, with several narrow strips of rawhide in their hands, but, just as they were about to bind me, Jack, the dog, thought that things had gone far enough, and that he would interfere. As one of the men attempted to secure my arms, the animal made a powerful leap, and, with an angry growl, fastened his sharp teeth in the neck of the ruffian, and held on as though my life depended on the power of his jaws.

"Maldito perro de presa!" was the exclamation, and the vaquero reached for his long knife, but, before he could lay his hands on it, Lewey sprang forward, grasped Jack by the neck, and choked him until he released his

held, and then the French lad held the struggling animal in his arms so that none of the injured man's friends could get at him with a knife, and end his earthly career.

"On with the lashings," shouted Sanchos. "It is one more charge against the sospechoso. You shall be revenged for this, as well as I for my injuries."

"Pobrecia muchacho," murmured the young ladies present, and I have no doubt but that they did pity me, for their faces showed it, and more than one shed tears at the cruel treatment I was receiving.

Two men grasped my arms, and held them behind my back, while a third under Sanchos' inspection, tied my hands in such shape that I could not move them. The lashings cut into the flesh, and were very painful, but I did not permit my enemies to see that I was suffering, for I would not let them enjoy such a triumph as they counted upon.

Lewey said it was a shame, and that he would like to punch the heads of the men who surrounded me, but, as Captain Fitch warned him to keep quiet, he was forced to be content, and grumble in French his deep displeasure.

"Leave everything to me," the captain said. "I know these scoundrels better than you do, and can manage them after a fashion. I will see you in the morning, at the calabozo, and you shall find a good breakfast at your disposal."

"Where to?" asked one of the vaqueros, turning to Sanchos for instructions.

"The calabozo," was the reply. "Lead the prisoner along, and see that he does not escape."

"Me go too," Lewey said, "I no lose sight of mine friend."

"We will go together," Captain Fitch remarked. "I shall not leave the lad until he is under lock and key."

He turned to his guests, and said simply, —

"I shall be absent but a short time."

Here the old ladies uttered a dismal groan, and looked the consternation they felt as they thought of the feast.

"But," continued the captain, "I shall order the supper to be placed upon the tables immediately, and request my friend, the alcalda, to preside and act as host, in my absence."

"Bueno," was the general exclamation, and the old ladies looked as though they wanted to give three cheers, while the men muttered a complaint at the captain's consideration for their hunger.

Two of the dirty greasers took my arms so that I could not bolt and make a run for it, and, with the triumphant Sanchos leading the way, and a flank guard of four or five men, Captain Fitch and Lewey following in my wake, we left the house where we had expected so much pleasure, and passed into the street. A dozen or twenty Indians and low, half-breed Mexicans were hovering near the door, waiting for the feast to be over so that the remnants would be turned over to them. They only stared at us, and asked the captain how much longer they would have to hunger for the old viands, the scent of which they were patiently sniffing, at the open windows and doors?

The captain encouraged them to be quiet for a little while longer, and assured all that there would be no lack of food, and so passed on. He was very pleasant to the crowd, and it was policy on his part to be civil, for he wanted friends just then, and as few enemies as possible.

The streets were dark, but the houses were lighted, and in some of them fandangos were going on. We could hear the twanging of guitars, the notes of an occasional harp, and once in a while the shrill yell of some female as she tried to amuse her auditory by a song of sentiment and love.

I knew where the calabozo was situated for I had seen it many times when in town, the temporary residence of some unfortunate sailor, who had attempted to clean out the village, when under the powerful influence of aguardiente, and, as a result of his spree, found himself in prison, and compelled to pay a fine of five or ten dollars, just according to the amount of damage he had committed.

Sanchos strode along, his bright colored scrape thrown over his shoulders, and whispering to a minion who appeared to be in his confidence. This fellow, as I afterward learned, was Sanchos' brother Carlos, the next wickedest ladrone in California. They were concocting some scheme between them, but what it was I could not even guess. But I suspected that it boded me no good, if the villains had their own way.

When we arrived at the prison the keeper was absent, and the only signs of life about the premises were the howls and yells of two or three drunken Indians, who had been arrested for disturbing the peace, and the next day would be flogged, fined, or set to work on the road, just according to their pecuniary standing, or that of their friends.

Some of the men were despatched in various directions to find the keeper, who, in company with his daughter, was attending a fandango, or other entertainment, and it was half an hour before the old fellow and girl could be hunted up. When he did come he growled at being disturbed, but changed his complaints to compliments after he saw Captain Fitch, for the American was the richest person in San Diego, and was quite free with his money, when he had a point to carry.

"To the devil with you," the old Mexican said to those who had discovered his whereabouts. "Why did you not state that the Senor Fitch was inquiring for me? I cry your mercy, good sir, for keeping you waiting. Take the key, girl, and open the door. Whom do you wish to lock up? and what is his crime? Not murder, I hope."

"Worse than that," reported Sanchos. "It is for being an enemy of our glorious republic. He is a traitor to Mexico, and his doom certain death, if the charge is proved before a drum-head court-martial."

"So may all the enemies of Mexico perish," the old jailor said.

He had formerly served in the army, and entertained a great opinion of the republic, and the responsiblity of his charge.

The young girl, his only child, opened the heavy door, and I was pushed into the building, while the keeper struck a light with flint and steel. An oil lamp was then found, the wick picked up until it smoked vilely, and by its aid the keeper took a square look at me, and his astonishment was expressed on his face.

"What the devil do you bring this boy here for?" he demanded, "I have seen him a hundred times during the past few years. I have visited his ship, and once he gave me some dinner, because I was not cabin company. He is no enemy to Mexico. If we are at war with the United States our great republic does not measure weapons with a mere muchacho like this. Take him away, and God go with you."

"Peace, you old fool," Sanchos said, in a stern tone. "I am an agent of General Castro, and my word here is law. The alcalda has examined my papers, and pronounced them correct. There is no power in San Diego but such as I choose to exercise. Lock the boy up, and your life shall answer if he escape."

"Is this true, Senor Fitch?" the jailor asked, turning to the American, or, rather, the man who was formerly an American, for he had become a naturalized citizen of California, for the benefit of business interests, which were of some magnitude.

"I regret to state that it is true," was the quiet response.

"Then the more shame for Castro and California," exclaimed the jailor's daughter, rather a pretty girl, to whom Lewey had been paying a little attention, regardless of my situation I thought that I detected him squeez ing her hand, when no one was looking, thus taking a mean advantage of me, knowing, as he did, that I could not rebuke him before the crowd.

"Hold your tongue, girl," growled Sanchos. "General Castro is a soldier, a patriot, and knows what he is doing, and what is for the best interests of California. We want no spies or traitors here. Long live the republic, and no mercy to los gringos," the fellow shouted, and his followers took up the cry, and the drunken Indians in the prison, thinking that death was staring them in the face, uttered howls of fear, and begged for pardon.

"If the military authorities order me to keep a poor boy confined, I suppose that I must obey, but it is a maldito shame," and the jailor cut the lashings that bound my arms, and then led the way to a small room, with grated window, and, for a wonder, tolerably clean. At least it was well ventilated, and there was not such a bad smell as many Mexican prisons can boast of.

"Not in there," cried Sanchos, seeing that I was to have an apartment to myself. "Let the sospechoso share the calabozo with the rest of the inmates. He must receive no favor at your hands."

"But the prisoners are only Indians, and they are drunk," pleaded the jailor.

"So much the better. Put the spy with them, and keep him there until I call for him. On your head be his care," and once more he gently rubbed his scar, and motioned for me to enter an apartment that was hot and dirty, and reeking with a stench that almost made me sick. The drunken Indians were wandering around the room, and howling at intervals, for the purpose of expressing their sense of grief at the punishment they were likely to have doled out to them on the morrow, when arraigned before the alcalda for justice. All of them were naked, except breech-cloths, and, with their long, coarse hair hanging over their shoulders, and wild, black eyes, they did not look fit company for even the most desperate of white criminals, much less a boy who had been reared with some regard for Christian principles, and felt degraded to have to associate with such scum as was now before him.

"O senor," cried the young girl, who began to take more of an interest in me, all owing to Lewey's interference, and soft pressure of the hand, "you will not insist that the muchacho shall occupy the same room as these wild beasts?" and she looked at Sanchos beseechingly, but the Mexican was blind to her blandishments, and deaf to her entreaties. He had resolved that I should suffer all the humiliations it was in his power to inflict, to pay for the jab of the boat-hook, and nothing seemed to move his pity.

"I have not offered you money," Captain Fitch now said, addressing Sanchos, "for the reason that I know a high-toned and honest Mexican can neither be bribed nor bought."

A groan of contempt and doubt from Lewey, a sniff from the young girl, and a toss of her head, as though she knew that Captain Fitch was stating what he did not believe, just for the purpose of accomplishing his ends.

"But," continued the captain, still speaking to Sanchos, "I will do this much on my own account. Let the boy occupy the vacant room, and I will give you fifty dollars tomorrow morning."

"No, senor, he herds with the Indians," was the firm rejoinder; but this was a little more than Don Carlos Sanchos and his fellows could endure. They had come to San Diego to make money, under the leadership of Don Antonio, and here was the first chance they had seen to obtain a peso at the expense of the residents. They did not like it, and expressed themselves in decided terms on the subject. They wanted vengeance, but dollars more, and plenty of them, and, now that the silver stream was ready to play, and lead to their pockets, the chief of the villains seemed determined to turn it aside. They growled, and Sanchos saw that he had made a mistake. His power lay in the hold which he had on the men. He wanted money, yet desired revenge much more, but thought, after a moment's hesitation, that he could obtain both. So he spoke in a conciliatory tone as he said, —

"I have no desire to offend so good a friend to California as Senor Fitch. Let him give us the fifty dollars, and the boy can remain a prisoner in the single room. Is it a bargain? Have I spoken well?" turning to his followers.

"It is bueno," was the unanimous growl, and Lewey once more squeezed the girl's hand, and she looked pleased at his attentions, and even smiled on him. He had a handsome face, and that went a great way in winning her favor. She was not the only girl who had been captivated by his good looks, and pursuasive tongue, for, Frenchman-like, he could make love even when he did not feel it.

"The money shall be paid tomorrow," Captain Fitch said, in reply to Sanchos' question. "Come to my house and obtain the pesos after breakfast."

I could only thank the captain for his consideration and kindness, and then, as the Indians continued to howl forth their complaints and fears, the jailor gave the lamp in keeping of his daughter, took the end of a stout lariat, which must have been used for such cruel purposes, rushed into the cell, and began to thrash the inmates over every part of their bodies that was most convenient, — heads or haunches, it did not matter much to the Mexican. He wanted a quiet life, and was determined to have it, unless his strength gave out.

The Indians dodged from side to side, but all of them received a liberal allowance of blows, and, when silence was at length commanded, bleeding and bruised, the miserable brutes retreated to a corner, glowered at the jailor, and were told to keep quiet for the rest of the night, or there would be another raid in their midst, and more stripes.

The Mexicans looked on, and laughed at the exhibition. They rather enjoyed it, for they had no pity for Indians, or any one else, and, when peace was restored, and Lewey had squeezed the girl for the last time, promising that he would come and see me in the morning, a coarse blanket was thrown into my cell by the jailor, a pillow of straw by the young girl, the door was locked on me, and I was left to my own reflections, with a pipe, tobacco, and a few matches. I filled the pipe, lighted it, curled down on the blanket, and in the darkness thought of my desperate situation, and wondered how I was to escape from it. Again did I reproach myself for leaving the ship, and casting my lot amid strangers, but all through the night, when I was awake, I did not utter a murmur against Lewey who had induced me to do so, and fell asleep at last in defiance of the fleas.

When I awoke it was sunrise, the Indians were quiet, and I could hear the sweet voice of the jailor's daughter, as she moved about the premises, singing a love song, and probably thinking of Lewey, his hand-squeezing and tender glances.

No one came to me until nearly seven o'clock, and then the girl unlocked the door, and looked into my prison.

"Caro chico," I said, "have my friends been here to see me this morning?"

"Not yet, muchacho," she answered. "There is time enough for them What can I do for you this fine day?"

"Could you give me enough water to wash in, and some to drink?" I asked.

"Yes; but if I should bring it into your cell, will you swear by the holy saints not to kiss me?"

As I had no thought of such an outrage the question set me to thinking, and I resolved to be firm, and promise nothing that would in the least compromise me. Besides, I remembered the previous evening's work, and how Lewey had obtained an advantage over me, because I was a prisoner, with secured hands, and he was free.

"Senorita,' I said, " the saints put temptation in our way so that mankind can be tested, and made good for a great future. Alas, I am a Protestant, and a heretic, but a just one, so must not disdain the nice and beautiful things of this world. Do not make me pledge my word, as I fear that I shall break it if you come near me, sweetest of Mexican girls."

She tossed her head in a coquettish manner, and smilingly showed her white, even teeth, but, as she did so managed to ask, —

" At least you will promise me one thing if I enter your cell with the water?"

" Name it, senorita," I cried.

" You will take no more than a single kiss. Say that you will not, and I shall enter without fear. Ah, if you were as nice as your friend I should have no doubt. He is so honest and good."

I could only groan, and then answered, —

" I will not lie, even to a beautiful lady like yourself. I fear that the saints would never forgive me for such a crime. I will promise nothing."

" But surely two kisses will content you? My padre has gone for the breakfast, and will not be back for half an hour. If he should return, and find me being kissed by a heretic, and a prisoner, he would be very angry. Be a good boy, and content yourself with two, or at the most three. But if you are quick, and do not dwell too long upon my lips, four. I am firm at the last number. I feel sure that your companion, who was here last night, is a much more modest boy than you, and not nearly as greedy. He would be contented with one, and think himself fortunate. But you — I do not know what to make of you,"

" Bring the water, dulce," I cried, and, before she could turn to obey, I had slipped my arm around her waist, and stolen half a dozen kisses. Then she broke away from my embrace, and pretended the indignation she did not feel.

" I am ashamed of you," she cried, while her dark eyes sparkled with the fun she was having, and her bruno cheeks showed the warm blood as it leaped through her veins, and dyed neck and shoulders with a deep crimson. Then she ran away, as if in anger,

But after a few moments' delay she returned with an earthen jug of water, a calabash to wash in, a towel, such as it was, for it looked as if cut from a second-hand grain bag, and a cracked cup to drink from. Then she left me alone for a while, to make my toilet, and, even before I had completed it, the young lady came to my room to shake up the blankets, and to tell me that coffee would be served in a little while, and, if I wanted anything more substantial, I would have to wait until Captain Fitch sent food from his house, for her breakfast would consist of tortillas and fruit, and she supposed I was not accustomed to such slender repasts.

"If you will let me drink my coffee in company with yourself and father I should not care for much else," I whispered, as she accidentally passed near me.

"Look here," the girl cried, as she suffered my arm to remain around her waist, and gazed steadily into my eyes, "I am afraid that you are a bold, bad young man, and I do not feel safe with you in the calabozo all alone."

"You forget the Indians," I remarked. "There are three of them in the large room."

"They are asleep, and the door is locked," was the prompt reply.

"There is no fear. Your padre will soon arrive," I urged.

"Not for fifteen minutes as yet, and if I should scream who could hear me? The saints protect me, but it is a fearful thing to be in the house all alone with a heretic, a man who does not believe in the church, the holy Virgin, and a candid confession."

"You can lock me up in the cell. I swear to you that I will not resist if you are disposed to do so. I am a good lad, and mean no harm to any one," I asserted, in a positive manner, for I did not know but that she might be a little timid, on account of the treatment she had received, and yet I had kissed her but six times, in the most innocent manner possible.

"No," she said, in a determined tone, "I will not turn the key on you. I think you bad, but I remember that a prisoner is always entitled to pity, and so I can keep you at arm's length, and expend some of my sympathy on your unhappy condition at the same time, for, do you know, I think Don Sanchos means to have you shot, and, if you should be killed, I declare to the saints that I would cry my eyes out. I heard the miserable tell his companions that if you escaped the gallows a bullet would end your career. He is a bad man, also, but ever so much worse than you. There is no telling how quick you will be led to death, and, as such may be the case today or tomorrow, you can kiss me just once for friendship's sake."

She put up her pretty lips for the kiss, but failed to rebuke me when I captured four or five. I could not stop to count them.

"Now I know that you are bad," the jailor's daughter remarked, but she could not make an effort to break away from my arms, although I could see that she had one ear toward the door, as though on the watch for the footsteps of her father. "Oh, what a miserable life I should lead if you were my husband," the girl remarked suddenly.

This was coming to close quarters, and getting a little more sympathetic than I bargained for. I had not thought of the little girl as a wife. In fact I had never spoken to her until the night previous. She seemed disposed to push matters to a crisis, and win me in an off-handed manner, if it was possible.

"Why do you think I should not make a good husband?" I asked, a little nettled at the insinuation.

She blushed a rosy red, and held down her head, as she quietly answered,—

"Because you want to kiss me all the time, and, if we were married you might pay too much attention to other girls instead of your wife, whom the blessed saints gave you, sanctioned by the priest. Oh, I am afraid when I think you would break my heart, for I know that you could not be true. Men never are. They don't care to kiss their loving little mates, but women who are not their wives."

It seemed to me that the girl was doing the wooing, and that I should find myself engaged before I knew it, unless I was very cautious.

"Americans," I said, as soon as I could think of something to say, "make the best husbands in the world. They are constant, always true, and loving. It is rarely they flirt."

"Then," the eager girl cried, as she put up her lips to be kissed, "I will marry no one but an American, and you are one."

This was a little more than I had expected, and I did not know how I was to extricate myself from the difficult position in which I found myself placed, for, as a general thing, I would not advise prisoners in a foreign country to make an enemy of the jailor's daughter, if it is possible to retain her as a friend. There are many chances for her to make your lot an uncomfortable one if so disposed. All this I knew, so did not feel like wounding the girl's self-respect, or her maidenly pride, if I could avoid it. But marriage was out of the question, for, if I was to wed any one, I must take little Anita, of Ranche Refugio, to whom I had pledged my heart and hand months before. But the young lady who was now standing by my side did not know it, and I was well satisfied to keep her in ignorance of the fact, or until I left my prison a free man, or was removed to some other. While I was framing some masculine story in my mind, so as to keep the girl good tempered and friendly, I heard heavy footsteps on the street, near the calabozo.

"Go in your cell," the young lady whispered. "It may be Don Sanchos, and if he should see you free would not like it. He might think that I had allowed you to make love to me, and that is always injurious to a poor girl's reputation."

She pushed me into the cell, locked the door, and then unfastened the outer one, and threw it open. I heard a person enter the prison, and soon distinguished the sound of Don Sanchos' voice, asking in gruff tones about the manner in which I had passed the night, and if I was safely confined in the calabozo.

"How should I know?" answered the girl. "I have much to do without attending to the prisoners. The boy may escape for all that I care. I am sure that he will give us enough trouble before he is discharged. Here, take the key, and look in at him if you want to, but see that he does not rush past you, and go clear."

"No fear of that," was the confident answer. "He is unarmed, and I have my knife, and can cut him to pieces before he gains the door."

This was good news for me, for I had thought for a moment of making a bold strike for liberty, but now I concluded that I had better remain where I was, and take no risks.

The ruffian took the key from the girl's hand, unlocked the door, and as I looked up from my reclining position, pretending to be just awakened, I saw the evil face of Sanchos, and in his right hand he held a long knife, as if prepared to use it in case I threatened violence.

I bel'eve that the scamp would have rejoiced had I shown fight just at that moment, for he could have killed me easily, but I remained motionless, and did not speak, as he regarded me with savage joy in his dark eyes.

"You are still here," he said.

I did not speak.

"Caramba! am I an oso, that I should not be spoken to?" was the fierce exclamation. "Dog of a Yankee, do you know who I am?"

Still no answer from my lips, for I knew that if I spoke I should say som thing to enrage him much more than if I kept silent.

The ruffian took one step into the cell, and Heaven knows what his inte ions were. He might have thought how pleasant it would be to drive his long knife into my heart, and so end his plan for revenge at once and forever, or he may have desired to test me, and see if I was game enough to stand his wild threats. But, before Sanchos could further insult and threaten me, the old jailor returned, and, as he entered the room, his daughter sprang forward, laid her hand on Sanchos' shoulder, and pulled him back.

"You have no right in this cell," she said. "All prisoners must be interviewed in the presence of a witness, and in the main room. My father will tell you that such is the law."

Sanchos allowed himself to be pushed from the cell, but I doubt if he would have moved had not the old jailor put in an appearance, and supported his daughter's position.

The door of my prison was closed and locked, but, as the keyhole was as large as a baby's fist, I could look through it, and see all that was going on in the living-room of the jail. The Mexican held a whispered conversation with the keeper, and pointed in my direction several times, as though to charge upon the man the importance of being vigilant, and seeing that I did not escape. Then he took his departure, and the girl and her father sat down to a scanty breakfast of coffee, bread, and fruit.

"Hullo," I shouted through the keyhole. "Am I not to have anything to eat this morning? Am I to be left to starve while you feast on all the luxuries of the town?"

"Patience," said the old man. "Your breakfast is to come from the kitchen of the Senor Fitch. The cooks of his house were up late last night, and the lazy ladrones have not stirred themselves as yet. All in good time, muchacho. My girl here will not let you suffer. She has a warm heart for all good-looking prisoners, especially when they are white gringos."

"Just as though I cared for the enemies of Mexico," cried the girl, with a toss of her head. "I love my country, and not those who seek to destroy it."

This I thought was rather refreshing, considering all that had passed between us since the girl was stirring, but, as I supposed she knew her own business best, did not not think it prudent to cavil at her words, or to remind her of having hinted she would like me for a husband. So I returned to my blankets and pipe, and wondered at the duplicity of women, especially Mexican women, when holding confidential relations with a father, and a lover hearing all that was said.

The old jailor finished his breakfast, lighted a cigarette, smoked it quite calmly, and with a certain dignity, then unlocked the door of the cell where the Indians were confined, stirred them out of their profound slumbers, with the aid of a piece of reata, striking to the right and left, I judged by the sound of blows, and at last the whole gang of vagabonds were driven into the street, and from thence to some court, where the alcalda, I presume, passed sentence on the lot, for they did not return to the calabozo, so the place was free from their yells and stench the rest of the day.

The young lady removed the few dishes, and was singing a little for her own amusement, and provoking me to wish that I was with her, when I heard a well-known bark, and into the room bounded Jack, and following him was Lewey, but he did not have in his hands the breakfast that I stood so much in need of.

"You here?" asked the girl, as Lewey entered the room. "I was in hopes that I should never again see you. Look at my hand. Gracias dios, but last night I thought you would squeeze it all out of shape, and the pobrecita muchacho, the sospechoso, looking at us all the time. You are a maldito hombre, and I believe you to be bad, very bad."

Confound the girl. She had used the same words to me. Did she have a regular formula for all the young men she flirted with?

"Ah, caro mio," that bad friend of mine exclaimed, "how could I help pressing the smallest and most delicate hand in all San Diego?"

And then the impudent lad put an arm around her well-developed waist, bent his head, and kissed her lips a dozen times or more, before he stopped to take breath.

This was a little more than I could endure. It was bad enough to be a prisoner, but to be confined in a cell, and peek through a large keyhole, and see your best friend kissing a pretty girl, one whom you thought a little spoony on yourself, was altogether too much. I kicked at the door, and yelled like one of the drunken Indians the night before.

"Wretch," I shouted indignantly, "is that the way you show your friendship? For shame! Or are you lost to all sense of honor?"

Instead of replying, and desisting from his detestable exhibition, the French lad simply winked one of his blue eyes in my direction, and then renewed the kissing, and, confound the girl, she seemed to like it, for I heard her murmur in very low tones,—

"I am afraid you are a bad man. I don't believe your friend would be guilty of such improprieties."

Confound the little coquette. She was repeating the very words to Lewey that she had used to me only an hour before.

"Ah, he is not a good man like me," the most perfidious of friends said. "He is not the same devoted lover I would be. He kisses a girl, and soon forgets her. I never forget the sweet face of a women I love," and then he kissed her some more, and the sight nearly drove me frantic. Once more I kicked at the door, and yelled out a strong protest.

"Vile son of France," I cried, "let me out of this so that I can punch your head. Is this the friendship that you profess for me?"

I spoke in English, so the girl did not understand me, but, even if I had addressed her in the native tongue, I don't believe that she would have paid any attention to me, for the lady only clung the closer to Lewey, and managed to lisp,—

"I should be fearful if you were my husband. I don't believe that you would be true and constant. You might flirt with other women, and break my heart."

This was a little too much for human endurance. I wondered how many more men she had spoken to in the same way, and with the like tokens of affection. I gave the heavy oak door, studded with spike-heads, a desperate kick, and said, in a tone of deep contempt,—

"Oh, bah! don't you believe a word she says, Lewey."

"I 'm attendin' to dis ding," was the consoling reply. "You attends to your business, and I look arter mine. You keeps cool, and goes to sleep, and not roar like von calf vot is hungry," and then the wretch took another kiss, and squeezed the girl a little more energetically.

"I am one of those men," said the scamp, speaking to the girl in Spanish, "that loves once and forever. With such a little beauty as you for a wife what more could a man desire? I should not care to look on any woman but you, to kiss no one but you, and thus we could go through life, hand in hand, and never a word of dissention between us."

I could not repress a groan at hearing such heartless lying from a young man who had French blood in his veins, and, consequently, thought it gallant and becoming to make love to every pretty face that crossed his path. He was so different from me that I wondered why he had not learned a more correct course of conduct.

"O you wretch," I cried through the keyhole, "stop your yarns and love-making. You make me sick with such stupid lies," while the young girl seemed to place full confidence in all he said, and actually put up her lips for an extra kiss, as a reward for the pretty words he had uttered.

"Yes," she said, "I could love you much better than your friend. He is so cold and distant, and pays no attention to the young girls that he meets."

This was good. The woman was as big a story-teller as the Frenchman. I thought the pair well matched.

"He is an Americano," Lewey said in a tender tone. "He belongs to a country dat is cold as its religion. The Americanos are like ice, which you never saw, and can form no idea of. Vhen dey talk of love a fire is needed to heat their words or they would freeze. But a Frenchman is as de sun at noonday, and as such he alvays remains."

"If you keep on that way much longer I shall need no breakfast," I exclaimed. "As it is, I'm sick at my stomach hearing such trash as you utter. Let up on the love-making business, and get me out so that I can have a share."

"Mine friend," asked Lewey, "do you dink I'm doing all dis to please mineself?"

"Well, it looks confoundedly like it as far as I can judge," I answered. "At least you might have the decency to get out of the range of the key-hole, so that I cannot see all that is going on before me. Now I understand the value of your friendship. It is to kiss pretty girls, and keep me locked up, so that I can't have a show. For shame on you. I would not treat you in such a scurvy manner."

"If you dinks I puts mineself to all dis trouble for de sake of de fille you is mistaken much," Lewey said. "It is for your good dat I does all dese mean dings," and then he kissed the girl again, because she expected it, and the fellow did not seem to shrink from the task, as though it was a disagreeable one.

"How is kissing the girl going to help me?" I asked.

"You vill vait and see. All in good time. I does much for mine ami, and I gets no danks for it, so it appears."

Just at this moment two peons appeared with a basket that contained a pot of hot coffee, some bread, and cold meats, all sent from the kitchen of Captain Fitch. The lovers separated, and the girl took the key of my door, and unlocked it, and then Lewey threw his arms around my neck, and embraced me.

"I vork as hard as ebber I can for you," he said. "Ah, vot vould not I do for you?"

I did not feel good-natured, so failed to respond to his greeting as readily as I might have done. I had seen too much. Besides, the girl was distant and cold, and seemed like a different person from the one I had joked with in the morning. She treated me more like a prisoner, as though rejoiced to show her power.

"Now eat your breakfast," my friend said, "and den ve vill smoke our pipes, and talk of de dings dat vill interest us. You is in a bad vay, but ve hopes for de best. De dog o' a Sanchos is a vile man, and vants your life, but de Cap'en Fitch send a courier off dis bery mornin', and he vite to General Castro, and de alcalda do de same. But drink your coffee, and not talk all de time."

I had not spoken a word, except to the dog Jack. The animal was so delighted to see me that I had bestowed more attention on him than Lewey. However, as I was hungry, and the breakfast was a good one, I soon finished it, then lighted my pipe, and prepared for a long talk.

"The Americano must go into his cell again," the girl said, as soon as the peons had departed with the basket and dishes. "It is against the rules of the prison for any one to be here, except the keepers and visitors."

Lewey winked, and whispered, —

"Leave her to me. I understand vomen, and you don't. You believes all dat dey tel's you. But me, bah! I discounts ninety per cent, and den makes a little profit."

He turned to the girl, and put on a sweet smile, as he said, —

"If my friend must go into de cell, I shall follow, for I have much to tell him. Think, caro mio, of locking us both up, vhen ve can be more comfortable here, and we swear dat no effort shall be made to escape."

The young jailor saw that there was no chance for a further tête-à-tête with Lewey, and, as she could exchange a few words with him while in the reception-room, but none if locked up, readily consented to break the rules, only stipulating that if any one should come to the door I could run to my cell, have the key turned, and was not to come out until all danger was passed. This suited us, and we readily agreed to it, for we did not know when Sanchos would again drop in to see how I was enjoying my imprisonment.

"Now," said Lewey, after our pipes were lighted, "you vill understand vy I makes love to de girl."

"I understand nothing of the kind," I answered, a little testily.

"Vell, you vill, if you listens to me in patience, and not scowl like a pirate. In de fust place, you is here."

"Confound you, I know that well enough without being told of it."

"Dat is right. Dar are some peoples dat has to be told many times, and den dey no understand much. Now out of dis you is to go, and dis bery night."

"I can understand all that. But how is it to be accomplished?" I asked eagerly.

"Ah, here comes in de finesse of de vise man. You may have noticed dat I make a little love to de fille?"

An indignant puff of smoke from my pipe was the only answer.

"Vell, it vas ah for you dat I does it. She now dinks dat I vants to marry her. I let her dink so ebber so much, but I is no fou. I is a Frenchman, and knows bery vell vot I talks about. Tonight dar is one big fandango in de town, and de jailor go see it, and dance. All de old men do dat, and de older dey am de more dey like it, if dey has a bonne fille to squeeze for de partner. He no hab vife, and he sure to go. I tell de daughter to stay at home, and I come see her, and court her much. Den I promise her eberyding if she let mine friend out, and she vill. I knows de vomen, and just vot dey vill do. If she no consent, I take de key, and unlock de door, and avay ve goes."

"But how shall we get away from the town?" I asked.

"Nebber you minds. I take cares of all dat. Vonce out of dis place, and Sanchos and his gang no lookin' on, I find de vay for escape. You leaves all to me, and no hint to de girl dat I am not a good boy, and means all dat I says. Ah, mon ami, I does much for your sake, and many disagreeable dings."

"Does Captain Fitch know of your designs?" I asked.

"Yes. He talk vid me all dis mornin' on de subject, and he laugh and approve. Nice man dat, and see great vay ahead."

"But where are we to go if I make my escape?" I questioned.

"To de hide-house."

"Why, that is the very place they would seek for us," I remonstrated.

"Yes, I know, and Captain Fitch know," was the confident answer. "But in dat hide-house Sanchos and his men no dare to come if ve say s and off."

"And Scotch Jack, what will he have to offer on the subject?" I asked, for it was important that the master of the hide-house should be with us, and help protect us.

"He all right. Dis mornin' he vake up all sober, and den ve gives him one big drink of aguardiente, and tell him to go to de beach, and get all ready for us tonight, and he swear dat he vill blow de head off de greaser dat comes near him. De government is bound by de treaty, you know, to protect de property of all foreigners in case of var, and dar is vhere ve vill hab 'em."

"Is that true? or is it a bit of imagination on your part, Lewey?"

"Captain Fitch say dat, and not me. He know eberyding, so I s'pose it

Lewey and I.

is true. But dar is one ding more. De alcalda say ve must be matriculadored if ve stay here in de country, and dat he has sent vord to General Castro dat ve has announced our determination to become citizens of de State. Dat is bad, but one oath dat you no intend to keep much no hurt any one, much less you and me. Ve forget him in a little vhile, if ve vants to."

"What does Captain Fitch advise on the subject?" I asked.

"He vink one eye, and say it is good for us; much better dan bein' shot as a spy by de rascal Sanchos, and his men. De alcalda come here dis arternoon, and make you take de oath, and sign de paper. Only dink, in a little vile ve can be full-grown greasers. Yes, ve must take de swear, and do de best ve can."

"The oath you mean, Lewey."

"Vell, it is de same ding, I s'pose. I swear all de day if dey vant me. Always do, mine friend, as de party vot is strongest vants you to, and den you vill hab no trouble."

I thought the matter over for a while, and at last concluded to be registered, as the preliminary for full citizenship, which could be accomplished in the course of time, if we were persistent in our demands for the precious boon.

At the same time there was one advantage in being matriculadored. We could exhibit our certificates in any part of California, and take up a section of land, five miles square, if we desired as much, and settle on it, and, after the lapse of time, receive a clear title from the Mexican government. The only stipulations made were the usual ones, — actual settlement on the property, and the raising of grain and cattle. California, at the time, was the most liberal country in its grants to foreigners that the sun ever shone on, and the acres given away were the best in the world, near large rivers, like the Sacramento or the American, with tablelands that extended for miles in all directions, and with not a stone on thousands of rods that was as large as a filbert. The soil was a dark loam, that extended downward for many feet, and the only disagreeable feature was the occasional overflow in the rainy season. But there were higher lands, just as good, and not subject to inundations, and those were usually selected, but the United States government made short labor with some of the claims, when the American Commission got to work on titles, and the just had to suffer with the unjust. Old families were ruined, for they had not always taken out deeds in a proper form, hardly thinking it worth their trouble, as land was of no value before annexation to the United States. Then the speculators hungered for farms which did not belong to them, and they scooped in all that they could lay their hands on, and proved by forgery and perjury that they possessed old Mexican grants, and sometimes the commissions passed them.

All of these things, or, rather, the advantages, passed through my mind, and I said that I would matriculador, or sign what the alcalda required. I had hardly given my consent, when we heard some one at the door, and I darted into my cell, and the girl locked me up, and then gave Lewey a kiss before she admitted the new-comer, who was no less a person than the alcalda, accompanied by Don Sanchos, the latter to see that I took the oath of allegiance in proper form, and signed my name to the same.

Lewey exchanged a few words with the new-comers, and then the official ordered the young girl to unlock my cell, and conduct me to his presence. Sanchos scowled at me as I entered the room, and looked the disappointment that he appeared to feel, for he had not supposed I would take the steps I did to secure myself from his persecution. To be sure, he could keep me imprisoned until General Castro was heard from, but he had no power to have me shot or hanged, without a formal trial, and that he was not disposed to do, as he knew nothing could be proved against me, and his charge of my being a spy must fall to the ground.

"Well, muchacho," the alcalda said, "I understand that you desire to matriculador. The Senor Fitch thinks you had better do so, and I can see no objections."

"Let him understand one thing," interrupted Sanchos, with an evil glance. "If he registers he will be liable to military duty, and have to serve with the Mexican army if called upon, or be treated as a traitor to the State."

"Will I have to act against the forces of my own country?" I asked, a little staggered by the information.

"Yes, just as freely as a Mexican-born citizen," was the alcalda's answer.

"Vot care you?" whispered Lewey, in English "You no shoot vell enough to harm any one. Me! Oh, I swear to anyding ven it suits me to do. Let us get out of dis, and trust to de good luck for de next time. You hear me make de love to de girl, and dell her strange dings? Vell, dat is vorse much dan takin' one stupid oath, vot no one cares for."

"What are you saying?" asked Sanchos, speaking to the free-thinking French boy, suspicious of words which he could not understand.

"I tell him dat I vill take de oath at de same time," was the prompt answer. "Vot care I? A Mexican is as brave and good as a Frenchman or Yankee any time."

Sanchos was not quite satisfied with the explanation, but he grunted his approval of the sentiment, while the alcalda smiled, as if he coul I testify in any court of justice that the words were correct, and such as would meet with approval in any part of the world.

"I will take the oath," I said, but resolved to make a mental reservation that none of my people should be injured by the course which I was obliged to pursue to save my life.

The alcalda produced his papers, and then Lewey and I raised our right hands, swore that we would bear allegiance to Mexico, and do all that we could to confound her enemies.

"Now sign the papers, and the deed is done," the official said.

The jailor's daughter produced pen and ink, after some little trouble, showing that they were seldom used at the calabozo to record the titles of committed or discharged prisoners, and then the alcalda arose, and held out his hand to the new candidates for citizenship, or as soon as we had signed our names to the document he did so.

"May you defend the honor of Mexico as readily as you would that of the countries to which you formerly belonged," the official said, and we shook hands on it, but did not do so with much gusto. Lewey looked upon the whole matter as a good joke, and even smiled and winked at the girl, when he thought no one was watching him.

"Have you concluded, Senor Alcalda?" asked Sanchos, as soon as the official had finished his pretty little speech.

"Yes, senor," with a wave of his thin, dark hand.

"Then let me say a few words, for they are important," and the scoundrel laghed in my face, and then caressed the scar on the back of his hand, with a zeal that was full of meaning. "The boys have announced their intention of becoming citizens of Mexico. They have signed matriculadors. They are now registered under the laws of the State and country."

"Yes, certainly, senor. But what then?" demanded the alcalda, looking the surprise he felt.

"Only this, Senor Alcalda. Read one more paper that I had the honor to receive from the hands of General Castro and Pio Pico, I did not deem it prudent to present it last night, when I gave you the others, for certain reasons best known to myself. I suspected just what has taken place, and wished for the result."

The alcalda opened the document, and from it we learned that the trusty and beloved Don Antonio Sanchos was empowered to raise, impress, and gather together all the able-bodied Mexicans he might deem proper to select, enroll them in the army, and forward them to Monterey as soon as possible, to act against the treacherous los Americanos.

This was a stunner. We saw the trap into which we had fallen, but it was too late for retreat. The fellow had drawn us along for his own purposes, and now we were in his power more than ever, for the State was under martial law, and Sanchos was its representative in San Diego, all civil courts being set aside for the time being.

" You would not take the boys away from this place, would you?" the alcalda asked, as he returned the paper to its owner.

"Is this document correct?" Sanchos cried, not heeding the question, and tapping the paper with the fingers of his maimed hand.

" It is," was the quiet answer.

" And you acknowledge the power that it gives me?" the scoundrel demanded.

" Yes, senor. I dare throw no impediments in your course. You are supreme here, under martial law. I must obey, or resign my office," the alcalda said.

" That you will not do, for I forbid it, and, if you should persist, I will arrest you as an enemy of the State, and forward you to Monterey for trial. Better be with me than against me."

The official was silent. He saw that he had an unscrupulous villain to deal with, and desired to save his own life, and that of his friends. Besides, the alcalda was a rich man, and knew what it was to be squeezed by the leading men of his State. He did not desire to lose anything he held most dear just for the sake of two gringo boys. He would have helped us if he could without danger to himself, just because he was naturally kind-hearted, and desired to oblige Captain Fitch, who really had an interest in us.

At this instant the old jailor returned to his charge, having been gossipping all the morning with the neighbors, and to him the military agent addressed himself.

" Lock these boys up, and see that they do not escape. I shall hold you responsible for their safe keeping," Sanchos said, pointing to Lewey and myself.

" Do you mean to imprison me?" the French lad asked, a little anxious for the first time during the day.

" Yes. You and your friend are conscripted for the Mexican army. In a few days I shall have the pleasure of forwarding you to headquarters, at

Monterey, in company with such others as I shall select. My brother Carlos will have charge of the squad, and he is not a person to be trifled with. Lock the lads up."

"You are the meanest, blankest cur in all California," Lewey cried, in a paroxysm of rage, speaking in Spanish, but the Mexican only smiled, and rubbed his scarred hand.

"Did you think that you were to escape all revenge for the injury you inflicted upon me at San Francisco?" asked Sanchos. "Do you remember how you pulled my hair, and banged my head, in the boat?"

"Yes, and I wish that I had been ten times more rude," was the frank exclamation of the French lad. "We let you off too easily that time. If we have another chance you shall not escape so lightly."

"Do you threaten me, you French dog?" asked Sanchos, and, as he spoke, raised his hand, and aimed a blow at the flushed face of my friend, but Lewey dodged, and countered on the dark visage of the Mexican, and then blood flowed from his nose in large drops, and the fellow reeled, and would have fallen had he not caught at the table for support.

But in an instant the Mexican had recovered himself. He reached for the long knife that he carried in the legging of his right leg, drew it, and would have stabbed my friend to the heart if the young girl had not sprang forward. She knew what her countryman was capable of, and, as she threw her arms around his form, so that he could not use his hands, she shrieked to her father,—

"For the love of God lock the muchacho in his cell, and put the key in your pocket. If you do not there will be murder committed here."

The father understood the situation, and so did the alcalda and myself. We all seized the struggling, wild, maddened Frenchman, and dragged him to the cell, and then the jailor turned the great key, and we were safe for the time being, but could hear Sanchos uttering fearful oaths of what he would do to us when the proper time arrived, and thus cursing left the calabozo to consult with his associates.

"He is a big coward," Lewey said, as the fellow left the prison, in company with the alcalda. "I could vip him vid one hand, if he no use de knife. You know it vas his brudder Carlos dat fire at us last night, vile ve is on de vay to San Diego. I hear 'em talk it ober, and dat Sanchos scold 'cos he no shoot better. Dey is a bad lot, and it vould hab been much better if ve had stuck to de old ship, and let de girls go to dunder."

I thought so also, yet did not express my sentiments in the same manner.

"But you trust to me," the confident Lewey exclaimed. "I do much for you. I eben make love to de girl, and you see how I succeed ven I commences. Oh, yes, I throws mineself avay for you," and the boy sighed, then lighted his pipe, and we had a good smoke, and went to sleep for an hour or two.

During the afternoon Captain Fitch called to see us, and advised us to be patient, for he had great hopes of buying our discharge from military service, and, when Lewey hinted to him that we intended to effect our escape that very night, and make the best of our way to the hide-house, he did not offer any objections, except to say that he could not furnish us with horses, as such an act would be equivalent to bringing down the wrath of Sanchos and his gang on his head. We would have to travel on foot, and then he recommended that we get on board an American vessel, and leave the coast as soon as possible. He would forward our money to any point we might designate, or give it to us in doubloons at the hide-house, provided we succeeded in reaching the place in safety.

This we agreed to, and then the gentleman promised us some dinner at five o'clock, and left us. He sent the food, as agreed upon, and, after he had partaken of all we wanted, we lighted our pipes, and waited for darkness.

We could hear the old jailor dressing for the fandango, and urging his daughter to go with him, but she complained of a dolor de cabeza, and so excused herself. Then, with directions to keep an eye on the prisoners, the old fellow ambled off, and the young girl commenced singing, to show that she had her own thoughts for company, and did not desire anything better.

"Now, mine ami, you shall see de sacrifices dat I makes for you," and, putting his mouth to the keyhole, Lewey commenced sighing forth the most ardent protestations of love that the young girl had ever listened to in her short and uneventful existence, and, confound the fellow, he put so much life in his prayers that I believe he rather liked it, and thought it not such disagreeable work as he pretended.

CHAPTER III.

LEWEY MAKES' LOVE, AND QUITE SUCCESSFULLY. — DON SANCHOS PAYS US A VISIT, AND IS CAUGHT IN A TRAP. — A GALLANT FIGHT IN WHICH OUR DOG TAKES PART. — ESCAPE FROM THE CALABOZO. — A VISIT TO THE HIDE-HOUSE BY THE MEXICANS. — AN ATTACK, AND A DEFEAT. — THE SOIREE WHICH JACK GAVE. — INDIGNANT SAILORS AND KANAKAS. — THE FIRE. — A RETROSPECTION.

"MY little darling," sighed Lewey through the keyhole, "does she hear me? does she still think of the young sailor who loved her from the first time he let his eyes fall upon her beautiful face?"

Then the lad turned to me, and said, —

"All dis I does for your sake. It is no pleasure for me to lie so to any voman."

"Go on," I remarked. "Lying comes to you so naturally that there is no fear of your injuring yourself in my estimation. Say anything that you please. Perhaps the girl can be induced to believe you. But I do not see how it is to benefit us."

"You vait and see, mine friend. Dat girl vill let us out of dis place, or know nothin' I of de female heart."

Once more he whispered through the keyhole, and said, —

"Caro chico, are you listening to me?"

"Yes," she answered. "I hear all that you say, but no words that you utter can induce me to unlock the door of your cell. My father has forbidden it."

"Ah, beautiful one, what is a father to a devoted lover? I burn to once more kiss your hand, to smooth the tresses of your luxuriant hair, to look into your eyes, so black and brilliant, to feel your sweet breath on my face," and then Lewey turned to me, and asked in a low tone, —

"How is dat for puttin' on de tenderness?"

"You are doing nicely," I rejoined; "but think of your soul."

"Nebber mind de soul now. It am de bodies dat I am dinkin' of most,' and once more Lewey turned his attention to the girl, who still hovered near the door, as though there was a certain fascination in its vicinity.

"I thought that I should never marry," Lewey continued, still speaking in Spanish, and whispering through the keyhole, "but now I have changed my mind, and I can never be happy unless in your presence. Ah, dulce, if you would but unlock the door so that I could be with you for a moment."

"I dare not," the girl replied.

"What do you fear, O best of women?" was the next question. "I love you. My friend is asleep, and hears me not. He knows nothing of the words I am addressing you. Let me press your hand but for a moment, and then I shall sleep in peace. Your heart is not like stone to withstand my prayers."

"If I should let you out will you return to the cell when I bid you do so?" the girl asked, and I knew that the smooth-tongued hypocrite was about to conquer, for I heard the girl remove the key of the cell from its accustomed place.

"I promise everything to one so beautiful as you," was the response. "Only let me remain in your presence as long as possible, for all is dark and dreary when absent from your side."

"Of all the liars that I ever heard you are the worst," I managed to whisper, as the key was put into the lock by the deluded girl.

"You shut up, and pretend to snore, for no girl like love to her be made ⁀annouder one listen to de pretty talk," my friend remarked, and, agreeable to his advice, I gave vent to some unmusical-like sounds as the door was thrown open.

"Come out, kiss me just once, and then return to the cell," the girl whispered.

There was no second invitation needed. Lewey rushed to her, enfolded the lady in his arms, then I heard some vigorous salutes, and but few struggles to prevent them.

"Hush," cried the girl. "Your companion will awaken, and what will he think?"

"He sleeps," answered the boy. "He is a cold-blooded American, and cares nothing for the beautiful girls of your nation Do not fear. All the kissing in the world would not awaken him."

"Still, I thought him very nice this forenoon. He is not bold and forward like you. I think he would marry me if he had the chance," I heard the girl say, as soon as she could recover her breath.

"Why should you desire to marry a man like him, when you can obtain me?" was the next question Lewey asked, showing the conceit of the boy. I wanted to get up and kick him, I felt so indignant.

"Perhaps you would not desire me as a wife if you knew me better," the girl remarked, in a coquettish tone, and, I supposed, toss of her head.

"Can you doubt me? I am a Frenchman, and a son of France never deceives the fair sex."

"But when should you want to marry?" asked the girl, who was a practical young lady, and desired some tangible pledge before she was ready to believe all that was poured into her willing ears.

"Just as soon as you please," was the prompt answer, and a kiss that made me gasp with envy.

"Would next week be too soon?" the lady asked.

For a moment there was an ominous pause, as though even the impulsive Lewey was a little daunted at the shortness of time that was allowed him to make his peace with the world, and a father confessor.

"You hesitate," the girl said. "You do not love me."

"If I did not answer it was because I regretted you should make the time so long before my happiness arrived. A whole week must I wait for you, dulce. Ah, why do you act thus coldly toward me?"

"Then we will say in four days," and the girl was rewarded with a kiss for her compliance to the French lad's pleadings.

"Now that all is settled you must do me a favor," Lewey said, after a little exchange of billing and cooing.

Then I knew that the crisis had arrived, and I paid much attention to what followed.

"Whatever you ask of me shall be granted, if it is right and proper," the prudent girl remarked.

"Do you think that I would demand anything not just and correct?" in a reproachful tone. "No, I am a Frenchman, and honorable, like all of my countrymen. We die for those we adore."

I could not repress a groan. This was a little too much for a listener, one who knew Lewey as well as I did. My stomach almost revolted at the nonsense he was pouring into that girl's ears. They both heard my exclamation, and the lady whispered, —

"Your friend has awakened. Do not speak so loud."

"Do not fear him," the lad cried. "He is always a sound sleeper. I have known him to slumber during the most terrible gales. Nothing would awaken him but a call for breakfast or dinner. When food was ready the slightest whisper was enough to bring him to his feet."

I determined to quarrel with Lewey if I ever got out of prison. But I would not punish him as he deserved, simply let his conscience do that provided he had such a thing, and I really began to doubt it more than ever.

"Now," said Lewey, "as we are to be married you must let my friend escape from the prison. Take that big key from your pocket, and open the outer door."

"Gracias dios! but I dare not do that," was the reply. "My father would kill me for violating my trust."

"Listen to me, caro dulce," pleaded the boy. "We must both escape tonight or we shall soon be separated forever. Did you not hear Don Sanchos say that we were to be impressed for the Mexican army? Our courage is so great we should be killed by the gringos in the very first battle, and then you could not marry a dead man, for he would be of no use. In a few days Sanchos will leave this part of the State for Pueblo los Angeles, or Santa Barbara. Then I can come from my place of concealment after all danger is passed, and no one can prevent our marriage."

Even our dog, which had been perfectly quiet during all the conversation here arose, shook himself, and uttered a subdued howl. He must have understood my friend, and become disgusted at his strong statements, one portion utterly devoid of truth.

"I dare not," sobbed the girl, and now I began to pity her, for who can withstand a woman's tears?

Even Lewey seemed a little contrite, for his voice lost some of its assurance, and he was more considerate, as he said, —

"Chico, we must leave this prison tonight, and with your aid. You can say we took the key from you by force. That you let us out of the cell for a moment, to get a bit of supper, and we rushed upon you, and made our escape. That is the story you are to tell, and no one will disbelieve you."

"But where will you go? There is no place that is safe from Sanchos. He will hunt for you in every direction, and, if he finds you, death will be your lot," and the young girl showed her anxiety by her tears.

"Fear not for us, little one. Once beyond these walls we can take care of ourselves. You will aid us, O sweetest of San Diego maidens?"

"Yes, you shall go."

I heard a shower of kisses on the girl's lips, which so disgusted Jack he uttered another growl of contempt, and I did not blame him, for it was enough to make a human being sick.

"Thom," cried Lewey, calling to me, "de noble-hearted Mexican girl vill release us. Ve is free. Avake, and let us be off, for ve hab no time to lose, and I has vorked harder tonight dan eber did i .iore. Lying does not easy to me come. But, O mine friend, much dors I do for you. May you nebber be called upon to act as I hab dis night."

I did not expend many sympathetic words upon the boy, for I thought they would be useless, not believing that he suffered as much as he pretended.

The girl had just taken the key from her pocket, and handed it to my friend, when we heard a footstep at the door, and then the harsh voice of Sanchos.

"Open, in the name of the law," he said.

"Quick, enter your cell," exclaimed the young assistant jailor. "He will kill me if you are seen in this room. Do not delay a moment; vamous muy presto."

"You will not lock the door?" asked Lewey in a low tone, as though he had a suspicion that she would do so, and I saw a shade pass over his face, as if he had been suddenly inspired with some new idea, that was of importance.

"Open the door," repeated Sanchos. "Caramba! do you intend to keep me here all night?"

"Go in your cell," the girl said, her face showing the terror that she felt at the sudden appearance of the agent of General Castro. "Do not delay a moment. I will not lock you in," and then, to show how sincere she was, added hastily, "Take the key, and lock yourselves in. I will tell the man that father has carried it with him to the fandango, in case he asks for it. Go," and she pushed Lewey into the cell, and thrust the key into my friend's hand.

He did not delay a moment, but entered the room, locked the door, and then the girl yawned, as if just awakened from a deep sleep, and admitted the Mexican.

"Did you not hear me call to you?" Sanchos asked. "Por dios, but I thought you were deaf."

"I was sleeping soundly, senor," the lady answered. "Last night I had but little rest on account of the drunken Indians, and today I have been busy with your prisoners. I did not expect any one here tonight, and fell into a doze. What is the hour, senor?"

She yawned, and Sanchos was deceived by her actions and words.

"I wish to see the prisoners," the Mexican muttered. "I desire to be sure that they are safe. In a day or two I shall start them toward Monterey, in company with Indians, and perhaps they will arrive there in safety. Quen sabe."

"The prisoners are all right," the girl said. "Look in the cell, and see or yourself. Try the door, and you will find that it is locked. The key my padre has in his pocket. He feared to leave it at home."

"Americano," Sanchos cried, as he endeavored to get a view of me through the keyhole.

"Go to the devil," I retorted. "We wish to sleep."

"You are not polite," laughed the Mexican. "I shall teach you to be more complimentary in the course of time. Kick that Frenchman into life, and let us see what he has to say for himself."

"Go to the devil," was the response from Lewey, in the same tone and words I had used.

"Not until I have sent you two boys to see him, and prepared a reception in my behalf. Would you like to come out?"

No response on our part, but Lewey grasped my arm, and whispered eagerly, —

"Is you game to dings do? Vill you lend me a hand? and in dis place he comes, and ve lock de door on him."

I squeezed back a willing response, and then we inserted the huge key in its proper place, and waited for our opportunity, when we could make a rush, and turn the tables on our enemy.

"I shall see you in the morning, and mind you have more civil tongues in your heads, or the worse for you. A few dozen blows with the end of a reata, on your bare backs, will be apt to improve your tempers and manners. Remember, I am master here just at present, and my word is law to all whom I address."

We wanted to punch the scoundrel's head for his insolence, but restrained ourselves.

"Stand ready," whispered Lewey. "You take de man's arms. I vill look out for his neck, and Jack him much vill bite about de legs. Be careful dat he does not de knife get hold of. If he do, cut vill he, and ve may come second best off."

We heard the Mexican move away from us to speak to the girl, and, at

this moment, Lewey used the key, flung open the door of the cell, and we sprang out, and toward Sanchos, Jack at our heels.

The Mexican turned at the noise we made, and, when he saw us, his surprise was so great that for a moment he forgot to reach for his long, sharp knife.

"Go for him, Jack," I yelled, and then Lewey and myself threw our arms around the man, the French boy at his throat, while I seized the elbows, and pinned them at his side, and the dog did some beautiful tearing in the neighborhood of his ankles.

"Diablo! help!" yelled Sanchos. "Give the alarm, girl. The prisoners will escape. A thousand curses on you."

He struggled fearfully, but we had the strength and muscle to cope with him. Besides, we had been trained to hard work for three years, pulling and hauling ropes, furling sails, and rowing, and were not easily exhausted, while the Mexican had led an indolent life, the only exercise he was accustomed to was riding horseback. I will give the scamp the credit of being a good equestrian, and he could throw a lariat with the precision of a rifle-ball.

"Down him," cried Lewey, as the fellow continued to yell, and we feared that he would alarm the neighborhood, while the girl was in a corner, wringing her hands, and almost frantic with terror.

We tripped the greaser up, and let him fall with a heavy thud, his head striking first, and it rather confused his senses for a moment, but the instant he recovered breath a yell issued from his mouth that must have been heard in the street, had any one been listening.

In the mean time Jack had torn off the Mexican's leggings, and was now down to hard pan, every bite telling, as we could judge by the fellow's kicks, for he was moving his legs quite lively, and sometimes the dog was in the air, and then on the floor, but at no period did he release his firm grip of flesh and clothes. Jack knew his business, and was attending to it with promptness and despatch.

"Call off your blanked dog," gasped the Mexican, but, as he opened his mouth to speak, Lewey jammed a piece of the leggings in between his teeth, and gagged the greaser effectually, so that he could no longer shout for help. To prevent being bitten by the desperate man my friend used the iron key with much force and happy results; then I reached down and seized the long knife, which had fallen from its sheath, and put the point to the owner's throat.

"Be quiet, or I'll kill you as you lie on the floor," I said, and Sanchos saw that I was in earnest, for he made a motion that he had yielded, and would make no more resistance.

"Turn him ober," cried Lewey. "Ve must his hands and arms lash to keep all quiet,' and over on his stomach we rolled the man, and then took the sash he wore around his waist, and tied his elbows together so that he could no longer assail us, had he been so disposed.

We drove Jack from his sport, dragged the greaser to the cell we had recently occupied, threw him in, and then said,—

"For the present we are quits. We won't kill you, as you deserve for your treachery, but hereafter let us alone, and we will be satisfied."

We could not see the man's face in the darkness, but it must have been expressive, as he lay on the floor powerless. He moved his legs, however, and kicked at us, but we were beyond his reach. Then, wishing the Mexican good-night, we passed out of the cell, and locked the door.

"Caro," said Lewey, to the frightened girl, "here is the key. Better run with it to your father, and tell him to swear that it has not left his possession for even a moment. Sanchos will think the gringos made one like it, so shall you and yours escape all harm for what has occurred."

"But you still love me?" sobbed the girl.

"Of course. Have I not said so?"

"And you will marry me very soon?" pleaded the woman, and she looked hard at Lewey, a little suspicious of his intentions.

"You must wait with patience until I return," the French lad said. "We are surrounded by danger, and this is no time to talk of matrimony."

We were moving toward the door, which was unlocked, when the young lady sprang toward us, and laid her hand on my friend's arm, thus detaining him for a moment.

"You are two bad men," she cried, "and I do not believe that either of you ever thought of marrying me. I have got to lose my prisoners, and a husband at the same time."

"But think of the kisses that you have received. Don't those count for something, little darling?" asked the hard-hearted French boy, as he continued to move toward the door.

"Ladrone of the devil," she yelled, "you have cheated and deceived me. You have no love for me," and, by Jove, she made a grab for the boy's thick head of hair, fastened both hands in it with a firm grip, and screamed like an enraged panther when deprived of its young.

"Take de blessed lunatic off," cried Lewey. "She vill mine head pull from de neck. Sacre, vot a little fire-spit."

I feared the girl would attract attention from some one passing the calabozo, and, although convulsed with laughter, strove to disengage her fingers, and at last succeeded, but, as she let go her hold, the girl turned, and fetched me a blow on the face that made me see quite a number of stars, and for a moment I thought I was in the presence of a prize-fighter.

"That will teach you better than to interfere in my affairs again," were the last words we heard from the girl, for she immediately tumbled to the floor, and kicked her heels on the planks until the noise sounded like the tatoo of a drum.

"By gar, vot a vife she vould make for a nice young man like me," was all the comment Lewey made as we darted out of the door, followed by Jack, and closing it after us.

As we ran down the dark street we could hear the hysterical screams of the disappointed candidate for matrimony until we turned a corner, and then the sounds of a harp and guitar came from an adobe house, showing that a fandango was in full blast near us.

"I must hab one leetle look," the French boy said. "I vish to see de ladies, God bless 'em, and to note if dey is booful. A Frenchman nebber miss a chance to pay his respects to de softer sex."

I rubbed my face, and wondered if all the girls of San Diego had hands like the jailor's daughter, and then attempted to point out to my friend the danger of stopping, even for a moment. But he was deaf to my prayers, and was not going to walk five miles to the hide-house until he had refreshed his eyes with a glance at the girls, and he had his way, for argument was lost on him, being so impulsive and reckless.

The door of the house stood open, and there was sound of scuffling feet, as the ladies and men waltzed. We kept in the shadow of the building, and looked in. There was a roomful of dark-faced greasers, and brilliant-eyed women, and in the corner, near a sort of bar, we saw bottles of wine and aguardiente, and a scamp we did not care to meet, it being Carlos Sanchos, brother of the fellow we had placed in our cell, and the same person we had good reason to suspect of firing on us the evening we made our way toward San Diego. Carlos was drinking aguardiente, with several of his gang near him each having a glass in hand, and a half-breed girl in close proximity to the party.

"I 'd like to fetch him a crack ober de head," muttered Lewey, as he watched the movements of the greaser, and just at that moment a woman came to the door to get a breath of fresh air. Before we could dart away she had caught a glimpse of us, and, with Mexican courtesy, said, —

" Entrer, muchachos."

We heard a stir in the room, and dropping of glasses, but did not halt for further demonstrations. We ran down a street, turned a corner, and saw before us the house of Captain Fitch, with a light burning in the dining-room. We did not stop to let the gentleman know we were out of prison, but kept on, as we heard the sound of footsteps behind us. We knew that we could outrun any greaser in the town, but were not disposed to give the fellows a chance to try conclusions, as we feared pursuit on horseback, and from several directions, which might be fatal to our fortunes and hopes.

As we passed Captain Fitch's premises we saw a low adobe wall, not more than five feet high, and enclosing a garden, the residence of a rich Mexican, who was collector of customs, or something of the sort.

"Ober ve goes here," panted Lewey, and he made a spring, vaulted on the wall, and then jumped to the ground, on the other side.

I caught up Jack, who seemed to think that the race was gotten up for his especial benefit, pitched him over the wall, and then followed the animal, and, just as I landed, a whole troop of greasers came down the street, followed by all the dogs in the neighborhood. Luckily for us the latter were worthless curs, and without the power to follow a trail, unless it was fresh and broad, like that of a wild animal. Man they had never been taught to hunt, although a few of them could track an Indian, if encouraged to do so by their owners.

As the greasers passed down the street we could hear them panting from the unusual exercise. Then they stopped near us, and all talked at once, like a group of school-girls, who expect an invitation to a party. We had to keep a firm hold of Jack's mouth, for he made considerable exertion to free his mind by the way of growls and angry barks.

"They did not come this way," one fellow said. "They turned to the right. I know they did, for I caught a glimpse of them."

"Who were they?" asked Carlos. "Does any one know?"

"They were the two boys confined in the calabozo," a greaser said. "I caught a glimpse of them as they ran from the door of the house."

"Diablo, impossible," cried Carlos. "They are in the calabozo, safe under lock and key. You must be mistaken."

"I know that I am not," was the positive reply. "I remember the boys very well. I have often seen them when they belonged to a ship that was on the coast."

"How could they have made their escape, if such is the case?" demanded Carlos, but, as no one seemed able to answer the question, a man suddenly asked, —

"Where is Don Sanchos, your brother? He should be here, and advise us."

No one could say where the chief scoundrel was located just at that moment, although I heard several of the greasers laugh, as though it would not answer to tell all that they knew about the fellow's movements in the night-time.

"I will wager a medio peso that the boys are at this moment in Don Fitch's house. They would naturally go there for protection and advice," a Mexican said, one who had not before spoken, and whose head seemed clearer than the others.

"Well thought of," was the exclamation of Carlos. "We will go and ask the senor if he is sheltering suspicious persons."

The fellows moved off in the direction of Mr. Fitch's premises, not more than one hundred feet from our place of concealment. Under the shadow of a fig-tree we watched the crowd hovering around the adobe house of the American, and we wondered what their reception would be like by the sturdy ex-whaleman.

"Now is de time for us to cut de stick," Lewey whispered, and we stole through the garden grounds, still holding on to Jack, to prevent his giving an alarm, passed to the other side of the premises, and climbed the wall, dropped once more into the street, and struck out for the hide house.

"By gar," Lewey said, as we walked along at a rapid gait, "ve sheats 'em booful."

"Yes, but we should have had no occasion to cheat them had you not been so obstinate," I remarked. "When will you learn a little prudence, you hot-headed Frenchman?"

"Bah, I runs more risk den dat to see de booful girls. A true Frenchman nebber dinks of danger vhen de softer sex is concerned. He risk all, eben his honor, for one sight of a nice face, one dat he can make love to. Me true Frenchman."

"Yes, I believe it," I sighed; "and, confound you, that tongue of yours, and desire to make love to everything that wears a petticoat, will cost you dearly some day. Oh, why will you not imitate me, and keep out of all danger?"

The boy passed an arm around my neck, as we walked, and then whispered, —

"You is here now, in dis place, all 'cos I talks to one female dat like to be made love to. Don't you say one vord about de prudence, and all dat, as I knows you kiss de girl afore I comes to your help. Deny it can you not."

I did not reply, for just at that moment we heard a roar from the mob in the town, and we suspected that Mr. Fitch was having his hands full in explaining to his visitors that no one was in his house, except those who had a just right to be there.

In fact, we afterward learned that the sturdy old captain had explained that he knew nothing of our whereabouts, and advised the Mexicans to go to the calabozo, and find out if we had made our escape from the prison. This the greasers did, and, when they released Don Sanchos from the cell, and his lashings, the profanity of the man was shocking, and he swore that he would yet have revenge for all of his injuries. In the mean time, in spite of his imprecations, Antonio did not lose his head. He directed that horses should be mounted, and search made for us on all the roads, and along the beach, thinking that we might secure a boat, and paddle to the hide-house by water, the safest way if we had been sure of finding a skiff on the flats. But we did not dare to run the risk, and so continued our course by the road, and soon left the town behind us.

It was near ten o'clock, we judged by the stars, and just cool enough to make walking agreeable. We had jogged on for half an hour or so, when we heard the galloping of horses in our rear, and suspected that our Mexican friends were in pursuit of us. We left the highway, and entered the bushes, waiting for the greasers to pass. We had to hold our dog very hard as the horsemen clattered by, at a full gallop, and, as they disappeared in the darkness, we continued our journey, knowing that we could do so with safety, as a Mexican never walks if he can ride, and we thought that the noise that the animals might make, if they returned to town, would give as ample time for concealment.

And so we pushed along, looking sharply on either side of the road for an ambush, and by eleven o'clock we were warned that the Mexicans had started on their way back to town. They had been to the hide-house, and seemed satisfied that we were not there, and supposed that we had not left the limits of the village. We once more secreted ourselves in the scrub, and waited until the cavalcade had passed. There were four men, and they discussed the probability of overhauling us, while one greaser, who seemed to have a little more humor than the rest of his companions, actually laughed as he related the finding of Don Sanchos, bound and gagged, in the cell. He even complimented us by saying that we were smart boys and had played a sharp Yankee trick on the agent of the government.

When the Mexicans were out of sight we resumed our journey, and were soon at the entrance of the hide-house. All was dark within, and there was not a light on the whole beach. Every one had retired except the dogs, and they came toward us with a rush and roar, then saw Jack, and recognized us as friends, and so left us to seek their usual sleeping quarters, or bark defiance at the coyotes on the sand-hills in the rear of the houses.

I pounded on the door of the premises to awaken Scotch Jack, the keeper, but he seemed disposed to pay no attention to the summons, even if he heard us, and it was not until we had beaten a rappel with two sticks for ten minutes that the old man condescended to move, and then he uttered a choice assortment of oaths, as he yelled out, —

"Go away from this, you blanked greasers, or you will get hurt. The boys are not here. I wish they were. You would n't get 'em, now I tell you."

"Jack, old fellow," I said, "don't you know us? It is Lewey and Thom. Let us in, for we are tired and hungry."

"You don't mean to tell me it 's you two boys?" the old sailor said. "Well, this beats the Dutch."

He unlocked the door, and the next instant the old Scotch salt was shaking our hands, and petting us, as if he had not seen us for a year.

"Come in, lads," he cried, "and let me close the door. The bloody greasers stopped here a short time ago, and insisted that you were in the building. I told 'em you were not, and, when they was too polite in their attentions, I jist drew on 'em with one of the old muskets, and they left in a hurry. The gun was n't loaded, but they did n't know it, so it was jist as good as if it had been. Now tell me all about it, and how you got clear of the swabs?"

We soon satisfied the Scotchman's curiosity, and then he roused out the kanaka, set him to work making a fire and a cup of coffee and, after we had eaten enough to satisfy our hunger, all hands lighted pipes, an I held a council of war as to the best method to be adopted to protect ourselves in case an attack should be made the next morning, for we did not for a moment suppose that the Mexicans would let us escape without further molestation.

"We 'll fight 'em," the old salt said. "They can't take you as long as I 'm alive. I can whip a dozen greasers when I 'm mad, and has done it time and time agin."

He meant when he had a cargo of aguardiente on board, but we thought it not prudent to hint such a thing at that time, as we did not care to lessen his enthusiasm in our behalf.

"In the fust place," Jack said, as he knocked the ashes from his black, strong pipe, "we must load up the old muskets, and get 'em ready for action. No takin' us by surprise, boys, in the mornin'. The greasers will come agin, and we 'll be prepared for 'em. Some of the men at the other hide-houses can lend us a hand if we want 'em to, I 'm sure. I 'll jist put t.e American flag over the door, and blank the cuss that dares to pass under it when I tells him not to. Don't you be afeard, boys. I 'm on deck, and commands this craft, and knows what I 'm about every watch."

We loaded the two old muskets with heavy charges of powder and small shot, and Jack got out a rusty cutlass, which he knew how to handle, and then we put out the lights, and turned in, tired and sleepy with the exciting incidents of the day and evening.

We were not disturbed during the night, and awoke refreshed, and feeling able to cope with any disagreeable incidents that might occur during the day. When we turned out the kanaka was preparing breakfast, and Scotch Jack was absent from the house, and did not return for some time. When he came back we noticed that the old cutlass was at his side, held in place by a stout leather strap, which served the double purpose of keeping his trousers around his hips, and as a sword belt. He appeared as proud of the weapon as a captain of a man-of-war in full uniform, and assumed the airs of one. He seemed to run away with the idea that the greasers, if they came to the beach in the course of the day, would be impressed with his war-like appearance, and make a hasty retreat.

"I have been around to the other hide-houses, and tipped the crews the word as to what we might expect, and the boys will lend us a helping hand, if we wants 'em to," the old sailor remarked, as he took his seat at the table, and laid the cutlass on a spare chair, with all the dignity and precautions of a military chieftain. "I hopes the greasers will keep away from us, 'cos I don't want no row, but if one comes the hardest must fend off. Blank the man what won't fight for a messmate, say I."

We certainly hoped the Mexicans would give us no more trouble, but had our doubts on the subject, as we expected the Sanchos family would not relinquish all thoughts of revenge so readily. They were vindictive scamps, and had the power to make it uncomfortable for us, at least for a time.

The day was pleasant, as no rain fell, but the sky was overcast, and the wind light from the southerd. The air was delicious, pure and invigorating. Great flocks of brant and ducks, geese and snipe, filled the flats of the harbor, and made lively music with their quacking and honks, while the waters of the bay were covered with gulls and pelicans. We looked at the fowl as they fed at low tide, and longed to make an expedition against them, but when we hinted as much to the Scotchman he repudiated the idea with scorn.

"You jist stay where you is," he said. "Keep in the house, and have an eye on me. I'm skipper of this craft, and mean to command it. No liberty today for any one," and we did not care to disobey the order, knowing how much we were dependant on the old sailor for protection.

About ten o'clock some one on the beach shouted "Sail oh," and we rushed to the door, thinking that a ship had entered the harbor, but the alarm was false, as it alluded to a party of horsemen who were galloping along the road leading from the town. We counted twelve Mexicans, and thought that we could recognize the two Sanchos at the head of the cavalcade.

"Stand by for stays," cried Jack, and took up his leather belt one more hole, and laid his hand hard on the hilt of the cutlass. "Get the guns all ready, and don't fire till I gives the word of command. I'm goin' to have a little talk with 'em."

As Jack's Spanish was rather limited we did not see how it was to be done with satisfaction on either side, but made no objections.

The horsemen dashed up to the door of the hide-house, and we saw the evil faces of Antonio Sanchos and his brother Carlos among the greasers. They did not dismount, but sat on their horses for the first half hour, and talked, as if reluctant to come to blows.

"Senor maestro de la casa," cried Antonio, addressing the Scotchman, "you have two fugitives from justice under your protection. We want them. Will you surrender the lads to us, or shall we take them by force?"

"Go to the devil," roared the Scotchman, who understood only the first few words spoken by Sanchos. "Jabber English, you blanked fools, if you desire to palaver with a gentleman like me. I don't know your hog Latin, and don't want to, but I can patter the John Bull tongue, or the Gaelic of old Scotland, with any able seaman of my weight."

"We do not comprehend a word that you say," replied Sanchos, who had listened attentively, in the hope of catching a sentence or two of the old sailor's meaning, but had to give up in despair. "Let the young men interpret for us. They at least know what we say, even if their Spanish is faulty."

"Hear de cheek," muttered Lewey, "and he know I speak de lingo booful."

"What do the greasers say?" asked Jack, turning to us. "I don't get the hang of their habler."

We informed the Scotchman of the Mexican's wishes, and, although Jack wanted to do all the talking, he grumblingly allowed us to take a hand in the palaver.

"Tell the greasers," the old sailor said, "that they had better tack ship, and head for the town once more, for it's no good for 'em to remain here. They won't get you without a fight, and some one will lose the number of his mess. Let them put that in their pipes, and smoke it, if they will."

We translated the speech, not exactly in the form in which it was delivered, but as near as we could, so as to convey a firm defiance, and, after Antonio Sanchos had heard us to the end, very patiently, I will admit, he said, —

"War has been declared between Mexico and the United States, and we have the right to destroy all the houses on the beach, and arrest every person who has sailed under the American flag. We do not desire to proceed to extremities, but we will have you two boys, by force if necessary."

"That yarn is as long as the mainto'-bowlin'," muttered Jack, as the Mexican ceased speaking. "It takes a sight of words from a greaser to say a little thing what has no meanin'."

We related to the old sailor all that the man uttered, and Jack assumed the dignity of an officer, as he handled his cutlass, and replied, —

"Tell 'em that they may go to the warmest place they can think of, and stay there forever, and then I won't give you up."

As soon as the words were conveyed to the Mexicans Sanchos seemed inclined to be angry, for he gave an order, and all of his companions dismounted, drew keen, long knives, unbuckled the heavy spurs from their heels, waved them in their left hands as weapons of attack, and then advanced toward us, thinking that they could carry our stronghold with a rush, but, as they came on, Lewey and I brought the old muskets to our shoulders, and covered the crowd, while Jack brandished his cutlass in a defiant manner, and the kanaka cook whirled a hatchet around his head, something after the style of an Indian's tomahawk.

The Mexicans took six steps forward, but, noting the warlike display that was prepared for their reception, halted in an irresolute manner, and once more opened a parley.

"We wish to spare the shedding of blood," Don Antonio Sanchos said "because, if we make an attack, some brave men will have to die. This we desire to avoid. Let us decide the question in a just manner. Come back with us to the town, go to the calabozo, and remain there until General Castro is heard from. After that we will see what can be done for you."

Now this might have been just and fair, except for the reason that we knew Sanchos would never forgive us for what we had done, could chain us to a gang of pressed recruits, and hurry us toward the headquarters of the army, and then conveniently murder us on the way. He and his brothers were none too good for just such treachery, so we determined to keep out of their power, if possible, and accept of no compromise.

"Come on, you black-hearted scoundrels, and feel the weight of a Scotchman's arm," Jack yelled, seeing the Mexicans halt, and fearing that there would be no fight after all. He did not wait until we had translated the greaser's speech. It was enough for the old sailor that there was a decided tendency to indulge in words, not blows, and he preferred the latter when his blood was up. The property in the hide house, the house itself, might be destroyed during the melee, but there was a great principle at stake, and he was not going to lose sight of it for a moment.

"Tell 'em to hold on for a moment," the old sailor cried, and entered the hide-house, took a small American flag from his chest, wrapped the end around his left arm, and then boldly shook the banner in the eyes of the greasers, and, as he did so, shouted, —

"Blank you for worthless, cowardly curs. Do you see what I have in my hand? It is the American stars and stripes. I 've served under 'em for twenty years, and blank me if I won't die under 'em afore I stirs hand or foot from double your numbers. Now come on, and remember that every knife aimed at me is a blow at the nation this flag represents. Somebody will get hurt if this fooling continues much longer."

If the Mexicans had understood him they might have been deeply impressed by his words, but, as they did not, there were several broad grins on the faces of the greasers, for they cared no more for the flag of our country, at that time, than a United-States ship did for the Mexican bandera, which waved occasionally over the presidios along the coast, and had but little power to back it.

"Blank 'em, if they a'n't laughin' at me," cried the indignant Scotchman. "I 'll give 'em somethin' to laugh at afore long, unless they minds their eye. They don't know me yet," and Jack put on some more quarter-deck airs, and swelled up, just as he had seen certain captains of ships do, when their dignity was called in question.

"We can't stand here talking all day," the elder Sanchos cried, as soon as he and his gang had allowed the grins to pass from their faces. "We care no more for your Yankee flag than we do for the green banner of the false prophet. Once more, will you give up the boys?"

"What does he say?" demanded Jack.

"He say," cried Lewey, with a little stretch of imagination, "dat he care no more for de American flag dan he do for all de Scotchmen in de vorld, and dat he can lick us vid one hand."

"Hold hard," muttered the indignant sailor. "He slights a true-blooded son of old Scotland, does he? Why, blank that greaser's eyes, I could eat a dozen like him."

The Mexicans seemed to think the time for argument had expired, and that a good chance for an attack now presented itself. They came forward with a rush, but dreaded the sight of the two old muskets, and Jack's formidable cutlass. Once more they halted, and seemed disposed for another palaver, but just then a new idea struck the elder Sanchos.

"Compadres," he said, "we will burn the coyotes out of their holes. Let us set fire to the building, and destroy it, and the nest of the enemies of the State."

This was a scheme I had feared would enter their minds, and it was one fraught with danger to every person on the beach, for, if one hide-house was fired, the others would surely go, as they were close together, and built of rough boards, a little damp on account of the recent rains, but still inflammable, and easily destroyed.

We hastily told Jack of the threat, and, as the words passed our lips, he snatched the musket from my hand, took a hasty aim, and fired at the greasers. I do not think that he intended to hit any particular person, but, as luck was on his side, planted the charge just where it would do the most good, for Don Antonio Sanchos had turned for the moment back to us, for the purpose of giving some instructions to his men. The light shot entered below his sash, and the fellow clapped his hands on the seat of his pantaloons, uttered a yell that set our dog to howling, jumped more than two feet in the air, and then came down on the soft sand, and blasphemed like a pirate.

His compadres drew back in surprise and consternation as they witnessed the antics of the wounded man. None of them wished to be injured in a cause that was not likely to bring them pesos. It was money they desired more than glory or hard blows. Shooting was all very well as long as they were not the recipients of the shot, and, while they were willing to do a little fighting, and much thieving, did not see that they were particularly interested in making an attack on a hide-house, that was barren of all treasure except a few hundred queros, and those were of no use to men who were traveling around the country, restless and anxious.

"Gringo of the devil," yelled Sanchos, as soon as he could recover his breath, and found that no vital part was injured, "you have insulted the State in my person. You shall suffer for this."

"You and your State be blanked," retorted the Scotchman. "I made a good line shot, and can do the same any day," then, as he noticed that the Mexicans still looked dissatisfied with the treatment their leader had received, and fearing that the greasers would carry out their threats to burn the building, the Scotchman put his hands to his mouth, speaking-trumpet fashion, and yelled, —

"All hands ahoy. Tumble up here, and help douse sail."

The cry was heard all over the beach, and understood. The masters and gangs of the several hide-houses had resolved to come to our assistance, in case of necessity, but not to make their appearance unless they were called upon in earnest. As the sailors and kanakas poured out of the buildings, armed with hide-hooks, clubs, and muskets, they presented a formidable appearance to men who were only provided with knives and spurs.

"Away, boarders, away," howled Jack, who somehow had the impression that he was on the deck of a frigate, alongside of an enemy, and been ordered to head a boarding party. As he uttered the words the Scotchman flourished his cutlass, struck at an imaginary enemy with a one, two, three motion, and dashed at the bewildered greasers, while Lewey the kanaka and myself followed our leader, clubbing the muskets, and prepared to do frightful execution on the heads of our enemies.

The Mexicans saw the formidable crowd advancing in their rear and front, and, alas for Don Sanchos' adherents, they were not capable of standing before such a charge. For only a moment did they hesitate, then, turning, fled for their horses, but even those could not be reached with safety, as the crews of the other hide-houses cut off their retreat, so there was but one resource, and that was to run, and they did scamper along the road toward San Diego, using their legs as they never had been used before, the infuriated Scotchman following close in the rear, with our dog far in advance, and snapping at every heel that was convenient for a nip from his well-armed jaws.

We were all mixed up in the chase. The guns were so heavy that Lewey and I could not make much headway, and, therefore, were glad when the old sailor, panting with his unusual exertions, the perspiration streaming down his rugged face, called a halt, and ordered a retreat to the hide-houses, as he had won glory enough for one day, in his own estimation.

We saw the greasers making the best of their way toward the town, and stopped for a while to see if they were disposed to return, and renew the fight, but, as they did not do so, we retraced our steps homeward, and then Scotch Jack delivered a short address, in which he said that the battle we had engaged in was equal to that of Waterloo, and, with such men as had backed him that day, he could overrun the whole country. We cheered our shipmate's speech, and all the rest joined in.

Then Jack said if he had a bottle of aguardiente he would treat the crowd, but was rather disconcerted when an old fellow wanted to know how far he thought one bottle of rum would go in such a collection of warriors, who had n't had a drop of spirits for a week?

However, Lewey and I saw a chance for popularity, and said that if a messenger was found we would send up to town for a gallon of spirits, and pay for it out of our own money, and three cheers were given for the proposition and the proposers, and a kanaka volunteered to start immediately for the village, armed with a one-gallon jug, which Jack owned, and kept for just such service.

We did not suppose that any one would harm the kanaka, as he was a quiet man, and never interfered with other people unless imposed upon. The result justified our expectations, for the native of the Sandwich Islands went to the town, and, when questioned by Sanchos' gang, said that every hide curer had a musket, and plenty of powder and balls, and were determined to kill all who visited the beach in a war-like manner. This was a slight flight of imagination on the part of the kanaka, but his word was believed, and, as Don Sanchos was busy having fine shot picked out of his person, it was thought best to let us alone for a while, or until a surprise could be effected, and no danger incurred.

We turned the horses loose, — those that had been left behind by the visiting Mexicans, — and they galloped back to town riderless, and were probably secured by their respective owners.

The kanaka returned with the aguardiente about four o'clock in the afternoon, and, from his appearance, we judged that he had sampled the liquor on the way down to the beach, for he was the silliest man we had seen for some time. He could do nothing but grin in an imbecile manner, and stagger along, first on one side o the road, and then the other, and say, —

" Me fighte greaser any day he like. Blank all Mexicans, and love good boys from Boston," which was complimentary to my nativity and to me, but was purchased at the expense of several drinks.

Scotch Jack was so indignant he wanted to try the messenger by court-martial, and sentence him to the chain-gang, but when some one asked him where he found his authority for doing so, the blunt, tough old sailor replied, —

"By the authority of right and might. A man what steals a shipmate's rum is too mean to live. See, that black scamp has taken half a dozen tots out of the jug, and what good has it done him? To appreciate liquor the drinker must be white."

"And a Scotchman," shouted some person in the crowd, but no one knew who uttered the words, for everybody laughed, and that made Jack so mad he wanted to fight his best friends.

"I 've shot one man this morning, and can lick half a dozen this afternoon, and not feel tired," he said. "Who slung that insult at my head?"

There was a deep silence. No one cared to answer, for Jack was a hard man when aroused, and could do his share of fighting on land or sea, as I had good reason to know, when he knocked Charley, the Dane, out of time and authority in the forecastle, one morning in the Admittance.

"I 'm a square man," the Scotchman said, finding that no one responded to his challenge, "and I 'm a charitable man. I 'm not going to drink all of this rum myself."

"Oh, no," in mocking tones from the crowd, who appeared to have their doubts on that point. But Jack went on, —

"Although my shipmates paid for the aguardiente I 'm no hog. They are good lads, and lets me do what I pleases with it."

We did not remember saying anything of the kind, but deemed it not prudent to contradict such a general statement, for reasons which were perfectly satisfactory. We owed him a debt of gratitude, and were glad to pay some portion of it.

"I has been thinking what is the best way to dispose of the rum,' Jack continued, after a moment's profound thought.

"I 'll bet you have concluded to drink it yourself," one old fellow responded, and then every one laughed.

Jack wanted to get mad, but thought better of it, as the speaker had charge of a rival hide-house, and the two men were on good terms.

"Now, boys, what does you say to a good tub of punch this evening?" e Scotchman asked.

"But who will mix it?" some one demanded.

"I will," was the old sailor's dignified reply.

"Then the saints help us, for no one else will get a smell," a man remarked, and every one laughed.

"I can lick you in two minutes," Jack cried indignantly.

"Well, you won't, for, if you did, I should n't feel like having any of that punch. Let 's take the rum first, and the lickin' arterwards, if you please," persisted the sailor, whose head seemed to be clear on that point.

"I 'll let my two shipmates, the lads, help me do the mixing," Jack said at length, and this decision seemed to please every one, so it was agreed that seven o'clock was the proper hour for the drinking to commence, and, with this understanding, the hide-house people separated, while Lewey took charge of the jug of rum, and, to prevent a great shrinkage before the proper time arrived, locked it up in his chest, and put the key in his pocket.

After supper we procured some limes, brown sugar, and water, a pan that had done duty for various purposes, but was clean as the kanaka cook could make it, and concocted a punch, and, after Jack had sampled it several times, he said it was as good as anything could be that had so much water in it, and yet taste of rum. As far as he was concerned he did not like to have his liquor sweetened. Pure aguardiente was the best for him, and for every one, but, as there was not enough to go around, he must do the best he could by the aid of water.

Our friends came trooping in at the appointed time, and each man brought a tin pot and a chair, as our establishment could not boast of glasses or seats sufficient for all hands. Scotch Jack did the honors, and welcomed every one with that quiet geniality which he could so well assume when good-natured.

"I have axed you all here," he said, as soon as the company was seated around the room, "to take a drink in honor of the way we licked the greasers, and to say that I thanks you for the hand you lent me in sendin' 'em off to the town in a hurry. I could have whacked 'em alone, single-handed, but I a'n't mean, and wanted to give all a chance."

Here he took a tin pot, bailed out a liberal supply of the punch, threw back his head, and allowed the liquor to course down his throat in a tantalizing manner to the observers.

"If you keeps on that way there won't be much chance for us at the punch, at any rate," one of the rival hide-house keepers muttered, and there was a murmur of assent all around the room from men whose mouths were watering for a taste of the mixture.

"Don't you be in such a blanked hurry," cried the Scotchman. "I knows what politeness is, and how the quality does the business when shipmates meet for a social glass. We is going to have toasts and sich like. I now gives you the first regular one. Here it is. Confusion to all greasers."

He put the tin pot to his mouth, and took a long pull, and there were deep groans from all the company present, for no one was invited to second the toast, or to drink to it.

Jack did not appear to heed the ominous growls. His thoughts seemed to be on other and more interesting matters. He looked around the room, his weather-beaten face all aglow with the hospitality which he was dispensing in so liberal a manner. But he paid no attention to the imploring looks and deep frowns of his audience.

"I 'll now give you the second regular toast," the Scotchman continued, after he had regained his breath, and then dipped his tin pot into the punch once more, not owning a ladle, and this time every one supposed the liquor was to be passed around, and their eyes were full of anticipation, and their mouths of tobacco.

"We has all heard," Jack continued, "that the United States and Mexico is at war. We don't know if it is true. If it is true, we will drink to the best man, and may he win."

He swallowed a liberal allowance of the punch, and, as the pot left his lips, gazed around at the mourners, and remarked, in a mild and encouraging manner,—

"We'll now give three cheers for the States."

No one responded to the call. The company were too indignant to cheer anything, or any one, but more than a dozen old salts breathed hard, and looked the fight which they felt. As for the kanakas, they chattered in their musical tongue, and wondered what kind of a party the white sailor had invited them to, where one man did the drinking, and all the talking.

"You don't seem to like that toast," Jack said, after a moment's reflection. "You act a little backward in cheerin' for the flag under which you have sailed for so many years, and eaten the bread and beef when it has been doled out to you in full rations, and no minister's faces to make weight."

"Blank yer yarnin' and chinin'," growled a sailor. "Give us a chance at the grog-tub, and then we 'll cheer fast enough. It's blanked dry work seein' a shipmate do all the swillin', and we as dry as an old hulk, what is laid up in ordinary."

Jack appeared a little surprised at the complaint. In an absent-minded manner he dipped his tin pot into the punch, tasted it, to see if it was to his satisfaction, yet did not seem quite suited, as he muttered, —

"I told the lads that they was puttin' in too much water. It allers spiles punch to add water."

"Give us a chance to see what it is like," one man said, but Jack did not choose to hear him. He was so well satisfied with himself and position that he appeared not to catch all the complimentary remarks which were addressed to him by the company. Neither did he seem to care for the ominous growls of discontent that were heard on all sides. If he did notice them he probably imagined that they were laudatory for the able manner in which he was presiding at the feast. Lewey and I were anxious to interfere, and distribute the contents of the grog-tub in a fair and impartial manner, but knew that if we interposed Jack would become angry at our intrusion, and use hot words. We needed him as a friend just at that time, and had no wish to provoke his quick temper, which we expected to see break out before the evening's festivities closed.

"I 'll now give you the third regular toast," the Scotchman said, as he filled his tin pot, "and I 'm sure all will jine me in it without bein' taken aback."

"We might all be taken aback, and get starn-way on us, if you should ax us to take a drop of that 'ere blessed punch," growled the master of the rival hide-house.

"Patience, mate," Jack remarked, "All in good time. Don't hurry me, and I 'll do more work than if I had an officer at my heels all day. The next toast what I offers you is " —

"Blank yer toasts. Give us the drink, and keep the toasts to yerself," was the universal growl, but the Scotchman did not notice the interruption. He continued, —

"I gives our own noble selves, and with three cheers. Now, one," Jack yelled, but no one present responded.

He went through the programme, and then dipped out another liberal supply of punch, and his hand was unsteady as he performed the difficult job.

"I will now sing you a song," the Scotchman cried, with drunken gravity, as he looked around the row of scowling faces. "It is one of Bobby Burns' songs. Ah, what a poet he was. Does any one here dare to say that Bobby Burns was not the greatest poet what ever lived?"

As but few present had any acquaintance with the Scotch bard, or, in fact, knew what a poet was, there was no response to the question, although an old sailor said that he knew the ship well, and had sailed in her from Glasgow to Hong Kong, one voyage, and a very wet vessel she was for'ard when there was a chop-sea on, and a stiff breeze blowing.

Jack did not correct the misunderstanding, even if he heard it. He took a sip of punch to clear his throat, and then, to my amusement, commenced to sing, —

"Flow gently, sweet Afton, among thy green braes."

As his voice was cracked, and none too melodious, the long-suffering patience of his audience was exhausted. What between a refusal to allow them a chance at the grog-tub, a call for three cheers every few minutes, when they did not feel like yelling, harangues that interested them not, it is no wonder that the company sprang to their feet, as one man, and, just as the Scotchman's voice gave token of breaking all to pieces, while his eyes were closed, to give full effect to his song, and he was waving the tin pot in his hand for the purpose of emphasizing the tune to which the lines should be sung, many hands grabbed him, he was lifted up bodily, hustled from the room, and pitched on the sand in front of the door, where he remained for a few minutes, too astonished to make a remark, or to comprehend the method employed to get him out of the house.

Then, like a pack of hungry coyotes, the residents of the beach swooped down on the grog-tub, and in one minute there was not a spoonful of the punch left, and all the company filed out of the hide-house, homeward bound, while Lewey and I looked at each other in amused consternation at the scene that had taken place before us, and changed so quickly.

From our wonderment we were aroused by hearing Jack's voice, and into the house he crawled, on all fours. As the light of the candles struck his head, he sat up, looked around, and asked, with a thick tongue, and drunken grin, —

"Boys, was there a hearthquake just now, or what was the matter?"

We helped the man up, laid him away in his bunk, and the kanaka turned in, and both were soon snoring, but the room was so warm that we did not feel like retiring just at that moment. We doused the lights, filled our pipes, and went outside to have a quiet smoke, and to talk over our future prospects, for they did not look any too bright just then, and once more we wished ourselves on board the Admittance, and homeward bound.

We sat on a spar, near the hide-house, in the deep shadow of the building, and talked for a long time, and, just as we had knocked the ashes from our pipes, and thought of retiring to our bunks, two dark forms stole out of the chapparel, and came toward us. They did not notice us where we sat, so we kept perfectly still, and waited to see what the visitors desired, as they had come from the direction of the town. Jack, our dog, was in the house, fast asleep, or he would have given an alarm, and the rest of the canines were off on the hills, making lively music for the benefit of a coyote that had ventured too near the beach, for the purpose of getting a supper of refuse fat and scraps of hide.

We said nothing, but waited. The men stopped, and listened for a moment, but, hearing no sound, went to the corner of the house, knelt down, and we could see them pile some dry material, which they had brought with them, against the boards, and then there was the scratching of a match, but it did not ignite readily, and a second attempt was made.

"Dey am about to set on fire de buildin'," whispered Lewey. "Vot skall ve do?"

"Bang them over the head with a club," I answered, and the proposition just suited Lewey.

At our feet was a lot of fire-wood, which had been cut at odd intervals, when there was no work to be done on hides. We selected heavy sticks, crawled on our hands and knees toward the visitors, for we suspected they belonged to the Sanchos' gang, and were to secure revenge for the treatment they had received during the forenoon.

The Mexicans were too much occupied in experimenting with matches to notice us. In fact, one of them uttered a strong "caramba" at the failure of the lucifer to blaze up, owing to the fact that the boards of the house were a little damp from the late rains.

"Make haste," one of the Mexicans said in a half whisper. "The dogs will return in a short time, and bark their heads off if they see us, and then the whole colony will turn out, and give us a lively chase all along the road."

"No fear," responded the other. "The gringos are asleep, and nothing will disturb them until morning. If we knew where the boys slept we would make short work of them with our knives."

"The risk would be too great," the other answered. "We might stumble on that accursed Scotchman. His fist is like a stone, and his strength is that of a bull. We will burn the shelter of the accursed heretics, and then they will be at our mercy. We can clean out the whole gang after the houses are gone."

Another match was lighted, flared up, and we saw by its blaze the dark faces of Carlos Sanchos and another greaser, whom we did not know. The kindling stuff was ignited, and, just as the men arose to beat a hasty retreat, we sprang to our feet, and struck the fellows two heavy blows on the sides of their heads, and they fell as if lightning had hit them, and did not move, except their feet, which kicked convulsively.

"I am afraid that we have killed them," I whispered to Lewey, rather awed at the crime we had committed.

"So much de better," was the cheerful response. "Two of our enemies out of de vay, at any rate," and then we stamped out the fire, bent down and examined the bodies of the insensible men, removed their long knives from the sheaths, and went to arouse Jack, and tell him what had happened.

But the punch had such an influence over the Scotchman, that all he could say in response to our appeals was that he "would sing just one more song, and then take a drink," and, pull as we might, there was no getting him to realize the sense of danger that the hide-house had been in, so we gave it up as a bad job, and went back for the injured greasers, but they had disappeared in some mysterious manner, and left no traces behind. They had recovered from the blows, which were not as bad as we thought, and left the premises. We called ou. dog, and put him on the trail, and he followed it, Lewey and I close to his heels, until he came to a lot of scrub oak, and there we saw that our nocturnal visitors had taken their horses, tied to the trees, and gone in the direction of San Diego. It was useless to attempt to follow them, so we called off our dog, and went back to the hide-house, thinking the fellows' heads were aching too badly for a second attempt to fire our building that night, and we were correct in our surmise, for no one disturbed us, but we took the precautions to lock the outer door, for fear some villain might wander in, and use a knife on our persons, remembering what one of the greasers had said on the subject.

The next morning Jack had but a hazy remembrance of the previous night's doings. He knew that he had enjoyed himself, and supposed that every one had done the same. We did not remind him of his scant hospitality, his attempts to sing, or even of the indignant rush of the suffering people, who pitched him on the sand, and then attacked the punch. It would have done no good to recall such matters, but we did point out the place where the Mexicans had attempted to fire the building, and showed the long, sharp knives, as proof of our assertion, and that all was not a dream.

This set Jack to thinking, and he called around at the various hide-houses, and proposed that an anchor watch should be established hereafter, to guard the property, and the project was adopted, until all danger was passed, and then the men had every night in, as usual.

We did not hear from the Sanchos gang for several days, and, in the meantime, took care not to wander from the protection of the beach, or even to go gunning, for fear of a surprise. But one morning Captain Fitch rode down to see us, and stated that he and the alcalda had received papers from General Castro, and that the military chieftain sent us permits to remain in the country, and do as we pleased, as long as we did not take up arms against the State. This so disgusted Sanchos and his gang that all had gone to the Pueblo los Angeles, and taken forty or fifty military recruits. We were now free, for the time being, from any molestation on his part, but we were advised to keep at a distance from the man, as he was dangerous, and might prove more troublesome in the future.

"My advice to you now is to ship on board of some American vessel that is on the coast, and get away from here as soon as possible. In time of war no one will be safe on the land. Even I have been molested several times by bands of greasers calling at my house, and asking for money. There is a girl, the jailor's daughter, who gives me no peace, she is so eager to know where you two boys are located. She says one or both of you promised to marry her. It is wrong to trifle with the affections of young ladies," and he grinned as he spoke, as though knowing more of our doings in the calabozo than he was disposed to tell.

Lewey blushed, something he was capable of doing once in a while, as he said, —

"You no tell her ve here. She is one good girl, but ve has trouble enough vidout vomen boderin' us just now."

"Except the girls you desire to marry?" hinted the captain.

'Oh, yes, dem ve skall dink of all de time," my friend said.

"Well, think of them as much as you please, but don't marry if you know what is good for your future welfare," then the captain, seeing no signs of approval on our faces, continued, "I suppose that I am only wasting my time in talking to you on a subject that you have set your minds on. I give you the best advice that I am capable of administering, and you refuse to take it. Some day you will think of all that I have said, and regret that you had not acted a little more sensibly. However, go your way, and remember that, if you get in a hard box, you have a friend in me at all times, and don't forget to appeal for my aid if necessary. Here are the papers from General Castro. Take good care of them, for they may be of service to you, in case some Mexican is disposed to make trouble, as armed men are riding about the country. But your safest place is on board ship, for the vessels on the coast will not be molested, so I am given to understand."

Then Captain Fitch produced a small bag of gold, and counted out fifteen doubloons for Lewey, and the like amount for myself, the wages which had been left in his hands by Captain Peterson, when we were discharged from the Admittance. The sum looked like a small fortune to us, and we thought that we could see many months of happiness and idleness before us on the strength of the amount.

"I need not tell you that it is just as well you should keep secret the fact that you possess this money. Give out that you have not a peso in the world, for there are lots of greasers who would cut your throats for a tenth part of a gold piece, and think they had committed no crime. If you go through the country beg your way, and return courtesies with profuse thanks, but give no silver in exchange, so shall you escape some of the dangers of California. I am talking to you now just as though you were my own boys, for I know that each of you must have relatives and friends at home who would thank me for my advice, if they knew you needed it as badly as you do just at present."

We were quite affected at his words, and I was more than half inclined to promise all that the gentleman desired, but a glance at Lewey's face prevented me. He had made up his mind to carry out the programme marked down months before, and I was weak enough to acquiesce in his decision.

It would have been better for both of us if we had listened with more attention, and weighed well his words, and let the girls we thought we loved so well go in search of other husbands. The captain was a man of experience in the little world in which he lived, and knew the Mexican character most thoroughly. He was familiar with their good qualities, and all of their bad ones, and so moved along in the society in which he was thrown almost without a jar, making money out of those who desired to borrow, and taking his interest of twelve per cent, and sometimes a little more, when the security was doubtful, with charming frankness and good-nature, as men who loan money generally do. The principal was never paid, as a matter of course, for the fascinating game of monte was more attractive to the average Mexican than the payment of debts, and so, as years rolled on, the captain grew richer, and the natives of the State poorer, and the more poverty-stricken the latter became the greater their pride and arrogance, and the more urgent their entreaties for fresh loans, on estates already encumbered with mortgages.

"I will send you a few notes of introduction to various parties on the coast, and in the interior," the captain said, after he had waited for us to digest his words, and saw that he had not produced the effect intended. "They may be of use to you. At any rate they can do no harm. In them I shall state the reason why you were discharged from your ship, and your desire to become rancheros, or cattle-raisers. Without such papers the Americans at the Pueblo, Santa Barbara, and other places might think you were deserters, and so turn the cold shoulder to you when there was need of their assistance. You must not expect that every American or Englishman on the coast will receive you with open arms, for they won't. If you are asked to dine with them, it may be in the kitchen where your food will be served, and not in the best room in the house, for we have an aristocracy here as well as in other countries, and the line is drawn at sailors. I know," the captain added hastily, seeing that we were inclined to interrupt him, "what you would say. I have not the slightest doubt but that you are as good, and belong to as respectable families as any on the coast, but you have served as sailor boys on vessels, and that cuts you off from all acquaintance with the better classes of the State."

"But if ve skall rise up, and become rich. Den vot vill dey say to us?" asked Lewey.

"When you arrive at that position you will be able to answer the question to your entire satisfaction, and need no help from me," was the gentleman's reply.

Some years after, a French corvette, of thirty guns, anchored in San Diego harbor, and all the officers were welcomed and made much of by the élite of the town. Among those who strove to make the French gentlemen content was Captain Fitch. He gave a grand soiree at his house to the commander of the corvette and the officers, and, while drinking toasts, took occasion to compliment the master of the man-of-war on his excellent English. The latter smiled, as he turned to the host and said, in our tongue,—

"Do you dink dat I could be admitted to any of de heuses in dis country on a perfect equality you know?"

"Most certainly. Why should you not be? Your rank will cause all to pay the most marked respect to a gentleman like yourself," Mr. Fitch answered.

"But s'pose I should inform you dat at one time I vas only a sailor boy on a vessel under de American flag?" the captain of the French ship-of-war continued.

"That would make no difference to us in this State," Mr. Fitch responded. "We judge a man by his merits alone."

"But if I should further inform you dat I vos vonce a prisoner in your calabozo, den vot vould you say?" asked the French gentleman, with a smile, as he thought of other days, and glanced around the room in which he was seated, surrounded by all the handsome ladies of San Diego, and influential gentlemen.

"I should think that your excellency was joking with me for some purpose," Captain Fitch replied.

"But I is not joking. I is very serious. I comes in dis port jist to see de old place some more. Vill you believes me vhen I tells you dat in dis bery room I vonce, in company vid a bery bad American boy, mine fast friend den, my best of friends now, gives vhat ve calls a performance of legerdemain, for de amusement of you and your guests?"

"Impossible," Captain Fitch cried. "I do not recollect the circumstance. You must be poking fun at me, for some purpose or other."

"Listen to me," the French gentleman remarked, in a calm tone. "One day, some years ago, vhen mine friend and mineself vas at de hide-house, on de beach, you ask us to gib de performance for de fun of your friends, and you tells us ve can hab de supper in one room by ourselves, but ve cannot eat at de same table vid your guests. Dat did not hurt our feelings, 'cos ve cared more for de viands dan ve did for de company. Ven de performance vas about vot you call ober, von Mexican greaser, named Sanchos, entered de apartment, and arrest mine friend Thom, and take him to de calabozo, on de charge of being a spy. You no recollect de ding now?"

Captain Fitch was astonished, and well he might be, at the singular tide of fortune that had carried Lewey from a hide-house to the quarter-deck of a French ship-of-war. The circumstance all came back to the gentleman, and for a moment there was much astonishment to see the Frenchman and the former American rise from their places at the table, shake hands with great eagerness and cordiality, and then stand and look at each other for a long time, their hearts too full for the words that wanted to flow, but did not, on account of gladness and surprise. The two men could not realize the great change that had occurred in their positions in life, and the captain of the ship-of war, as he wiped away the moisture from his eyes, was heard to mutter, —

"I 'd gib one dousand dollars if Thom vas here on dis occasion to take part in it, and I knows dat he vould gib anuder dousand for de chance."

Lewey and I.

The Captain Fitch, when he could recover his breath, and get over his astonishment, told the wonderful story of our experiences in San Diego, to his Mexican and American friends present, and Lewey, in the French language, related his exploits as a legerdemainist, not only at Captain Fitch's but at Monterey, and, to judge from the laughter of the naval officers, my old friend must have said some funny things, but I hope he told the truth about me, and took his share of the blame, where the latter came in, especially all that related to the firey serpent.

I have since been told by the French naval officer, and those who were with him on that memorable day, that there was more champagne drunk at the feast than was ever known before or since, and, when all hands were as full as possible, Captain Fitch proposed that the whole company should march through the streets, and visit the calabozo, a suggestion that was received with cheers, and, arm in arm, Mexican and Frenchman, ladies and caballeros, the party passed along the calles, and visited the prison, and the only unpleasant incident that occurred was when a dry, black, wrinkled woman threw herself into the French captain's arms, and called him her treasure, and a bad man at the same time. It was the jailor's daughter, married, and the mother of six children. The host had privately sent her a dollar, and instructions what to do, and the right time to make the demonstration, the most laughable episode of the day, for even the ladies present screamed with delight at the spectacle of a naval captain, in full uniform, being embraced by a half-naked Mexican woman. Justice to Lewey compels me to state that he treated the whole matter as a good joke, although he swore by all the saints in the calender, that he had never seen the woman before, made love to her, or promised to marry her, and that she had mistaken him for some other person, and meanly hinted that I was the man, but no one believed him, I hope.

Lewey gave the female, after he had extricated himself from her embrace, a twenty-dollar gold piece, sent her from the ship some jewelry, a few gaudy shawls and handkerchiefs, but never sought a second interview. Thus do the loves of our younger days pass from our minds, and lie buried in the grave of youthful fancies, and, when I think of the matter, I am inclined to the opinion that Lewey's graveyard of affairs of the heart must be well stocked with broken hopes and forgotten protestations of eternal fidelity on his part.

But all this is foreign to the fact that we were seated at a table in our hide-house, and listening to the kind words of Captain Fitch, who promised us letters of recommendation to his friends, and, when he had taken his leave, we made up our minds to make the journey overland to Ranche Refugio, where we hoped to join Anita and Engracia, and with them we thought our trials and troubles might cease, and that happiness would shine on our heads every day of our lives, or as long as we resided in California, which might be for years, or only a few months. How much we were mistaken in the life we were to lead will be revealed as this yarn progresses, for who could have imagined the trying scenes through which we must pass, the hardships we were to endure, the dangers to be encountered, the cruel enemies we must face and defeat, the warm friends we were to meet, who protected and sheltered us so that at last we escaped with our lives, and thus lived to rejoin our relatives at some distant day, older, wiser, and better young men.

CHAPTER IV.

PREPARATIONS FOR A LONG JOURNEY. — FAREWELL TO SAN DIEGO. — EN ROUTE TO RANCHE REFUGIO. — A VAQUERO AND BULL. — THE LONELY ADOBE HOUSE, AND A PRAIRIE-FLOWER. — THE MOUNTAIN LION. — LEWEY IS AGAIN IN LOVE. — AN INTERRUPTION TO A MIDNIGHT COURTSHIP. — THE THREAT. — WILD INDIANS ON THE TRAIL.

WE were in no hurry to start on our long and dangerous journey to Ranche Refugio, for it was the winter season, and sometimes the rain fell in torrents, so we knew the streams would be swollen, and dangerous to cross. We had thought of obtaining passage in a sailing vessel bound up the coast, but none entered the harbor for several weeks, most of the ships being at San Francisco, lying there for security, while the northwest and southwest gales prevailed. One bark, the Don Quixote, came to an anchor at San Diego, and loaded with tallow for Callao. We could have shipped on board of her, and were urged to do so by the master, but Lewey had set his heart on being married, and I could not bear to disappoint his sanguine anticipations, and so the chance passed away.

At one time we thought of taking an otter-hunter's boat, and skirt along the coast, landing at night for shelter, but the people to whom we spoke on the subject, men who knew just what we would have to encounter, protested against the scheme as being too dangerous and impracticable in the winter season, when gales were frequent, and the surf fearful. They said we might be capsized, or driven to sea, in a sudden squall, before we could make a landing, and that no boat could live in such waves as were prevalent between San Diego and Santa Barbara.

Jack was in no hurry for us to leave the shelter of the hide-house. He was accustomed to our society, and knew that he would miss us when we took our departure for good. He talked to us with all the seriousness of a father on the unwise course we had marked out, and declared that no good would come of it, he was sure. We were welcome to remain with him as long as we desired, and do no work unless it suited us. But all his arguments were lost, and at last he spared his breath, as he saw that no impression was made on our plans.

It was rarely that we heard from the North. Once in a while a courier would arrive with despatches for the alcalda, but no battles were reported, excepting a few slight skirmishes with Captain Fremont and his explorers, on the shores of San Francisco Bay, or the banks of the Sacramento River. But it was stated that General Castro had the Americans just where he wanted them, and that the whole gang of invaders would soon be captured. We did not think there was much probability of a long struggle, as we hoped the Californians would remain neutral during the war, as Captain Graham, of Santa Cruz, advised, and so we went on with our preparations for departure, just as though the country was at peace.

We had much to do before we commenced our journey, and many things to pick up. We found at one of the hide-houses two light rifles, which some trappers had left there years before, and never called for. They were in good order, and needed only a little oil to work perfectly. With them were bullet moulds and powder flasks. There was no trouble in securing caps and ammunition at the town, so that in this respect our equipment was complete. We purchased the rifles for the sum of ten dollars, and the seller thought he got a good price for the guns, as he never used them, preferring the old-fashioned ship's musket to any other firearm that was ever invented. Then we hunted up, by the aid of friends at San Diego, two pairs of small pistols, not of much use, except at close quarters, but, as they were light, we thought it desirable to possess them. We made straps to sling our rifles over our shoulders when traveling, some strong belts to wear around our waists, for the purpose of securing our gold pieces, and bags of canvas to hold our discharge papers, the permits from General Castro, and letters of recommendation of Captain Fitch, addressed to people along the route.

Our next business was to seek to purchase two mustangs and saddles, and this we were enabled to do, yet horses were cheap, and saddles dear. But our friend, the captain, had some old second-hand equipments, which he had taken for debts from drunken greasers, years before, and he let us have them at a cheap rate, lariats and all. We exercised our animals every day, after we obtained possession, and thus got accustomed to their ways, and enured ourselves to the use of the saddle. At night we would let our horses feed on the grass near the hide-houses, or, rather, just back of them, for the country was then brilliant with a green covering, and the flowers were in full bloom in every direction, or where the sand was not too dense for them to obtain a little nourishment.

We were in high spirits over our anticipated excursion, as we thought of the pleasures of riding through the country, and seeing its wonders, camping when we pleased, and moving on when it suited our convenience, our own masters, and under no one's control. But Scotch Jack was dissatisfied with all of our arrangements, and uttered ominous growls of warning as to the hardships we might have to encounter, for he had a much greater appreciation of the difficulties of the journey than we did.

It was near the first of April when all of our arrangements were completed, and we were ready for the journey. The steady, heavy rains had ceased, but there were occasional showers night and morning. The whole country was verdant, and filled with the perfume of thousands of strange and brilliant-hued flowers. The gales had degenerated into soft breezes, that came from the north and west, invigorating and healthy. The lungs seemed to expand under their influence, and we could bathe in the morning in the salt waters of the bay, stand on the soft sand, and inhale the delicious atmosphere, then go back to the hide-house, and create consternation in the mind of the kanaka cook at our desperate attack on the fried beef-steaks and coffee.

The night before we were to leave, in consideration of the kindness we had received from every one on the beach, we resolved to give a farewell party to our old friends. We readily obtained Jack's consent to the project, only stipulating that, as we were to be the hosts, it was necessary he should not boss operations, as he had done on one memorable occasion, and drank nearly all the punch before the indignant guests rose up, and smote him to the right and left, and then deposited him on the cool sand, as a warning against further exhibitions of selfishness.

It was some time before we could get the Scotchman to promise that he would not interfere, but we had to consent to his petition for permission to make a speech, and sing one of Burns' songs. When this was arranged all the rest was clear work. We went around to the hide-houses, and personally invited the sailors and kanakas. All reluctantly agreed to come, although the keeper of the rival establishment said he 'd be blanked if he was going to any more shindies where one man did all the talking and drinking, and gave no one else a chance at the grog-tub.

" But this time," we pleaded, " Jack will not have the serving out of the punch. He will be anchored in a chair like the rest of you, and we'll see that you have your full share when the mainbrace is spliced, if you will only come."

"You don't know that Scotchman as well as me," the hide-house keeper said. "When it comes to drinkin' and fightin' he wants more than his share. Howsomever, bein' as it is you, and 'cos you is about to up anchor, and sail away for foreign parts, I don't mind if I comes over for a little while this evenin', just to see the boys, and help along the fun."

We sent up to San Diego for two gallons of aguardiente and some lemons, but took the precaution of despatching a different messenger from the kanaka we had previously entrusted with such a delicate duty, but it made no difference, the English sailor, who was called upon to go, getting more than half drunk on the way to the beach, so our package suffered a little depletion on its passage to the owners.

Jack was indignant at such rank treachery, and swore that there was not a person on the shore who was fit to be trusted with rum, excepting himself, and that the next time an entertainment was given he would do the errand, and then all could depend upon him.

When Lewey heard this remark he winked very seriously, but uttered never a word, for we knew that Jack had no fear of rum, and would attack it every time there was a chance for an encounter, and yet he was thrown by his enemy just as often as they came to close quarters. But the Scotchman never knew when he was vanquished, and still foyght on, against desperate odds.

We made a nice punch, and at seven o'clock our friends had all assembled at the hide-house, bringing tin pots and chairs. Their eyes glistened as they fell upon the grog-tub, but all were patient, even if uneasy glances were cast upon Jack, as if fearful that he might disappoint them at the last moment, and go in for more than his share of punch.

But Jack behaved very well, all things considered, and, after we had given each person a liberal supply of liquor, and all had tasted and approved, lighted their pipes, and prepared to listen, I stepped to the table, and made a short speech.

"Messmates and shipmates," I said, "we are about to break ground, up anchor, and sail for other parts. Before we square away, and shape our course, let me, in behalf of Lewey and myself, return thanks for the sailor-like treatment we have received at your hands."

"Three cheers for the lads," roared Jack, and they were given with a will, and then all held out their tin pots for a further supply of punch.

We complied with the mute, but significant appeal, and I continued my address.

"When we were threatened with arrest by a gang of land-lubber greasers you stepped to the front, and drove the scoundrels to their dens. We shall never forget it, and hope some day to again see you, and to once more fill the grog tub at our expense."

There was a roar of applause, and, at its conclusion, Jack sprang to his feet, and replied to my speech.

He said that he was an old man, and had knocked about the world for fifty-five years. He had served in line-of-battle ships, frigates, and in merchantmen, and he wanted it understood that better shipmates he had never fell in with than Lewey and myself. We reminded him of one of Burns' songs, which he could not remember very well, but would try and sing it for the gratification of the company present, if any one desired him, and forthwith, without waiting for a vote on the subject, commenced howling the old song,—

"A man 's a man for a' that,"

but the noise and confusion was so great that we could not see the connection between the song and ourselves, and, after Jack had yelled himself into an intense state of perspiration and thirst, there were loud calls for more punch, and thunders of applause for the song.

We did not drink any of the mixture except once, in response to a toast honorable to ourselves, and to show that we were not too proud to share in the fun of the people on the beach. Had we refused to partake of a glass, in company with our guests, there would have been strong mutterings of discontent, and this we desired to avoid, wishing to leave a good impression behind after we were gone.

At nine o'clock the punch was entirely consumed, and wistful glances cast around the room for more. No person was intoxicated, but all had enough for one evening at least, and, when some of the kanakas commenced to yawn, and Jack proposed to sing another song, the people stole quietly out of the room, and sought the seclusion of their own quarters for the night.

The Scotchman looked around in a dazed sort of manner, as though wondering why men should be so lacking in good taste, then blanked some one's eyes to his heart's content, and went to bed, while we cleared up the room, gave it a good airing, and turned in also, thinking of what kind of a place we should find to sleep in the next night, when on our journey.

The following day was bright and pleasant. We were up at an early hour, had a good swim, fed our horses with a little barley, packed our blankets, dressed in full suits of Mexican clothes, — sombrero and leggings, spurs and knives, — and, after breakfast, saddled our animals, and then prepared to take leave of our old shipmate.

"You know, boys," the Scotchman said, as his voice grew husky, and his eyes moist, "that I is agin the whole thing. But you is bound to go, and so that 's the end of it. But if you wants to come back your old bunks is ready for you at any time, and you will always find a friend in Scotch Jack."

"We know it, old shipmate," we answered, "and perhaps we may return sooner than you expect. We shall leave all of our effects here, — chests and bedding, — and if you never hear from us consider the property your own. Use it just as you please. We make you our heir-at-law."

"I don't care so much for the dunnage, lads, as I do for you," was the answer. "Come back to me, and the chests may go to blankation. But," and here the thoughtfulness and prudence of the Scot came in play, "jist you put them sentiments of yours in writin', and then everythin' will be shipshape in case anythin' should happen to you."

We readily complied with the request. We drew up papers, stating that Jack was to inherit all of our property, in case of death, and called in the master of the rival hide-house to witness our signatures, and, after that duty was performed, the question arose, for the first time, what we should do with our dog Jack. The animal knew that we were making preparations for departure, and he was restless and anxious, for fear he would be left behind. He moved about the house, around it, and then returned and looked in our faces, as if he desired to speak, and express his sentiments, if he was to be deserted. In this respect he was almost human, and his bright black eyes pleaded for consideration at our hands, as dog never did before, it seemed to us.

"Vot skall ve do vid him?" Lewey asked. "Vill ve takes him, or leaves him here vid our friend?"

"I 'll look arter him, lads, if you desire me to do so," the Scotchman said, but the dog did not notice the kindness expressed. He whined, and gazed at us in a pitiful way, and almost barked his head off, as I remarked, —

"He will be lots of company for us, and a good lookout nights, when we camp out. Yes, let us take old Jack with us."

The dog uttered a series of joyful yelps, and made frantic efforts to reach my face, so that he could slobber kisses upon it, and, when he found that I was not inclined for such demonstrations of affection, turned his attention to Lewey, and the French lad received his full share of Jack's expressions of delight.

So it was settled, and then we packed up in a bag a stock of pilot bread, some sugar and coffee, tin pots, salt, and a huge piece of old junk, all boiled, and ready for consumption, in case we should not encounter a ranche during a day's journey After we had stowed all the articles on our horses, the members of the various hide-houses gathered around, and insisted upon shaking hands, and, as soon as we had done so, the Scotchman called out for three cheers, and they were given with a will, and then we mounted our impatient mustangs, ambled down the road, and the last words we heard from the people was the fatherly advice of the master of the rival hide-house, as he yelled out, —

"Boys, don't you marry no greasers, or have anything to do with 'em. They is pizen."

We waved back a recognition of the intended kindness, and then we were loping along at a slow gait, and the dog was nearly crazy at the prospect of a journey. If he had known all he was to encounter it is quite probable he might have been disposed to remain on the beach, and live in idleness, the king of the whole tribe of dogs, being the best fighter of the lot, and there were some good ones.

We knew something of the trail that led to Los Angeles, as we had made careful inquiries of couriers and vaqueros who had crossed the plains and mountains in summer and winter, and they had told us how to proceed by the shortest possible route. They said that the passage through the canyons of the Sierra Madre Mountains was the worst part of the journey, and that in some places we would have to dismount, and lead our horses, as the trail was too difficult to ride. We were also advised to keep a sharp lookout for grisly bears, and mountain lions, and to shun both if possible, as a fight with either would not add to our renown in case of defeat. Of game there was an abundance, such as rabbits, deer, and quail, with an occasional rattlesnake thrown in, by the way of variety. We needed no words on the part of the couriers to avoid the latter on all occasions. We had seen quite enough to satisfy our curiosity while in California. There was no danger of starving if we could shoot with some degree of accuracy, or had hooks for catching fish, as all the streams were filled with trout, and no one but the Indians ever molested them.

This last information had been timely enough to enable us to provide lines and hooks, in case we should find occasion to use them on the journey, and we hoped that such would be the case, for we did not mean to travel rapidly, as time was no object with us, thinking that our fiancées could wait a few days, more or less, for us, and not be rendered uncomfortable, as wedding trousseaux, with girls of their position in society, were not extensive or costly. An overskirt and one under-garment being all that was required, as a general thing.

"Dis," said Lewey, as we struck the trail, and headed North, leaving the sleepy little town of San Diego in the rear, "is de sublimest of happiness Now ve is free, and de vorld is afore us. Ve is our own masters. I could shout vid joy."

I did n't feel so excited, for, the truth was, I saw the dangers and trials of our journey much more vividly before us than my friend, whose happy nature was like mercury in a glass, — constantly going up and down, and rarely stationary for any length of time.

"If we should meet with a grisly bear, Lewey," I asked, "you would not attack it, I hope?"

"Vould n't I?" was the indignant answer. "Vy, Jack and me could knock de vust bear in California end for end, and dink nothin' of it."

I harbored doubts on the subject, but did not express them, as I knew that Lewey had made up his mind what he could do, and only reality would convince him to the contrary, and so we loped along the narrow trail, indulging in conversation when in the mood, and walking our horses as soon as they showed the slightest signs of warmth.

We left the last hacienda, a farm-house, where there were ten thousand cattle grazing near, all looking up at us in a strange, wild manner, and so threatening were their movements, because Jack had invaded their retreat, — they did not like his looks, thinking he was a strolling coyote, — that to save him from violence, and ourselves from a desperate charge, I dismounted, and took the dog on the pummel of my saddle, where he clung quite contentedly, as if he was aware of my kindness, and could appreciate it.

The cattle were too much accustomed to horsemen to care for us, yet they knew we were strangers to that part of the country, and one lordly old bull, that had seen many a conflict, and beaten the young males time and time again, uttered an angry bellow, and moved slowly toward us, as if on an investigation.

"Ve must quicken de pace," said Lewey, "or de blanked bull vill be afoul of us, and carry avay our spare."

This was his nautical manner of expressing fear that the bull would knock us over, in case he should use his horns in desperate earnestness.

Just as we were about to touch our horses with the spurs, out from the high chapparel and tall grass, on the side of the trail, burst a wild-looking ranchero, with long black hair, two-thirds Indian and the balance poor Mexican blood, mounted on a splendid mustang, that was quivering with life and excitement, under the stimulant of a pair of cart-wheel spurs, which jingled as the fellow rode toward us, circling a lariat around his head, and uttering fiendish shouts, whether of welcome or defiance we could not tell.

"Prenez garde," whispered Lewey, forgetting his English for the moment, and we would have halted, and awaited the approach of the vaquero, to see what his intentions were, but that confounded bull was near the heels of our horses, and we did not care to encounter the horns of the animal.

We unslung our rifles, and laid them across our saddles, all ready for use, in case there was danger in that whirling lariat, but, whether the half-breed saw the motion, or did not intend any demonstrations except those of a friendly nature, he swept past us like a whirlwind, and brought the reata down upon the rump of the angry bull, beating him until he changed his course, and was glad to seek shelter among the members of his harem.

It was all done so quickly, and so easily, that we could not prevent a loud exclamation of approval.

"Bueno, senor," we shouted, and the fellow grinned, and curled up his lariat on the pommel of his saddle, then removed his sombrero, and saluted us with the grace and politeness of a prince of the royal blood of most any kingdom you might happen to think of.

"Buenos dias, senors," the ranchero said, as he advanced, and reined up alongside of us. "The bull is apt to be troublesome to strangers, but a few blows on his flanks are enough to teach him a lesson for a short time. If it had not been for your dog he would have failed to notice you."

We returned his salutation, and re-slung our rifles over our shoulders, as we saw that he had no evil intentions respecting ourselves. We also thanked the man for his services, not that there was much danger, for we could have easily kept out of the animal's way by spurring our steeds to full speed.

"Where are you from? and what is the latest news?" the stranger asked.

"We left San Diego this morning, and are bound for Los Angeles," was our answer. "There is no news in town, except that queros are a little dearer, and tallow is firmer," giving him news that we hoped would please him.

"That is good," he said. "I shall kill many cattle this spring, and I 'd like to get much money for the hides and tallow. Is there any news of the war? I hear that there is trouble between Mexico and the States. Do you know anything of the matter?"

"Only rumors," was our ready answer. "We trust the cloud will soon blow over. Mexico is a great nation, and her people are very brave. She can afford to be magnanimous toward the United States."

"Si, senor, it is true," and the man's face was expressive of pleasure at the compliment. "Is either of you senors an Americano?"

"Oh, no," was Lewey's ready response. "We are both French, and like California so well that we expect to remain here all of our days."

"That is bueno," the ranchero said. "But, as you are traveling through the country, of course you have papers from the authorities permitting you to do so. If not too much trouble I should like to see your documents. I have been told to be on the lookout for all who journey to and fro."

"There is a paper from the alcalda of San Diego," Lewey remarked, "asking aid for us in case we need it. Read, if you please," and the document was handed to the ranchero, who looked it all over, even to the seal of the official, but, as he could not comprehend a word that was written on the paper, it was passed back to us in a grand and dignified manner, just as if the half-breed was an intelligent scholar. Any piece of writing would have answered as well, as far as the vaquero was concerned. A written document was a mystery in his eyes, and yet he would not let us know that he was incapable of understanding all that passed his examination.

"The paper is correct, senors," the Mexican said. "Pardon me for asking for it. I wish that you had time to go to the casa, and partake of refreshments."

We shook our heads, and intimated that we had not the time, and hoped to see him some other day.

"Then perhaps the senors have a piece of tobacco that they can spare?" asked the ranchero, in a polite tone, and with a profound bow.

We had a good stock on hand for our pipes, but did not let the fellow see all that we possessed, as we feared it might excite his cupidity, so we cut a large piece from a hand, and the man was just as well satisfied as if we had given him a pound.

We asked about our route, and were told to follow the trail, that we should find an abundance of water at the various springs, at the foot of the mountains, and were advised to avoid large herds of cattle, if possible, or else keep our dog out of sight, as the animals did not like perros, as a general thing. Then we waved our hands, and said "Adios," and separated, first depositing Jack on the ground, to his great delight, as the bullocks were some distance from us, and no longer paying the least attention to our party.

"A very courteous ranchero," I said, as we rode along, and, looking lack, waved our sombreros at the stranger, who returned the salute, and then disappeared in the chapparel.

"So courteous dat de scamp vould hab cut our throats for de tobacco vot ve hab vid us, if ve had not been armed," Lewey remarked, with a sneer at my estimation of character. "You don't know de greasers yet, and you von't till you is dead."

"At least it was lucky that we had our papers to show him," I remarked.

"Vot good did dat do?" was the question. "He cannot read or vite, and anyding vid de letters on 'em answer for him. If he had vanted to fight I was all prepared for him," which was quite true, but still I was glad that Lewey's great readiness in killing people was not tested, for I did not think it pleasant to shoot Mexicans, and ride off laughing at the feat.

"You noticed," said my friend, "dat I stated ve vas both French. I does dat 'cos de Americanos is not in de good oder jist at dis time. But de Frenchman, he respected eberywhere, for de France is a great nation, and all love him."

As his impudence was so sublime I let it go unchecked, but readily agreed that I would pass as a countryman of his where we deemed it advisable to conceal my nationality.

About twelve o'clock we came to a spring of running water located near some trees, at the foot of a high hill, where the pasturage was good. Here we determined to halt for a time, eat our dinners, and feed our horses. We unsaddled the beasts, and piquetted them by the aid of lariats, so they could not return to the town, and then built a fire, made a pot of coffee, and ate some of the salt beef and pilot bread we had brought with us. Not a house or a human being was in sight. We were in one of the wilds of California, yet better land, or a finer location for a farm, could not have been found in the whole State, as the grass was rich and luxuriant, and the water supply ample, at that season of the year. I suppose all that portion of territory is now cultivated, and covered with fields of grain, and orchards of oranges, figs, and lemons, and vineyards of grapes. But the solitude was oppressive at that time, and, after we had smoked our pipes, and rested, we were glad to once more resume our journey in search of pleasanter places.

As we rode away, still following the trail, we saw a number of deer on one of the hills, and seemingly indifferent to our presence. Lewey wanted to have a shot at one of them, but I coaxed him to let them alone, as we did not need food, and could not very well carry a carcass to our next halting place. I told him we should have plenty of chances to get all the deer we desired, if he would only have patience, and, for a wonder, he acquiesced in my views, and saved his powder and shot.

The sun was warm, but a fresh breeze was blowing from the high mountains, seen in the far distance, and we loped on at an easy pace, so that we would not tire our horses and Jack, although the latter displayed no sign of fatigue, but bounded along cheerfully, smelling of every suspicious bush, or high chapparel, always on the watch for game, or something that wanted a little brush, in the shape of a fight. He looked upon the journey as a picnic, gotten up for his especial benefit, and, when we drew rein, and walked our horses, glanced up at us, his eyes expressing the fun that he was having in our company. Once in a while he saw a sneaking coyote or deer, and, ambitious of renown, started off in chase, as if confident of overtaking all that he pursued, but a sharp whistle or word brought him back, wagging his tail, as if to tell us that it was only his fun, and he did not mean anything by it. He seemed aware that it was wrong, and would do so no more, yet forgot his good resolutions in ten minutes, and would rush with angry growls for something that was more fleet of foot than himself.

As the day declined we began to look for a place to camp for the night, where there was water and wood, but, when we had climbed a hill, and gazed down in the valley below, saw an adobe house, and smoke in front of it, and a woman bending over a fire.

"Dere am de blessed signs of civilization," said Lewey "A voman and a petticoat. De one goes vid de udder. Alons, mon ami, ve is in de luck all de time. Ve skall hab a place to stop for de night. Let me speak to her de fust, 'cos you has not de perlite vays of de great French nation, you know."

We descended the hill at a walk, as we did not wish to be too abrupt in calling on strangers, and, as we approached the house, the woman heard the footsteps of our horses, looked up, and then darted into the building, and banged too the door, as she happened to own one. That was a sure signal she was afraid of us, or doubted the honesty of our intentions in thus intruding on her privacy.

A cur came bounding around the corner of the house, — a cross between a coyote and a sheep-dog, — and made a dash at Jack, but our game little animal uttered a growl of defiance, seized the canine by his neck, gave him one rough shake, and then the stranger uttered a howl of regret that he had made such an attack, put his tail between his legs, and ran away, and, when at a safe distance, stopped and barked at us. He imagined for a moment that a mountain lion had been encountered by mistake.

We dismounted from our horses, tied them to a post near the doorway, and then Lewey opened a conversation with the female of the house, endeavoring, in his usual seductive way, to assure her that we had no evil intentions.

"Senorita," he cried, as he pounded on the door, "we are amigos. You need not fear us. We intend no harm. We are strangers, and have lost our way."

There was no response to this touching appeal, and Lewey looked a little discouraged, but still did not relinquish all hope that he might induce the woman to communicate with him.

"Will you not speak to us?" the French lad exclaimed. "We are travelers, and the best of Catholics, and respect women next to the saints," and still the lady of the house showed no signs of relenting, and, just as my friend was about to tempt her with some more pretty words, we heard the sharp click of a gun-lock, and, glancing around, saw that we were covered by a musket, enormous in its proportions, as far as length and bore were concerned, and at the stock of the gun was a villainous-looking face, and the uncombed, long hair of a dark, dirty, tall, lank, wrinkled, half-breed greaser.

"Vamous," said the owner of the gun, a flint lock concern, that would carry about half a pound of buckshot, and powder in proportion, and, confound the fellow, he held the musket perfectly steady, and covered us in such a manner that one of us would have been blown all to pieces had the man fired in our direction.

Jack made a motion to rush on the Mexican, and give him a sample of his jaws, but we called to the dog, and forced him to lie down, and wait for fresh negotiations.

"Amigo," said Lewey, who would not show the slightest fear, although I have no doubt he felt a little tribulation in the presence of that awful blunderbuss, "put up your gun, and join us in a friendly smoke. We have some nice cigarettes, and know that a caballero like yourself will enjoy them."

"Who are you?" asked the greaser, apparently willing to listen to reason, for he removed the gun from his shoulder, and the scowl left his face.

"We are travelers on our way to Los Angeles, and would stop here to-night, if it please you and the lady of the house."

"You are not agents of the government then? You do not come here to spy out my possessions so that a tax can be laid on them" asked the Mexican.

"No; we are gringos, and you have nothing to fear from us," was Lewey's ready answer.

"What country do you belong to? You are not Mexicans. That I can tell by your words," the half-breed said, as he grounded the stock of his formidable gun, and took a step forward.

"We are Francia marineros, and traveling through the country for the sake of seeing it. We have no money, but a little tobacco, and a gentleman like yourself shall share it."

"Where is Francia?" asked the greaser. "I have heard of Americano and Inglaterra, but no other country, except Mexico, the powerful."

"France," cried the indignant Lewey, "is the greatest country in the world, and has more soldiers and ships than there are cattle upon your plains. It is the land of the great Napoleon."

"Never heard of him," was the reply. "Was he a ranchero? Did he own many horses and cattle?"

For a moment Lewey was speechless with astonishment and disgust. He had to lean against the hitching-post for support, and his breathing was laborious, as he looked at me in a mute appeal for help to find words wherein he could express his consternation that there lived a man, forty years of age, or more, who had never heard of the deeds and battles of the "Great Napoleon."

"Napoleon," I said, coming to the relief of my friend, in a timely manner, "owned many horses and mules, and, when the latter turned on him, the great man vamoused the ranche."

"Now you dink dat is funny, don't you?" asked my French friend, in a low tone, for we did not care to let the Mexican hear us speak English.

I did not answer the question, for the owner of the premises laid his gun one side, touched his broad, stiff-brimmed sombrero, and said, with the grace which even a beggar of Spanish descent can assume, —

"You are welcome, senors. Such as the house affords is at your disposal. All that I possess is yours, to do with as you please. Stay as long as you wish, and return when you desire. The door will always be open for my friends. And now I will try one of your cigarettes, if you have no objections."

We gave him several. He lighted one, and smoked away with evident relish, while we proceeded to unsaddle our horses, and to stow our blankets and traps in an adobe store-room, where there was barley in bags, hens and mules, and such odds and ends as a man who is isolated from all civilization would be likely to accumulate in the course of many years. The Mexican did not offer to lend us a helping hand. It was none of his business how guests arrived or departed. He furnished shelter, and such food as he was able to procure, but the labor of removing saddles, or putting them on horses, was something he did not care to incur. It was not the custom of the country, unless the host kept half a dozen vaqueros in his employ, to look after cattle, and perform odd jobs of work.

We piqueted our mustangs where the grass was good, and then returned to the Mexican, still squatting near the fire, and throwing his whole soul into the enjoyment of smoking, so it was evident he had not tasted tobacco for many a day.

"Senor," I said, as we joined him, "do you not think that you had better allay the fears of the lady of the house? We noticed that she fled at our approach, and perhaps she will be pleased to learn that we are friends and not enemies. Her anxiety must be intense."

"Diablo," he answered. "I had forgotten the women. They passed from my mind like the smoke from my nostrils. I will call them," and then he raised his voice, and shouted, so that all could hear him, "Senora Juana, Senorita Florencia, come forth. We have friends here who will be glad to see you."

The door was unbarred, after a moment's hesitation, and then a dirty-looking, half-breed woman, without shoes, feet that were hard and dry, and stiff with dirt, clothed in a skirt and under-garment, came out of the house, and saluted us with a half-shy, half-sullen glance, as though she was not prepared to welcome or repudiate us until better acquainted.

We knew the customs of the country, also the weaknesses of its women, and, when we saw that we were not greatly admired, I arose, removed my hat, and proffered the senora a bunch of cigarettes, with the request that she would take them as a token of our appreciation and respect.

The frown left her brow, and a more agreeable expression took its place.

She lighted one of the cigars, and joined us in a quiet smoke, but the eyes of her husband were fixed on that bunch of cigarettes like a hungry animal's on food that is beyond its reach, and we feared he would take it by force and violence.

"Where is Florencia?" asked the Mexican. "Why comes she not out to welcome our distinguished guests?"

"She is timid," was the answer. "She fears to meet the eyes of strangers."

"The senors are good caballeros, and will harm no one," the husband said. "Go and tell her that a Mexican gentleman has offered shelter to travelers, and that his family should second the proffer of hospitality."

Lewey winked at me as we heard this grandiloquent address. I glanced at the surroundings, and mentally calculated that everything within sight was not worth one hundred dollars, and yet the greaser was assuming the airs of a grandee of Spain, with millions at his command.

The woman finished her cigarette in a cool, contented manner, then arose, and entered the house. We could hear a little struggle, a few shrill whispers, and at last the wife dragged forward a young girl, who held back, and averted her face, as if ashamed of being picked to pieces by two men she had never met before. We were a little amused at the scene, and did not take much notice of the girl until she turned her head to steal a look at us, half in surprise and half in fear. Then we leaped to our feet, removed our hats, and bowed low before the prettiest little half-caste specimen of femininity that we had seen for many a day, as she was dazzling in her beauty, with the most luscious black eyes, large and liquid, and veiled by lashes that were wonderful in their length and thickness. Her form, what we could see of it, and she was scantily dressed, seemed the very perfection of a sculptor's dream, and, although her feet were bare, and soiled by constant contact with the earth, yet they were small and exquisitely shaped, and her ankles were worthy of the face. We could not have been more surprised had an elegantly dressed lady stepped out of that miserable adobe hut, and saluted us in the choicest of French expressions.

The girl, not more than thirteen years of age, was born and reared in that out-of-the-way place, and probably had never seen her sweet face in a looking-glass during all of her short life, and did not know that she was as handsome as some of the rarest flowers that blossomed around her parents' ranche. I never saw such a piece of rustic beauty in my life as that little girl, whose name, her mother informed us, was Florencia, a fitting appellation for one so rare in beauty of face and form.

Lewey, always on the lookout for a handsome countenance, and desirous of making an impression, sprang forward, hat in hand, to salute the little lady, and, as he poured forth a torrent of compliments, the girl looked up full in his face, and, for the first time, seemed to awaken to the fact that a nice young man was addressing her with more respect and politeness in his tones than she had ever heard in her uneventful life, or could hope for again. The look of timidity passed from her classical features, and her glorious black eyes appeared more brilliant than ever.

"Confound the fellow," I thought. "He will play the mischief with that girl's heart unless I interfere, and save her," and, for that laudable purpose, stepped forward, and made a few remarks that I thought quite appropriate.

With all the coquetry of a girl's nature the little lady turned her attention to me, and actually smiled at my endeavors to speak Spanish as fluently as my friend. She thought that heaven was near, for here were two white young men paying her marked attention, and treating her with a deference she had never before experienced, so she gave us each a word of good-nature, and then drew the inner garment of her dress a little more tightly over her shoulders, so that a finely formed bust should not be exposed to our rude gaze.

"Confound you, what did you come and poke your nose in this mess for?" asked Lewey, in French.

"To keep you out of mischief, you bad boy," I answered. "I know you, what you are capable of, and what you are thinking of. For once in your life please not to exert the power of your fascinations. This little girl does not know the meaning of love, and, if you continue as you have begun, we shall leave behind us a sad heart tomorrow."

"But why should we leave tomorrow?" my friend asked. "We are in no hurry. Time is no object with us. If we do not start for a week no one will blame us for delay on the route," still speaking French.

"I shall go tomorrow even if I have to travel alone," was my response. "I will not let you play havoc with the girl's peace, just to gratify your confounded vanity. You are already half in love with her, and in a day or two there will be promises of marriage, and you never would fulfill them. The girl is no match for you. Let her alone, and treat her coldly as I do," and then, when the little lady asked me what I was saying in a strange tongue, I had to lie a bit, and say that we were complimenting her eyes and face, and she tossed her head and smiled in a manner that showed how much of a woman she was in feeling, in spite of the disadvantages under which she had labored all her life.

The mother and father looked on, and smoked, in quiet enjoyment. They did not understand the dangerous position of the daughter, for love had long since died out of their hearts, and they would have laughed at such a sentiment. I think that if either of us had asked the padre to bestow his daughter's hand in marriage, he would have consented without a thought of the future, only stipulating that the husband should be a good Catholic. That would have been the only proviso he cared to make on such a solemn occasion, so fraught with the future welfare of a girl.

At last the smoking was concluded, and then the mother and daughter commenced preparations for supper. The stone for cooking tortillas was heated, the corn soaked in the usual way among Mexicans, an earthern pot was put on the fire, filled with bits of meat, peppers, and some vegetables, then Lewey went with the girl to a spring, and brought fresh water in a calabash. He was making himself useful, but if the daughter had not been pretty he never would have cared to do the labor that he did on that occasion.

" Ve vill contribute toward the supper from our own stores," whispered the French lad. " Ve vill not be mean here, not one bit."

" Especially since there is a pretty girl to share in the feast," I suggested, but Lewey would admit nothing that was detrimental to himself.

" I is a Frenchman," he said proudly, "and one of dat nation alvays admire de booful. Get out de coffee, de sugar, de bread, and say no more about it, or, by gar, I dink you jealous of your old ami, and love de girl yourself."

We surprised the people with our contributions, and what pleased them more than words can express was the taste of coffee, well sweetened with sugar, and a few cakes of pilot bread, something they had seldom seen before, except when a visit was occasionally made to San Diego, and even then the mother and daughter were not invited to make the journey only at rare intervals.

It was not such a bad supper, for we were hungry, and had good appetites for sauce. There was a lack of spoons, knives, and forks, but fingers were convenient, even if not clean as soap and water could make them. Lewey loaned his spoon to the young girl, and she was pleased with it, while the father and mother were content with such as they had carved from wood, neither small nor graceful, but large enough to hold about a gill of liquid, so the owners could fill up quite rapidly when hungry, and had a hot olla before them.

While we ate our meal the Mexican told us all of his history. He liked the country where he was located, as he had unlimited quantities of land, and no neighbors to interfere with his rights. He owned a few thousand head of cattle, and one or two hundred horses, but the latter were of little value, and nearly wild. The only disagreeable incidents of his life were when the Indians made a raid through the country, from what is now called the southern part of Arizona, crossing the mountains through deep canyons, the existence of which was known only to themselves, as the Mexicans had never organized, or dared to follow the lawless bands, or punish them for driving off stock, and capturing prisoners. More than two years had now elapsed since the Indians put in an appearance, and the father seemed to think that they would trouble him no more. He once scattered a band that approached his house by firing a broadside from his formidable old musket, and in that one discharge killed two painted warriors, and wounded as many more, and it seemed to satisfy the Indians that the vicinity of the adobe building was a dangerous place, so they left him, but made fearful work with his stock, driving off nearly half that he owned, and more than fifty horses. The latter he cared nothing about, and the savages were welcome to them.

"Think," said Lewey, "how dangerous it is for your wife and daughter to reside in such an exposed place. What if the Indians should make a raid, and capture them some day, when you were absent from home?"

The greaser shrugged his shoulders as he answered,—

"It would be the will of God. But the Indian who laid a hand on my wife might never forget it," and the Mexican smiled in a significant manner, and glanced at the tough, boney hands of his spouse, as if he had some experiences in domestic affairs that were valuable.

"But the daughter? Surely you would feel badly if anything happened to one so young and beautiful?" Lewey said.

"She can see an Indian, or signs of them, better than a hawk. Her eyes are like eagles, and her speed, when she runs, is only equaled by that of a deer. Florencia can take care of herself when I am absent from home, and if she was in distress Tobias would come to her relief like the wind, with his fleet steed and sturdy lariat."

I stole a quick look at the girl's face, and so did Lewey, but no blood rushed to her cheeks and dyed them with a deep crimson. She continued to pick at the pilot bread as unconcerned as if she had not heard the name of the nearest ranchero, the one we had met in the morning. It was evident that her heart had not been touched by his bold horsemanship and wild-looking eyes.

Darkness gathered, and settled down upon the distant mountains and prairie, and already the coyotes were abroad, and calling to each other from neighboring hills. The fire was fast dying out, only occasionally flickering as a faint breeze swept through the palio, and stirred the embers into life. The husband and wife smoked our cigarettes with great relish, and the pretty daughter, with a serape over her shoulders to keep off the heavy dew and cold night air, neither looked at us, nor moved from her position, but gazed at the dying embers, as if she was endeavoring to read her future in the hot ashes, and then, as I glanced at her sweet face, so sad and yet so beautiful, just as the last flame leaped up, and expired with a faint crackle, I saw Lewey's blanket move, — pulled a little carelessly over his left hip, — and knew that under cover of that useful article he was holding and squeezing one of the girl's dark but well-formed hands, and that, for the first time in her life, she was drinking in all the bliss that a young woman can imagine when half inclined to be in love with a good-looking man.

"For shame, Lewey," I said in English, but he made no reply, neither did he remove his hand, and, just as I was about to rise, and terminate the scene, we heard a shrill scream, a yell, so loud and terrible, that I sprang up, and only had time to seize Jack, who had been sleeping by my side, and prevent him from darting forth into the darkness, and investigating the noise, for his hair was standing erect with the rage that possessed his great heart. He struggled to free himself from my hold, and growled angrily at all interference in his movements.

Lewey also jumped up, dropping the girl's hand, but the rest of the group did not move or manifest any great amount of agitation or fear.

Again that shrill, fierce scream fell upon our ears, but this time nearer, and in the direction of our horses, which were piquetted near the courtyard. We could hear them snort and paw the ground in their fear and desire to break away from the stout reatas that held them fast.

"What is it?" we asked, as we sprang for our rifles, which were leaning against the house, all loaded, and ready for use.

"It is a mountain lion," answered the Mexican, puffing at a cigarette with admirable nonchalance. "He will not venture near us as long as there is fire among the ashes. But you had better bring your horses nearer the buildings. The beast may be hungry, and, if he is, there is no knowing how quickly he will leap on one, and make a hearty supper. This thief of the devil has been on the ranche for the past two weeks, and some night I shall have to kill him. Quien sabe ? "

We took our rifles, and, as we did so, the greaser's dog came creeping to the fire, his tail between his legs, and ears drooping, trembling all over. He looked at every one in a pitiful sort of manner, as if ready to protest in case he was kicked out from his safe position into the darkness.

" Down, Jack," I said, as sternly as I could, when releasing my hold of the dog, for he showed no sign of fear, and wanted to dart off in pursuit of the strange beast, and I have no doubt but that he would have tackled the brute if he had been encouraged to do so. There was nothing he feared except an unkind word from his masters.

Jack obeyed, but uttered an angry protest, and growled defiance at the prowling foe. If we had allowed the game little fellow to follow his inclinations it would have been his last night on earth, for the mountain lion could have crushed him with a blow of his powerful paw, strong as that of a leopard (an animal of a similar species), then thrown the dog over his shoulder, and strolled off toward the mountains to feast at his leisure.

When the savage beast uttered his shrill scream, the coyotes on the hills ceased their sharp barks, and seemed to listen so that they could denote the presence of their fearful foe, and not disclose their own position in the darkness.

" Take care that he does not spring on you," the Mexican father said, as he threw on a few more fagots of wood, and kindled up the fire, just as we were ready to go the rescue of the horses, who were struggling and straining at the reatas, and shaking with terror.

The host did not seem inclined to lend us a helping hand, which we thought strange, and a little impolite, but the man supposed we were just as much accustomed to the ways of that vast solitude as he was, and that no assistance was required on his part. In this he was mistaken, but to preserve his respect it was necessary to show no fear. Just as we were moving off the young girl arose, threw off her serape, and said,—

" The senors are strangers, father. They may not know the ways of a frightened horse, or the cunning of a mountain lion. I will go with them, and speak to the caballos. They always respect a woman's voice, or the touch of her hand, because it is more gentle than that of a man, and inspires them with courage. Come, senors, I am ready."

But we held back. We did not desire to involve the little girl in any danger, and waited for the father and mother to utter a remonstrance, but none was spoken by them. They seemed to think that the offer on the young lady's part was a natural one, and not worthy of remark or protest. By Jove, what courage the little beauty possessed. She was not one to squeal at the sight of a mouse, or to go into spasms if a spider alighted on her dress, or a grasshopper tickled her ankle. I could not help admiring her as she stood near us, her well-formed head thrown back, and her bright eyes sparkling like the stars above. I was enabled to note her pose and flashing orbs by the aid of the fire, that was now burning up brightly, revealing the girl's form, long black hair, and scant dress. How little did I think that it was on Lewey's account she was anxious to go, and, if possible, save him from all harm.

"No, no, you remain by the fire," the French lad said. "We need not your help. The wild beast is terrible in his rage, and we fear for your safety if he should make a spring."

"Have no fear for me," was the response. "I can take care of myself. Come; the horses are again uneasy. The lion is near once more."

As she spoke there arose another shrill yell, and then, in the rear of the animals, we saw two firey eyes, large as silver dollars, it seemed to us, and, before we could utter a word, the young girl bounded toward the savage beast, and I uttered but two words.

"Vamous, maldito," she cried, and the lion disappeared in the darkness, uttering sullen growls of protest as it slunk away.

We followed her, and found that she was stroking the horses with her little hands, and talking to them in a soft, soothing tone, and they seemed to comprehend her, for they ceased to tremble, and put their velvet noses on her rounded neck, and uttered the peculiar cry that mustangs use when pleased, or are favored with the presence of one they like.

Although the night was cool the animals were reeking with perspiration, through fear, but, when we unfastened the reatas, and led the beasts toward the house, their expressions of joy were quite human.

"Fasten them near the out-building, Florencia," the father said, "and give them a mess of barley on the ground. One of us will have to sit up all night to keep the fire going, and the lion at a distance, otherwise the horses would not be safe, unless let loose."

"How do the caballos and cattle on the plains escape the ravages of the savage beasts?" I asked, as we secured our animals, and the girl emptied a measure of barley on the ground before them, for which they appeared quite grateful, as they fed readily.

"It is only the weak calves or colts that the lion attacks and devours; those which have been separated from the herds," was the answer. "The stallions and the bulls form a line of defence, and kick and toss anything that dares approach the mares or cows, night or day. Even a grisly bear is cautious how he plays around a mob of cattle, for there is death in a stud's heels, and gaping wounds from the quick play of a lively bull's horns. Let a horse or bullock be secured by the head, or hobbled, and a mountain lion will pull it down, and devour it in a short time. There is the diablo again, prowling around, and seeking a supper. He must be hungry to act so bold. Florencia, throw a brand toward the brute, and then go to bed. It is time your eyes were closed for the night. The senors will excuse you."

"I will sit by the fire, and keep it burning," she said, without looking up.

"No, it is useless," was the response. "The strangers can do that by taking turns. They have guns, and can shoot the beast if it approaches too near."

"Why can't we do that now?" Lewey asked. "We have rifles, and know how to use them."

"The mountain lion is a hard beast to kill," the Mexican remarked. "You can test your guns if you wish, but, to prevent mistakes, think I will have my old escopeta at hand. Bring it to me, girl, also the machete. It may come in play if the beast makes a spring."

The girl arose without a word, and brought from the house the old musket, and also the machete, or heavy chopping-knife, such as the Mexicans used for cutting down brush, or thick chapparel. She placed them in his hands, and once more sat down by the fire, and did not speak a word, although, when she seated herself, I noticed that she took a different position from the first one she assumed, that is, she was between Lewey and the prowling mountain lion, and if a spring was made by the ferocious beast she would be more likely to receive the encounter than my French friend. Was it an accident or intentional that she thus placed herself in so much danger? No one could tell by the expression of her face what was her thought, for it betrayed neither emotion nor fear.

"The women will enter the house," the father said. "It is safer for them. Men only should fight lions."

The mother lighted a fresh cigarette, and entered the building. The daughter did not stir.

"I will remain, and help the strangers," she said, and displayed a second machete, which she had concealed in the skirts of her dress.

"She is not afraid," the father said, and nodded toward his child. "She has faced many dangers, and never yet quailed. She is a true daughter of Mexico, and I am her father."

We were about to utter some complimentary remark, but once more the wandering lion uttered a shrill yell, and this time not more than five or six fathoms from us. We could see his firey eyes as he surveyed us, and hear his jaws when brought together with a snap, as he gave expression to his disappointment in not obtaining an early supper.

"Now," whispered Lewey, and up went the rifles to our shoulders, and they were both discharged the same moment, full at the great, burning eyes, that looked so savage and threatening.

There was a yell, a roar, and then we could hear the beast rolling on the ground, scratching and tearing at the grass, and snapping its jaws in savage fury.

"By all the saints, but I believe you have hit the diablo," the Mexican said, as though surprised at the accuracy of our aim. "Girl, throw a brand in the direction of the beast, and let your father see if another shot is necessary."

"No, no," cried Lewey, stopping her as she was about to obey the command. "It is dangerous for the senorita to do so. Let me incur all risks."

He snatched the burning fagot from her hand, and threw it with all his strength in the direction of the wounded beast, and, for a moment, by the light of the flaming brand, we could see a body rolling over and over, and tearing and biting at wounds on the head and shoulders.

I had lost no time in ramming down another bullet in my rifle, thinking that it would be needed, but, before I was ready to fire, the Mexican brought his heavy escopeta to his shoulder. There was a blinding flash, a dull, uncertain roar, and the greaser was kicked across the courtyard, and against the adobe house, and for a moment I feared that the man was badly injured, but he picked himself up, and muttered,—

"Bueno, I know I have finished him," and he was nearly correct in his supposition, for the struggles of the lion ceased, and, when I told Jack to go for him, the dog uttered a shrill bark of delight, and bounded out into the darkness, and the Mexican's cur followed. Then we heard some angry snaps and snarls, and our dog came back to us after a moment's delay, and wagged his tail, as much as to say, "I have finished our mutual enemy, so there is nothing to fear."

We stirred up the fire, and sent one more brand in the direction of the lion. He was lying quiet, and the cur was lapping some blood that flowed from the wounds.

The girl lighted a fagot, and walked toward the dead beast without sign of fear.

"He is muerto," she said, and held the flame of the stick so near the lion's mouth that she singed the long whiskers around his nose.

"We have done well," the Mexican cried. "See, here are three wounds. But my shot did the business after all."

And so it appeared, for the charge from the escopeta had made a most hideous hole in the lion near the right shoulder, while the balls from our rifles had lodged in the head and neck, either of which would have caused death in time, but not immediate dissolution. At any rate, if he had charged on us we might have been injured, and perhaps the little girl maimed for life, before we despatched the brute.

"A good night's work, senors," said the Mexican. "The lion has been roaming over the plains and hills for the last few weeks, and worried the cattle. Caramba, but he can do no more damage. Tomorrow I will skin him, and sell the quero the next time I visit San Diego. Senors, accept mil gracias for the part you have performed. It was a lucky moment when you made my house your home for the night, and as much longer as you please to stay."

The girl said nothing. I was inclined to doubt the truth of the man's assertion. I was afraid that it would be the most unprofitable incident for the senorita that she had ever experienced in her young life, for I imagined that she had looked upon my friend's face, and lost her heart and peace of mind at the same time, as I knew Lewey well enough to know that no inducement on earth could prevail upon him to remain and marry the girl, thus burying himself from all society and civilization. He was a flirt, and it was born in him, and no experiences on his part, no dangers that he encountered, were sufficient to restrain his roving propensities, or keep him from pouring compliments into willing ears. I doubt if age has even yet dulled his interest in a sweet face and graceful form, married man that he is, and the father of a family, small, but as large as French customs will allow at the present time among the aristocracy of his country.

"Shall we have one more cigarette before we retire for the night?" asked the Mexican, and the girl seemed to second the request, for she stole a quick look at Lewey, and then dropped her eyes.

"By all means," cried my friend, and out came his pipe and tobacco, but I put a veto on the measure.

"The senor I know will excuse us," I said. "We have traveled far to-day, and under a warm sun. Tomorrow we must start early, and make a

good journey toward Los Angeles. We need rest, and will now retire if you have no objections."

"You is always spulin' de fun," Lewey grumbled in English. "Vy can't you keep still, be good, and not see dings? Vot a particular boy you is. If a young girl like you I say not one vord, but vink at it all de time."

But on account of that pretty little child of nature I was firm, and resolved that the lad should no longer trifle with her affections, if I could prevent it. His blue eyes had done damage enough already, and I feared that it would be a long time before the senorita forgot him or his jaunty ways, his soft words and warm looks, so well calculated to move a girl's heart, especially such a child as Florencia.

"Well, senors," the host said, when he found that I was firm, "the best place that I can offer you for sleeping quarters is the shed. There is nothing in it but some barley, hens, fifty hides, and a few other necessary articles, which will not interfere with your slumbers. Pleasant dreams to you, and may the saints have you in their keeping now and forever. Go to bed, girl. Why do you remain up until this late hour, when it is your custom to lie down with the sun? Your mother has been asleep for half an hour. May the saints pardon me for being profane, but, caramba, note her snoring, and she will keep it up all night, and in the morning vow her sleep is like an infant's. Santa Maria, but hear her go it. I wonder she does not strangle."

"Let me help arrange the room in which the senors will sleep, padre?" pleaded the young lady.

"Nonsense. The senors are travelers, and need not be particular in this part of the country. Good-night, caballeros. You need not fear for your horses now, as there will be nothing but coyotes prowling near, and no one cares for them. They will be sure to keep at a distance from the heels of the caballos," and, with these words, the father motioned the girl to enter the house, and then followed her, but did not close the door, as we expected he would do.

"Cool it is," muttered Lewey; "but den it am de custom of de country, so ve vill not complain."

By the aid of a burning fagot we cleared a space where we could spread our blankets, and, with our saddles for pillows, lay down. If we had not been impervious to flea bites we should have been eaten up before morning, for the insects swarmed over us by millions, and must have enjoyed the rare treat of sucking fresh blood to fill their hungry bellies.

But, troubled as we were, I dropped off to sleep, and could have had but a short nap, for I was awakened by an unusually loud bark of a venturesome coyote, and looking out upon the courtyard saw a large, lank animal near the door of the house, as though engaged in reconnoitering, to see if it was safe for him to enter, and hunt for a supper. I threw a club at the intruder, and told Jack to keep quiet, for the dog was restless, having been tied to a beam, to keep him out of danger while we slept, and then turned over, and, to my surprise, found that I was alone, Lewey having disappeared while I slept.

In an instant I was wide awake, and on my feet. I understood the matter as plainly as if I had been informed of all that had transpired while I slept. Out of the building I went, and walked away from the house some little distance, but saw no one. Then I turned, and strolled in the direction of the dead mountain lion, which the coyotes gave a wide berth, for fear it might not be as defunct as it appeared. Near the animal I heard low voices, and one of them was that of Florencia, and the other my friend Lewey's.

"I swear to you," the French lad was saying, "that I loved you the first moment my eyes rested on your face. It is beautiful; more charming than the fairest girl in San Diego. Give me but one kiss to prove you do not dislike me, and let me hope that when I am gone from here you will not forget me in a day, or a week. Assure me of that, and I will think of you so often, until I return, that even your warm nature will rejoice."

"Take the kiss," the girl answered. "It is not much to give one like you. But as for thinking of me when you are in another part of the State, I do not believe it. I wish that I could, for then I should be happy even if I am separated from you."

The wretch put his arms around the form of the girl, and took not only one kiss but a dozen, and she did not seem to shrink from his embrace, as she should, and would have done, had she known the French lad as well as I did.

I thought it time to interfere. I was resolved that the artless little girl should not further commit herself, even if Lewey's assertions were sincere, and I had good reasons to doubt them, for although he could fall in love with much rapidity, it was also certain that he got over his passion just as swiftly, and without a particle of heartache. He was a true Frenchman in this respect, and did not believe in moping when it was possible to be gay.

As I advanced the girl sprang from my friend's arms and muttered, —

"Santa Maria, I thought it was my padre. If he should find me here it would be death to both of us. He would chop us to pieces with his machete, and laugh at our prayers for mercy."

"Fear nothing, Florencia, it is my amigo. He will not lisp a word," Lewey said, in a hasty tone, and then, turning to me, asked in English, —

"Vot in de devil's name did you come here for to spoil de fun?"

"Fun for you, but death to the girl. For shame, Lewey, to make love to such a little wild blossom," I answered. "Let the girl alone, so that she can return to the house, and talk no more of love to her, for I do not think it desirable to break her heart, and you know that marriage is an impossible thing at the present time. Confound it, you miserable flirt, how many girls do you desire to be engaged to at the same time?"

"I do vish dat you vould mind your own business, and let me all alone to mineself," my friend said, in a petulant tone. "I interferes vid you nebber. Vy, you might de love make to all de females of California, and not one vord say I vould. Go back to your blankets, and let alone me. See I nothin'."

The girl stood listening to the conversation, carried on in low tones, so that the terrible padre would not be awakened, and with her head bent down. She could not understand a word that we uttered, but she must have known that we were conversing about her, for once in a while she would raise her face to Lewey's, and ask, —

"What are you talking about? Speak in Spanish, if you please, so I may know all that is going on."

"Lewey," I said, in a calm tone, "I will not take offence at your words, for we have been friends for many years, and never had but one quarrel during all that time. I now appeal to your better nature as a man, a young one to be sure, to let the girl enter the house, and promise to see her no more tonight."

"And if I does not," he asked, in a sullen tone, "vot den?"

"Simply this. As soon as daylight comes I shall saddle my horse, and return to San Diego alone. We part forever."

"But I loves de girl," he pleaded, after a moment's pause.

"Nonsense. You think so, but in a day or two you will acknowledge your mistake. If you love her so much, remain here, and marry her. I will give you all the gold I possess to start you in life, and try and make you happy on this solitary ranche, so far out of the world. Come, be a man, and tell me if you will take the little child for your wife without delay, for I would not trust you an hour."

"I vill do as you vish," was the answer. "I am not de kind of man to make dis girl happy, and yet I vish dat I could, for she is booful, and I do love de booful faces."

"Go into the house, senorita," I said. "Your father might awaken, and then there would be trouble. Do not stir out again this night."

The girl looked at Lewey for advice. He pretended not to see the pleading face, but was watching the stealthy movements of a sneaking coyote very attentively. For a moment she hesitated, then, receiving no word from my friend, turned toward the house, but, as she did so, suddenly raised forward, and seized my hand, pressed it to her lips in a hurried manner, and whispered, —

"Senor, I know not what you have said, but mil gracias for your words and presence here tonight. May you both be happy will ever be the prayer of pobrecita Florencia," and she was gone.

I heard a sob, and saw Lewey brush away some dampness that had gathered in his eyes.

"You poor boy," I said, as I sprang forward, and threw my arms around his neck, "are you as hard hit as this denotes? Do you really love the girl?"

"Yes, I dink I does," was the answer. "But I skall get ober it in a little dime. I is a fou vare de vomen is concerned."

"How many do you think you could love at one time?" I asked.

"I knows not, but I skall like to try. I dink dat I could vorship a million if dey vas all booful, and did not plague me vid der jealousy. Now mine ami, I is all right vonce more, and ve vill sleep to go till de morrow."

There was no other incident during the night. Lewey slept, and, perhaps, dreamed of the object of his worship, but he did not move out of the shed until I called him a little after daylight, just as the people in the house were stirring. Then we arose, packed our blankets and traps, piquetted our horses out to graze, filled a large calabash with water, and had a good wash, a proceeding that made the greaser look on, and wonder, and the wife to smile in a sarcastic manner, as though she could not see the need of such useless proceedings, while Florencia wet her face and hands at the spring, and dried them on a cloth that must have been in the family many years, and had never been what the women call "boiled out."

The senora started the fire, and mixed the usual dish of torti'las, and prepared an olla, which she was to cook in a black earthen pot, one that had been licked by a coyote the night before, and, to prevent our stomachs from being turned, Lewey snatched the crock up, and went to the spring, giving the utensil as thorough a cleaning as it was possible without soap, sand, and hot water.

The wife did not seem in the least offended at my officious friend's proceedings, but the rich blood mounted the dark cheeks of Florencia, as she witnessed the act, and she felt the shame that did not find vent in words. I have no doubt she contrasted her surroundings with what she imagined were ours when at home, and lamented her fate more bitterly than ever before.

Again we contributed our share to the breakfast, — a little coffee and sugar, — and, after a hearty meal, smoked until the sun arose, and warned us to be on our way. Then we saddled our animals, packed our traps on them, and were ready for our long journey over the trail, and towards the mountains.

"Adios," we cried, as we swung ourselves into the saddles. "May God be with you," and we touched our sombreros, and the Mexican repeated the salutation. The wife smiled on us, and bade us come again, as she would be glad to see us at any time.

We glanced around to bid Florencia farewell, but the girl was not in sight. She had disappeared when we put the saddles on the animals.

"Give our regards to the senorita," I said, then we ambled out of the courtyard, and took the trail, Jack at the horses' heels, glad to be once more in motion.

Lewey did not utter a word, but he often looked back to see if he could get a glimpse of the young lady. For ten minutes or more we galloped along, and then, suddenly, just ahead of us, the chapparel parted, and Florencia sprang on the trail, and stood in our path. I uttered a groan of dismay, but Lewey paid no attention to me. He spurred on his steed, and, when he neared the girl, jumped from the saddle to the ground, and threw his arms around her, and kissed her several times without any remonstrance on her part or mine.

"I could not let you leave me without saying one word of farewell," she said, "and I did not wish my padre to notice our parting. Now go, and God be with you."

The French boy took one of the girl's little dark hands, and kissed it very gently, as he said, in a voice meant to be sincere and tender, —

"I swear to come back," and, as he uttered the words, there was an angry growl from the dog, and he rose up from his resting-place, and sniffed the air in a suspicious manner, and then, just about fifty fathoms from us, across the trail, four horsemen dashed from the thick chapparel on each side of us, and uttered a shrill yell of triumph, and brandished long lances, on which were hung locks of human hair and feathers, and it did not take a second glance to reveal to us that the strangers were wild Indians, admirably mounted on hardy mustangs, and sitting the animals without the aid of saddles or stirrups, bridles or head gear of any kind to guide their horses, as untamed as the riders. All this we saw, and then realized that we were in the presence of a roving band of Indians from the other side of the mountains, scouring the plains in the hope of securing plunder, in the shape of cattle and women, scalps and horses, and, in the days of which I write, the savages did a large business in the southern part of California, crossing the mountains when they pleased, for there was no one to make them afraid, or drive them back to what is now known as Arizona, then a wilderness, and the home of the fierce, treacherous Apache Indians, and members of this tribe were now before us calculating on an easy conquest.

CHAPTER V.

THE APACHE ATTACK. — PAINTED WARRIORS, AND THEIR CHARGE. — DEATH TO THE INDIANS. — RETURN TO THE RANCHE. — THE GOVERNMENT COURIER. — A HORSE TRADE. — OUR JOURNEY RESUMED. — THE FEAST OF THE BUZZARDS AND COYOTES. — TROUT FISHING. — RANCHE VALLECITO. — A PROPOSITION. — THE NIGHT CAMP, AND A STARTLING APPARITION.

THE only Indians we had ever before seen were those met at the missions and ranches of California, and were called tame, because they had received some enlightenment by the aid of priests, whose willing servants the peons were, receiving only food and a shirt for the labor which they performed, not very arduous at any time. The tame bucks we had always looked upon with perfect contempt, as not possessing the feelings or courage of a warrior, but here, just ahead of us, was something different from what we had been accustomed to, for the half-naked visitors sat their horses like centaurs, and there did not appear to be much tameness about them, for they uttered a yell that denoted triumph, and shook their lances in our direction, and then, seeing there were but three of us, counting the girl, and leaving out the dog, prepared to charge down the trail.

"Holy Virgin, mother of Jesus," Florencia cried. "Fly to the ranche for your lives. The Apache Indians are on us, and will take your scalps. Turn your horses, and escape if possible."

"And what will you do?" asked Lewey, who felt more anxious for the safety of the girl than for his own. I will give him the credit of saying that his first thought was for the little beauty, and not personal preservation.

Even if we had turned, and spurred our horses to their utmost speed, we could not have reached the ranche in time to escape a spear thrust, as the

Indians were better mounted and far more expert horsemen than we could ever hope to be, even if we had spent a life in taking lessons from the best ranchero in California. Consequently, in our surprise, we did the very best thing that was possible under the circumstances. We did not fly as the Indians expected we would do when they first sighted us, and this made them a little suspicious of an ambush, which the rascals dreaded above all things. They feared that there might be Mexicans hidden in the nigh chapparel, on each side of the trail, and for that reason hesitated to bear down, and crush us at a blow.

"Never mind me," Florencia cried, in answer to Lewey's appeal. "The saints will have me in their keeping. Ride for your lives, or you are dead men. Those warriors know no fear, and have no mercy on all they capture. There are four of them, and only two of you. Be warned in time," and the young girl knelt at my friend's feet, and raised her hands in supplication, so that he would be moved by her appeals.

"Never will I leave you like a coward," Lewey exclaimed. "I would have acted a treacherous part toward you, but may the devil fly away with me, as I suppose he will some day, if I don't make it warm for the savages before they take you prisoner."

He snatched up his rifle as he spoke, and then glanced at me, and, as his eyes met mine, I thought that he was not the worst boy in the world, even if he did like to flirt with pretty girls, and tease them, when he should have been honest and frank.

"You vill stick by me, old friend?" the lad asked. He spoke in English, and hurriedly, for there was no time to lose, as the Indians showed signs of charging toward us, seeming to divine that we were without supports.

"As long as I have life," was my answer, and the French boy's face lighted up with the joy he felt at the words.

"I knowed it," he cried. "Dismount, and let de girl hold de horses, so dat avay dey vill not run. Ve can much better shoot on de foot den in de saddle."

Down I dropped to the ground, and threw the bridle of my horse to the girl. She understood the meaning of the action as well as though we had explained the matter by half a hundred words. Florencia started the animals along the trail that led 'to her home, and when the Indians saw the movement, and understood that there was a prospect of the girl's escaping, —a prize that they coveted more than a dozen head of cattle, — they uttered a fierce yell, lowered their long lances, and dashed toward us, swaying their bodies from side to side as they advanced, so that our aim would be disturbed, in case we fired on them. I think they did not expect a volley, as all the Mexicans they had encountered on the raid, it is very probable, had fled at the first glimpse of the painted fiends, terror-stricken at the thought of being scalped, and hacked to pieces.

"Take de von on de starboard side," my French friend said in a whisper, "and I vill de von on de larboard side look aiter, and den pistols to 'em take as fast as possible, and no mistake make."

Even in that moment of peril Lewey did not forget that his nautical expressions conveyed more meaning to my ears than if he had used the words of a land-lubber. I nodded, and by this time the Apaches were not more than ten fathoms from us, riding like a whirlwind, and looking hideous in their paint and feathers, yelling in concert, and shaking their lances.

"Now," said Lewey, and at the word we discharged our rifles, and then jumped as far as we could into the chapparel, on each side of the trail, dropping the rifles as we did so, and drawing our pistols.

It was well we made the leaps we did, for in another second we should have been spitted on the lances of the two uninjured warriors. Our aim had been true, for a wonder, and both the Indians we had singled out, a little in advance of the others, tumbled from their horses, and the trained steeds instantly stopped, and waited for the owners to remount, but they did not seem to be in a hurry, for good and sufficient reasons, as we afterward discovered, both painted brutes having small bullet holes in their breasts. The pellets of lead had gone completely through the bodies, and out near the shoulder blades, a dose sufficient to settle their accounts for all time, and yet the wounded Apaches did not lie still even after touching the earth, but rolled into a thick clump of chapparel, and with their last strength sought concealment in the long grass, so that in death they could preserve their scalps from enemies.

As I have said, we dropped our rifles, and drew our pistols, and, as we landed in the rushes and grass, nearly as high as our heads, we turned and fired them at the pursuing Indians, when they were not more than three fathoms from us. The ball from my pistol struck the knee joint of the Apache nearest my side of the trail, then glanced from the bone, and entered the spine of the mustang he was riding. The beast dropped as if struck by lightning, throwing the Indian to the ground, nearly at my feet, and, had not Jack come to my assistance, the warrior might have given me an ugly jab with his spear, for, in spite of his injuries, and the pain he endured, the savage was about to make a lunge at my stomach, as I was too astonished to get out of the way, or discharge my remaining pistol full at his head, as I might have done, had I possessed proper presence of mind at the time to consider my danger.

The Apache had raised his spear, as I was looking at his hideous face, streaked with thick layers of paint, and thinking how fortunate it was he had managed to dismount so suddenly, when Jack thought that the time had arrived for him to take a hand, and show what he could do to prove that he was a dog of courage and resources. He did not need to be told to pitch in, for instinct prompted him to make a sudden attack, and, while the warrior was just on the point of giving me a thrust, Jack made a mighty bound, and landed full on the back of the Apache's neck, and commenced chawing at the flesh and muscles, as if desirous of securing a little lunch of Indian meat, just to see how it would taste.

The savage was not prepared for this demonstration. His lance's point fell, as he turned to meet the new enemy. He reached for the long knife in his leggings, and, if he could have secured it at the first attempt, Jack's life might have ended then and there, but the angry snaps that the dog gave disconcerted the savage, and, muttering some malediction in the Apache tongue, he made a second attempt, but by this time I had come to my senses, no longer fascinated and dazed by that terrible face. He had exerted over my senses some such spell as the rattlesnake is supposed to have over human beings, birds, and animals.

As the savage again reached for his knife, feeling the pain of Jack's long and sharp teeth tearing at the flesh in a fury of rage and desperation, I sprang forward, tore the long lance from the hand that held it, and then plunged it through the body of the prostrate Indian. He uttered one cry of rage and defiance, the hand fell to his side, the eyes grew dim, a shudder ran through the body, and the warrior was dead, and the instant life ceased Jack relinquished his attack, and uttered a howl, as though to bark a requiem for the spirit that had gone to its happy hunting-grounds.

Then, for the first time, I had a chance to turn my attention to Lewey, and see what had become of the boy. He missed the Indian that was on his side of the trail, because his pistol hung fire. It had failed him just at the wrong moment, and, before he could cock the second one, the Apache dashed on in pursuit of the girl and horses. Lewey had followed as rapidly as possible, thinking of the safety of Florencia, and supposing that I had fatally wounded the savage who had tumbled from his horse, and fell at my feet. He imagined that I was more than a match for a dismounted, half-dead Apache, but he was much mistaken. I afterward warned him to be

CALIFORNIA

more careful the next time, and see that I was doing well before he left me to aid strangers.

I noticed Lewey tearing along the trail as fast as his legs could carry him, and I would have taken one of the two mustangs that were standing near me, all riderless, and waiting for the word of command from their owners, and followed in pursuit, but did not care to mount a horse that had neither saddle nor bridle, for fear it might take me to a part of the country I had no desire to visit, perhaps in the midst of the rest of the raiding tribe, which I imagined was not far off.

I picked up my rifle, and Lewey's also, for he had left it behind, in his eagerness of pursuit, and then slung one of them over my shoulder, and loaded the other as I trotted after my friend. I did not know how many Indians were near, but was determined to be prepared in case there was another attack.

I had not run more than fifty fathoms before I heard a roaring report. It sounded like the Mexican's musket, for there was no other weapon near us that could make so much noise, it appeared to me.

In a few seconds there was a shout of triumph, not from Lewey, but the ranchero, and I surmised that the old fellow had done some damage with his blunderbuss, perhaps killed the fleeing Apache, and such was the case, for on the ground, when I arrived at the spot, was the body of the dead Indian, the whole side of his head blown away, and presenting a disgusting sight to those not accustomed to such wounds.

And that Mexican was as proud as a peacock over his deed, and pointed with much gusto to the wounds, and then to the large muzzle of his musket.

Florencia was safe, and was in the yard with our horses. The old Mexican had heard the firing soon after we had left his house, and, thinking there might be Indians near, as his wolfish dog was uneasy, and sniffed and growled, a sure sign that danger of some kind was abroad, he had gone through the chapparel, and remained in ambush until the Indian came along in pursuit of his daughter. Then he understood the whole matter at a glance. The girl was allowed to pass, and, when the Apache hove in sight, a handful of shot was lodged in his head, the very best place it could have been deposited, just at that time.

There were mutual congratulations indulged in, and then the Mexican insisted upon our returning to the spot where we had been first attacked, so that he could see if the rest of the Apaches were dead, or only wounded. The Mexican did not think that there were any more savages in the vicinity, as he said that they were apt to break up into small bands, and scour the country in every direction, meet at some spot near the mountains with all the plunder and prisoners, and then depart through a secret canyon for the southern portion of Arizona, from whence they came. This was the first time in two years, as he again told us, the Apaches had made a raid, and he rather suspected the Indians, that is the main body, had gone in the direction of San Diego, where there were more cattle and females for prisoners. At any rate, it would not be safe for us to continue our journey for a day or two, as we might fall into the hands of the prowling ladrones, and lose the number of our mess, although he did not express himself in such nautical language.

As we returned to the scene of the charge, the two dogs followed at our heels, a common feeling of danger seeming to make them fast friends, for the time being, as they did not snap or growl at each other like the night before, and in the morning. Indeed, the animals appeared to express to each other a feeling of satisfaction that they had done so well when hard blows were called for.

As we neared the spot we saw the two horses standing motionless, waiting for their masters who would never mount them again. The Mexican looked at the brands on the flanks of the mustangs, and knew them as well as if they had been printed matter. Much better, in fact, for he could not read a word of Spanish.

"They are from the Ranche Vallecito," he said, and pointed toward the north, in the direction of the trail. "They must have been stolen two years ago, when the great raid was made, for it takes an Indian a year to break in a mustang, and teach him all the tricks necessary to be an Apache's best friend, something that can be trusted night and day, will come at his call, and stand until told to go. I will let them mingle with my herd, if I have any left, and in a few weeks' time they will forget some of their wild training, and not sniff at a white man, as you see these do."

As he finished speaking the Mexican attempted to lay his hand on the nearest mustang, but the horse reared, and struck at the greaser with his fore feet, and then bit at the man in a vicious manner. The Mexican did not seem surprised at the attack. He easily avoided it, and then hit the brute over the flank with a stick, and the animal loped along the trail for a few fathoms, then stopped suddenly, and glanced back, as if he had forgotten something, and could not tell what it was.

"He is looking for his savage master," the Mexican remarked. "It is curious that the mustang should love one who treats him as ill as an

Apache warrior. The more abuse, the longer the journey, the greater regard. It is singular, but true. Now let us find the bodies of the dead if they are dead. Here is blood on the grass. You must have hit them hard to make them fall from the backs of their horses. Ready with your guns, and be on the watch, for there is no knowing what the diables may be up to in the tall grass. If they are not dead they can do us mischief. Be very careful."

We sent the dogs into the chapparel, and then followed them very cautiously, our rifles all ready for action. We did not have far to go, as the trail of the wounded savages was quite distinct, and well defined by drops of blood. In a clump of grass one Apache was lying, still alive, but in the agonies of death. He looked at us with a scowl of hate on his painted face, and then commenced to chant his dying song, for he knew that there was no mercy in the dark, swarthy face of the Mexican.

"Ladrone of the devil," the greaser cried, "your time has come. Go to the fiend who created you," and, before we could interfere, he had seized the warrior's lance, and drove it through the red man's body.

"So perish all the enemies of Mexico," the greaser shouted, and repeated the blow.

The Apache gave a gasp, and was dead.

"It was a cruel deed," Lewey remarked, and turned away with a shudder.

"If you knew the painted devils as well as I do you would not think so," was the reply. "They will torture the life out of you, and laugh at your groans. They spare neither women nor children. Should I save him from the death he so well merits? Let the buzzards feast on his flesh, and the coyotes pick his bones, for his race has ended forever."

We sent the dogs on the other trail, and found the body of the Indian, but there was no life in his hideous carcass. He must have been a petty chief, for his lance was ornamented with several long locks of hair, looking like a woman's, and his leggings were embroidered with the quills of a porcupine, the work of some squaw he had left at home to mourn for his absence, or rejoice at his death, just according to his domestic relations, for I suppose Indian females are like their white sisters in this respect at least, and judge of a husband by his treatment.

We left the bodies where we had found them, the horses waiting patiently for their masters, and returned to the ranche, where the Mexican wife received us with a smile of approval. Our animals were safe, and Florencia had taken the precaution to remove the saddles, and piquette the beasts near the house, where the grass was abundant and fresh. She evidently did not intend that we should resume our journey immediately, and her father was of the same opinion, for he said, —

"You must wait until tomorrow before you start. There may be more Apaches on the trail, and if you should meet them perhaps they would be better prepared for a fight than those who have fallen. This is the safest place for you for a short time at least."

The young girl's face showed some of the pleasure she felt at her father's words, but she did not raise her eyes from the ground, or appear to hear her parent's advice. Lewey stole a look at me to see how I received the announcement. I was a little perplexed. There was danger in advancing, or in remaining where we were, but my friend, in a tone of great sincerity, remarked, —

"You can trust me, Thom. I swear to you by our friendship dat I vill not say one vord to de girl I should not be villing for you to hear."

I had confidence in his word, trusted him, and agreed to remain where we were until the next morning.

"By the way," said the father, as he lighted a cigarette, an example which his wife followed, as soon as we had passed them a package, and he looked at his daughter a little suspiciously, "what were you doing so far from the house this morning? and why did you not remain to bid our guests God speed?"

"I did not think they would care for my good wishes," was the reply, thus showing that a Mexican girl can equal an American maiden in equivocating when there is occasion to deceive a father, and keep secret her love.

"But you were a long way from the house," the Mexican said. "Had it not been for these senors you would now be a prisoner in the hands of the Apaches. You must be more careful in the future how you take solitary rambles."

"I was in search of quail's eggs. I know where there is a covy in the chapparel," the girl answered, and a blush mantled her dark cheeks as she spoke.

The reply seemed to satisfy the father that her errand from home was a legitimate one, so he did not deem further explanation necessary. He again thanked us for saving the child from the hands of the Indians, and in this the mother joined most heartily, and, to prove that she was sincere, made ample preparations for a dinner, and an olia that should surpass all of her previous efforts.

The sun came out hot. We lounged in the courtyard, our rifles and pistols all ready in case more Indians should make their appearance, and we did not know but a few of the tribe might put in an appearance, searching for their lost comrades. We neither saw nor heard any suspicious movements, however, until about eleven o'clock, when both dogs grew uneasy, and uttered short yelps of anger.

The Mexican, as he noticed the movements of the animals, dropped on his knees, placed one of his ears close to the ground, and listened long and attentively.

"A horseman is approaching us on a swift lope," he said. "He is not an Indian, and the beast is guided by bit and bridle. To prevent mistakes, however, let us be prepared to give the stranger a warm reception."

We could hear nothing, but in a minute or more the swift beat of a horse's feet were noticed, and along the trail, from the direction of Los Angeles, came a Mexican half-breed, superbly mounted on a showy mustang, his serape streaming over his shoulders as he dashed along, his broad sombrero on the back of his head, and his long, black, coarse hair fluttering in the wind.

"It is Pedro," the Mexican said, as he dropped the butt of his heavy musket.

"And who is Pedro?" I asked, as the horseman approached.

"The government courier. He rides between San Diego and Los Angeles with despatches. It is a lonely journey for him, and full of danger, but the man is well paid, and likes his work. There is no better horseman in California than Pedro," and our host prepared to give the new-comer a warm welcome, for it was evident he intended to stop, as he waved a hand in our direction, and shouted out a Mexican salutation and greeting.

Pedro, who was about twenty-five years of age, thin and muscular, short, but graceful in the saddle, threw his horse on its haunches when within a short distance of us, stopping him so suddenly that the feet ploughed up the dirt and grass for some distance. Then the vaquero sprang from his saddle, and, as he touched the ground, saluted all present by removing his sombrero, and said, —

"Buenos dias senora, senorita, y senors," and, leaving his steaming horse where he had halted, tip'oed to the fire, lighted a cigarette, and took a survey of the company present.

He was a smart-looking fellow, with eyes as black and keen as a hawk's, just the kind of a man who would do a little fighting if there was any occasion for it, or running, if that was better and safer than rough work.

He unbuckled the huge spurs from his heels, laid aside the light carbine which he carried slung over his shoulder, placed the long, sharp knife and pistols with the gun, and then asked, —

"Who are these senors?" and motioned toward Lewey and myself.

"Two French caballeros, on their way up the coast," our host answered.

"Bueno," was the response. "I feared they were Americanos."

"Why should you fear they were Americanos?" asked our host.

"Because war is declared between the United States and Mexico, and we cannot be too careful of all sospechosos."

"It matters but little what country a man comes from if he helps me at a pinch, as these young caballeros have done this morning," our Mexican host answered. "American or French, they have my thanks."

"Ah, you have had a brush with the wild Indians?" asked the courier. "I saw a dead horse on the trail, and flocks of buzzards hovering over the chapparel, as if they were about to make an attack on a corpse or injured bullock. Did you kill any o the ladrones?"

"Four of them have gone to their happy hunting-grounds, three by the hands of these young senors, and one by the aid of my old musket, which you always laugh at."

"I will laugh at it no more, amigo, if you have sent an Indian to the infernal regions where they belong. What were they? Apaches?" asked the courier.

"Yes, and on a raid for cattle and prisoners. These senors saved my daughter this morning, and shot those beasts who would have captured her. Think how much I owe them, and why I should not stop to ask where their country is located," and the Mexican looked some of the gratification he felt.

"Diablo," the courier said, as he removed his sombrero, and extended his hand, "it was a deed worthy of a Mexican. Frenchmen or Americans should be proud of killing an Indian, and doubly grand when it is an accursed Apache, whom the saints may consign to the eternal region of fire for all I care. Senors, I am pleased to shake hands with such bueno hombres. Hereafter command me in everything."

We shook hands with great heartiness, and offered the courier a fresh cigarette, which he accepted with a profusion of thanks.

"You ride fast today, Senor Pedro," the Mexican host said, after the ceremony had been performed. "Is there such pressing news that you must scour the earth with your horse's feet?"

"Santa Maria, I should say so. The American gringos are mustering at the North, and General Castro has shaken them up, and is preparing to drive the accursed heretics into the mountains, where they can starve. A war ship is at San Pedro, and the people of Los Angeles fear that the marineros will march by land, and attack the town. I have despatches to the alcalda of San Diego, praying him to put in order the presidio, at the entrance of the harbor, and to give the heretics a warm reception, in case they should dare to venture near in one of their ships. Our people are aroused, and will fight for California until the last drop of blood is shed."

Considering that the presidio at San Diego had but two brass pieces, and those were spiked and useless by neglect, we did not think our ships would suffer much while rounding Ballast Point, and could not believe that all the greasers of the State were prepared to die for the Mexican flag just at present. The news did not alarm us in the least, as we had heard just such rumors before. We thought that Captain Fremont and his men could take care of themselves, and not get much hurt, and the result justified our crude opinions.

"This is indeed news," our host said. "You must rest here, and eat, so that you can go on in the afternoon. I will give you a fresh horse when ready to start, and you can take yours when returning, if the accursed Indians do not run it off with the rest of the stock."

This was a common practice, and excited no expression of gratitude. I looked with admiration at the courier's steed, for it was a noble animal, and gentle as it was fast.

"Let me exchange with you," I said to Pedro. "I like your horse. Mine is fresh, and can carry a man to San Diego by midnight. I will give you a dollar, — for, although I am poor, I have that amount of money, — in addition to my caballo, for yours."

"Senor," said the courier. "the horse is no longer mine. May you be happy with him. He is a noble brute, and true as gold," and the man held out his hand for the eight-real piece, took it, tested it with his teeth, to see that it was not counterfeit, and seemed satisfied with his bargain, for he grinned.

This may seem a cheap price, but our host would have been g'ad to have disposed of all the horses on the ranche for a dollar each, and thought himself well paid.

"Courage, amigo," the Mexican said, as he noticed Lewey's face, a little downcast at the thought of my being better mounted than himself. "You shall have a caballo equally as good, and it sha'n't cost you anything either.

"Florencia, can you find the bay bronco, the one I have ridden so often, and drive him to the corral this afternoon?"

"Yes, padre," was the ready answer. "I know where he is feeding when the sun goes down," and a flush of pleasure passed over her handsome face, as she thought of the happiness she was to render her lover.

Pedro looked at the girl with the admiration he did not attempt to conceal, and I thought that I could account for the rest he was taking at the lonely ranche, even if his despatches were urgent. He was in love, like my friend, but was a more suitable match for the girl than Lewey, and I wondered she did not fancy the dark-eyed vaquero, who had all the brilliant qualities calculated to win a doncellito in her station of life. But she preferred a white face and blue eyes, as the contrast was more striking than a dark skin such as she possessed.

I went to my purchase, stripped the saddle from his back, and then piquetted him where the feed was good, rubbed the perspiration from his flanks and back, and the brute seemed to like the attention, for he put his nose against my shoulder, and uttered a whinny of delight at such treatment, something he had never experienced at the hands of his former owner.

Our Mexican host and the courier laughed at the exhibition I was making, and even the wife smiled in a sarcastic manner, but Florencia seemed to approve of my doings, for she gave me a glance from her expressive black eyes that would have made Pedro happy for a day, had he been the recipient of the great favor.

Not content with my ministration, I led the horse to the spring for a drink of fresh water, but he did not seem to care for it, as it was not his usual time for drinking, morning and evening being the hours in which he was accustomed to quench his thirst, when water was convenient, and his master not too indolent to turn him toward a river or pond. Then I procured a couple of quarts of barley, and had the satisfaction of seeing the animal feed as if he liked the grain, and appreciated the attention.

"You would spoil a mustang in two weeks," Pedro said, as I returned to the group sitting in the shade of the house, and awaiting with patience for the olla which the wife was tending. "Our horses are hardy and do not need any care. They can pick up a living on the plains, and think themselves fortunate if they do not have to lope a hundred miles on an empty stomach. The more you pet a broncho the less reliable he is," and the I. trod led confirmation of the words, but I loved animals, and did not like to see them suffer, or be abused, and in this instance my kindness was well repaid by the mustang I bought that day for a dollar and a poor specimen of horse flesh thrown in to boot.

"Did you hear or see anything of the Indians on your way?" asked our host, as we gathered around the olla, which the wife pronounced ready. It was made of cheque, barley, onions, red peppers (rather more of the latter than we relished), potatoes, and a few herbs to give it taste and seasoning.

We once more produced our stock of coffee and sugar, and gladdened the heart of the courier by giving him a strong concoction, in which grounds and dulce struggled for supremacy. It was as nectar to him and the others, so no one found any fault.

"I left the Ranche Vallecito last night," Pedro said, in answer to the question of our host. "There were no signs of Indians at the time in that vicinity, and I saw no one on the trail. I think the band you killed were out of their usual course, and that nothing more will be seen of the ladrones between here and San Diego, unless they strike Francia's ranche, an I, if they do, will hurry the captured cattle towards the canyons of the mountains, and so escape all pursuit, even if our people were prepared to give chase, which I don't think they will be. The Mexican is brave, but he loves not the yell of wild Indians," and I did not blame him if all the Apaches screamed like those we had encountered in the morning.

The courier then gave us some valuable information concerning the route, what streams we would have to ford, and canyons to pass through, mentioning especially the Seco Canyon as being dangerous, dark, and dreary, with high and rugged mountains on either side, and a little stream of clear, sparkling water meandering down the course, and emptying into the Pacific Ocean, at some distant point. In fact, we found the journey we had before us was more difficult than we had contemplated, but we were determined not to give up the undertaking, but to push on, and hope for success as we advanced.

We hinted that we should like to wait at some point on the way until the courier made his return journey, but Pedro did not seem to favor the plan.

"In the first place," he said, "I do not know when I shall again pass this way. It will depend upon the alcalda of San Diego. He may desire that I remain for important information, and when I do start I shall spare neither horse-flesh nor myself. You could not keep up with me for ten hours without tumbling from your saddles with fatigue. Better go on alone, and follow the trail as well as you can. Stop at the few ranches you may see, rest, and inquire your way, and may the saints have you in their keeping," and then the courier, with his great appetite satisfied, threw himself upon the ground, under the shadow of the adobe house. and in an instant was fast asleep, resting himself for the work before him that afternoon and evening, on his lonely ride to San Diego, the trail of which he was not certain was clear of Indians.

Our Mexican host, seeing no more signs of Apaches, skinned the dead mountain lion, and then sent out his daughter on a spare horse to drive in the bay broncho which he had promised to present Lewey. The young girl accepted the mission as one of no particular danger or importance. She sprang into the saddle as light as a cat, and did not assume the position that ladies usually do, for her feet were thrust in the stirrups on either side of the animal. In fact, she rode like a man, and did not think it unbecoming to her modesty to do so, as she had never been taught that her style was unwomanly. She was right, for a side saddle would have been out of place in that wilderness.

Florencia sat her horse as gracefully and easy as a trained caballero, and, as she struck the animal on the flank with the end of a reata, coiled up on the pommel of her saddle, and darted out of the courtyard, Lewey could not help expressing his admiration in warm words of praise, for he turned to me, and said, —

" Dat is de most booful sight dat I have seed for many a day. Ah, mon ami, she is grand on de foot, but in de saddle she is von bonne fille, and I adore her."

" Has your love for Engracia vanished so soon ? " I asked.

" No," was the hesitating reply; " but den dis girl is somehow so different, and a real Frenchman can love many times, and many dings, and be none de vusser for it."

" Remember your promise," I said. " That courier Pedro loves the girl, and would cut you into mince-meat if he thought you had the slightest affection for the senorita. A Mexican's jealousy is only equaled by the intensity of his love. A sharp-pointed knife has put many a rival under the sod, and out of the way. Be warned in time, my friend, and keep your feelings to yourself."

" She loves him not," was the answer, with a doleful sigh. " She has told me dat she likes me, and I believes her.'

She must have made the confession the night before, when I interrupted the tête-a tête, showing that love sometimes makes quick work with young and susceptible hearts.

In an hour's time Florencia returned with the promised bay, a horse of great beauty and power, but not so handsome, I thought, as my own. She drove him into the corral, and then secured the rather wild steed, shifting the saddle from the mustang which she had ridden, to the animal which she had brought in.

"Why do you do that?" asked her father, for we had gathered around to see the new-comer.

"The beast is wild, and needs discipline," she said. "He has not been ridden for a month, and the senor to whom you have given him is a stranger to all of a mustang's unruly movements. I will tame him by a short ride, and then tomorrow he will carry the visitor away from us like the wind, and perhaps we shall never see either again."

It is probable that the girl meant more than her father comprehended, for he made no reply, but allowed his daughter to carry out her designs. Alone she put on the thick sweat-cloth and heavy saddle, thrust the cruel curb into his mouth, even if the broncho did resist, adjusted the bridle, vaulted into her seat, and dashed from the corral as if pursued by a pack of hungry coyotes, and, as her graceful form swayed with every motion of the fiery beast, and her long black hair streamed in the air, like a thousand tiny pennants, bare headed, without shoes or stockings, her position on the horse revealing a generous view of little ankles, and well formed legs, I could not help feeling enamoured with this child of nature, who knew how to love, but did not understand many of the refinements of civilized society.

"Ah, she grows more booful every moment," Lewey muttered, and I mentally cursed the Apaches, and our luck in being detained another night at the ranche, as I feared for my friend and the girl, and that Lewey's admiration would overpower his reason.

Florencia returned after an hour's ride, her horse covered with foam, but quite subdued, and ready to obey the slightest wish of his rider. The girl did not think she deserved any particular praise for what she had done, and seemed surprised at our compliments. She had been accustomed to cattle and horses from the time of her birth, and for many years had helped her parent round in his stock, when it was necessary to do so for the sake of branding the calves and yearlings.

The girl reported that she had met with no signs of Indians, and that her father's stock appeared to be undistrubed, so we arrived at the conclusion that the courier's supposition was correct, and that the Apaches we had killed were but a portion of the band, and had wandered our way in the hope of securing new fields for plunder, and had met with a just fate.

By this time it was four o'clock, and Pedro was awake, and ready to resume his journey. He saddled the horse I had traded with him, and did not seem to think that I had cheated the government official very badly, and I came to the same conclusion as soon as Pedro mounted the mustang, for the animal appeared to be a different beast when the skillful vaquero was in the saddle, as he knew how to manage him much better than myself. He did not spare the spurs, or the heavy curb, and, when he raised his sombrero to Florencia, and waved his hand to us, and said, " Adios, senors," dashed away at a rate of speed that I thought impossible in the broncho, and I imagined my new acquisition would have had some trouble in keeping in line.

Florencia had given Pedro a little smile in return for his salutation. It was not much, but the best the poor fellow could obtain, and I wondered, as I saw him press his steed up the steep trail, and then glance back to the house for a final salutation, if he felt encouraged by what he had received. The next moment he was on the other side of the miniature mountain, and that was the last we saw of him for some days, and then he made his appearance at a most important moment, as far as our destinies were concerned, and the good he rendered us was not forgotten.

The afternoon and evening wore away in a listless manner. Lewey kept at a distance from Florencia, and she rather avoided him, I thought, so I had nothing to worry about, and, when the time arrived for us to retire, the Mexican advised us to have our rifles handy for immediate use, as he did not know but a marauding party of Indians might visit us. He kept no watch, however, as he said that his dog would give us all the notice we needed, in case there were prowlers near, as he could scent the Apaches for a long distance.

To prevent Jack from getting into trouble with prowling coyotes, or adventurous Indians, we tied him in the out-building, close to where we slept, and, after a smoke by the fire, turned in, and slept all night, and I do not think that Lewey moved, or even rolled over, until daylight, thus showing he was a lad of his word, and was honest in what he said when we returned to the house after the fight with the Indians.

We fed and watered our horses, and they seemed in perfect order for the journey, and then the wife had our breakfast all ready, and, just about an hour after sunrise, we prepared to depart. This time Florencia did not disappear from the house. She sat in the doorway, and watched our proceedings with a listless look, and not a word did she exchange with us until we were ready to mount and away. Then, hat in hand, I went to her, and said good-by, took her dark little hand in mine, gave it a gentle squeeze, and uttered a few words of civility.

"You are very kind, senor," she said. "I hope you will come back to us some day not far distant.

I stood aside, and let Lewey take my place. He spoke in a low tone, so I could not hear what he said, even if I had cared to listen, but I noticed there were tears in Florencia's eyes as she arose, and passed into the house, and that was the last we saw of her for some months.

We shook hands with the Mexican and his wife, mounted our impatient mustangs, and were off, the woman asking the saints to protect us during our journey, and to come again when we desired.

As we loped along, not speaking a word, we came to the scene of the encounter the day before. The bones of dead the horse were picked nearly clean by coyotes and buzzards, while in the chapparel, where the Indians had died, were large numbers of the bird scavengers, gorging themselves with their disgusting feast, and striving with the sly coyote for a full share of flesh and bones. They did not move as we approached, except the latter, and they simply hid in the tall rushes, and returned as soon as we had passed on our way, shuddering as we thought what might have been our fate had the battle gone against us.

We pressed on during the forenoon, and about twelve o'clock stopped near a small stream that came from the mountains on our right, high and rugged, the tops appearing to be covered with snow, but we were so far from them that we could not be positive on that point, and for a while imagined that what we supposed was snow were marble ledges.

On the banks of the little brook, near where there was a ford, across which the trail was well defined, we halted for rest and luncheon. There were no signs of Indians, but the footprints of the courier's horse were distinct in the soft ground, and there were no others near, showing that he had not been fo'lowed by the Apaches.

We piquetted our horses, after removing the saddles, and they found plenty of feed near the stream. Then, while Lewey was gathering dry grass and fagots to start a fire, I took a fish-line, a bit of salt meat for bait, and tried my luck in the little brook. Lewey said that he would eat all the trout I caught, as he had but little faith in the experiment. The hook, however, had hardly touched the water when there was a rise, a rush, and I had my line a two pound trout, and was compelled to haul him in hand over hand, as I had neglected to cut a pole, and could not play the prize as I should like to have done.

I held the spotted fish up after it was landed, and uttered a yell of triumph. My French friend gave one look, and ran toward me.

"Dat is good, by gar," he said. "Let me de next one catch, and ebber so much obliged I to you vill be. I knows how de fish to take."

As a general thing all Frenchmen think they are great sportsmen and fishermen, and my friend was no exception to the general rule. I readily let him have the use of the line, for he would have humored me under similar circumstances.

"Now I vill you show," he said, and threw the hook into the water. There was another rush, a bigger trout, an anxious boy, a struggle, and then over the bank went Lewey, for, in his eagerness, he had not noticed where he stepped, and tumbled in the stream.

"Hold on to the fish, Lewey," I shouted, as soon as I could do so, for I laughed so heartily that I did not speak for a moment. Really it was very funny to see the French boy blowing the mud and water from his mouth, uttering not the choicest of Spanish and English expressions, yet retaining his hold of the line, and the trout at the same time.

As the brook was but little more than four feet deep, not much damage was done, except to the boy's clothes, and, when he had frightened the life out of the fish, or drowned it by his pulling and hauling on the line, we laid the prize on the bank of the stream, and then Lewey uttered a mighty shout of triumph.

"Did you ebber seed such fishin' as dat?" he asked, as soon as his transports moderated.

"Never," was my answer. "Do you usually fish that way in France?"

"Alvays. Ven ve gets a big von on de hook ve goes overboard arter him," which I have good reason to believe was a lie, but, as I had never seen a Frenchman fish before, I was compelled to accept his statement as a fact at the time.

We had all the trout we needed for our dinner. We could have caught hundreds in the same rapid manner, but did not desire to destroy that which we could not consume, thus proving that we were not genuine sportsmen, but the veriest amateurs.

Lewey stripped off some portions of his clothing, and dried them in the warm sun and gentle breeze, while I dressed the fish, wrapped them in leaves, and laid them among the hot ashes and coals, and when they were done we had a feast that epicures might have envied, so delicious was the flesh of the trout. Even Jack signified his approval by eating all that we could not dispose of, and looked a little disappointed when the last bones were picked clean, to think that there was no more for his consumption.

We lighted our pipes, and remained under the shade of a tree until nearly two o'clock, taking a little siesta in the meantime, then saddled our rested horses, and resumed our journey, crossing a ford where the water was not more than a foot deep, an embankment thrown up by some great flood of the rainy season.

As we galloped along the trail, looking sharply to the right and left for signs of Indians or wild beasts, we again admired the action of our steeds, as they moved along like perfect machinery. The only trouble was their desire to go faster than we wished. They had been accustomed to being ridden by men who spared neither spurs nor horseflesh when in a hurry, and we had to coax and pat our caballos to restrain their impatience, and keep them down to ten miles an hour, instead of fifteen or more.

They understood our wishes at last, and kept side by side, but if one poked his nose an inch in advance the other was not happy until he had made up the deficiency.

It was a magnificent country we passed through that afternoon, as all the land was good for raising cattle, the grass being rank and plentiful, with here and there a spring or a water-course. I suppose that the whole of that region is now covered with fields of grain, and vast herds of bullocks, with houses and orchards all along the route we crossed. Once in a while we would come to a sterile district, where the sand was heavy, and hardly a shrub was to be seen for miles, and on several occasions we saw great rattlesnakes in our path, too indolent to move out of the way, and all ready to strike if we approached them, which we had no great desire to do. At first we had some little trouble with Jack, as the dog wanted to go in pursuit of everything that he scented, and a rattlesnake he thought was something like an eel, to be well shaken, and then devoured. But a few warning cries, and some gentle blows with the end of a reata, brought our pet to a sense of his danger, and then he gave snakes a wide berth, following directly in the wake of our horses' heels, so that he would be sure and make no mistake.

Once the mustangs shied out of the trail with a sudden leap, and both of us reeled in our saddles. If they had not been of California construction — deep, and high in front and rear — we would have had a narrow escape of falling to the ground, and near two large rattlesnakes, basking in the sun, on a strip of hot sand. The fright made Lewey so angry that he checked his horse, and swore that he would go back, and kill the reptiles. As his blood was up I held his mustang until he could accomplish the job.

My friend, armed with a lot of stones, retraced his steps, followed by Jack, and then vented his rage on the snakes. Even where I sat I could hear the rattles, as the tails were waved in defiance, but Lewey hurled stone after stone at the vermin, and first one head was lowered, and then the other, and a club soon beat the life out of their ill smelling bodies, for they gave out a peculiar odor when excited that was powerful and pungent.

"Dar," said Lewey, as he returned from the attack, "dey von't unsh'p any more men in dis vorld, and for de vorld to come peoples must take care of demselves, for I can't look out for eberybody," and that reasoning seemed to satisfy and restore him to a good-humor, for he smiled and laughed all the rest of the afternoon, and did not even allude to Florencia, so I hoped the magic of love was disappearing from his mind, and that, with his usual consistency, he was forgetting her. Once I had said, in a musing sort of tone, —

"What do you think Engracia and Anita are doing at the present time?" and he answered, —

"Eatin' de frijoles, I s'pose, if dey has nothin' else to do," and then I knew that his love for the woman he was engaged to was wavering, as men do not like to think that the girls they admire have occasion to eat anything but the daintiest of food, expecting them to turn with disgust from the sustaining and nutricious bean.

I said no more, but thought of the boy's protestations and devotion, and how he had led me along, and finally prevailed upon me to leave the ship, so that we could be married to the young ladies of our choice, and I wondered if he would jilt Engracia when the proper time arrived for him to say yes or no. I was firm in my determination to make a wife of Anita, but I wanted Lewey to wed as well as myself, for the sake of company. I hoped he would do so, and supposed that he ultimately might consent, if we encountered no more pretty faces on our route.

A little after five o'clock we crossed a small mountain, and at the top looked down upon a pleasant valley, and there spread before us were herds of cattle and horses, and a large adobe house and out-buildings, with a corral in which were a dozen animals, all ready for use, in case the owners desired to saddle them for a little gentle exercise over their vast possessions.

Our approach was the signal for some little excitement among the inmates of the house. We could see two women beat a hasty retreat into the building, while three vaqueros made their appearance with huge escopetas, and watched with interest for the first hostile demonstration that we were disposed to make.

Three or four dogs bounded toward us, and Jack was all ready to make friends, or be enemies, as they should elect, but the Mexicans called the curs back, and so we were enabled to approach the house without a collision, as we feared would be the case.

"Que quiere usted?" one of the vaqueros shouted, and brought his escopeta so that it would cover us.

"Comida y dormir," we answered, meaning that we desired food and rest.

"Usted amigos?" was asked, a little more pleasantly, and the musket was lowered.

"Si, senor, todas amigos," was our prompt answer, intimating that we were friends.

"Come along then," the Mexicans said, and, as we advanced, they saw that we were not Indians in disguise, so the guns were put aside, and we were welcomed with looks of surprise, and words of deep courtesy from the three men.

This was the Ranche Vallecito we had heard the courier speak of, and the people knew his horse at once, for, as I dismounted, one of the vaqueros looked at the brand on my steed's flanks, and said, —

"We have seen that mustang before. It is the courier Pedro's horse. He was here yesterday."

The Mexicans glanced a little suspiciously at me, as the words were spoken, but I answered carelessly, —

"Yes, Pedro is now at San Diego. We exchanged bronchos yesterday afternoon at Tobias's ranche. I gave my mustang and an eight-real piece for this animal, and made a good trade."

Then all three men laughed in unison, and one of them said, —

"Pedro is smart. When he makes an exchange he always gets the best of the bargain. We have a hundred horses that we will sell you for eight reals each, and ask no caballo in addition."

"Gracias," I answered, with a laugh, to show that I was not offended, "this animal pleases me, and I want no other."

As we knew the customs of the country we did not wait for an urgent appeal to remain, but proceeded to unsaddle our mustangs, and by this time one of the Mexicans, a young man about our age, offered to aid us. Jack, by his resolute demeanor, had inspired the greasers' dogs with a wholesome respect. so they did not molest him, but kept at a distance, and looked the the astonishment which they felt at seeing a stranger in their midst.

We piled our saddles, blankets, and equipments in an out-building like that at the last ranche, and then turned the horses into the corral, where they would not escape during the night, unless the gate was thrown open.

"What is the news from Tobias's ranche?" the father of the family asked, as we returned from the corral, having rubbed the perspiration from the horses' backs, much to the amusement of the Mexican muchacho, who had never seen such pains taken with animals in all his life.

"We had an exciting brush with the wild Indians yesterday morning, just before Pedro arrived," I answered, quite indifferently, as though it was something that I had been accustomed to all my life.

"Gracias Dios, you don't mean to tell me that the Apaches are on a raid?" asked the aged Mexican.

"Yes; there were four came near the house, and tried to capture Senorita Florencia."

"The saints have us in their keeping, but they did not succeed, I hope," cried the two sons, thus showing that the girl's charms were known even in that part of the country, and had produced their usual effect on the young men.

"No, we beat them off, and saved the girl," I said, in a complacent manner.

"And killed three of the savages, while Senor Tobias blew off the head of another," the impulsive Lewey exclaimed.

"Glory to God the highest," the old Mexican cried. "Four Apaches slain by your hands. My house and all that it contains are at your service."

He called to his women folks, — the wife and daughter, — and bade them prepare a feast that would reflect honor on the establishment. The girl was not remarkable for her beauty, so Lewey did not make love to her, as he would have done under other circumstances. The mother was dark, smoke-dried, and wrinkled, with hands that were none too clean, but she made us welcome, and called us heroes, because we had saved the life and honor of a girl, as though we deserved credit for such a just deed.

The Mexicans were very particular that we should give them a minute account of the fight and death of the wild Indians, and felt a little fearful that the Apaches might make a raid in their direction. So much importance did the father attach to our communication that he compelled the youngest of his children to saddle a fleet mustang, and scour the country in several directions, to see if there were any signs of the savages. But the boy returned at dark, and said that he could see nothing of a suspicious nature, and so the stock was considered safe for the night.

We helped ourselves to a measure of barley, and fed our horses, ate our supper with a relish that a long day's journey had given us, and, after a liberal distribution of cigarettes, and a pipe of tobacco for ourselves, retired to the out-building, spread our blankets for a bed, and prepared to sleep, and just then the rain descended in torrents, and we felt thankful that we were under shelter for the night.

The fleas were as voracious as usual, and full as numerous, but their feeding did not disturb us, and, when we awoke at daybreak, the storm had passed away, and there were promises of a pleasant day. The air was fragrant with the perfume of flowers and herbs. The quails called to each other from the chapparel, and wild pigeons passed over the fields in countless flocks, while on the little mountain we had descended the night before stood a herd of deer, watching the movements of life at the house, and caring nothing for our presence, so tame did they appear. The leader of the drove was a large buck, with monstrous antlers. I was more than half tempted to give him a shot, and secure them as a prize, but, when I reflected that I could not carry them with me, I gave up the idea, and let the graceful animal live, and depart in peace.

We piquetted our horses where the grass was fresh and sweet, and let them feed while we washed, and smoothed our hair, a proceeding that caused a quiet smile to pass over the faces of our hosts, for they thought that it denoted a weakness of mind on our part, but it had its reward, for, while I stood watching our mustangs feed, and quite ready for the breakfast that was cooking on the fire, the father drew near, and suddenly asked, —

"To what country do you belong, senor? You do not speak Spanish well enough to be a Mexican, and your skin is white, not dark like mine."

I remembered in time not to declare my nationality, and answered, —

"I am French. My companion and I are brothers, and we are travelling through the country just to see what it is like. We are bound for Los Angeles, and have papers of protection from General Castro. Would you like to see them?"

"No," was the short answer. "They would be of no use to me. I can't read or write, neither can my children. But are you a good Catholic?"

"A most excellent one," I replied, not thinking of the meaning of my words, only knowing that Protestants were not loved or respected by the bigoted greasers.

"It is good," he said, with a smile, as I thought, of relief. "Now I have a proposition to make you. Look around, and see land and cattle on either hand. All are mine. Is there a more lovely place than this?"

I was forced to admit that the region was a paradise, under that cool, spring breeze, with the sun just rising from the mountains, and tinging with a golden hue the distant hilltops, and the Sierras, covered with snow, while the air was filled with humming bees, seeking in the numerous flowers an early harvest of honey. It is a little singular, but I have recently been informed that this region, at the present day, produces more honey, through domestic attention and protection, than all the other parts of the State combined.

"You like the place?" asked the Mexican, waiting until I had taken in all the surroundings before he spoke.

"Yes. Who can help admiring nature in her solitude and grandeur?" I answered, willing to please the Mexican, and make myself agreeable.

"It is well," the man said. "You can remain here all your days if you wish. If you desire to ride, there are hundreds of horses at your disposal. If you love hunting, the mountains and plains abound with deer, and game of all kinds. If you prefer work, cattle are to be rounded in once a year, and branded, or barley to sow, and be gathered. In many ways you can make yourself useful."

What did the Mexican mean by his broad hint? Was he disposed to keep me a prisoner in that wilderness, where a traveler or stranger was rarely seen, and the only recreation was such as he had described? No books or papers were in the house, and when the people were tired they went to sleep, and when hungry ate their coarse fare, and thanked the saints it was no worse.

"Why do you thus tempt me?" I asked, resolved to learn all his thoughts by a direct question.

For a moment the Mexican hesitated, and then said, speaking very slowly and distinctly, —

"You noticed my daughter did you not? I saw you look at her with admiration in your eyes, or I am mistaken."

I began to feel warm and uncomfortable, for I feared the conversation was taking a serious turn, and one dangerous to myself.

"Yes, senor, I admired the lady. She is muy hermoso," I answered.

"She is beautiful," the host repeated, with all of a parent's pride, for, as a general thing, fathers think their daughters perfection, even if they are far from it. "I am glad you admire her," the Mexican continued, "for the feeling is mutual. She likes your appearance, and will marry you."

I almost staggered under the sudden announcement of my contemplated happiness, but I was in a dangerous position, and knew it. The least offensive word, or contemptuous gesture, would be the last that I should ever make in this world. A sharp knife, and a ready one, could reach my heart, even if the dark eyes of the senorita failed to do the business.

"Do you mean to tell me that your daughter is willing to marry me?" I asked, as soon as I could recover from my daze, and speak plainly.

"She has admitted to me and her mother that such is the case. Say the the word, and I'll send to San Mateo for a priest, and in a few days the knot can be tied."

This was unexpected happiness, but I had to keep my head clear, and think rapidly, for there was no chance to fool away time and words with the determined greaser at my side.

"Ah, great is my misery," I said, on the spur of the moment. "Why did I not dream of such happiness before I pledged my word to another?"

"You are then engaged to some woman?" he asked, a little disappointed.

"Woe is me, but I am. How could I think that such a beautiful senorita as your daughter would lift her eyes to me, a poor man?"

"But you can read and write?"

"Yes, senor."

"Then you are not poor, and raised to an equality with my child. She is rich in land and cattle, but has no education. Take her, and the saints bless you."

"How gladly would I do so, if I could only be free of the girl who is expecting me, and seeks to be my wife."

"Shake her off," was the advice, in a sullen tone.

"Tell me," I said, laying a hand on the angry father's arm, "what would you do if a man should seek your daughter's heart, agree to marry her, and then desert her at the last moment?"

"My knife would find a place between his ribs before he had enjoyed his honeymoon," was the savage answer.

"And serve him right," I exclaimed, in apparent frankness. "The father and brother of the girl I am about to marry would treat me in the same manner. They, like you, are Mexican caballeros, and ready to revenge an insult to their relative with death. Let the matter rest just as it is for the present. I am a man of honor, like yourself. I will seek my betrothed, and tell her all. Perhaps she is already married. I hope that she is. I have not seen or heard from her for months. If she is untrue, or gives me back my freedom, I shall hasten to your ranche, and then proudly demand the hand of your beautiful and innocent daughter."

This was not exactly true, but I was not going to infuriate a man when he had the power to do me a serious injury, and perhaps take my life, as readily as he would have slaughtered one of his lively bullocks.

I could see that the greaser did not like the idea of relinquishing his hold on me. He knew when he had come across a prize for his daughter, even if other people did not, and the lady was a girl of most excellent taste and judgment, as I admitted at the time, and have always thought that she was inspired when she selected me for a husband. She must have been a wonderful character reader, for one so young and unaccustomed to the world, and when she did obtain a partner, how striking the contrast must have been in her eyes, and how bitterly she probably regretted that she had not married her first love. I have often spoken of the unexpected proposal that I received at the Ranche Vallecito, and what an honor it was for one so young and tender, and sometimes regrets have been expressed by those who should take an interest in my fate that I did not yield to such solicitations, marry, and settle in the wilderness, where my genius could have found full scope in fighting fleas, Apaches, and a very dark and wrinkled mother-in-law, with hands none too clean for mixing tortillas, and other fancy dishes.

For a few minutes the Mexican father, who was so anxious for an advantageous match for his daughter, and saw the prize slipping from his fingers, remained silent, watching the bees and the herd of deer, revolving in his mind what course to pursue to make two young hearts happy.

"Let us understand each other," he said. "If you find the senorita you are expected to marry unfaithful, or can get out of the engagement with honor, you will do so, and return here?"

"Can you doubt it? I should fly as fast as horse-flesh could carry me," but I did not say in what direction.

"That is enough. I will tell my daughter all, so that she will not think her love is slighted. You do not mean to express contempt for her wishes?" and the host's hand rested on the hilt of his long knife in a careless manner, and his eyes showed some of the fire of an untamed ranchero.

"The saints forgive me," and I crossed myself, "but if I was free you would see how quickly I should welcome the priest, and be proud of such a wife as the senorita will make. Ah, she is lovely and gentle. Happy will the man be who wins her."

All the time I was speaking I kept my eyes on that long knife, for I feared its sharp point, and the owner. I was determined to get out of a bad position the best way possible.

"I have a great mind to detain you," my host said, with a wistful eye, "and defy the family of your intended. If they should come here for the purpose of making complaint, we could ambush the whole party, and put them out of the way with but little trouble."

I almost shuddered at the free expressions of my would-be father-in-law, and longed for the hour when I could mount my horse, and escape from such a dangerous locality.

"The plan that I have laid out is the best," I remarked. "Let us separate with that understanding."

"Bueno," the Mexican responded. "We will shake hands on it," and we did, then and there. "When you leave today, if you must resume your journey, I desire you to salute my daughter with a kiss. It will prove to her that you are anxious for more. Be careful that you do not forget it."

I promised compliance with his wishes, although the task was not one that I felt anxious for, as the girl was far from being handsome, and I had not seen her wash her hands or face since she got out of bed. But I had promised, and meant to carry out the programme, and so escape a cut or stab from that long knife.

"Vot vas you and de greaser talkin' about so long?" asked Lewey, when the Mexican and I separated.

"He desires me to marry his daughter," I answered proudly. Perhaps there was a little more pride than there was any occasion for, but it was the first proposal that I had ever received in that line, and young men are apt to be vain of their conquests.

"Does de girl vant you?" asked Lewey, his eyes opened to their widest in astonishment.

"So I have been given to understand," was my reply, in a complacent tone.

"Parbleu, de girl is crazy to pick you ven dar is me. Nebber heard of sich foolishness in all my life. Hope you said no."

"Well, yes, I did plead that a previous engagement would prevent me from accepting the offer, and I suggested that you might do."

"And vot did de greaser say to dat?" demanded my friend.

"Oh, not much. He thought that he would prefer a sedate, stable man to a fickle boy as a husband for his child, and so declined to take you into account. I quite agreed with him."

"It is von lie," roared the French lad. "He say no sich ding, and I don't believe he ax you to marry de girl."

"You will see when we get ready to leave. I shall then kiss the girl a good-by, and if you attempt it some one will get a boxed ear."

"I vould not kiss her for von million dollars," with an expression of disgust, and then I knew that our host's daughter must be very plain to repulse such a boy as my French friend, who was not over scrupulous as to what he kissed, and where he kissed, as long as it was a woman, and young.

We had a very good breakfast, and, after it was finished, saddled our horses, the young Mexican lending us a helping hand, and expressing regrets that he could not go with us, and see the world. He thought that everything great and beautiful were centered at Los Angeles, which he had heard so much about, and yet had never visited, for the ranche was his home from the day of his birth, and he supposed he should have to remain there until his death.

Just as I was about to mount my horse, I caught the glare of the Mexican father's eyes. He was reminding me of a certain contract which the bustle of departure had made me forget for the time. But, as soon as I saw a hand go to the hilt of his knife, I knew what he meant. Off went my hat, and thus uncovered I approached the young girl, who really did look a little regretful at our departure.

"Senorita," I said, "in a few weeks I hope to have the happiness of again seeing you. Until then will you allow me to salute you?"

She put up her lips just as though she had been instructed what to do, and I kissed her as fervently as I could under the circumstances, and that bad Lewey, who forgot his bold words, sprang forward, and offered to salute the girl in the same manner that I had done. But she drew back, and gave the boy a haughty look that delighted me. I desired to laugh, but did not dare to in the presence of a man who wanted to ambush families, and put them out of the world, in case it suited his convenience.

Lewey covered his confusion and defeat by asking a few words about our route and stopping-places, and this our host was kind enough to give.

"Push on," he said, "and you will reach San Felipe Creek by noon. After this late rain you may have to camp on the bank of the stream for a few hours, or even a day, until the water recedes, and the ford is passible.

If the creek is low you can be at San Mateo by night, where you will find a ranche, and comfortable quarters; and now the saints above have you in their keeping. Adios."

He waved his hand, the women did the same, and the sons shouted out a hearty farewell, and, with Jack at our heels, delighted to escape from the companionship of curs of low degree, we gave free rein to our impatient mustangs, and were off, following the trail that led to the North.

The morning air was delightful, for the rain of the night before had freshened the grass, and revived the flowers, and the atmosphere was impregnated with perfume. The bees hummed around us, and the whistling quails sprang up all along the narrow trail, and flew in large coveys for shelter among the thick chapparel and short grass. Wild pigeons winged their way in immense flocks toward the mountains, and honking geese headed for the shores of the ocean, or some large lake north of us that supplied the waters of the San Felipe Creek, and then emptied into the Pacific. Ducks quacked as they rose from the marshes on our left hand, and their variegated plumage shone like gold, silver, and bronze, as the strong sunlight fell upon their feathers and wide-spreading pinions. Coyotes crossed our path, and looked with hungry eyes at Jack, but the dog was obedient, and did not stray from the trail in pursuit of game of any kind. A dozen deer were roused out of thickets by the noise of our horses' feet, but they only gazed at us in wondering amazement, and did not turn and fly, as if they knew man, and what he was capable of doing. It is probable the bucks and does had never heard the crack of a rifle in that vast solitude, and at most were only occasionally hunted by Indians, when bullocks were not convenient. Once a black bear crossed our path, and sat up on his haunches, and looked a little surprised to see such early visitors, growled angrily at the dog, was answered by a savage bark from Jack, and then the game little fellow looked in our faces, as if he wanted permission to make an attack, and show what he could do with an animal ten times larger than himself.

But a shake of the head was enough to restrain the little bulldog, and he winked one of his eyes, as much as to say, " I was only fooling you, and had no intention of going near that monster. When I fight it is to win."

Our horses scented the bear, and were a little uneasy for a few moments, but, when they saw that we were not disposed to make an attack, settled down to their work, and soon we were some distance from such a dangerous neighbor, and when we came to a spring Lewey checked his horse, and dismounted for a drink of the clear, pure water.

"You had better get off, and vash your face," my friend remarked. "Dat greaser girl vas none too clean, and she might have left some dirt on your cheeks, 'cos you has enough of dat for both of us," and then, when he saw that I was not pleased with the words, his sunny nature broke out. "Did you dink dat I vas in great earnest, O mon ami? Little much care do I for de girls vot you kiss. Do you dink dat I let von nice boy like you marry a fille same as dat? ' take her mineself fust," and that is the way e would have proven his devoted friendship, and could man do more?

And so the cordial relations between us were resumed, and there was sunshine on Lewey's face for the rest of the day.

We stopped at what is now called Julian City, I believe, or near it, and ate our lunch, fed our horses, smoked a pipe of tobacco, took a few winks of sleep, and resumed our journey, but not always at a gallop. as the trail was so indistinct that at times we had some trouble in keeping it, consequently we were late when we reached the banks of a small stream, which we supposed was San Felipe Creek. We hunted for a place to ford, but the water was pouring down at so lively a rate that we did not dare to venture, for fear of losing our horses and stores, so at last concluded that we would have to remain where we were, and camp for the night.

There was plenty of good grass and wood near at hand, and water in abundance, but the place was lonely, and we did not feel quite at our ease, as we thought of the long night before us. But we could not go on until the stream had fallen, and we expected that it would by morning, as the landmarks showed a decrease had taken place in the course of the day.

We looked all around us, toward the mountains, and in the direction of the ocean, although we could not see it, but the position of the sun showed where it ought to be, and not a human being, except ourselves, was in sight. We even failed to get a glimpse of smoke from some distant ranche, and hen, after we found that camping was inevitable, removed the saddles from our horses' backs, piquetted them where the feed was good, and, while thus engaged, I saw, near a clump of alder-bushes, a solitary doe looking at us with great, wondering eyes.

For the first time during our journey we needed meat, as our salt junk was all gone, so there was no reason why we should not have venison for supper, if we could get it. Lewey held Jack, while I took my rifle, and stole around in the rear of the doe, and, when within thirty yards, fired, and had the satisfaction of seeing the deer bound away for a few rods, and then drop, badly wounded. Another shot put an end to its suffering, and when I carried my prize to the camp was quite proud of my achievment.

We dressed the deer, and cut off such steaks as we needed for supper, and then hung the balance on the bough of a tree, to use for breakfast. By the aid of a roaring fire we soon had some nice chops on the coals, with coffee boiling in a tin pot, and our pilot bread spread out all ready, and Jack was just quivering with anticipation for the good things to come, as the perfume of the burning flesh was grateful to our hungry stomachs, and we had no doubt but our dog was as eager for a meal as ourselves.

"Dis is not so bad," my friend said, as the sun disappeared, and darkness gathered around us. "Ve vill much eat, and den de n orn come all de quicker vid de stomach full. Ah, by gar, de coffee am made, de meat am done, and — Vot de devil am dat?"

I did not wonder that the French boy asked the question, for Jack gave a sudden yelp of rage, and made a dive at a tall, dark, but rather handsome Indian, a young fellow not more than twenty years of age, and a great chief, — that we could tell by his dress and ornaments, — as he stood leaning on a long lance, near our fire, and looking at us in a cold, defiant manner, expressive of contempt, we thought. We had met a wild Apache Indian we imagined, and the sight was not an agreeable one, for we suddenly remembered our bold deeds in slaying some of his tribe, and how proud we were of the fact, but now it seemed to us that such matters were not to our credit, and that our scalps were in danger of being raised to pay for our temerity.

CHAPTER VI.

A SURPRISED GREETING. — A MIDNIGHT VISITOR. — AN ANGRY BEAR. — AN OWL'S TOOT. — A BAND OF WARRIORS. — THE CHIEF'S COMMANDS. — ESCAPING WITH OUR SCALPS. — THE SULPHUR SPRING AND BATH. — THE RANCHERO'S FEARS. — THE NIGHT CAMP AT THE FOOT OF THE MOUNTAINS. — THE PROWLING LION. — HOMESICKNESS. — A STRANGE MEETING. — THE LONELY CANYON. — LOS ANGELES. — DON SANCHOS APPEARS.

FOR one moment we gazed on the savage without speaking, after Lewey's exclamation. No wonder my friend thought that our visitor was the devil, for he did look diabolical, as the flames lighted up his dark, painted face and hair, the latter ornamented with eagle's feathers, while the handle of his lance was decorated with human locks and long strips of red flannel, probably taken from the shirts of dead Mexicans or trappers, whom the warrior had encountered during his raid from the southern part of Arizona, and through lower California.

All this we had time to note, as Jack made a bound for the unwelcome and unexpected visitor, but we were not prepared to see our dog, just as he was within a short distance of the Apache chief, receive a kick that sent him end over end, and finally landed the little fellow in my lap, where I held him fast, quivering with rage and disappointment, as I wanted to see how many companions the Indian had, and if his visit was peace or war, before proceeding to extremities. Our rifles were some distance from us, and out of reach, and, had we jumped to our feet, and ran to obtain possession of them, the savage could have thrust his lance through and through us, and hardly stirred from his tracks.

"How?" asked the Apache, as he held up one hand, the palm turned to

ward us, which must have signified good will, for he made no effort to use his weapon, or move toward us.

"How?" we both exclaimed, and imitated his example, still retaining our seats, and that probably saved our lives, as the savage saw that we had no hostile intentions.

"Mexicano?" demanded the Indian, with a sharp look from his bright eyes. as he asked the question.

"No," we both answered with one accord, as we supposed the chief had no love for people of that race.

"Quien?" our visitor demanded in Spanish, showing that he knew something of the language.

"Americano," Lewey replied, at a venture.

The face of the Apache lighted up at once, lost some of its sternness, and a slight smile passed over his rather good-looking countenance, even if it was fierce.

"Speakie you de Yankee?" asked the warrior, to our great surprise.

"Yes. Where did you learn to talk English?" I demanded.

The savage extended his hand, and came forward, dropping his lance as he did so, to show that his intentions were peaceable.

We shook hands with the visitor, and motioned him to take a seat by the fire, while I released the struggling Jack, who smelled of the Apache, and no longer threatened the savage who had saluted him with an unceremonious kick. But it was evident our pet remembered the rough treatment, for he looked at us as much as to say, "Just let me try that dodge over again, and you will see if I don't do better."

"Me speakie good Yankee," the Apache said. "Me learn of white trapper away off," and he pointed toward the mountains.

"Is the chief hungry?" I asked.

"Yes, me eat."

We cut off some steaks of venison, and threw them on the coals, and then handed a pot of coffee to the Indian. He drank all that there was, smacked his lips, and said "Good," then proceeded to rake the burning flesh from the fire, and to eat as though a long ride had given him a sharp appetite.

We handed him a cake of pilot bread, and a pinch of salt, and then the chief must have thought that we were not bad friends, for he no longer glanced around, and peered in the darkness, stopping his mastication every few seconds to listen for unusual noises, or to note if strangers were lurking near.

In half an hour that savage disposed of large quantities of half cooked meat, not minding the few ashes that adhered to the chops, and at last, when his appetite was satisfied, he drew back from the fire, and murmured, —

"Tobac."

We handed him a dozen cigarettes, and he lighted one, took a long whiff, swallowed the smoke, seemed to relish it, then asked, —

"What do here?"

"On the way to Los Angeles."

"Hum! Heap big town. Me know. There," and he pointed in the direction of the place.

"And what are you doing here?" I asked.

"Steal cattle,' was the candid answer, and he looked a little proud, as he uttered the words.

"Where are your warriors? A big chief like you should have many companions," I remarked, thinking to flatter the savage.

"Me chief. Warriors all around here. Me call, they come. No call, no come."

I thought the Indian was lying, but pretended to believe him, as it is not just the thing to doubt a man's word, when you are in his power, or he has influential friends to back him up in all he asserts.

"How far have you traveled today?" I asked.

"Oh, heap. Me come from the mountains this morn, when the sun rise. Tomorrow me go there get much cattle. Mexican no fight. They run when they hear the Apache's war-cry."

He pointed in the direction of the Vallecito Ranche, and I pitied my would-be father-in law, if they took him by surprise, and wished that I could give him warning of the intended raid, for I had no ill feeling against him, even if he did want me to marry his only daughter, a girl not remarkable for beauty or cleanliness.

We hoped that our visitor had not learned of the death of four of his people, and that we were concerned in their early decease, for if such was the case, it was probable that he might desire to avenge their great loss to the world and his tribe. We mentally resolved to make no boasts of our deeds in the killing line until we were beyond the haunts of the Apaches, for just then we were not ambitious to shine as heroes. We would wait before boasting.

"We met none of your warriors on the road today." I said. "We have traveled many miles, and seen no trail."

"You is much lucky," was the quiet answer. "Apache see you to-day, kill you, and take scalp."

"What if they should see us tomorrow?" I asked.

"No hurt the white Yankees. Me give you pass. Apache know it, and let you go, if see you."

We had our doubts on the subject, but at the same time concluded not to express them in a defiant manner. We thought it best to be on good terms with the savage.

"For dree years me live with white trapper over de mountains," the chief said, as he puffed away at his cigarette. "He show me how to shoot, to speak de Yankee tongue, and to be a big warrior. He and de Apache great friends. We love each other. S'pose you Mexican, me not stay here and eat at your fire. Me kill you, and take scalp."

"Why did you not wait until we were asleep, and then kill us?" I asked.

The young savage smiled, and a cunning look passed over his face, as he answered, —

"Me trail you all de arternoon. Me see you camp, and kill de deer, and me crawl up, and listen. Den me hear you speak de Yankee lingo, and I know you no Mexicans. We friends," and he held out his stained paw for another shake of our hands.

We thought that the chief could be trusted, but were not sure of it. However, we sat and talked with him for an hour or more, and then got up, and looked to our horses, and, as they had fed enough for the night, we changed their location to a tree close to the camp-fire.

"Chief no steal our horses?" I said, as we secured the animals by strong reatas so that they could not break away.

The young fellow smiled, as much as a warrior who is on a trail dares to look pleased, and shook his head.

"Me good Indian now. No steal friends' horse. Take Mexican's all I want. See me bring in my mustang for de night."

He put his fingers in his mouth, and uttered a shrill whistle, and then a wild broncho dashed out of the chapparel, and galloped toward the savage, stopped when within a few feet of its owner, and waited for further commands.

Our horses uttered dissatisfied snorts, and manifested symptoms of uneasiness at the approach of the half-tamed and half-wild mustang, but we quieted them by words, and then the Indian hobbled his steed, tying the fore legs together, and turned it loose, to feed as it might during the night

We gave the chief our horse-blankets to lie on, examined the caps on the rifles, to see that they were all correct, and then lay down, the Indian with his feet to the fire, and his lance by his side. He might have been playing 'possum, for it seemed to us that no sooner was his head on the ground than he fell asleep.

"Lewey," I whispered, as we pulled the blankets over our shoulders, "is the cuss honest?"

"By gar, Thom, dat is somethin' dat I can't answer much mineself. Ve ill put our trust in de saints, and hope to avake in de mornin' vid de hair on our booful heads. If he moves eber so little in de night, and mine eyes is open, den I shoot him like a coyote, you see."

And, even as the French lad spoke, his voice grew a little indistinct, and he uttered a snort, that sounded like snoring, but, as Lewey always vowed that he never snored in all his life, I supposed that I must believe him.

In a few minutes I should have followed his example, except the nasal sounds, but kept my eyes open by a powerful effort, and watched the flickering fire, saw the embers grow dim, and heard the loud calls of the numerous coyotes, as they summoned their clans for an inspection of our camp. The horses were not easy, and seemed to fret at their confinement, while Jack uttered a few low growls, then curled up under the blankets, and went to sleep, for the poor little fellow was as tired as the rest of us, and needed repose.

By and by I dropped off to sleep, and was half awakened by feeling something snorting at my ear. I imagined that it was Lewey trying to get more than his share of the blankets, so spoke sharply to him, and said, —

"Lie still, you Frenchman, and let me sleep," and then something hit me a clip alongside of the head, that was far from pleasant, and I gave my companion a kick on his body that made him utter a choice expression in his native tongue, and roll over, and then Jack darted out from under the blankets, gave some shrill barks, and when I looked up over me stood a huge, hairy animal, with glowering eyes, and a monstrous paw, that was raised to let fall on my face. By the faint blaze I saw that my nocturnal visitor was a bear, and not a small one, even if he was of the common black variety.

"A bear! a bear!" I yelled, and rolled out of the reach of the heavy paw, and grabbed my rifle.

"A bear! Vare?" yelled Lewey, and, as he struggled to his feet, he felt where, for the visitor laid a paw on the seat of his trousers, and I heard above the uproar the sharp tearing of cloth and buckskin, and then the shrill voice of my friend, as he exclaimed, —

Lewey and I.

"By gar, dat hurts."

As I jumped across the fire I looked for the Indian, but he had gone as suddenly as he appeared. I snatched up a burning brand, and dashed it in the face of the bear, which was snorting around the camp, causing our horses to be nearly frantic with terror. But the brand stopped pursuit, for a moment, and thus I was enabled to seize my rifle, and send a ball into his body. That only rendered the beast more furious, and, with a savage roar, he charged on me, but I jumped aside, and escaped the deadly embrace. Then Lewey fired, and, as he did so, a dark form bounded forward, and thrust a lance into the beast, near the fore shoulder, and, before the brute could snatch at the weapon, and break it, the Indian had retreated a few paces, and waited to see if there was occasion for another prod, while Lewey and I got behind a neighboring tree, loaded our rifles, as well as the darkness would permit, and little Jack made music and work as he tugged at the rear of the savage beast, yet kept out of harm's way by his agility and carefulness.

The fire leaped up, stirred into life by the tumult that was raging, and then we saw the young Apache chief once more leap forward, and thrust his long lance into the body of the bear, and this time his stroke touched the heart, for the animal uttered a faint roar, and tumbled over, bit at the grass and ground, and was dead.

"Hum," said the chief. "Big feast tomorrow. Good meat for warrior. Make brave heart for Indian on the trail."

We piled on the wood, and lighted up the surroundings, so that we could see our prize. It was a black bear, not one of the ferocious, fighting, grisly kind, but a beast formidable enough to weigh about five hundred pounds. We did not care to encounter many during our journey, especially in the night.

It was a long time before we could calm our horses, or get Jack to settle down in peace and quietness. As he labored under the impression that he had done most of the killing, he required us to pat and praise him a dozen times before he could be induced to curl up, and go to sleep, and even then he would dream of the battle, and growl himself awake, dart to the carcass, and sniff at it to see if there was any life existing. Satisfied that there was none, he would retire for another nap, and repeat the performance in the course of half an hour.

"Yankees heap brave men," the Indian said. "No run all the same Mexicans. We friends now more than ever," and he extended his paw, and we again shook hands. He seemed to think that there was some special significance in this ceremony, which he had learned from his white trapper friend.

We piled up some wood on the fire, to keep the coyotes from gnawing the carcass of the bear, and once more went to sleep, and this time we were not disturbed, for we did not awake until after daylight, and then only by the loud honking of thousands of geese on the borders of the stream

The young Indian had disappeared, but his blood-stained lance was leaning against a tree, and his hobbled horse was near our own, making advances that were scornfully received and rejected by our animals, as they kicked and bit at the mustang every time it approached to exchange morning salutations.

We wondered where the Apache chief had gone, but did not suppose that he was far off, and our surmises were correct, for the Indian came into camp, bearing on his back eight fat geese, which he had shot with his bow and arrows, and with hardly an effort.

"Cook goose," the Indian said, and, drawing his knife, cut off neck and legs, then run the blade across the breast, stripped skin and feathers from the carcass at one grand pull, and there was the flesh and fat before us, clean and tempting looking.

The chief did not seem to think that it was necessary to remove the crop and entrails, and smiled in a disdainful manner when we performed the office before laying the fowl upon the coals. However, he offered no objections, and watched the cooking with the concern of a hungry man, and, when the goose was done, and the coffee made, we fell to, and there were only bones left for Jack to pick, but he satisfied his hunger on broiled venison. Then we lighted our pipes, and, while we were smoking, heard at a distance, the gruff hoot of an owl. The Indian listened for a moment very attentively, then put his hands to his mouth and repeated the cry. Five minutes later a dozen painted Apache warriors burst through the chapparel, and dashed toward us, shaking their long, ornamented lances in an ominous manner.

"White friends no move," was the chief's command, as we were about to spring for our rifles, as we thought our time had come. "Hold dog fast," the Indian continued, noticing that Jack was struggling to escape from my arms, and make a rush toward the visitors, to investigate them, and see if he could not defeat them single handed. "Keep still. Me friend yours. No hurt Yankees, if you no hurt them."

We sat still, but were a little apprehensive of trouble. We could not do much in the way of defeating twelve well-mounted Apaches, and escape was not to be thought of, as our horses were neither saddled nor bridled, and fastened to a tree.

As the Indians charged toward us, with yells that were far from cheerful, the young chief held up one of his hands, and then the visitors checked their steeds, and remained motionless, looking at us with no friendly feeling in their wicked eyes, and probably wondering why they were not permitted to tear the scalps from our heads, as is the pleasant custom of the fierce devils, when on the war path.

The chief very deliberately emptied a tin pot of the last drops of coffee, lighted a cigarette, puffed out volumes of smoke from his nostrils, then calmly arose, and went toward his companions. There was an interchange of gutterals and grunts, and we knew the conversation was concerning our welfare, for the young Indian pointed toward us, and then to the dead bear, as if inviting his warriors to a feast. They needed no second invitation, but sprang from their horses, whipped out their knives, and commenced skinning the animal, while some gathered firewood, and made a roaring blaze, but, even while the Apaches were thus engaged, they did not fail to glance at us with fierce eyes, as though longing for the time when we should be given up to torture and the scalping-knife.

"I vish," whispered Lewey, "dat I vas on board de old ship Admittance, and poundin' de chain-cable, or even lushin' down de masts. Anyding but dis."

I also had the same desire, but we sat still, smoked our pipes, and watched the painted scamps as they moved about the camp, preparing their breakfast, for we saw they intended to have a feast of bear meat, before moving on a rail.

Presently one of the warriors, who seemed to have nothing to do, strode toward our horses, appeared to admire them, and then laid a hand on the reatas, as though to cast them off, and appropriate our property to his own use.

We made a movement as if to start up, and prevent the fellow from stealing our animals, but the young chief noticed the act, and said, rather sternly, —

"Yankees quiet keep. Me big chief, and take care of friends."

He spoke in his native tongue to the Apache, the one who was making free with our mustangs, and, while the fellow seemed to hesitate for a moment, he did not relinquish his grasp of the reatas, as though the temptation to steal was too strong to be overcome.

Again the chief spoke, and this time a little more impatiently. The war rior retained his hold of the horses, in spite of their plunging, for they smelled the savage, and did not like his odor or wild looks. Then the Apache thief muttered some words which must have been impudent, or "back answers," as we used to say on ship-board, for the eyes of the young Indian flashed like those of an enraged mountain lion. He bounded to his feet, snatched his long lance, that leaned against a tree, poised it for a moment, and only for a moment, and then sent it whizzing through the air apparently without aim.

But it was aimed true, and went with the force of a tornado. The warrior tried to dodge the flying lance by ducking his head, but the barbed point struck him on the shoulder, and down he went.

The warriors suspended their labors on the bear for a moment, and looked at their wounded companion, but no one offered to resent the injury.

The chief muttered some angry words, and waved his hand. It was an order to one of the Indians to return his lance, and the youngest of the gang sprang forward, tore the weapon from the shoulder of the prostrate Apache, regardless of his injuries, and then handed the instrument to the chief with every mark of respect, and the latter received the spear without even a word of thanks, or a cold nod of recognition. He seemed to be accustomed to having his commands obeyed, and no wonder, for he was the eldest son of the most powerful and popular chie in Southern Arizona, the celebrated Plomo, or lead, a savage now forgotten, but a well known character forty years ago.

The wounded savage staggered to his feet, and disappeared in the chapparel, where I have no doubt his injuries were dressed by a comrade, but no one sought to avenge the honor of the disgraced Apache, or took any further notice of the incident.

"Now ready you get," the young Indian chief said, as soon as he had shown his authority. "Me show you place to cross de river. Ride hard, and no say nothin' about Apaches to Mexicans. Me spoken, you hear?"

We nodded, and lost no time in preparing for our journey. We thought it was best to put some miles between us and the painted savages. Our horses were in good order for a long gallop, and we mentally agreed not to halt until we had gained the shelter of the ranch at San Mateo, where we hoped to pass the night.

As we gathered up our blankets and stores, the Indians piled on the fire huge lumps of bear and deer meat, and hardly allowed them to be warmed through before they were pulled from the ashes, and devoured, the grease and blood running down each side of their ugly and dirty mouths, and from thence trickling to their naked, painted breasts.

As we put the saddles on the horses, many a wild, savage look was directed to our blankets and stores, but not a word was uttered, or a hand raised to help or restrain us from leaving. Our rifles seemed to excite admiration, but no one ventured to lay a finger on our guns, much as they wanted to. The chief appeared to keep his eyes on his followers, and his lance was near at hand.

In half an hour's time we were ready to depart, and looked anxiously toward the chief for permission to move on. He spoke a few words to a warrior, and the latter went in search of the mustang that had been hobbled the night before. It was not far off. Without saddle or bridle the young Indian sprang on its back, and motioned for us to follow him.

"Good-by, red men of de mountains and plains," said Lewey, turning to the Indians, for he could not resist the temptation to say a few words, like a woman who is mad all over, and desires the last expression of her opinion. "May ve nebber meet agin in dis vorld, or de vorld to come, but of dat ve has no fear. A long farewell to all of you now and forebber, amen. Now I lay me down to sleep," and here the boy forgot the rest of the petition, and did not wait for the gruff exclamation of astonishment from the savages, who were not aware of the benedictions he was calling down on their heads in so serious a strain.

"How," the Apaches said, and waved their soiled hands in token of farewell.

Jack gave a final bark of disgust at the painted devils, and then trotted on ahead, glad to get out of such disreputable company, and even our mustangs tossed their heads, and manifested pleasure at being free of such dirty society as they had been forced to consort with for the past few hours.

We followed the young chief along the bank of the stream for a mile, or less, and then saw a place where his band had forded that morning. The water was not more than two feet deep, we judged, and we could see the trail that led to it for a long distance, sharply defined through the grass and high chapparel.

"Here cross you," the chief said, with a significant wave of his hand. "Now part we, and nebber meet each other agin. If you see more Indians of my band show 'em this, and no hurt."

He tore off a feather from his headdress, notched it in a peculiar manner with his knife, and handed it to us.

We thanked him for his kindness, and then I offered to bestow a hand of to ....., a, some sort of recompense for his protection. He took it, nodded and once more pointed to the ford, as if impatient for us to go without delay.

We shook hands, started our horses, and crossed the creek in safety, and, when we reached dry ground, turned in our saddles, and saw the Apache still standing where we had left him, watching our movements. We waved our hands once more, touched our mustangs with spurs, and hurried from the scene as fast as possible, and that was the last we saw of the young chief.

"I vonder," asked Lewey, "if he did not much regret, ven he seed us goin' from him and his dirty gang, dat he no keep us?"

"To be sure on that point let us hasten our steps," I answered, and away we went at a lively lope, and did not check our horses until we saw that Jack was suffering at the pace, and needed a breathing spell. Then we walked our steeds, and talked of the lucky escape we had made, and how thankful we should be that we had claimed America as our home instead of Mexico or California. Nevertheless, we still resolved to call ourselves Frenchmen at the next stopping-place, unless it was occupied by Indians. For the sake of our lives we determined to be anything and everything,— Yankee, gringo, greaser, Mexican, or French. It did not matter to us as long as we saved our persons and scalps, for we thought more of them than country.

As the hour was early and cool, we got over considerable ground before noon. The trail was at times a little indistinct, but we pointed our heads toward the north, and could tell by the sun in which direction we were traveling. About twelve o'clock we saw a spring bubbling up from a little sand-hill, and thought it a good place to stop and rest. Jack went for the water, took a lap, then uttered a yell, rubbed his mouth, and backed off, disgusted.

"Vot is de matter vid de dog?" asked Lewey, and took his tin pot, dipped up some of the water, and put it to his lips.

Then he uttered a strong exclamation, such as he had learned on ship board, spat the water from his mouth, and said,—

"It is hot as de infernal regions, and taste just like de place you go to ven you dies."

It was a hot sulphur spring, bubbling out of the earth, and killing all vegetation where its waters flowed, and mingled with the ground. In these ..... h. . .... would attract thousands of visitors, for the sake of bathing and drinking, and I have often wondered if that spring has ever been utilized in the present modern times, or if an earthquake has directed the source of its flow to any other quarter.

We hunted around for cold water, and found some in the immediate vicinity. It was heavily charged with iron, but sweet and pure. There were no signs of Indians or bears near us, so we thought it would be safe to unsaddle our horses, and give them a good feed and rest. The grass was plentiful, and we could screen ourselves from the hot sun under some trees, it disposed to take a few winks of sleep after our lunch. Then, for the first time we realized that we had nothing to eat except bread and coffee. We had left the carcass of the deer with the Indians, glad enough to get away from them without claiming our property. There was a prospect of being hungry, but just then I happened to hear some cooing in a distant tree, and on going to it, found that there were thousands of wild pigeons roosting in its branches, sheltering themselves from the noonday heat. Here was food before us, and in abundance. Besides, there were plenty of small stones and clubs lying near, so that we could kill all the birds we needed, and not waste a shot, sending some lurking Apache to our retreat, in case he should hear the report of a rifle.

It seemed cruel to kill the gentle, pretty little things, so innocent of any contemplated wrong on our part, for they did not offer to fly even when I was under the tree. But we were hungry, and the stomach stifles conscience and generous resolutions. I picked up a club, and threw it with all the strength of my arm. The weapon struck a thick covy, and down tumbled eight birds. The uninjured ones just cooed a little louder than usual but did not offer to fly.

I gathered up my spoil, and, as we had all that we could eat for one meal, left the birds without further destruction.

Lewey was rejoiced when he saw what I had secured. He started the fire, and then we plucked the pigeons, cooked them over the coals, and there was enough for us, including Jack, who had a whole one, beside the bones we tossed to him, which his looks gravely assured us were welcome.

A few whiffs from our pipes, a short nap, and we were ready to resume our journey, but Lewey proposed that we should have a hot sulphur bath before we started, thinking that it would invigorate us for a long ride in the afternoon. The project was a good one, and, with towels in hand, we went to the hot spring, but the waters were so warm that we could not bathe, so contented ourselves with filling tin pots, and throwing the contents over our persons, when sufficiently cool. In this way we had quite a little wash, and felt much better for it, although Lewey said that the sulphur bit some portions of his skin, where the bear had hit him the night before, and which riding horseback had not improved to any great extent, to judge by the way the French lad danced around on one foot, and uttered startling exclamations in several different tongues, and seemed inclined to be indignant because I laughed at him, as I felt not his smarts. It is easy to laugh at another's woes.

We started on our journey about three o'clock, our bodies and horses refreshed for the ride to San Mateo, where we expected to find a ranche, and quarters for the night. As we left our camping ground, which is now a railroad station, and called Vista, we almost regretted that we could not pass the night in such a pleasant place. But the fear of Indians was on our minds, and we did not dare to tarry any longer in such a lonely place.

The trail for the afternoon led us over rough hills and sandy plains, and toward sundown we looked on a pleasant valley, and saw an adobe house and out-buildings, and more than a thousand head of cattle grazing on the rich grass. Two rancheros, mounted on strong mustangs, were dashing over the plain, but as soon as they saw us, uttered a loud Mexican yell, and spurred their horses toward the houses, as though to seek shelter from suspicious visitors.

We did not quicken our pace, but moved along slowly, so that the people could get over their scare, and receive us as Christians, and not as Apache warriors, as they probably thought we were.

We rode up to the corral, and then waited for some one to make an appearance. Two dogs were in the dooryard, but they only barked at us, and did not venture near, for reasons best known to themselves.

Presently we saw the door of the adobe house cautiously opened, and a wild looking greaser's head thrust out, and a long, big-bored escopeta was pointed in our direction.

"Who in the devil's name are you?" was asked in Spanish.

"We are friends," was our response, "on the way to Los Angeles. We crave shelter for the night, and God will reward you for your kindness, as we can't, being poor."

"Where do you come from?" and the door was opened a little further, so that a more distinct view could be obtained of our persons, and honest-looking faces.

"San Diego, and we are French boys, traveling through the country for pleasure."

"Have you papers granting you permission for the journey?" was next demanded.

"Lots of them. Come and read them if you will," was our response.

"No one in this house can read," was the answer.

We had expected the reply, so were not disappointed.

"Then come and look at us. You have nothing to fear. We have ridden hard to escape the Apaches, whom we met this morning," I shouted.

"Santa Maria, do you mean that you have seen wild Indians near us?" and the greaser threw open his door, came toward us, gun in hand, followed by a son, also armed, and ready to shoot at the first provocation.

"Yes" was our answer, as the men drew near and looked more friendly, seeing that we were not formidable appearing. "A party of Apache Indians is at San Felipe Creek. We escaped by hard riding, but, as they did not cross the stream, it is probable that they have gone south on a raid."

"Thank the saints for that," and both men crossed themselves. "Dismount, senors. Our house and all that it contains are at your service."

We did not require further urging. Our saddles were taken from the horses and stored in a shed, where we knew the night would have to be passed, for it was the guest chamber for strangers, and then we piquetted our animals where the feed was good, and by this time Jack had licked the greaser's dogs into respectful treatment; consequently he was happy, and made himself quite at home.

When we returned to the house two women had made their appearance, one the wife of the old Mexican, and the other the spouse of the son. Neither was very clean, nor handsome, so Lewey had to content himself with grumbling because they lacked beauty, and there was no chance for him to flirt and utter soft nonsense, as was his usual custom, when he had nothing better to do. The ladies of the house were a little diffident, and hardly raised their eyes to our faces, for the presence of strangers was embarrassing, they saw so few in that lonely location. But they commenced the usual deliberate preparations for supper, and soon the smell of tortillas arose on the air, and the mysterious olia was simmering on the fire.

We had to relate all of our experiences with the Indians, but did not deem it best to confine ourselves strictly to truth in so doing. We said that as we were about to cross the stream, a band of Apaches had appeared in our rear, and uttered yells and threats, but did not pursue us, and that the last we saw of the savages they were headed south. We did not deem it best to boast of our friendship for the young chief, for it might have made the Mexicans suspicious. Neither did we hint that we had killed three Indians in the vicinity of the lonely ranche, and thus saved the life of a very sweet young girl. We did not care to have the information reach the ears of the Apaches, as we might desire to cross over the trail at some distant day, and perhaps meet the savages a second time.

"Why did not the Indians pursue you?" asked the old Mexican, as soon as we had concluded our yarn.

"Because we were better mounted than themselves, and had rifles," was our answer. "They feared our guns, and sure aim," making it appear that we were dead shots, and terrible fellows.

"Your horses are two of the best in the country. One of them we know well. It has been ridden by the government courier Pedro. He passed by here but a few days ago," the old greaser remarked, and there was a tinge of suspicion in his tones.

"Yes," I said, in an indifferent manner, "we met him at Tobias's ranche, and there made a good trade, — our horse and eight reals for his."

The son laughed, and the old man grinned.

"Pedro is sharp and bright," the former said. "Holy Virgin, but he will be a rich man one of these days, unless he is killed by the Apaches. Only think of the rogue making such a bargain. Ah, to gain money one must mingle with the world. How often I have said it, padre, and desired to go to Los Angeles in search of fortune. There silver is to be picked up by the handfuls, and all the people are rich."

But the old man frowned upon such wild statements, and said many years before he had seen the wonders of the town, and pesos were as scarce as on the ranche, and food much dearer. None but a loco would want to live there, for the people were proud, and every door was not open to the stranger. So the son was silenced, but not convinced, in this respect resembling the farmers' children of our State, who tire of the homesteads, and want to see more of life than a little village can show. In the young man's eyes Los Angeles was like the capital of the world, teeming with wealth and opportunities to become suddenly rich. He had never read a page of a book, because he could not, and what he knew about life in other parts was gained from the courageous priests, who once in a while made a circuit of the sparsely inhabited districts, for the purpose of christening, marrying, hearing confessions, and celebrating mass, when there were a dozen or even less people brought together for the purpose of enjoying such religious consolation.

We produced our stock of tobacco after supper, and sat around the fire, and smoked cigarettes and pipes, until the cries of the neighboring coyotes warned us that it was near eight o'clock, and time to retire. The ranchero was not quite satisfied that the Indians would not swarm down upon him in the course of the night, so laid his huge escopetas where they would be convenient, and asked us if we would assist in case an attack was made, and to this we readily consented. He stated that he relied more on his dogs to give warning than his own watchfulness, as they hated the sight or smell of an Indian, and would make noise enough to wake us up in case the Apaches approached. The curs did not return the yelps of the coyotes, as they had become so accustomed to their barks that no notice was taken of the noisy pests. Nothing but the wild scream of a mountain lion, or the peregrinations of a hungry black bear could disturb the sleep of a greaser's dog, except the peculiar perfume of a savage Indian, and that the curs seemed to detect, even if the Apaches were at a great distance. They may have learned in some way that the Indians were partial to baked dog, and considered it a staple dish when at home, or in camp for any length of time.

To be on the safe side we secured our horses in the corral for the night, and then went to sleep, tired with our long ride, and the disturbed slumbers of the night before. We had as bed-fellows the usual number of fleas and bugs, but were now quite tough, could endure a large amount of biting and scratching, still remain quite comfortable, and not awaken to curse the obnoxious insects, as many bad men would have done, with less tender skins than our own.

The night passed without an alarm. We were up soon after daylight, and astonished the people of the house by washing our hands and faces, a proceeding that they thought savored of weak minds. The son showed us his paws and rather dark countenance, and stated in the most candid manner, that he had not used water on either for some weeks, and yet, he urged, they were not soiled. We did not dare to dispute the point with him, but took precious good care that he did not handle our food. The women's work we had to endure, but shut our eyes, and hoped for the best, as we lifted tortillas to our mouths, and wondered if we should die after eating a peck of dirt. If the proverb held good we feared that two nice young men would be taken off very early in their career of usefulness, for filth was cheap.

After breakfast we rewarded our host and son with half a hand of tobacco, to pay for our entertainment, fed our horses with a measure of barley, gave them a little grazing, and then made a few enquiries regarding our journey, and the trail. The old Mexican had been over it, and directed us as well as he was able, but did not speak in the most encouraging manner of the mountain gorges and canyons, while crossing the Sierra Madre, yet he wound up with declaring that the view from the summit of the most elevated portion of our route was something wonderful, and long to be remembered. He also gave us the cheering information that we might have to camp at the foot of the mountains that night, it being dangerous to attempt the canyons in the darkness, as a mis-step would cause us to fall hundreds of feet, upon the water-courses and rocks below. We were advised to keep a good fire burning, to frighten off the mountain lions and bears, and not to sleep both at the same time, unless we could rely on our dog to give us warning of the approach of wild beasts.

We thanked the Mexican for his advice, saddled our horses, and then bid farewell to the family, with a parting warning to keep their eyes open for the Apaches. The son whispered that he wished he was going with us, and we should have liked his company, provided he had washed his hands previous to starting on the journey, and continued the practice as long as he was in our society, and handled our food

We touched our hats to the ladies, said "Adios, senors," to the men, and were off, loping along at a moderate pace, to our own joy, and that of Jack, who was glad to be clear of the companionship of dogs covered with fleas, and who spent most of their time biting and scratching at the hungry insects.

The day was pleasant, with a warm sun overhead, and we had no fear of Indians in that part of the country, so rode on as unconcerned as men could who were not too well acquainted with the trail. Lewey was unusually cheerful, and confided to me how anxious he was to see Engracia, and that he would have been a fool to marry Florencia, and buried himself in a wilderness for the sake of any woman, no matter how handsome she might be, and when I said that he was as fickle as a spring morning, the boy only laughed, and intimated that he could not help it. He was born so, and could never change.

We passed through what is now called Aluchiola and Santa Ana, stopped for a brief space at a spring, where we had some more wild pigeons for lunch, obtained by the primitive method of knocking them from the branches of trees by the aid of clubs, and, for fear we should not fare well at supper time, killed two dozen of the birds, and packed them in a bag, where we carried some of our useful articles. Then, rested and refreshed, we pushed on for the mountains, and the long canyon that was to lead us to Los Angeles Valley, and the town of that name.

The sun was already near the ocean when we drew up, and concluded to camp for the night, for before us were rough and threatening canyons and dense gorges. We needed bright sunlight to lead us on our way over the Madre Mountains, the dangers of which we did not underrate. We found a stream of pure water, but it was not more than two feet deep, and easily forded. The source was from the snow-capped hills, extending as far as the eye could see, north and south, rough and shaggy.

We unsaddled our horses near the stream, where the grass was nutritious, and firewood abundant, washed down from the mountains during the floods of the rainy season, or when the snow was melted by the hot sun of the summer months. We found a huge pine-tree, under the branches of which we resolved to build our fire and sleep. To the trunk we could secure our horses for the night, having them within the protecting light of the flames, and so keep mountain lions and bears at a distance. We had been given to understand that it was not the common black bear that would be likely to molest us on the mountains, but the savage old grisly or a cinnamon one, the latter full as dangerous as the bigger animal, and a more active beast when wounded, for he never knows when he is whipped.

As there was still considerable daylight remaining, I took my fish-line, and tried my luck in the stream, while Lewey started a fire, and boiled the coffee. At first I did not get a bite, but near a dam, that might have been erected by beavers, I had a beautiful rise, and landed a pound trout, and out of one prolific hole I caught six handsome fish, enough for supper and breakfast, in connection with the pigeons, no mean help, when two hungry men sit down to a feast, and a dog is watching every mouthful they eat, and looks a little abused if they do not throw him a substantial chunk of flesh or fish every minute or two, and reminds them that they are neglecting certain duties by laying a paw on their arms every time he thinks he is not properly served with some choice bits.

But there was enough for all of us, and even Jack turned away in disdain from a pigeon's wing, or the tail of a trout, after he had eaten to repletion, and looked in our faces, as much as to say, "Do you think I am a glutton to endure all that you desire me to eat?"

We sat around the fire until the flames cast strange and fantastic shapes on the ground, and on the huge, rugged rocks, and, when we had smoked our pipes, darkness warned us that it was time to look after our horses, and get them near the blaze, and out of the way of the sudden spring of wild animals. Already the mustangs were impatient for our companionship, as they uttered soft whinnys, as if pleading for our presence, and the sound of our voices. It was indeed a lonely scene, and we could not help glancing over our shoulders as we sat on the ground, always expecting to see something uncanny coming out from the darkness, and giving us no room for a shot.

We looked to our rifles and pistols, tried the edges of our long knives, and, guns in hands, went to our horses, and brought them under the pine-tree's sheltering branches. We had just got them secured for the night when a shrill scream came from a canyon up the mountain, and we knew that a fierce lion was our neighbor, and likely to trouble us for some hours, unless we could dispose of him in a satisfactory manner. Our horses trembled, and even Jack did not deem it advisable to leave the vicinity of the fire, and seek an encounter with the beast.

We piled more wood on the flames, and watched for the mountain lion to show himself, but he did not seem disposed to venture near us for some time. We could hear him jump from rock to rock, and growl, and every few minutes utter a yell that made us quake with fear, but we did not go in pursuit, and so sat there for an hour or more, until at last the beast grew bolder, and came sneaking near the horses. Then we got a fair glimpse of his wicked eyes, and determined to test the effect of rifle-balls, and see if we could not kill or disable him, as the hungry savage was liable to make a spring at any moment, either on us or the mustangs.

"Aim at de eyes," whispered Lewey, and, as he spoke, we drew up our rifles, and fired.

The shots must have taken effect, for there were shrill screams of pain and rage, and then a huge, tawny-colored body, dimly seen by the flickering flames, bounded toward us, and landed directly in the rear of the horses, the worst place the lion could have chosen, for the now thoroughly maddened animals launched out their heels in spiteful fury, struck the wild beast square on the ribs and shoulder, sent it rolling over the ground, and in our direction. Before the brute could recover from its surprise we emptied the contents of our pistols in its body, but even then it tried to regain its feet, and renew the fight for life. Our dog now thought it time to show his spirit, and with a growl dashed at the hind-quarters of the animal, and nipped it near its tail, but the beast turned and struck at Jack so fierce a blow with its fore paw, that our pet's life would have ended then and there had the claws touched him. Luckily, the dog was so nimble he avoided the stroke, and, before the lion could make another demonstration, we seized two large stones, and dashed them on the head of the tough beast. This last assault seemed to finish it, but to make sure work we continued to pound the prostrate savage until no signs of life remained, and then Jack ventured near the body, and sniffed at it with perfect freedom.

"Dat vos vell done," Lewey remarked, as soon as we could take a breathing spell. "De brute vas vusser den de Injuns or de b..ar. Now ve vill get ready for de next von."

We loaded our rifles and pistols, dragged the dead beast some distance from our horses, so that they could not see it, or smell the blood, then petted the mustangs until they quieted down and no longer showed signs of fear. It was wonderful to note the actions of our steeds, how they craved our company and kind words, and seemed to have confidence in our presence and power to keep them from all harm.

Both of us did not dare to sleep at the same time after this dramatic episode, so we collected some fresh fuel, and then Lewey lay down and took a nap, while I kept the fire going, and watched at the same time. It was terribly lonely that dark night, lying as we were under the shadow of the mountains, with not a human being within twenty miles of us, as far as we knew. The air was filled with strange sounds, and the wind sighed mournfully through the canyons and gorges of the dark, ragged hills. The coyotes uttered sharp barks in the valleys, and called to each other for information as to the strange lights they saw, but did not venture near us, and we should not have cared much for them if they had, as we were accustomed to their ways, and knew their cowardly nature too well to fear their presence.

While I watched, and kept the fire going, I heard the gruff growls of a bear coming through one of the canyons, but he seemed so surprised at the flames, that he uttered his displeasure in angry sniffs, and then waddled off in another direction, not venturing near us, for which I was very thankful, as I had encountered all the adventures I desired for one night, and could not repress a sigh as I thought of my loneliness, and how uncertain was the future. Perhaps there were tears in my eyes for a moment, for I know that the stars seemed to suddenly become dim, and some of the constellations disappeared from sight. My head drooped to my breast, and a sob startled me so much that I brushed the moisture from my eyes. I knew that repining would not restore me to my old ship, now near home, so hummed a sea song, to keep up my spirits, and the unusual noise awoke Lewey.

"How goes it?" he asked, as he sat up, and looked around.

"Smoothly," I answered, but the lad must have noted a change in my voice, for he sprang to his feet, and came toward me.

"Thom, mon cher ami, you has been tear sheddin'," he said. "You deny it not. Unhappy is you."

"It is a trifle," I answered. "A little lonesome, nothing more, old boy."

"You lies down, and much sleep take," the generous-hearted fellow said. "De vatch vill I keep till daylight. You is tired, and the night has been a hard von for you. But, oh, vot booful times ve is habin'. Did you ebber seed anyding like dem? So much better den bein' on von old ship, dat smell of tar and vater bilge."

"Do you think so, Lewey?"

"Do I dink so? Vy, look here, ve is our own masters. Ve sees de country. Ve meets de nice adventures all de time. Von girl falls in love vid you today, tomorrow anuder von shins up to me, and so ve goes on, and has de fun all to ourselves. Ah, ve is habin' much good times, and you don't know it. Vy, I vould n't exchange dis life for anyding dat you can dink of. Now you lie down and sleep, as I has had de booful nap, and no more sighin', 'cos ve skall come out on top alvays."

He words inspired and made me forget the realities of my position. The tears were brushed from my eyes, and the stars and constellations looked bright and hopeful as I laid my head on a saddle, drew a couple of blankets over my shoulders, and the last thing I heard, aside from the hooting owls and the yelps of the coyotes, was the stirring hymn of the Marseillaise, as Lewey hummed it in his native tongue, between puffs of tobacco smoke.

I slept late. When I awoke the horses were already piquetted, a pot of coffee was steaming on the coals, and six beautiful trout were all ready for baking in the hot ashes. My friend had been hard at work since daylight in preparing breakfast, and getting ready for an early start. He pointed with pride to the fish, and said that he was a natural-born fisherman, but a child could have taken trout from that stream, there were so many of them in the deep hole I had fished the night before.

"Is you all right dis nice mornin'?" my friend asked, as I got up, and packed the blankets, preparatory to a good wash in the clear stream. "No more nostalgie, de bad homesickness."

"All right now," was my answer, in a cheery tone.

"Dat is bon. Today ve vill hab a booful time ridin' ober de mountain, and seein' de valley and de country, oh, for so many miles. Ve skall be above de clouds at some places, and can vash our faces in de dew if ve vants to, and de ladies say dat is nice for de complexion."

And so the lad chatted on, with the idea that I was dispirited, but the daylight had brought renewed hope to my heart, and I was no longer unhappy. The air was so exhilarating that it acted on the nerves like a stimulant or a glass of wine, and when the sun showed its warm and cheerful face, fresh from the base of the mountains, I would not have exchanged places with the whole crew of the old ship, captain and all.

As we picked the bones of the trout and pigeons Lewey related to me the incidents of his lonely watch, but there was nothing of a startling nature to tell. Our friend, the bear, had come near him once, and then gone away as soon as fresh fuel was piled on the flames, and once or twice venturesome coyotes had stolen near the mountain lion, and licked the blood that flowed from the dead brute's wounds.

We had just finished our breakfast, and were lighting our pipes, when we were startled to see a cavalcade of horsemen issue from the canyon on our right, and head in our direction. There were ten of them, well mounted, and all armed with carbines and sabres. They looked like military people, but if they had uniforms on they were concealed by bright-colored serapes, and we could only judge of the strangers by their sombreros, and gilt bands, which looked like those we had seen worn by the Mexican army in California.

The horsemen did not notice us for the first few minutes after leaving the canyon, and were only awakened to our presence by the sudden barking of Jack. Then the visitors looked up, saw that two young men were sitting near a fire, smoking, and very much surprised to see s rangers in that part of the country, and we nearly choked with laughter when the cavalcade turned, as if on a pivot, and dashed back toward the mountain gorge.

The strangers, all Mexicans, as we could see by their faces, supposed that we were Indians on a raid, and that there was no hope for those who fell into their hands, so a rapid flight was made for shelter, where a good defence could be undertaken if necessary.

When near the entrance of the canyon the Mexicans turned, and checked their horses, seeing that the wild Apaches were not in hot pursuit, as they supposed. This gave us a chance to act, and Lewey sprang to his feet, waved a blanket, and yelled at the top of his voice, —

"Amigos, amigos, senors."

Still the Mexicans did not put great faith in the protestation, but unslung their carbines, and pointed them in our direction. Even this act of daring did not frighten us as much as it might, for we knew a greaser could not hit a mountain with one of the guns he carried, as they were made for show and not use by the manufacturers.—But we did fear a stray ball would reach one of our horses, so peacefully grazing, and that was something to guard against, consequently, when the Mexicans assumed a belligerent attitude, and looked fight, both of us, without our rifles, showed ourselves, and renewed the shout of, —

"Amigos, senors, amigos."

Then one horseman, who seemed to be a guide, advanced a few paces, and said, —

"If you are friends come toward us without weapons. If you attempt any trick we will shoot you down like dogs."

We thought this a pretty lively threat, considering the whole party were quaking with terror, for fear of their lives, and that, if we had been so disposed, by the aid of our rifles we could have driven all hands through the gorge, pell-mell, and the devil take the hindmost, for they would have sniffed Apaches in the air, and that was enough to startle a whole company of soldiers, make them break ranks, and take shelter under cover of the nearest rocks.

"We are unarmed," we responded. "Have no fear. There are only two of us and a dog, and the latter will not bite."

"A Mexican fears nothing," the spokesman said, a little proudly. "He dislikes an ambushed foe, but can contend with one if there is need to risk so much. Who are you, and what do you here in this lonely place?"

"We are young men journeying to Los Angeles, and enjoying the country through which we pass. There are no Indians near, we think, so you need take no precautions. Come and cook your breakfast by our fire, as we shall soon start over the trail."

The guide returned, and reported to the leader of the troop, and at last all seemed disposed to believe our assertion that we were not warlike. But they approached very cautiously, still holding their carbines in their hands, and ready to use them if we raised a finger to some hidden foe. When, however, the party were within a few fathoms of us we recognized several persons we had known while members of the crew of the Admittance, and among them General Michaeltoreno, at one time governor of the State, and the person in whose honor an elegant fête had been given at Monterey, at which Lewey and I officiated in a grand act of legerdemain, and then let off a most wonderful fiery serpent, that astonished all who beheld it, and disgusted some.

"What are you young men doing here?" asked the general a little sternly. "The country is at war with the United States, and we are suspicious of all people who cannot give an account of themselves."

"Look at that dead mountain lion, senor," Lewey said. "We killed him last night while prowling around our camp. That is one good mark in our favor."

All the party seemed to think so, for they dismounted, and examined the beast, their horses refusing to approach it.

"Well, what else have you done?" demanded the general, after he had satisfied his curiosity about the lion.

"We have met a party of Apaches on the trail, and killed several of them near Tobias's ranche," my French friend replied, quite proudly.

"What!" cried every one. "You have encountered the wild Indians, and slain some of them? You speak the truth, we hope."

"A Frenchman never lies, senors,' was the dignified answer, and a look such as a great general put on at one time when asked to surrender at the battle of Waterloo.

But the statement seemed so remarkable that we could see glances of disbelief on the faces of the Mexicans. That two young men, mere boys, should kill Apache warriors, and then escape their vengeance, was to be taken cum grano salis, the effect of lively imagination and not reality.

"Why do you seek to deceive us by such a story?" the general asked. "The Apaches are cunning Indians, and do not allow muchachos to kill and destroy without resistance."

"The savages are no match for bold men with rifles in their hands. We met a party, and destroyed it, and you will learn the truth when you make enquiries at the ranche. We are not braggarts, but honest lads," my friend said, in such a confident tone that the Mexicans began to think there was some foundation for his story.

"Why are you traveling through the State in these troublesome times?" demanded the general. "You may be American spies for all that we know to the contrary."

"We are on our way to the Ranche Refugio to be married," Lewey answered, quite promptly, and then every Mexican just opened his mouth to its widest extent, and laughed so heartily that we were indignant at their levity over so serious a matter.

"Have you papers granting you permission to travel?" the general demanded.

"Yes, senor. We have one from General Castro," and here the late governor's face darkened, for he did not like his successor, "and also a paper from the alcalda of San Diego, recommending us to the good wishes of the people of Los Angeles. In addition we have letters from Captain Fitch to his friends, the Senors Temple and Stearns, of the Pueblo, so you see we are not sospechosos," and as Lewey spoke he produced all the documents from the bag which held them.

The general glanced over the letters and recommendations of the alcalda, and uttered a snort of contempt when Castro's pass was examined. He handed all back to us, and then asked, —

"Why did you leave your ship?"

"We were attacked by the smallpox, and compelled to remain at San Diego for fear of contagion to the rest of the people on board the vessel," Lewey remarked.

"But the disease did not leave any marks on your face," the general said.

"No, senor, the saints be praised, our beauty was spared," and Lewey uttered the words as though he believed what he stated, and once more the Mexicans roared with laughter at the impudence of the boy, he was so calm and cool.

During all this time I had permitted my friend to carry on the conversation as he spoke better Spanish than I could, and showed what he claimed to be, — a Frenchman, — while I was fear ul the Mexicans would recognize me as an American unless I held my tongue.

"General," Lewey said, as soon as the laughter had subsided, "we have met you many times in Monterey, and yet you do not appear to recognize us. When you first took the office of governor we had the honor of giving a performance in your presence, and the same night let loose a fiery serpent that was much admired."

The ex-governor and his friends took a square look at us, and then seemed to recognize our faces, for all grinned, as the general remarked, —

"Santa Maria, now I know you. What a fright you did give the people of the town that night. I hope your captain punished you as you deserved, for the joke you played us. Why, you bad boys, even I had to dodge my head to escape being singed."

"And I tumbled over a chair and nearly broke my neck," one of the officers said.

But the information we had imparted did not cause any ill feeling, and in a few minutes all the group were seated around the fire, and cooking breakfast, the materials for which were unloaded from a pack-horse. We were invited to partake, but declined, as we had eaten all we needed before the party arrived.

We gave the general all the information we were able about the route, and the Indians, and, while some of the people were anxious to retrace their steps to the Pueblo, others were in favor of pushing on as fast as possible for San Diego, from which place they were to travel overland to the Mexican ports of the Gulf of California, if such a thing was practicable. They had heard that the journey over the desert plains was one of great difficulty and danger, with but few residents, and those mostly degraded Indians of the sand hills and seashore, with scanty stores of water, inclined to be brackish. But, as business was pressing, the attempt must be made, no Mexican vessel daring to sail for Mazatland for fear of capture by ships of the United-States Navy, which were swarming on the coast, and in the Pacific, ready to overhaul any craft that appeared in sight.

Then the officers gave us directions how to pass through the canyons of the mountains, and, with mutual congratulations, we saddled our horses, and bade each other farewell. Whether the party ever succeeded in reaching the Gulf of California I never knew. It is a journey I should not care to make even at this late day, for the danger of starvation and thirst is too great to be undertaken without cachés of water and provisions at stated intervals.

As we entered the dark and cold canyon of the mountains we waved our hands, lifted our hats, and were lost to view of each other. The sun did not penetrate the deep gorge, and on either side of us arose the bare and rugged rocks, with living rills trickling from the seams, and in some places beneath us were running streams, which we had no doubt contained trout, or other fish, for they were deep and cool enough for a preserve. For a mile or more we did not see an animal, so we expected to escape all conflict with wild beasts, as we could not imagine what a lion or bear would find to eat in such a vast and sublime solitude, where a loud word reverberated from arch to arch, from crag to crag, and gorge to gorge, like distant thunder, and then rolled back and forth until the cries were repeated near our heads, just as we had recently uttered them, sharp and distinct. High over us, three thousand feet at least, sailed back and forth several huge eagles, looking for a breakfast on the surface of the snow or the hard rocks, ready to pounce on a rabbit or a dead coyote, and uttering screams of rage as a swift-winged hawk darted near them, and then sailed away with a croak of delight at the anger of the kings and queens of the air and mountains. A few green lizards clung to the walls of rock, or on the trunks of stunted pines, but they did not move as we passed, waiting for the sun to penetrate the canyon, and warm them into life and activity.

Some places we found were so steep, and the trail so narrow, we had to dismount and lead our horses, fearful they would slip, and fall into the gorges below. The mustangs clung to the walls, but showed no signs of fear as long as we walked near their heads, and had a hand on their bridles. It was the most wonderful pass that I ever saw, and even then I calculated how a few men could hold it against an army of brave soldiers, for a number of stones hurled down the sides of the mountain would have created a panic and rapid retreat.

Once we heard a movement on the right of the canyon, and a rock rolled into the stream below. We stopped to see what had caused the bowlder to become dislodged, and saw an immense bear perched on a craig, and looking at us with wistful eyes, and probably mentally calculating how many square meals we could furnish. When he saw that our attention was attracted he picked up another stone and sent it after the first one, and opened his capacious mouth, and actually grinned at the fun he was having, for the brute looked down the wall of rock, saw the missile strike the water, throwing the spray high in the air, and then glanced at us, as if to ask approval of the sport. We shouted back our applause, and the brute put his shaggy head one side, and listened until the reverberations died away, then growled out his thanks for our attention, and tried another stone. We were tempted to use our rifles on the beast, but the exhibition he had afforded us was too good to be interrupted by a useless infliction of pain, and so we let him alone. When we turned an angle of the canyon the bear was still on the spur of the wall, and gazing after us as though regretful at losing such charming spectators. For all of his friendly expressions we were rather glad that he was on the opposite side of the trail, and could not dispute our course over the mountain.

It was after twelve o'clock when we emerged from the canyon, stood on the summit of the mountain, and looked at the landscape beneath us. Far off on our left were the bright blue waters of the Pacific Ocean, ruffled by the strong morning breeze, with miniature white caps all along the shore, and some thirty miles distant we could see the rough island of Cataline, and also the miserable port of San Pedro, where we had carried many a hide on our heads in days past, toiling up the steep hill with heavy boxes and lumber, and cursing the men who compelled us to do such hard work for six dollars a month. I would n't do it now for two hundred. Almost at our feet were fine level lands, green with the spring rains, and one location particularly pleased me, for I had never seen a more beautiful spot. As near as I can understand it, the place that I thought so charming is now the prosperous little town of Pasadena, celebrated for its fruits and flowers, and intelligent inhabitants. But in the days I speak of not a house was to be seen on the mesa, although thousands of head of cattle were roaming over the plains, fattening on the rich pasturage, for the dry season had not commenced, and everything was fresh and verdant, not withered and seared by the hot sun. Then there was the San Gabriel Valley, which I could have purchased for a song in 1846, now representing millions of money. Some few miles from Los Angeles was the old mission, and its adobe walls, many years old, and at one time representing eighty thousand head of cattle. Then the priests were a power in the land, and commanded the services of thousands of peons, for their food and a shirt a year. But the Mexican government confiscated the property, and the Indians were dispersed, and the bullocks sold by some rapacious administrador, who fattened on the misfortunes of the holy fathers. The latter damned the officials, but the seizures went on just the same, for the Mexican authorities said that if they could get the money they would risk all chances in the next world. We shall probably never know who got the best of the matter unless we can summon spirits to testify on one side or the other, or wait for death.

The scene was so charming that Lewey proposed we remain where we were and cook our dinner, but we had nothing except coffee and hard tack to eat. There was plenty of sweet grass for the horses, and water near at hand, with a trout stream close by, so we gladly unsaddled our steeds, piquetted them in the bright sunshine, and, while Lewey started a fire, and put on the water for coffee, I took the fish-line, and went in search of trout in a brook that was rolling and foaming in its course toward the San Gabriel Valley.

I had nothing for bait but a little piece of pigeon wing, and this was enough, as good as the most gaudy fly, for the simple fish jumped at it with charming frankness, and were pulled from their native element in such haste that in half an hour's time I had secured eight trout, and they would average at least a pound each, enough for two hungry young men, and a dog that could eat more than both of us. It was a good lunch, and a glorious place to partake of it.

We put the fish on the coals, roasted them to perfection, and then sat and ate our dinners, and admired the landscape and view of the ocean. For dessert we had an abundance of ripe blackberries, the bushes being loaded down with them, large and delicious fruit, and we did not stir out of our tracks to obtain all that we wanted. Even Jack seemed to like them, yet would not take the trouble to for... to himself, on account of the briars on the bushes, but waited until we had gathered a handful, and then barked for them until his demands were complied with.

After the feast of berries, we lighted our pipes, and smoked, again admired the country, and then the enthusiastic Lewey, who was a lover of nature, could not restrain his happiness, as he thought of the dangers we had passed through, and that now all was plain sailing before us.

"Vell," he asked, "vot does you dink of dis? No more sick for de home sa.ne last night? Look all around you. Did you eber see anyding like it more? Ah, how happy ve should be dat ve is here and not on board a mean old ship. I could smile and jump in de air I feels so good. In a few days ve shall see Anita and Engracia, and how glad dey be to meet us. Den all de trouble ve forgets, and ve lives and dies in a pot of grease, as de story books all say."

I suppose that it was the air which inspired us, for we did feel happy and contented, although we had not the least idea where we were going to stop when we reached the Pueblo. But we expected something would turn up, and did not despond.

Toward two o'clock we saddled our horses, and resumed our journey, loping through the valley, past herds of cattle, and once in a while saw a vaquero, who was looking after the animals, seeing that they did not wander off too far from the usual runs. Those we met did not pay us any particular attention, but when we drew near the mission of San Gabriel we noticed that some strong glances were cast toward us, and we thought the people were struck by our distinguished appearance, and were disposed to give us a hospitable welcome after our long and dangerous journey over the mountains.

As we neared Los Angeles two horsemen, evidently caballeros, rode alongside of us, and looked our mustangs all over, as if admiring them, as well they might, for they were unexcelled for speed and beauty.

"Where do you come from, strangers?" they asked.

"San Diego, senors," was our reply.

"Did you meet many people on the road?" they demanded.

"Yes; this morning we encountered General Michaeltoreno and his suite, on the other side of the mountains."

"Who else, senors?" the caballeros demanded.

"Several bands of Apaches, who were raiding the country, and stealing mules."

"Santa Maria, and you escaped from them?" and here the gentlemen crossed themselves.

"Yes, senors, but we had to fight them, or be killed," for we thought it would not be a sin to boast a little, now that we were beyond the reach of the savages.

"Did you meet the government courier Pedro on the way?" was the next question.

"Yes, senors. We saw him at Tobias's ranche, and he was well, and hoped to get through the raiding parties, but who can tell his fate?"

"We see that one of you is mounted on his favorite horse. How did you happen to possess it?"

"By a trade and purchase, senors," we answered.

The gentlemen exchanged glances, but said no more, and just then we thought that we would ask a few questions in return.

"Can you tell us, senors, where we can find the Senor Abel Stearns's residence? We have a letter for him from a gentleman of San Diego," we said.

"Certainly," was the gracious reply, and we galloped along the main street, hundreds of people looking at us as we moved along, as the cavalcade seemed unusual.

At last we halted in front of a pretentious house, and saw a gentleman on the veranda, smoking cigarettes, and several ladies near. We knew him at once, and also two of the young senoras, for they had been on board of the Admittance several times while we were lying at San Pedro, at different periods.

We thanked the caballeros, and they galloped off, after touching their broad sombreros to the ladies, and making their horses perform wonderful capering for the benefit of the fair sex.

I dismounted and approached the gentleman. He looked at me with some degree of wonderment, for he did not recollect my face, and neither did the young ladies.

"I have a letter for you, sir," I said, as I removed my hat, and bowed to the young ladies.

I spoke in English, and that seemed to astonish my hearers, for I was dressed in Mexican costume, and burned black enough for a greaser, or half-breed.

"Why, man alive, you are an American," said Mr. Stearns, still staring at me. "Where did you come from?"

"Overland from San Diego, sir. We have just arrived, and want you to direct us to a place where we can remain for a few days' rest. We have had a rough journey, and feel tired, for we have fought Apaches, mountain lions, and bears, and think we deserve a few days of leisure."

"The devil, I should think so," was the frank exclamation, and then he turned to the ladies, and explained in Spanish what I had related. The story seemed to excite general interest, for the women all uttered the words, —

"Pobrecita muchachos," and crossed themselves at the name of the Apaches.

Mr. Stearns read the letter from Captain Fitch, and then looked at us, more puzzled than ever, as he said, —

"So you two young men were on board the Admittance, were you? I recollect you now. But what fools you are to stop in this country just as a war is raging, and every American is hated, except the old residents. And you think of getting married, my friend writes me. Well, well, this is a little too rich, upon my word," and the gentleman laughed until the tears came into his eyes, and then very correctly translated my story, and the contents of the letter.

But the ladies did not laugh. They thought it was a little too romantic for anything, as they expressed it in a terse way, and warm words of approval of our course were uttered. A woman always sympathizes with parties about to wed, and the poorer the match the more congratulations they bestow. So as soon as the young women heard that we were in love, and wanted wives, their hearts were in a flutter.

"Let them remain with us," they cried with one accord. "We will teach them Spanish so that they can converse with their future mates. It must be awful not to understand what a lover says."

I did not utter a word of the tongue they were conversing in, not wishing to break the spell of a good impression.

"Well, have it your way," the gentleman said. "They are not our kind of company, but we will take care of them in some manner, and give them enough to eat."

Then he called a peon to take our horses, and, as we removed our packages to the rear of the house, I looked down the street, and saw the dark face of Don Antonio Sanchos, our worst enemy in all California, and the last person we desired to see at that time, as we supposed he was in Monterey, and could no longer trouble us.

CHAPTER VII.

DON ANTONIO SANCHOS MAKES IT UNPLEASANT, AND ACCUSES US OF MURDERING THE GOVERNMENT COURIER. — TO THE CALABOZO. — AN EXAMINATION, AND SURPRISE. — HEROES OF THE DAY. — WANTED FOR THE ARMY. — OFF FOR SANTA BARBARA, AND INCIDENTS ON THE WAY. — THE CAVALRY, AND ITS HURRIED MARCH. — SANTA BARBARA AND SOME OLD ACQUAINTANCES. — RANCHE REFUGIO, AND OUR RECEPTION BY A STRONG-MINDED WOMAN.

I MUST confess that I did not feel comfortable when I saw the dark, revengeful-looking face of Don Antonio Sanchos, the man who had persecuted us so intensely at San Diego, and by whose orders we had been confined in the calabozo, and forced to sign matriculador papers, and declare our intention of becoming Mexican citizens. We thought the greaser was at Monterey, with his disreputable brothers and followers, where we had understood there was some prospect of a fight between the State forces and the command under Fremont. But the scoundrel was at Los Angeles, and saw us at the same time we noticed him. We would have avoided the man if possible, but it was too late, so were not surprised when the fellow halted in front of Mr. Stearn's house, and addressed the proprietor.

"Senor," he said, "two young men, one of them French and the other American, have just arrived in town from San Diego, and are on your premises."

"Well, what of it?" asked Mr. Stearns, with scant civility, for he did not appear to be on the most familiar terms with the visitor.

"Simply this, senor. I want those young men as my prisoners. I claim them under the law of California as sospechosos, as enemies of the republic," the greaser remarked, and there was a wail from the ladies at the words, as they thought of a wedding being postponed, and happiness destroyed.

"Nonsense," was the reply of our host. "The boys are all right, and I will vouch for them. I have known them for years, and they never had the slightest intention of injuring the republic. Go your way, Don Sanchos, and let them alone."

"The senor is not aware perhaps that I am the agent of the government, and have the power of making arrests when I will?" the Mexican asked.

"Yes, I know all that, but don't abuse those powers, Don Sanchos, for the same party that made can quickly unmake you, and I have a little influence at Monterey with the governor and Don Pio Pico," Mr. Stearns remarked.

"I know the senor is powerful, and that his wealth is great, but all that will not prevail when it is known that I, the representative of the State, have been ill-treated by the muchachos, imprisoned by their means, shot at and wounded by a gun which they fired at me, and that my brother Carlos had his head split open by the desperados. Think of the wrongs I have suffered, and then imagine if I can forgive them."

"How is this?" asked our host, and the ladies looked at us in wonder, thinking that we were a little worse than the wild Apaches they had heard so much about, while at the same time they were disposed to admire us for all that we had done, as women like bold deeds, even if they are not quite high-toned and honorable.

As Mr. Stearns seemed disposed to demand an explanation, Lewey, as the most fluent talker, stepped forward, removed his hat, bowed with French politeness to the ladies, smiled one of his most fascinating smiles, such as he knew would touch the female heart, and commenced the story of our wrongs at the hands of Don Sanchos, and in good Spanish, so that all could comprehend what he said.

"We were in love," he began, and at the words the ladies beamed on him, "and when we were discharged from our ship, sick with a disease that we feared would terminate our young and innocent lives" (Lewey was an awful falsifier when disposed to shirk the truth, and had an object in view), "our only regret was that we could not live, and marry the two girls we had become attached to at Ranche Refugio."

Here two pretty girls sobbed, and wiped the tears from their eyes. The romance was affecting them.

"But the good saints, under whose watchful care we recovered," and here the lad crossed himself in true Catholic style, "willed that our time had no. arrived, and so we lived, and were happy in thoughts of the future. — how we were to pass our lives as devoted husbands, and in a land that can show more beautiful ladies than any quarter of the globe. Even France, my native country, must yield the palm to California in that respect, and my American friend here, Thom, says that the United States has no such handsome girls as this portion of the republic of Mexico can produce."

The young ladies' faces glowed like a garden of roses after a summer rain, and Lewey glanced at me in a manner that I understood, for I nodded an acquiescence to all that he had stated.

The elderly women smiled as they thought of their early days, and the beauty which they had possessed, and was now represented in their children. They looked at each other, and seemed to come to the conclusion that we were young men of discernment and good taste.

" Under such circumstances it is no wonder we desired to remain here," my friend continued, " but, while we were making preparations to join those whom we so dearly love, this man, Don Sanchos, appeared at San Diego, and caused our arrest as sospechosos."

" I was serving the State," interrupted the greaser. " It was my duty."

" He did this," continued Lewey, not noticing the remark, "because at one time we had injured him for insulting two ladies at San Francisco."

" Muy bravo machachos," murmured the girls, and glanced at us with flashing eyes, showing where their sympathies were.

Don Sanchos held up his right hand, where the vivid scar was distinctly seen, made by the point of a boat-hook, as he said, —

" This is the kind of treatment that I received at the hands of the gringos, and for nothing. I have cause to remember it, and always shall."

" This man caused our imprisonment in the calabozo, but we made our escape," Lewey remarked.

" By professing love for the jailor's daughter, and swearing to her undying devotion," snarled Sanchos.

The ladies looked a little shocked, as though they had never heard of such depravity. The case was going against us, and Lewey saw it, but was not in the least dismayed. He remained cool, and was careful to take advantage of all the best points.

" We confided in the keeper's daughter, and told her that we were to be married, that our hearts were true to those we loved, but scorned to tell a woman that we fancied her when such was not the case," my friend went on, and Sanchos smiled in an incredulous manner, just as though he could not believe it. "The young lady did not let us out of our cell, but when we were in the ante-room escape was possible."

My friend was determined to shield the girl, even at the expense of truth, for he feared she might suffer for what she had done in our behalf.

"And before the ladrones escaped they bound, gagged, and threw me in the cell which they had occupied. Besides that their confounded dog bit my legs," snarled Sanchos, and the ladies did not seem to feel much pity for his misfortunes. In fact, the man commenced stripping up the bottoms of his slashed trousers to show where Jack had fastened his teeth, but suddenly recollected that the ladies would not be interested in old scars, so wisely refrained.

"Boys, that was wrong," Mr. Stearns said, but he looked as though he did not grieve very deeply for the part we had played. "The senor is an agent of the government, and should have been treated with respect. However, that is all settled now, I hope. I will be security for the young men's appearance and good behaviour as long as they remain at Los Angeles."

We bowed our thanks, and looked our gratitude.

"By the way," Mr. Stearns asked, "did n't I hear something about one of you lads being offered a commission as midshipman on the sloop-of-war Ceynne?"

"It was my friend, Thom, sir," answered Lewey, before I could deny the report. "He is rich, and has lots of money, but loves California more than his home."

Lewey was the most wonderful boy I ever met for ready answers, and some of them were not always true, I regret to say. But he never blushed when telling an untruth, as he looked honest and confiding, with the light of sincerity shining from his blue eyes.

The ladies were delighted with the answer. In their estimation I was no longer a common sailor, but a caballero, a gentleman of means, and their interest in me increased, although they might have had some secret thoughts that I was throwing myself away on a poor girl when there were so many rich ones who desired husbands, and wealth at the same time.

"Now, Don Sanchos, go your way," Mr. Stearns said. "I will see that these two young men are looked after, and taken care of. Let us have no more trouble. They have come to me highly recommended, and I understand that they also have a letter for Mr. Temple from my old friend Captain Fitch."

But Don Sanchos did not seem disposed to move off with this assurance. He smiled in a sardonic manner, as he rubbed his maimed hand, and said, —

"Your assertions are quite cheerful, and would be satisfactory, but as the agent of the government I have a more serious charge to make against the young men, and even you, senor, will not uphold them in what they have done."

We wondered what the greaser referred to, and on what track he was standing.

"Come, come, don't let us have any more charges," Mr. Stearns cried. "We have heard enough for one day at least," and the ladies all smiled an unanimous amen to the words.

"I regret, senor, that I cannot yield to your wishes," Sanchos said, and as he spoke waved his hand in a peculiar manner, and up the street we saw a dozen horsemen moving, and in the crowd we recognized Carlos Sanchos, almost as great a scoundrel as his brother.

Mr. Stearns looked the astonishment he felt.

"I arrest these young men," the greaser said, as he stepped forward, "for the crime of murder."

There was an exclamation of horror from the ladies, and wonder and surprise from us. What did the fellow mean? Was this some new dodge to get us in his power, and punish us?

"Explain yourself, senor," Mr. Stearns cried. "These are serious words. Be careful how you trifle with them."

"This is no light matter, senor," the greaser remarked, in a cool, determined way. "One of these young men has in his possession the favorite horse of Pedro the courier. He was due here yesterday, yet no word have we heard of him. It is rumored in town that the ranchero has been murdered on his way from San Diego, and that these boys committed the deed, and then took possession of the horse. Look at the brands on the animal's haunches, and you will see that they are Pedro's. There is no doubt of it. A dozen men can swear to them. They know the caballo well. Now what motive could these men have for making way with the courier except to steal his despatches, and give them to the enemies of the government? Therefore, in the name of the law, and by the power invested in me as an agent of the State of California, I do arrest these young men as sospechosos."

There was a flood of tears from the young ladies, and an angry denial on our part and when there was silence Mr. Stearns said, —

"Explain this whole matter, boys, so that we can understand it."

I did so, but spoke in English, as my Spanish failed me in my eagerness to show all the circumstances of the case.

"When we were at Tobias's ranche," I said, "after we had killed three invading Apaches" (here Sanchos smiled, as much as to say that was a gringo's lie, for he understood a little English) "the courier arrived with despatches for the alcalda of San Diego. He was pleased with our bravery, and commended us in warm terms, and, because I admired his horse, he was glad to make an exchange with me, I paying him eight reals in addition for the animal. Senor Tobias, the owner of the ranche, for the gratitude he felt because we had saved the life of his daughter, made my friend Lewey a present of the caballo he rode. You can see the man's brand, a large T in a circle. This is our defence, and is the truth, so help me God."

"I believe you," Mr. Stearns said, in all sincerity, and then he related the story I had told to Sanchos and the ladies, and the generous females were delighted when he came to that part whereby a girl was saved from the Indians.

"It is the lie of a gringo," the greaser remarked. "It will not do for me. The young men stand charged with murder. Until they can prove that Pedro is alive they must be kept in prison. Let no man keep in my way, or the worse for him. In the name of the law I arrest them."

The ladies uttered a series of shrill screams, but after they had been silenced Mr. Stearns asked, —

"Will you accept security for the appearance of the young men tomorrow before the alcalda?"

"No, senor. To the calabozo they must go, and await certain events," was the answer.

"You see, boys, I have done all that I can for you," our host said. "The man has the power to arrest you. The charge is a serious one, but I hope it will be disproved. I will be present before the court tomorrow, and, in company with Mr. Temple, do what I can to confound your enemies. Yield as gracefully as possible, and look for the best results. Be assured you sha'n't starve while in prison."

"Will you permit us to leave our property here until we are acquitted or sentenced?" I asked. "Our rifles, knives, and pistols, horses and blankets are valuable, and we should find it hard work to replace them."

"Give yourself no uneasiness on that point," our host said. "I will see that all are taken care of, and restored to you as soon as free, which I hope will be in a few days."

"And our dog, sir," I remarked. "It is not probable that the prison officials will permit him to go with us. Will you also feed him as well as the horses?"

"Oh, yes, but the animal will not remain with me."

"He will if we command him to do so. He is a knowing dog, and is already aware that some misfortune has overtaken us. You can tell that by his looks. Jack, old boy," I said, addressing the animal, "you must remain here until we return. Do you hear?"

He did hear, but a look of deep dejection passed over his expressive eyes, and he seemed to ask that we would rescind the order. But when he found that it was not forthcoming he lay down, and did not offer to stir until we moved from the house, escorted by the body guard of the agent of the State. Then he raised his head, and uttered a prolonged howl, but subsided when one of the ladies patted his head, and waved a farewell at the same time.

Our passage through the main street was quite an event for the sleepy little town. All the people had awakened from their usual afternoon siestas, and were refreshing themselves by yawning at the doors and on the verandas. The crime of which we were accused was repeated from mouth to mouth, and, as all had not heard our defence, we were generally supposed to be guilty, and there was some talk of hanging or shooting us without delay; and I really believe that Don Sanchos would have been only too delighted had such action occurred on the part of the populace, the majority of whom were none too good for such lawlessness, but the best people were just.

However, when we were half way to the calabozo, Messrs. Stearns and Temple appeared on the scene, and their presence seemed to have a beneficial effect on our fortunes, for the people kept at a distance, while the better-disposed women said that we were "pobrecitas," and hoped the saints would pardon us.

I wonder if that old calabozo is still in existence in Los Angeles? Probably the march of improvement has been the means of erecting a stately stone prison instead of an adobe one, where refractory Indians were confined, and foreigners were locked up after an extensive acquaintance with native rum, or aguardiente.

My friend Lewey told me, the last time I saw him at Cherbourg, some years ago, that he visited Los Angeles in 1854, his ship anchoring at San Pedro, and that he saw the same place in which we were confined, and entered the room where we were kept as prisoners, and that all remained as of old, but no one would believe that the polite naval officer had ever been under lock and key in the Pueblo, even Messrs. Stearns and Temple refusing to recognize the captain as the poor boy who had claimed their protection some years before, and he had to mention many particulars of certain transactions before he was credited with being one and the same person.

We were escorted to the calabozo with as much ceremony as was consistent with men who would like to have sold us our freedom for a small sum, provided Don Sanchos was willing. But, as he cared more for vengeance than money just at that time, his gang did not dare to make any opposition to his wishes.

Luckily for us there was no inmates of the prison at the time, so we had all the fleas and odors to ourselves, and, after the keeper had turned the key on us, and then went home to get his supper, we had an opportunity to do a little talking and consulting. Lewey's confidence never left him. He was as jaunty and self-possessed as a man who could command instant liberation in case he desired it. I think that much of the élan was put on for the sake of making me feel more comfortable and at ease.

We were about to light our pipes, and have a quiet smoke, when the keeper of the prison returned to us in hot haste, and brought some food, coffee, and fruit, and said that we were to be made comfortable regardless of expense, and forthwith he produced half a dozen blankets, a light, and blocks of wood for pillows, and when we inquired who had been so kind, he grinned, and showed us a Mexican dollar, which proved that some one had bribed him to look after our welfare. We had no doubt but that Mr. Stearns and his family were acting with energy in our behalf, and did not intend that we should starve or suffer if they could prevent it.

We talked of our situation, and confessed that it was not a comfortable one in case Pedro did not turn up, or was found murdered on the trail, and then fell asleep, and dreamed of the Admittance, surf, hide-droghing, and handsome women, and when we awoke the jailor brought us a calabash of fresh water for our toilets, and then followed a nice breakfast, sent from the house of our friends.

By eleven o'clock Don Sanchos came to the calabozo to escort us to the presence of the alcalda, and when we were arraigned in the hall of justice a crowd of men and women were there to gaze on us, and speculate on the crime we had committed.

Among the spectators were the handsome ladies we had seen the day before, and each of them gave us a smile, while Messrs. Stearns and Temple came to us, and exchanged a few words of greeting. They said that they intended to ask for a continuation of the case until another day, in hope that something would turn up regarding the welfare of Pedro.

As soon as the alcalda had taken his seat, a lawyer, who seemed to act for the government, stated the case in very clear terms, related the enormity of the crime, and then Mr. Temple put in a few words in our behalf. He had known us, he said, as honest, hard-working boys, and ridiculed the idea that we would commit murder. One of us was an American citizen, and the other a native of France, different from the usual run of sailors on the coast, left without a ship to call their home.

At this point Don Antonio Sanchos whispered a few words to the attorney for the government, and the latter said, —

"These young men are no longer citizens of France and the perfidious United States. They are subjects of Mexico, for they have signed matriculadors, thus taking the first steps to be naturalized. We must deal with them as with our own countrymen."

" Is this true ? " asked Mr. Stearns, turning to us.

" Yes, sir," was our prompt answer.

" What in the devil's name did you do that for? " was the next question.

" Because we were in love, and wanted to get married," we answered, quite innocently.

" Oh, what fools," was the cheerful response. " Did n't you know any better ? "

" No, sir. We supposed it was all right."

" Well, it 's all wrong, and now we must trust to luck, and get you out of the trouble the best way we can," and then turning to the alcalda Mr. Stearns said, " We acknowledge that the young men have signed matriculadors, but that only goes to show the honesty and good intentions of the lads. They were anxious to become citizens of the State for certain reasons which will appeal to the judgment and good sense of every lady and man present."

" What were the reasons, senor ? " demanded the alcalda, and he smiled as he asked the question, although I really believe he knew all about the matter at the time.

" Well, it seems the young men want to be married, and they supposed the ceremony could not be performed unless naturalized, or that they gave notice of their intentions to be."

At this explanation there was a general laugh from the male portion of the audience, and smiles and blushes on the part of the ladies. The latter looked as though they thought our ambition a notable one, something that should be commended, instead of ridiculed.

"We shall have to ask for a continuation of the case," Mr. Stearns said. "Let the matter lay over for a few days, and perhaps the courier will turn up all right."

"We can settle the subject at the present time just as well as though we waited a week," the advocate for the government said. "California now needs soldiers. Monterey is threatened by the United States. Already a horde of robbers and murderers has invaded the territory. We must drive them back to the mountains, or polute our soil with their graves. Let the young men volunteer for the army, and the case will be instantly closed."

"But the lads did not matriculador for any such purpose," Mr. Stearns remarked. "If there is any fighting to be done they prefer to do it after they are married," which candid remark produced a laugh from the men, and a pout from the women, the unmarried ones looking quite spiteful.

"Let the prisoners decide the question," the alcalda said. "They are old enough to choose between imprisonment, or freedom, and the gayety of a soldier's life."

"Vot shall ve do?" whispered Lewey, but, before I could answer the question by an indignant refusal, there were murmurs of astonishment, and then came a chorus of voices, and the cry of, —

"El correo, el correo," and pushing through the crowd we saw the muscular form and handsome face of Pedro, the government courier, the man we had met at Tobias's ranche, and with whom I had exchanged horses, and paid a little to boot.

Don Antonio Sanchos did not look happy when he saw Pedro's well-known face, and his eyes showed some of the disappointment he felt as the courier sauntered forward, and stood in front of the alcalda. Every one in the room knew the ranchero, and all were glad to welcome his return except our enemies.

Mr. Temple, a smile on his face, sprang to his feet, and addressed the alcalda.

"Senor," he said, "here is the caballero who was supposed dead, and whom these young men were accused of murdering. Let him be put on the stand, and questioned. You and I and every one present know him well, and are sure of his truthful character."

"Si, si," was heard all over the room. "Let the correo speak, and tell us what he knows of the young men."

But Pedro did not seem to take heed of the murmurs. He looked around upon the audience as though he did not quite understand what the tumult was all about, and, as his eyes roamed here and there, they suddenly fell on our faces, and a smile lighted up his countenance and black eyes, as he sprang toward us, and seized our hands, giving us a grip that almost made the tears start, and then patting us on the backs with both hands shouted, —

"Amigos, amigos, como sè va?" or in English, "Friends, friends, how do you do?"

There was a great shout from the audience, and the young ladies looked as though they wanted to kiss us, and we felt so pleased that we would have willingly cast aside our timid modesty for the time being, and consented to the embrace.

"Do you know these young men?" asked the alcalda, as soon as the noise had in some degree subsided.

"Si, senor," Pedro replied, in a loud tone so that all could hear.

"State what you know about them," was the command.

"One moment, senor. I am a government correo, and must deliver my despatches before I answer any questions, or talk on matters that do not concern the public welfare. Here are papers and letters from the alcalda of San Diego. I have just arrived from that town, and come to your court to deliver my messages. I was not aware that my two friends were under arrest. I know not 'or what."

The courier placed in the alcalda's hand a bag containing the documents, and the official glanced over the papers, but made no comment as he read them, yet the news was important as it announced plans for the war, and preparations for a vigorous defence.

"Now, senor correo," said the alcalda with a sigh, as he read the news, and realized what the result might be, "you will please take the stand, and tell us what you know about these young men."

"We have no desire to hear the correo, senor," the government attorney cried. "We are satisfied that no murder has been committed, and withdraw the charge."

"No, no," came from all parts of the room. "Let the correo speak at once."

"It is necessary for the reputation of these young men that the correo should be heard," Mr. Stearns cried. "They have told their story. Now let Pedro tell his, and we shall see if they agree in their account of the meeting."

"Go on, Pedro," ordered the alcalda. "You have met the young men before today?"

"Yes, senor."

"Where did you first encounter them?"

"At the ranche of Tobias, fifteen miles or more from San Diego, where they had remained over night."

"You are friendly to the young men?" was the next question.

"Gracias Dios, I should think so. They saved my life, and that of a young girl, Florencia, the daughter of the ranchero."

"In what manner?" and all the people in the room leaned forward to catch every word that Pedro uttered, as he answered the question.

"The senors had started on their journey for this place, but met on the road the Senorita Florencia, who was looking for the eggs of quails. While exchanging salutations with her on the trail, a band of four Apache warriors burst from the chapparel, and rode toward them, with the intention of making a prisoner of the girl and killing the caballeros."

At this stage of the story the young girls uttered sobs, and the elderly ladies crossed themselves, and said short prayers.

"Some men would have turned their horses' heads and fled," the correo continued, "but not so my friends. They said to each other, 'We will save the young girl, or die for her.'"

Here there were ripples of applause, and the ladies flashed bright glances at us, as though we were real heroes, and for a moment forgot their tears.

"Go on, and tell us what was the result," the alcalda commanded.

"As the murdering devils of Apaches charged on the young men, they dismounted, told the girl to make her escape with their horses, and stood their ground, and fired."

"Yes, yes," cried a dozen voices. "Go on and tell us the balance of the story."

"Two of the cruel thieves fell, and the third was also shot as he advanced. The fourth Apache was killed by Tobias, just as he was about to overtake Florencia. None of the wild Indians were alive when I arrived at the scene a few hours after the battle."

"Bueno," was the verdict of the people.

"But how do you make it that the young men saved your life?" asked the alcalda.

"In this way, senor. The Indians were raiding the district of San Diego. If the young men had not been present they would have killed me, the girl, and Tobias. They were concealed in the chapparel, and awaiting all who passed. I could not have protected myself against the sudden attack. For this reason I say that I am indebted for my life to the senors. I owe them muchos gracias."

The audience gave expression to their joy by a loud clapping of hands, and the ladies waved rich fans, and looked pleased at the result, so unexpected to all.

"How did you happen to let the young men possess your horse?" the alcalda asked, as soon as the confusion had subsided.

Pedro blushed a little, and looked abashed for a moment. Then he rallied, and said, —

"My caballo was tired, and I needed a fresh and fast horse to run the gauntlet of the wild Indians. The senor liked my animal. I favored his, as I knew that it could travel faster than mine, when properly managed. I made the exchange, and received eight reals to boot. It was a good bargain for me, but if the senor is dissatisfied I will return him the money," and at this point the audience laughed, and nodded to each other, as much as to say Pedro was a sharp one, and no mistake.

"The horse is government property, and the correo had no right to exchange it," the attorney for the State cried, inspired by Don Sanchos.

Pedro grinned at the advocate, as he said, —

"If the senor will look at my instructions he will see that I have full power to buy, exchange, or take horses where and when I please. It pleased me to exchange my steed for another, and I did so. But I will give him back to my friend, for I fear I cheated him."

Then the people once more smiled, and, when I shook my head, and said that I thought I had the best of the bargain, there was a general roar, and even the alcalda joined in the mirth.

"The case is dismissed," said the magistrate. "The young men are discharged."

Messrs. Temple and Stearns came to us and shook our hands, and congratulated us upon our escape. But just then Don Sanchos made his voice heard.

"I claim these young men for the army of California," he said. "We need just such people. As matriculadors they must serve when called upon. Let them be enrolled at once, and sent to headquarters immediately."

This was not a pleasant termination of our trials. We did not like the idea of being enrolled as Mexican soldiers, and compelled to fight against the United States, but the alcalda reassured us, as he said, —

"The young men can be enlisted among the brave defenders of the State, but they have the privilege of receiving a month's notice before being called upon to serve. This is the law."

"Then, in conformity to the law, I give the matriculadors one month's warning," Don Sanchos said, and he gave us a look that showed he would not forget the exact time. But we answered his glances with a gesture of contempt, for we had beaten him three times, and hoped to be enabled to do so again, if the occasion served.

The alcalda arose, bowed to all present, and retired, and then we found ourselves surrounded by the foreign residents, and congratulated on the victory which we had gained. One lady, an aged dame, kissed us on both cheeks, and called us blessed. She was a widow, and wanted a second husband, and probably thought we might answer, but she smelled of garlic, and her teeth were bad, so was out of the question as long as there were young girls ready to take us for partners.

We did not get to Mr. Stearns's house till near three o'clock. Pedro went with us, and told us how he had escaped the Indians on the route, and that it was thought the savages had returned to the southern part of Arizona. At all the ranches he had heard only praises of our conduct, and a fervent hope that we would return some time. We sent our compliments to Florencia and the other ladies, and Pedro said that he would deliver them when he again passed over the trail, which might not be for a week or ten days, just according to the news from Monterey.

Our dog Jack was frantic with delight when he saw us, and could not do enough to show his pleasure. He had been very good, and only manifested his loneliness by whining once in a while, and looking down the street to see if we were coming.

Our host gave us a very good dinner, and in the evening Lewey and I entertained the company with an exhibition of legerdemain that pleased the young ladies, and caused them to marvel at our skill.

The next day Sanchos and his gang left the Pueblo, and every one was glad that he and his followers were gone, and it was hoped would never return.

We remained six days at Los Angeles, and then announced our intended departure for Ranche Refugio. We were requested to stay, and none were more urgent than the ladies of the household, but we pleaded that honor and duty called us to go, and so one morning saddled our horses, packed our baggage, and were ready to start, but as we bade all a kind farewell. Mr. Stearns said.

"My lads, there are several American ships on the coast. Get on board one of them, and stay there. Do not come on shore if you can help it. Let the girls alone, and some day you will thank me for my advice, for it is the best that I can give you."

We promised to think of the matter, and then saluted all who were present to see us off, and trotted down the street, Jack barking himself hoarse with delight at the prospect of meeting more adventures, and once in a while, to vary the monotony, dashing at some greaser's dog, and sending him scampering homeward, his stub tail between his legs with every evidence of fear.

Pedro rode with us for ten miles or more, just as an act of courtesy. He gave us directions as to our route and halting places, and the most feasible way of crossing the coast range of mountains, between Los Angeles and Santa Barbara, and when he had commended us to his patron saint, said that God would watch over us, shook hands, and dashed back to the town like a whirlwind, Lewey and I pursued our journey all alone.

"I dink," remarked my friend, as we loped over the trail, "dat ve made von great mistake. Ve should have married two of de sweet little girls of Los Angeles, and settled dar."

"And let our wives starve?" I asked.

"Vell, ve skall starve vid dem, so de ding is equal. Ve might as vell take life easy in von place as anudder. Besides, I dink dem Pueblo senor Itas has more money dan de udders."

"And keep away from Anita and Engracia?" I asked, a little reproachfully.

"Vell, ve could hab gone and seed 'em vonce in a vhile," and then the bad young man gave me a wink that was suggestive of an easy conscience regarding the marriage relation.

But as I refused to encourage the ideas which he entertained the French boy dropped the subject, and we rode on in silence for an hour or more. It was quite evident to me that Lewey did not love the girl he had sworn to honor and remember as strongly as he might have done, or he would not have been attracted by the pretty faces we had seen since leaving San Diego. I feared that there would be some difficulty in getting him to give his hand unless his heart went with it. However, I trusted that the sight of Engracia's sweet features might produce the usual results on his fickle mind, and determined not to argue with him on the subject, as such a course would make him more obstinate.

By twelve o'clock we had climbed the summit of the coast range of mountains, and looked once more on the Pacific, and the islands that extend along the coast from Santa Barbara to San Pedro. The view was a magnificent one, and, while we halted to partake of a slight luncheon, and rest our horses, a Mexican ranchero rode toward us from a trail that led down into the valley, in the direction of Buenaventura. He was a young fellow, dark, and not prepossessing, and there was something in his face that resembled the features of Don Sanchos and his brother Carlos, bold and brutal.

The ranchero rode up and saluted us in a frank manner, asked where we were going, and the news at Los Angeles, and, when we had answered all of his questions in a satisfactory manner, intimated that he had a ranche a short distance from where we were resting, and would be glad to welcome us to his house and all that it contained, if we would honor him with a visit.

Lewey, in his usual impulsive manner, sprang up, and proposed that we should accept at once, but I felt such a repugnance to our visitor that I firmly declined, pleading the need of haste to reach the end of our journey.

"Vot a feller you is," Lewey remarked, in English. "Ve can go and see his home, and perhaps he has a booful sister dar."

But I was firm, and at last the visitor looked the disappointment he felt in not securing our presence at his ranche, and then in a sullen manner mounted his horse, and, as he did so, asked, —

"Are your rifles loaded, amigos?"

I do not know why, but I made a prompt response that was not exactly truthful, as I said, in a careless manner, —

"Oh, no, we did not think it worth while, as the mountains are safe, we have been told."

"You are sure?" was the next question.

"Yes, quite."

The fellow instantly put a hand to his mouth, and uttered a peculiar cry, and out of the bushes sprang three horsemen, all with long lariats in their hands, and swinging them as they dashed toward us.

"Surrender, you gringos," cried the man who had wanted us to visit his ranche, and accept of his hospitality.

We jumped to our feet, and laid hands on the rifles that were near, surprised but not dismayed by the advance and sudden appearance of the greasers. We saw at once that there was a plot and trick of some kind to capture us, but for what reason we could not divine, as it was unknown

that we had money on our persons, not having revealed the secret to a single person, since we had been paid the doubloons by Captain Fitch, at San Diego.

"What does this mean?" asked Lewey in Spanish of the greaser.

"It means that you are my prisoners," was the ready answer. "Surrender, or we will drag you down the side of the mountain at the end of our lariats."

"Keep off," we cried, as we backed against a pine-tree, the branches of which would shield us from the whirl of the unerring lariats. "If you dare to molest us we will kill you as we would a mad dog," and we raised our rifles in a threatening manner.

"Bah, we do not care for your escopetas," was the cry, as the horsemen formed in a line, and looked for a chance to ensnare us with their reatas, but the tree afforded shelter, and they could not touch us or our horses, as the branches extended for a long distance, and our backs were against the trunk of the stout pine, or red wood, I have forgotten which.

The new-comers seemed to fear the muzzles of our guns, and rather held back, until the owner of the ranche, and leader of the gang shouted, —

"You need not care. Their rifles are empty. Ride them down, if the gringos dare not come out and have a fair fight."

This was cool, even for a Mexican greaser. Four mounted, expert horsemen daring two young man to leave the shelter of a tree, and trust to their quickness in dodging the deadly reatas, which once over our forms was certain death, or maimed for life.

"Keep away from us," we cried, in a calm tone. "We warn you that there is death for two of you if an attack is made on us. Our rifles are loaded, and we know how to use them. Ladrones of the devil, leave us in peace, and we will not harm you."

The greasers laughed at the advice. They thought we were sure to be captured sooner or later, and while we were speaking the men dismounted to act to better advantage in approaching us, and then I noticed one of the Mexicans reached down, and drew a long knife from his leggings. I knew the meaning of the action as well as if the fellow had told me what he intended to do. He would poise the cuchillo for a moment, and then let it fly through the air, and it probably might hit within a few inches of the spot he aimed at. I had seen the trick performed many times, and was not unprepared for it.

"Lewey," I whispered, "the greaser is about to throw his knife at us. Take care."

"Den throw a little lead at him afore he has de chance," was the reply.

The Mexican raised his long, sharp knife, and the next moment it would have penetrated one of our bodies, but I stopped his pleasant little pastime, for, just as he was ready to throw, I aimed my rifle and fired. The ball struck the greaser's shoulder, and, with a yell of pain, the knife was dropped to the ground, and the fellow nearly tumbled over backward, so great was his astonishment.

As if in response to the report of the rifle, far down the mountain side, toward Santa Barbara, was heard the fan-fan of trumpets, the loud, shrill blast of cavalry music, such as the California troops were accustomed to march by.

The greasers listened eagerly for a moment, then mounted, and dashed spurs in their horses' sides, and disappeared down one of the narrow trails that led we knew not where.

"Dey got a stomach full dat time," Lewey cried, as the last of the Mexicans disappeared from sight, only the lad did not use quite such polite language as I have written. "You gib von of dem somethin' dat he vill remember for many and many a long day, and de pain vill keep him avake for some nights sure. Ah, to dink dat I vanted to go vid dat greaser, and felt cross 'cos you vould not consent. You vill forgib me, bon compagnon?" and the French boy extended his hand. He was always ready to be forgiven when he had done anything more foolish than usual.

Up the side of the mountain we heard the shrill blast of the trumpets, the sound re-echoing from peak to peak, and at last we saw a troop of Mexican cavalry winding about the narrow trail at a slow pace, for the ascent was difficult and dangerous, and at the head of the column were several officers in showy uniforms, with heavy sabres at their sides. There were about one hundred men in all, but the fellows were slight and lacked strength, yet they made excellent horsemen and capital scouts, quick and accurate in the information they obtained of an enemy's position and movements, as we afterward learned.

"Had ve better vait and see de sojers, or cut and run for it?" asked Lewey.

As the troops had already seen us, and were commenting on our unexpected presence in that part of the country, I thought that we had better remain where we were, and have an interview, but just as I spoke the squadron was halted, and a couple of scouts thrown out to see if there was a force back of us, and what it was composed of. It is probable that the commander imagined the wicked Americans were stealing a march on the Mexicans, and crossing the mountains to take Santa Barbara in flank and rear, as could have been done very easily, if so disposed, but as there was nothing to prevent an attack from the front or water side of the town, our government did not deem it expedient to compel men to march ninety miles instead of one. In fact, during the war, a midshipman from the frigate Congress or Savannah, with twelve men, held the pleasant town for several weeks, and then marched out of the rude stockade they had erected with all the honors of war, after being threatened by some hundred greasers, who should have eaten them up before breakfast, as a little lunch to sharpen their appetites for a more substantial meal.

The scouts came on very cautiously, halting their mustangs every few paces so that a good look could be obtained of us, but, when we rose up, and showed our powerful forms, the soldiers dashed into the bushes to get out of sight, for fear a shot might whistle around their ears. To prevent further complications, and not provoke the men, we waved a scrape in token of peace, and then the scouts came toward us, and looked with astonishment at our persons.

"Remember you is a Frenchman for dis day at least," Lewey said, as the cavalry advanced up the mountain, and halted near our resting place.

"Who are you?" asked the officer commanding, "and what are you doing here?"

"We are French lads," answered Lewey, "and on our way to get married."

Then men and officers laughed and shouted at the information. It was a little singular that people always smiled and joked us when we stated that we were about to be married, just as though there was something to make merry over in the announcement. We thought it was rather a serious piece of business, and most folks find it so before they die.

"When did you leave Los Angeles?" asked the commander, as soon as the laughter had subsided.

We told him, and also said there was no news of importance at the Pueblo. The colonel and men were going to the town to look after the Americans who might land at San Pedro, and march to Los Angeles, as they afterward did, and got licked by the greasers in an out and out manner, about the only victory the Mexicans gained over the United States forces, composed of sailors and marines, and not a field piece to offset the only one the Californians owned.

"Have you papers permitting you to travel through the country?"

asked the officer, after we had given him all the information we thought desirable.

"Certainly, senor," was our answer. "We have a pass from General Castro. Shall we produce it?"

"Yes, let me see it."

We handed the paper to him. He read it carefully, and then returned it to us.

"That is all right," and then his eyes fell on our rifles. The pistols we had put out of sight, as we feared the soldiers would be tempted to take them.

"I heard a shot as I came up the mountain," the colonel said. "What were you firing at?"

"A deer, senor," as we did not deem it advisable to tell him all that we knew.

"And you missed?" with a laugh.

"Yes, senor; the deer was a long distance from us."

"Let me see your rifles," was the next command.

Lewey promptly stepped forward, and held them up for his inspection.

"These are good weapons. I need them for my men to fight the Americans," the officer remarked in a very cool tone. "I will keep them."

"Is there anything else you would like that belongs to us?" Lewey asked in a sarcastic manner.

"Yes, your horses. They look like good ones, and well broken to the saddle. We will take them."

"And also the saddles?" demanded my friend, keeping down the rage that wanted to find vent.

"Yes, the saddles also."

"Perhaps you need our blankets?" Lewey inquired, with a sneer.

"We can use them," was the prompt reply.

"I'll be hanged if you do," my friend cried in Spanish, and then threw up his arms, looked down the side of the mountain, and shouted wildly, while he seized the two rifles from the officer's hands, tossed them to me, and continued, —

"Gracias Dios, here comes Fremont and his desperate gang of trappers and wild Indians. We shall all be murdered in cold blood if we are captured. Save me some one."

"Adelante," yelled the commander of the cavalry, not stopping to see if the report was true. "Vamous, muy presto," and with a yell the whole body of men struck their spurs into the horses' sides, and went on with a rush and a dash so charming to see that Lewey just laid down on one of the most convenient flat rocks, and roared until the tears blinded his eyes. The last we saw of the troop the colonel was a little ahead of his men, but not much, and leading the officers were the two trumpeters, their instruments over their backs, and pounding their spines at every jump of the mustangs on which they were mounted.

We did not lose any time in saddling our horses, gathering up our traps, and descending the mountain trail, only to ascend another that seemed higher than the one we left, and so we pushed on until near night, when we came to a lonely ranche in a valley, and craved permission to pass the night under the shelter of an out-building. The owner and wife were a little dazed, as they had been visited by the Mexican cavalry in the morning, and the bold warriors consumed everything they could lay their hands on, besides helping themselves to horses and two bullocks, the latter eaten for breakfast, only the choicest bits being taken by the dainty soldiers, and the rest thrown to the dogs.

While Lewey was looking after the horses, and piquetting them where the grass was good, I took my rifle, and sauntered along to the edge of some trees, and managed to stumble on a fat doe, which I shot, and carried to the house. We dressed the carcass, and had some nice venison steaks, and then the ranchero and his wife regaled us with a few Interesting accounts of the treatment they had received at the hands of their countrymen, and, when the lady said that the soldiers had insulted her by offering to salute her chaste lips, we thought that the depravity of the cavalry was something to be deplored, or their stomachs of unbounded strength, for Lewey stated that there was not enough money in all California to tempt him to do such a thing, which is sufficient proof that the senora was very plain, and smelled of garlic.

We were not disturbed during the night, except by the yelping of coyotes, and the usual terrific attack of fleas. But as we were accustomed to both nuisances we managed to have a fair quantity of sleep, and were ready for breakfast at sunrise, and on our way by eight o'clock, the host and wife requesting us to call and see them if we ever traveled that way again.

It was a beautiful morning, cool and crisp, and the heavy dew of the night had freshened the grass and flowers, and filled the air with perfume. Our hearts and spirits were light as we galloped along the valleys, or walked our horses slowly up the steep mountains, keeping to the trail, so blind in some places we had to pick our way to be sure that we were on the right road, and it was not until late in the afternoon that we stood on the last hill that overlooked Santa Barbara, sleeping quietly in the valley, with the white mission church, the bells of which were clanging for some unusual service for the pious. There, in front of the town, was the long, sandy beach, with the surf breaking white upon the shore, where we had landed so many times, got ducked so often, and passed so many happy hours while on board the ship Admittance, only at that period we did not know that we were enjoying life, but thought ourselves miserable and over-worked. The place seemed like a home to us, it looked so familiar, calm and content under the warm afternoon sun. Just inside the kelp was anchored a large ship, and we imagined it to be the Sterling, a Boston vessel, after hides, flying the American flag at the peak, in defiance of the Mexicans and the war that was supposed to be raging at the time, only Santa Barbara had not seen any bloodshed thus far, and the people were not holding meetings, and advising every one to go to the scene of strife, and die like heroes for their country. The male portion of the inhabitants at that time only wanted to be let alone, and allowed to sleep and eat their meals in peace.

For an hour we sat there on the summit of that hill, and looked at the town and the ocean, and enjoyed the prospect before us. Eighteen miles beyond us, to the north, was Ranche Refugio, the end of our journey, and Lewey's face glowed as he suddenly remembered the object of our trip, and some of his young love seemed to revive as he pointed toward the place, and said, —

"Dar is vare ve vill see de girls. Tomorrow ve vill clasp dem in our arms, and de next day ve vill talk ober vedder it is best to be married or remain single. Come on, mon ami," and we descended the hill, and rode toward the town, people staring at us, and wondering who we were, and whether we were Mexicans or foreigners.

We knew every public man and house in town, but did not feel like calling on our acquaintances and requesting hospitality, so concluded that we would pull up at some greaser's place, and pay our way, thus being independant of every one. We supposed the rich men of the town, the Robinsons and Noriegos, would be offended at our course, and desire us as guests, but we imagined that our explanations would prevent any hard feelings on their part, and thus break up the friendship that had existed so long between us. Beside, we did not really think the above-named parties would be likely to recognize us in case we made them a friendly call, and claimed bed and board for a few nights.

While we were speculating on these things, little thinking that my companion, in the course of a few years, would be escorted through the same dusty streets, the guest of the best people of Santa Barbara, and representing the French nation as the captain of a man-of-war, whom should we see walking along, in a brown study, as though calculating the price of hides and tallow, silks and cotton fabrics, but Mr. H. F. Teschemacher, our former assistant supercargo, and some years later mayor of San Francisco.

We looked at him quite hard, but he did not recognize us, and at last spoke to him, and even then it was some time before he could realize that the two browned, sun-burned boys were the same parties who had been on the Admittance for three years. To be sure our costumes were a little travel-stained, and in some places ragged, and we would not have passed as caballeros of the first class, or been considered good ornaments for a drawing-room, but our hearts and principles were first-class, as could have been detected by those who made a study of humanity under all sorts of guises.

"Where did you boys come from?" asked the astonished supercargo, as soon as he could realize who we were.

We told him all about our discharge, and travel by land from San Diego, and the object of our journey, and when we alluded to the expected wedding the gentleman smiled.

"Well, of all the fools I ever met you two boys are the greatest," was the candid remark, and we did not take offence as we had got accustomed to that kind of talk, and considered it complimentary to be men of our words.

"Don't you know that the country is turned upside down by the war between Mexico and the United States?" Mr. Teschemacher continued. "The ship Sterling is in the harbor. Tomorrow I will get you berths on board of her, and in a short time you can return home."

"Thank you, but we are not anxious to ship just at present," I said. "We intend to settle down, and be residents of the country, raise cattle, and get rich like other people."

"What nonsense," was the response. "You do not know the danger you are in. Have you any money?"

"Not a cent," was that blessed, untruthful Lewey's response, and the lad winked at me as he spoke.

"Here," said the supercargo, putting his hand in his pocket, and pulling out two Mexican dollars. "Take these, and tomorrow I will see about shipping you on the Sterling. You can find a place to sleep at most any of these houses, I have no doubt."

"Mil gracias," laughed Lewey, as he refused the coins. "Ve is not traveling beggars jist yet. Ve danks you jist de same though as if ve was in vant."

While we were thus expressing our appreciation of the gentleman's kindness another party drew near, and we saw that the new-comer was Mr. Robinson, whom we had met many times at Santa Barbara, the same gentleman who was at one time supercargo of the ship Alert and brig Pilgrim. Mr. Dana did not like him very well for some reason, but I had no fault to find with his conduct on the coast toward sailors, or any one else, as he seemed kind and considerate.

"Did you ever see these young men before, Mr. Robinson?" Mr. Teschemacher asked, as the former gentleman took a good square look at us.

"Not to my knowledge," was the answer. "Who are they?"

"Two of Peterson's boys. They were discharged at San Diego, and now want to marry, and grow up with the country."

"What fools," was the usual rejoinder, and then Mr. Robinson laughed, just as though he had said something funny, but we did not see anything to be merry about. It was rather serious business with us.

"Where do you intend to stop tonight?" asked the ex-supercargo.

We said that we did not know. We were looking for a place to rest and refresh ourselves.

"Well, go to that house near the mission, and you will find shelter for the night. Tell the ranchero to charge the bill to me."

"Thanks," I remarked, "but as my friend Lewey so forcibly puts it we are not tramping beggars just at present."

At this moment Jack, who wanted his supper, and was impatient at the long conference, uttered a doleful bark.

"Nice dog that of yours, boys," Mr. Robinson said. "Will you sell him?"

"No, sir. He is not for sale," was our prompt response.

"I will give you five dollars for him," the gentleman urged, a large sum considering that every house in Santa Barbara had from four to ten curs lying about the court-yards, and yelping at all hours of the night.

Perhaps he thought our poverty could be relieved in the way of trade, but if such was the case he was mistaken, for Lewey spoke hotly and indignantly.

"Not for five hundred dollars vould ve sell de dog vot has been vid us in trouble and in pleasure, loves all de same vot ve loves, him dot has stood by us ven ve vanted friends, and nebber turned his back on us ven an enemy appeared. He is part of us, and in good fortune or in bad, if ve has a bone or a crust, poor little Jack skall share it vid us, and receive de biggest part even if ve is starvin'. Dat is de kind of boys ve is, vot has a dog ve vill not sell for money, nor love, nor friendship. Five dollars," the indignant Lewey repeated. "No, not for five dousand vould ve take for de animile, and dat is our answer, now and foreber, amen."

The gentlemen laughed at the French lad's enthusiasm, but it was not a smiling matter for us, so I nodded assent to Lewey's impassioned speech, and believed all that he uttered, and agreed to it.

"How about the horses?" asked the ex-supercargo. "They are nice animals, and I will buy them if you have the power to sell."

"The mustangs are ours," I answered. "We came by them in a fair and honorable manner, but where we go they will also go, and no sum that you can offer will purchase them. The horses and dog are the only friends we have in California, and those we will keep as long as we have the power to claim them," and off we rode, leaving the two gentlemen to speculate as to the temper of the boys they had encountered, lads who would not sell what they owned, a new idea for California, where money had its purchasing power among all classes of officials.

We did not notice the adobe house that was pointed out to us, but found another where we saw a ranchero standing in the doorway, a man whom we had seen many times on our ship, and whom we had laughed and joked with when he brought hides to the beach for the rich ranche owners. He was glad to see us, and offered to give us some supper and breakfast, a feed of barley for our horses, and shelter for the night, all for a small sum, if we had money enough to pay, if not we were welcome to everything without cost.

We intimated that we could find a few spare dollars, and then piquetted our horses, fed them, had the usual supper, — tortillas and an olia, — and after it was finished strolled about the town, past Don Noriego's house, where I saw his young and handsome daughter sitting on the veranda of her residence, and playing some soft, low notes on a guitar. I stood leaning on the wall of the court-yard, near where I had eaten my first dinner in Santa Barbara, and listened to her performance for more than an hour, but she never noticed me, probably supposing that I was a ranchero visiting the town, and attracted by the music, as there were a dozen other people present as well as Lewey and myself, and we attracted no attention in the twilight, being in Mexican costume, and broad sombreros drawn well over our faces. We smoked two or three pipes of tobacco while waiting, and at last the moon came up, and its silvery wealth of light shone on the people who were close to the veranda. I noted the old don and family, and wondered if they would recognize me if I went forward, spoke to them, and told them who I was.

But I was fearful of a repulse, and to be mortified in the presence of a beautiful woman is a terrible disgrace in the eyes of a boy, and so, with a sigh, I turned away from the court yard, and we shaped our course toward the beach, and, because I was silent and reflective, Lewey also assumed a sad expression, and at last turned to me, and asked, —

"Thom, mon bon ami, is you still spoons on de gal?" just as though I was in love with the lady we had heard playing on the guitar, and Lewey's warm heart went out of its way to meet and sympathize with me in my loneliness.

"Thom," the French boy asked, "does you love her more den you does me?"

And he put out his hand in a beseeching, half-timid manner, and there, near the beach of Santa Barbara, with the full moon shining down upon our heads, and Jack at our feet, wondering at the quietness of our proceedings, we shook hands, looked into each other's eyes, and then, without a word being spoken, resumed our walk, and presently sat down on the damp sand, and gazed at the white surf, as it rolled and tumbled on the beach, and roared mildly in a language that we could understand, for it told of gales at sea, and reefed topsails, wet jackets, and hard work.

While we sat there the Sterling's boat came on shore for the captain, and we watched the boys as they landed through the rollers, and contrasted their labor with our own, when we had the same duties to perform. The lads came toward us, but we did not speak to them, and, as they supposed we were greasers, who could not understand English, they paid no attention to us, but tumbled around the beach, and blanked the master for being so late in coming down from the town.

But he made his appearance at last, and the boat was pulled through the surf to the ship, and then we heard the men hoist the gig up, and over the water came the ringing, clear tones of the bell, as it struck half past nine, or three bells, in nautical parlance.

We strolled back to the town, past the houses where fandangos were flourishing, to our quarters, saw that our horses were resting quietly, and then lay down on our blankets, and, with saddles for pillows, went to sleep, Jack nestling close to our heads, and occasionally dreaming of fighting mountain lions or coyotes, but only a sharp word was necessary to awaken him to the fact that he had made a mistake. Then he would sigh to think that all was not real, scratch or bite a flea, and go to sleep again, sometimes snoring like a human being, he was so tired with his long journey through the day.

Our host returned from a fandango about twelve o'clock, and did us the honor of stumbling over us in his course to a rude bed, where his wife had been slumbering for some hours, as he had not thought it necessary to invite her to accompany him on his tour of pleasure, acting like many husbands of modern times, outside of California.

At sunrise we were aroused, even the sleepy ranchero being stirred up by the shrill-voiced spouse, who scolded in the choicest of Spanish for the man's misdeeds of the night before, all of which he received with an imbecile grin, as though long custom had taught him the folly of replying to her sharp tongue.

The lady was kind enough to prepare our breakfast, and then, as this was the last day of our long journey, we took a little more pains with our costumes, washed some of the accumulated dirt and dust from our persons, put on a fresh flannel shirt, and at eight o'clock were ready for our gallop to Ranche Refugio.

"How much shall we pay you for our entertainment?" we asked the host, but the man shook his head, and said, as he glanced anxiously toward his partner,—

"Not a medio. You are welcome," and then added, in a whisper, "The wife is a little loco this morning, because she thinks I danced with the girls last night. If you desire to make her a present I shall have no objections. Anything to keep peace in the family."

I gave the woman a four-real piece, and she was satisfied, for her face lost some of its sternness, and she even asked us to come and remain another night when we were disposed, a request that her husband seconded.

We rode slowly down the main street to the beach, and took one more look at the calm, beautiful bay, and the roaring surf. A boat was on shore from the Sterling, taking off hides, the men up to their hips in water, none too warm at that season of the year, and we could hear the sailors blank California every time there was an unusually large roller, which almost lifted the persons who held the boat's bow in place off their feet. This sounded so natural that we could not help snickering, for it reminded us of other days, when we performed the same kind of work, and indulged in the same strong expletives.

The sailors heard us laugh, and one of the men said, with a growl and an oath,—

"You bloody greasers, we wish you had to do this job. Then you would grin out of the other side of your mouths."

"Gently on the oaths, shipmate," I remarked in a quiet tone. "We did that kind of labor for most three years, and had our share of surf and duckings."

"Who in the bloody thunder are you anyhow?" the man asked, for he did not recollect our faces, although he had seen us often on board the Admittance when the Sterling first came on the coast.

Our Mexican costumes had so changed our appearance that even messmates would not have recognized us very readily. Besides, a little soft down had began to appear on our upper lips, and we were very particular to cultivate it for all that it was worth, as it made us look a little more manly, relieving us of the green, boyish appearance we had assumed for so many years.

As all the shore party were attracted by the conversation, I thought it only right that the sailor should have an answer, so said, in a dignified tone,—

"This gentleman," pointing to Lewey, "is the governor of the State, while I am only the commander of the army, and have the title of general."

"It is a blanked lie," roared the old salt. "You are two bloody beachcombers, and run away from some whale ship. I can tell by the cut of your jibs."

We thought it was not worth while to continue the conversation as we were getting the worst of it. The man had not come far from the truth, so, with a laugh at the sailor's remark, we turned from the hard sand of the beach, and struck the trail that led to the ranche, our route being on and near the seashore the whole distance.

It was a delightful ride that morning, for the ocean was on our left, and the coast range of mountains on our right, and a gentle breeze from the northwest ruffled the surface of the water, cool and bracing. A late shower had laid the dust, and revived the drooping grass and flowers. There was no mud to splash through, as would have been the case in the early part of the wet season, when water sometimes falls in torrents for several days.

We were seemingly all impatience to see the girls for whose sakes we had made such sacrifices, and wondered how they would receive us, if with joy or coldness. Yet we dreaded to reach the goal of our hopes, and soon after passing Point Arena let our horses walk for half an hour, each of us busy with his own thoughts. When Lewey looked up, and saw that I was watching his face, the lad laughed, and said, —

"I dink de same ding dat you does. Ve has been fools, and now ve must go on and be bigger vons, hey?"

"I still love Anita," I sighed.

"Dat is not so, and you knows it," was the candid remark. "If you vas von caballero grand you vould not take de girl for a vife, but look in some udder quarter, vare you vould not ashamed be. Dat know I quite plain. But ve has pledged our vord, and a Frenchman nebber go back on dat — nebber. His honor is at stake."

"Especially when you made love to Florencia at the lonely ranche," I remarked.

"Vell, dat vas von exception," was the candid reply. "I lose my head dar, but now de honor of a Frenchman all come back, and he remember his vord and his vows." Then he hesitated for a moment, and continued, "But I vish dat dey had uttered been nebber, and if de girls is married cry shall not I."

Perhaps he expressed my sentiments in a measure, for it must be remembered that we had not seen the objects of our affection for several months, and a boy's love is not supposed to last forever when separated from the one he thinks so beautiful.

After a while we loped along, and by twelve o'clock were near the gulch that led to the ranche, where we had landed so many times in the surf. We walked our horses up the ravine to the house where the pretty sisters resided, and with whom Lewey and I had waltzed one afternoon. How the old days came back to us as we recognized familiar scenes and sights. My heart was beating so strongly that I could hear its motion, and felt nervous and weak, so much so that I dismounted, and went to the young ladies' house, and asked for a drink of water.

Both of the senoritas were at home, and readily complied with my request. Then they politely asked us to partake of some fruit, and sent a peon for it when we did not decline the offer. They saw that we were foreigners and travelers, and tried to make our rest agreeable. They did not recognize us until we made ourselves known, and then expressed astonishment at our being where we were, as they supposed we had arrived home long ago, even if the matter had been considered for a moment by young ladies who had no special interest in us or our ship.

We did not inform the girls that we were on a matrimonial errand, as Lewey, in his usual careful manner, thought that it was just as well not to, the beauty of the ladies beginning to make an impression on his susceptible heart, and he said that it was always best to have an anchor to the windward, meaning, I suppose, that if we did not find Anita and Engracia all we desired, we could repudiate them, and fall back upon the sisters, in the hope that they might be induced to smile on us, but they were far above us in rank and fortune, and could look higher in every respect for a matrimonial market.

We did not offer to leave the house of the pretty sisters until we had controlled our agitation. Then we bade farewell to the senoritas, mounted our horses, and went to the well-remembered adobe hut where Anita and Engracia resided. With flushed faces and beating hearts we dismounted and approached the door, which stood wide open, with a fire in front of the premises, and an olia simmering on the coals, showing that dinner was nearly ready.

The noise we made attracted attention, and an old woman came to the door, and looked at us in wonderment and surprise.

"Engracia," Lewey asked. "Where is she?" and to have judged by the lad's face one would have thought that on his question hung a matter of life and death.

"Anita," I said. "Tell me where she is, and that she is well."

Still the old woman looked at us, and did not answer a word. A feeling of gloom took possession of our minds. The girls were dead or ill, we thought.

"Who are you?" the woman asked at last.

"Do you not recollect us? We are the boys who used to give you bread and tobacco. The same ones who made love to your daughters, and presented them with stockings, money, and other things," we both cried eagerly.

The old woman advanced toward us in a hurried manner, and a look of peculiar determination on her face. Ah, she recognized us at last, was all ready to give us a kind, mother-in-law embrace, and call down blessings and prayers for happiness on our heads, and we were willing to fall upon our knees, and receive the orisons that were to ascend to heaven in our behalf.

"Mother," cried Lewey, with a sob, "for such we must now call you, speak to us of those we esteem so much. Let us see them, so that we can feast our eyes on their beauty, and tell them that we have never ceased to think, even for a moment, of those we adore, and have loved so many months. But now our reward is to come, and with joyful hearts we will greet your beautiful daughters."

"Will you?" asked the old woman, in a tone that was intended to be sarcastic. "Ladrones of the devil, what sent you here to an honest woman's house? Get you gone, or there will be trouble."

Did we hear aright? Were those peppery remarks directed to us, to boys who had supplied the old woman with pounds and pounds of pilot bread and tobacco, who had been encouraged to call at all times, and never a word said against our engagements? No, there was some mistake, or else it was all a dream, and we should at last awaken from it, and laugh at our fears and strange fancies.

"My good madre," began Lewey, in a soothing tone, " you do not recognize us. Look at us well, and see your future sons-in-law, who will be proud to labor for your welfare," and then the lad added in English, " I kick her de house out de fust day I is spliced. I nebber live vid her near me, no nebber, by gar."

"Mal vagabondos," the old woman remarked, " I know both of you, and have heard enough. Get you gone from here, or I'll scald the life out of your heretic carcasses, as sure as I have a patron saint."

"Vell, dis beats me," my French friend said. "I vould rudder face a mountain lion dan dat dreadful voman at any dime. Is dis de veddin' feast to invited vich ve are?"

I could only look on, and wonder what had changed the sentiments of the mother. Had we come all the way from San Diego to listen to such abuse? To be called thieves and vagabonds? To be grossly insulted by an old hag, who had eaten our bread, and smoked our tobacco, and glad enough to get them?

This was putting our love to a severe test, but one thing I was resolved upon. Never should that old woman live in the house with me and mine. I had heard enough of her tongue to last a life time, and what could I expect if she was always near me?

"What shall we do?" I asked Lewey, who was inclined to stand his ground, like the boy on the burning deck from whence all had fled.

"I vill nebber run from a voman," he answered. "A Frenchman is brave, and can fight, but he nebber runs, no nebber," and as he spoke the woman raised an earthen jar from the fire, and the way that lad walked backward to get out of her reach was suggestive of a panic if she had but pursued.

"Don't be afraid of her, Lewey," I said. "She is harmless."

And just as I uttered the words the old lady snatched up a burning brand, and was about to hurl it at my head, when Jack thought that he would take a hand, and show what he could do as a peacemaker, as he feared some desperate assault was about to be made on his best and most loved friends.

As the senora raised the burning fagot, having dropped the vessel of hot water, it being too cumbersome to use with facility, Jack supposed that an attack was to commence in earnest. He uttered a short, savage bark, and went for her bare feet and ankles, and perhaps a little above the latter, for he must have nipped the flesh, as the woman uttered a scream like that of an enraged mountain lion. Then she gave a jump in the air, and when she came down lost her balance and sat on the olla that was preparing for dinner. It was warm and liquid, and the soup must have burned her, for she clapped her hands to the after part of her thin and nearly the only garment she wore, and said some things that should not have been uttered by a woman who had prospective sons-in-law within hearing.

Her yells brought to the scene some of the neighbors, who came to sympathize and console her, and, as the people seemed to think we were to blame, Lewey motioned to our horses, so we mounted and rode swiftly away, not caring where as long as we were clear of that woman and her dreadful words and imprecations.

When we were out of sight of the home of our beloved girls we halted, and looked at each other in wonderment.

"Vell," said Lewey, "ebery von has said ve vos fools, and now vot does dink you on de subject?" a question hard to answer, for we did not know what we should do, or where we should go for even a night's lodging or a late dinner. Our love affairs wore a decidedly gloomy look, we thought, and what was to be our next move was a most important question, and one not easily answered. We had suffered and endured privations for the sake of two dark-eyed girls, and now we were thrown aside as useless lumber. But we had one satisfaction, — we felt as though our hearts were not quite broken even if we were jilted.

CHAPTER VIII.

A MUTUAL AGREEMENT. — AN OLD ACQUAINTANCE. — THE RANCHE. — A FANDANGO, AND AN UNEXPECTED MEETING. — A GRAND SURPRISE TO ALL. — DON ANTONIO SANCHOS PUTS IN AN APPEARANCE. — A STRUGGLE FOR LIFE. — A DISAPPOINTED GREASER. — ON THE MARCH. — A SWIFT EXECUTION. — A LADY'S GRATITUDE. — A NEW PROGRAMME. — THE ESCORT AND ENCAMPMENT.

MY French friend's question was an important one, and I took some time to answer it. We had not been received in a very hospitable manner, it was true, by the mother of the young girls we had hoped to marry, and our flight from the scene of her home was more like a panic than an orderly retreat. We had seen the old lady, and heard her in tones we could not fail to understand, but had obtained no glimpse of the daughters, and I wondered if they approved of such conduct on the part of their parent. We had not found plain sailing thus far, and what to do next was a question I could not answer, but did say in a frank manner, —

"Yes, Lewey, we have made fools of ourselves. Now what shall we do?"

"I tells you," he answered. "Ve vill go back to de pretty sisters, and makes love to dem."

Ah, what a boy he was for resources. Always ready with some plan to make life happy, and never casting a thought to the disagreeable part. He could turn from one girl to another without a sigh of regret for the failure of his projects, or a thought of the vows he had uttered.

The proposition he advanced was a tempting one, and I should not have hesitated to embrace it, except that my colder, northern blood convinced me that the plan was not a feasible one, for I doubted if the young ladies would be ready to listen to the ardent protestations of two penniless young men, wandering vagabonds, as the old woman had called us in her blind rage.

"But vot can ve do?" my friend asked, after I had refused to listen to his advice.

"We can return to Santa Barbara, and ship on board the Sterling, or some other vessel," I said.

"Nebber," was the candid reply. "I does no more vork afore de mast unless I is starvin'. Somethin' vill turn up for us. You see if speaks de truth do not I."

And, as he finished his indignant protest, a ranchero hove in sight, loping along a trail that led toward the mountains. The Mexican drew up when he saw two strangers, seated on horseback, as if undecided where to go and what to do, passed the usual salutations, and touched his sombrero.

"Buenos dias, senors," he said. "What can I do for you?"

He was a young fellow, not more than twenty years of age, and his face seemed familiar. We were confident that we had seen him before, but where was the question. All at once I recollected the boy who had escorted us to a fandango at San Luis Obispo, when we had been sent on shore to watch some hides at the Cave, while one-half of the number was stolen during our absence at the dance.

"Do you not remember us?" I asked, as soon as I was assured of the fact that we had met before.

"No, senors, I think not," was his answer.

We then recalled to his mind the night at the Cave, and the fandango, and the young fellow's face showed that he was pleased at seeing his old friends. At the same time I always suspected that he had a share in the purloined queros, or at least knew where they went, and who took them. But we were willing to forgive him, as we needed friends, and hoped we had found one in the person of the ranchero, whose name, he told us, was Alberto.

"What are you doing here?" the young fellow asked. "You are riding around the country like gallant Mexican caballeros while I supposed you were on board of your ship."

"We came here to be married," Lewey said, "but the girls we were to wed have disappeared, and their mother gave us such a warm reception that we were forced to cut and run for it."

When we told him the name of the girls his dark face and eyes were lighted up with merriment.

"You did well to escape with whole bones, for the old woman has the worst tongue of any person at the ranche. Her daughters are near, I know, for I saw them a day or two since as I rode past the house. Some one has poisoned the mother's mind against you, for she would marry the girls to the devil for the sake of getting them off her hands. No one dares to take them for fear of such a mother-in-law, as she would command the house."

This was not cheerful news to us, for men do not want wives who are thrown at their heads by ambitious mothers, anxious for a good match for their daughters. However, the woman had offered to pitch at us something more ardent than a spouse, and we thought she must be prejudiced against us, supposing we were fortune hunters, in search of heiresses, although the passionate parent was not worth fifty dollars, house and all, and we could command more than that sum in ready money.

"Come home with me," the young ranchero said, after the gravity of our situation had been explained to him. "I have recently obtained a ranche, and am stocking it with cattle. It is only a mile or two from here. I have an old Indian woman to cook, so you will not starve. Remain as long as you please. The deer are abundant, and once in a while a bear is seen. Come with me, and we will have lots of fun. There is a fandango near me once a week, and you will see the girls at some of them, I am sure."

This was a fair and unexpected offer, and we readily accepted it, because there was nothing better to do. So we thanked the young fellow, and rode along with him, giving full details of our adventures on the route from San Diego, but when we mentioned that we had encountered and killed Apaches his wonder and admiration knew no bounds. He thought we were first-class heroes, and deserved to be immortalized and made saints, for he had heard the most wonderful stories of the savage and cunning warriors, and thought that no white man could stand before them.

Then the young ranchero gave us a full history of himself. He had been left a fortune of five hundred dollars by an uncle, and with a hundred more which he had saved, bought a ranche, and a few head of cattle. His hacienda consisted of five thousand acres of good valley land, and he could have as much more as he desired for the asking. Lewey looked at me, and winked. Here, he thought, was the chance we had so long sought and desired. We determined to enter into partnership with Alberto, if he would take us, and become cattle raisers in earnest. But there was time enough to talk of such matters after we had seen the ranche, the stock, and its accommodations. With the Mexican's knowledge, and our business tact, we thought success would be an assured thing. We could hunt and fish, ride and play, and do but little work, except at the season for rounding in and branding. This was the life for us, and one we had depicted many times. If fortune crowned our efforts, in a few years we could become grandees of the country, men whom captains and supercargoes would look up to and respect for their wealth.

We found Alberto's adobe house not much in the way of pretention, yet it had two rooms and an out-building, where the usual stock of odds and ends had accumulated, — old saddles, hides, fleas, barley, tallow in quero bags, and a hammock for the Indian woman to sleep in. The furniture in the house was composed of two chairs, home made, with strips of hide for seats, a rude bedstead of red wood, a rough table, some cheap prints of various saints plastered on the walls, a crucifix, and four dogs, the latter disposed to resent Jack's intrusion, and then suddenly left our animal to his own meditations, when he showed a disposition to lick the Mexican's curs, without waiting for the formality of an introduction.

Don Alberto welcomed us to his home with all the grace and airs of a grandee. He made us at ease, helped us piquette our horses where the grass was freshest, stirred up his cook to get dinner, and, after we had dined on an olia that was not so bad as some we had eaten, mounted our horses, and rode over the hacienda, which we found well watered from mountain springs. The cattle looked fat and healthy, while there were about fifty horses on the place, which we did not count of much value, as there were more than enough for every man, woman, and child in California scattered about the various ranches of the State.

We were pleased with all that we saw, and retired that night with the firm intention of buying two-thirds interest in the ranche if we could come to terms with the owner.

The next day we took our rifles and went after deer, saw quite a number, so that there was no trouble in securing one for immediate want, and that evening, as we sat around the fire and smoked our pipes and cigarettes, proposed a partnership with our host. He was a little surprised at the thought, as he had not considered such a project possible. We pointed out how we could be of use in many respects, that the stock might be increased, and money made in the course of a few years, if there was no disease or drought. We urged him to name a price, and he said that he would think of the matter, and let us know the next day.

But the next day came, and Don Alberto had not made up his mind, like all Mexicans. He wanted more time to think of the project, and desired the advice of some friends. We made no objections to the delay, but went on just as though we were interested in the farm. Lewey and I made a bedstead of some red wood, a nice table, chairs of deers' horns, kept the larder well supplied with game, and even gained the good will of the sullen Indian cook, who rarely smiled, but seemed to be ever looking for that great liberator who was to free the peons from bondage and the hard toil of the country.

It must not be supposed for a moment that we informed Don Alberto of the fact of our having some gold on our persons, enough to buy an interest in the ranche. We were too well acquainted with the Mexican character to do any such thing. The fact would have been noised abroad, spread from mouth to mouth, and some day we might have found a knife at our throats, or one in our sides, and the belts of gold gone, never to return, or life either, for that matter.

No, we simply said that a foreigner at Santa Barbara would let us have all the money we wanted, when the proper time arrived, and that yarn was as good as any, for it left the impression that we were without money on our persons, and so escaped the avaricious attentions of the ladrones, who did no work, and considered gringos lawful plunder.

In our distant retreat we heard no word of the war, or how it was progressing. It was a rare thing for any one to come near us, and we did not venture in the direction of Ranche Refugio, for fear the spiteful mother would again give us a piece of her mind. The girls sent no word, and we supposed they had forgotten us, and turned their attention to men in their own class in life.

About a week after our arrival a neighboring ranchero rode up one morning, and said that he was to have a fandango at his house, and wanted Don Alberto and his guests to come over and enjoy the festivities. There were to be lots of pretty girls, and nice dancers, and no end of fun. We thought it possible that we might meet Anita and Engracia there, so said that we would go, but were so much disappointed in the conduct of the girls that we really did not care whether we went or remained at home. We considered that they had treated us badly, after all our endeavors to please them.

At eight o'clock we started for the house where the fandango was to take place. As it was not more than a mile from our quarters, and the moon was bright, we concluded to walk the distance instead of riding, as was customary in the country.

As we turned down the trail, we noticed a dozen or twenty mounted men gallop along the path, and disappear in the chapparel on one side of the road, but paid no attention to them, as we supposed they were some of the invited guests, and were crossing the country so that they could save time and distance. To be sure Alberto said, —

"The fandango will be a great success, for all the caballeros for miles in extent may be there, to judge by the horsemen who have gone on ahead of us. I wonder who they can be? I did not seem to recognize any of them."

We did not pay much attention to his words, but trudged on, and soon came to the adobe building where the dance was to be held. It was lucky we had left Jack at the house, for there were enough dogs present to have made him unhappy, every visitor bringing one or more, and they fought and quarreled in a lively manner, and when seven or eight had a roaring, combined fight the ends of reatas were applied to all alike to make them realize that no one was to come to blows except their masters.

When we entered the house there were twenty men and thirty women and ladies present. A guitar and harp furnished the music, and already the fandango was going on. We glanced around the place, but did not see the girls we were so anxious to meet. Every one received us pleasantly, and many a bright eye was cast toward us, in hope that we would ask for a waltz. We looked on for a few minutes, and then, finding the room warm, and the air uncomfortable, went outside, and, as we did so, saw some horsemen moving away to the right and left, in the shadow of the trees, as though to gain the rear of the house undetected.

We wondered, but paid no attention to the matter, for just then a soft hand was laid on my arm, and a sweet voice spoke my name. I turned, and there before me stood Anita and Engracia, looking more lovely than we had ever seen them.

Lewey held out his arms, and pronounced the name of the girl he had professed to love so deeply, and with a bound she was enclosed in them, and tender kisses were rained down on her face and neck, and he was calling her all the little angels he could think of in English, French, and Spanish, a jumble of everything, for he could not speak fast enough to satisfy his hungry heart.

"Will you let my sister be devoured, while I stand here idle?" asked Anita, for the girls' sudden appearance had deprived me of motion and speech, and I could only look at her in wonder, and imagine I was dreaming.

But her tender words recalled me to myself. I put an arm around her waist, drew her gently to my breast, and kissed the willing lips that were raised for the greeting. For five minutes I did not speak I was so occupied with looking at the girl's dark eyes and handsome face, but when I found my voice asked,—

"My little dear, did you know that we were near you?"

"Yes," she answered very softly.

"And you remained away from us all this time, although you must have known we were anxious to see you?" I said in a reproachful tone.

"Do not upbraid us," Anita remarked. "If you but knew how much we have suffered on your account you would forgive us."

"Tell me all," I said, as I kissed the lips that were so near my own, and glanced toward the French lad to see if he was similarly inclined, and it is useless to say that he was too busy to pay the slightest attention to me or the girl I held in my arms.

Anita hesitated for a moment, as though to recall the past, and said,—

"Some days since a strange man called at the house, and had a long conversation with our mother. He went away, and we did not see him again, but a few hours after he had departed the good priest of the parish came to the place, heard our confessions, and then talked with our parent. We do not know what he said, but after the holy father had gone we were told that you were vagabonds, ladrones, and no better than runaway sailors, unable to support wives, or to be true to them, and, oh, worse than all, you were denounced as heretics, and a curse and excomunion were threatened us if we dared to listen to you, or speak with you again. It was frightful, was it not?"

I thought that it was, at the same time I did not blame the padre, for he was right in looking after the welfare of his flock, and seeing that no harm came to its members if he could prevent it.

"We were told that you and your friend were on the way to the ranche," Anita continued, "but that it was probable you would never live to arrive."

I thought of the encounter on the mountain top, and saw that a trap had been laid for us, but by whom I could not just divine.

"For several days," the little girl went on, "our mother kept a strict watch on the trail that led to Santa Barbara, while we were imprisoned in a room in the house, and told not to stir from the premises, and when you were discovered approaching our mother alone received you."

"I should think she did," I remarked. "I remember the reception very well."

"We did not dare to speak to you, and say that we were near and true," the little girl continued, "but it was very painful to hear you called all manner of hard names, and when mother fell into the pot containing the olla you did not laugh, did you, dear?"

"No, love, but we desired to."

"Well, she says that you did, and that made her more angry than anything else. Mother has a sharp tongue and a bad one, so you can imagine what we had to endure after you were gone."

"Can you describe the man who came to your house and warned your mother and the priest against us?" I asked.

"Yes, I think that I can. He was an evil-looking person, tall and thin, and on his right hand was a vivid scar. I remember it well, for when he smiled he rubbed it with his left fingers. His frown was more agreeable than a smile. I hated him the moment I saw him, for his presence was evil."

I had no difficulty in recognizing the portrait. It was that of Don Antonio Sanchos, whom we supposed we had got rid of forever. But it seemed not. He had laid a little trap on the mountains, and it fell through, and one of his gang had got badly bitten by a ball from my rifle, while the rest fled at the approach of the cavalry. Sanchos had sought to destroy us by an easy method, but for fear of some miscarriage of his plans had hurried on to Ranche Refugio, and warned the mother and the priest of our coming, poisoned their minds, and thus defeated a happy reunion.

"Anita," I said, as soon as the girl had concluded her story, "the man who visited your mother is our most determined enemy. He has persecuted us several times during the last few months, but we have thus far defeated him. He now takes a mean revenge by seeking to separate us. Do you think we could change your mother's will by calling on her and explaining our honorable intentions in regard to yourselves?"

"No," answered the girl quite promptly. "She hates, and would not hesitate to scald you if there was hot water on the fire at the time you appeared."

I shuddered as I imagined such a woman for a mother-in-law. I thought I loved the daughter, but did not like hot water, so resolved to give the old lady a wide berth, and not cross her hawse if I could prevent it.

"If I should see the priest, Anita, do you think he would listen to me?" I asked.

The little girl shook her head, as she nestled still closer to me, and put up her lips for some more kisses, as though she was hungry for them.

"He says that you are a cursed heretic," she whispered, "and, oh, I wish you were not."

"But my friend Lewey is a Catholic," I remarked. "The priest can have no objection to him."

"Yes, he says that the Frenchman is worse than the Yankee, because while the latter has no particular religion the former pretends to believe in the saints, yet never calls upon them, goes not to confession, and eats meat Fridays like a sinner. Is he as bad as all that?"

Now here was an excellent chance to follow the example of the world and blast the reputation of a friend, but I did nothing of the kind, for although Lewey was far from being a pious young man he was not as bad as some people would have believed him to be.

"My friend," I said, "eats meat on Friday because he does not keep the run of the days. He has not confessed for the simple reason that priests are scarce, and time is too precious for him to hunt them up. After he is married you will be surprised at his goodness."

"I hope I shall," she sighed. "If you had only half of his religion I should be satisfied."

I did not feel complimented, and was about to declare that I was a model of goodness, when the faint blast of a trumpet was heard in the woods at the rear of the adobe house, and then a dozen horsemen showed themselves, and seemed to hold a conference. I thought it strange that the rancheros should act in such a mysterious manner, but supposed it was a peculiar method they had of enjoying themselves, and surprising their friends. The dance was going on in full force, and no one paid any attention to the bugle call, even Engracia and Lewey not noticing it, but it might have been because they were so occupied with their own affairs, much more interesting than the galloping of horsemen.

"Before I can marry you," Anita whispered, "you must become a good Catholic. Will you do so?"

"Even if I consent, my dear, the priest will not bless our union," I remarked. "What shall we do in that case?"

For a moment she dropped her head, and appeared to think of the matter, then looked up with love and confidence beaming from her dark eyes and blushing face.

"If the good father will not bless us, then take me as I am, without his sanction," she cried, and put her arms around my neck, and tears fell from her eyes as she thought of the deep significance of her words.

"Do you intend it, Anita?" I asked, for I knew that it meant ostracism from her church and home, from relatives and friends, a moral death for one so young, and all for love of a gringo.

"I mean all that I say," was the firm reply. "Take me when you will and let us hope that the saints will pardon us, and the good father act justly when he sees that we are firm in our loves."

This was a denouement that I had not expected in so sudden a manner I liked the girl and was willing to marry her, but I did not wish to subject her to unjust remarks and suspicions, or cause her a moment's unhappiness. No wonder I hesitated, and considered what I should do, but my thoughts were interrupted by Lewey exclaiming in a tone of triumph, —

"Thom, old boy, love has conquered at last, as it alvays vill ven urged by firmness and sincerity. Engracia has said she come to me vill vidout de blessin' of de holy fadder. Thus is my long and steady devotion revarded to be."

To have heard his rapturous exclamations one would have supposed he was a lover whose constancy had never been questioned, or whose thoughts had remained true to the one object of his adoration.

Before I could answer the young man there was another faint blast from a bugle, this time in front of the building, and a trumpet in the rear of us repeated the note. Then we saw horsemen closing in around the house, and by the moonlight we judged there were twenty or more caballeros near us.

Anita and Engracia caught the sounds, looked up, and then exclaimed hastily, —

"Enter the house, in the name of the saints. Oh, what is there in store for us at the present time?"

A lively fandango was going on, and we could see the performers posing and moving to the sounds of the guitar and harp. No one was outside except our own party. The dogs uttered some unmelodious sounds in response to the trumpets, but as they were always yelping no one paid any attention to them.

The girls dragged us into the house, and before we asked for an explanation we could hear the military command of, —

"Halt. Let no one pass. Shoot all who attempt to escape."

The words were uttered so loud that even the dancers I eard them, and suspended their gyrations, while the musicians' fingers no longer struck the strings of their instruments. The Mexicans looked at each other in surprise, while the women gathered in one corner of the room, and showed a disposition to give us the usual specimen of female hysterics. All but An ita and Engracia. They remained by our sides, and seemed calm in comparison with the rest of their sex.

We heard the clank of sabres, and the clinking of carbine locks, as though guns were got ready for execution, and in a minute more three men entered the room, and it needed no second glance to recognize two of them as Don Antonio Sanchos and his brother Carlos, while the third was an officer of the Mexican cavalry, dressed in uniform, and rather a good-looking young fellow. We imagined that we had seen him before, at Monterey, when we gave an exhibition before the élite of the town.

"Let no one attempt to escape," cried the elder Sanchos. "The door is guarded, and the man who crosses the threshold without consent will surely die."

The women uttered shrill screams, and the men looked at each other in wonderment, and felt for the long knives in their leggings and sashes. Sanchos noticed the movement, and said, —

"The ranchero who draws a cuchillo, and attempts to use it, dies like a dog. Keep your hands quiet. We come here in the name of the law."

The Mexican officer leaned on his sabre, and looked on. He did not speak, or appear to appreciate the part he was playing.

"Enganchadors," was heard all over the room, and it seemed as if Sanchos was not regarded with favor by the rancheros.

"No, we are not enganchados," Don Antonio said. "We are not crimps, as you call us, but Mexicans, loyal to our country and State, and anxious for its welfare. We have the warrant of General Castro for the enrollment of men for military duty, and we now call for volunteers. Monterey is in danger. The heretic Fremont, and his band of robbers, is on the way from the Sacramento River to the town of our devotion. He must be driven back, or captured. To do this we need brave men. No others are wanted. I will now enroll the names of all who wish to serve the State. Let each man step forward who desires to volunteer."

Not one moved. They did not see the fun of leaving their ranches, and fighting for a State government that paid no money for services.

"Come," grinned Sanchos. "Who speaks first? Who desires the honor of being the premier volunteer? What, no one comes forward? In a few minutes I shall select those I want, and when I name a man he will go. Think of promotion, and glory to be gained in conquering the gringos."

The rancheros were not impressed with the scoundrel's eloquence. The gringos might go to blazes for all that they cared. They did not want any of the fight that was going on.

"Perhaps these young men will volunteer?" Don Sanchos asked, and then turned full upon us, and his smile was not sweet. "I know they anticipate a life of happiness and ease as husbands of the girls whose hands they hold, but let them think how much more pleasant it will be for their prospects when they return to this place all covered with glory and honor. Shall I have the happiness of taking your names, muchachos?" and the fellow gave us a look that did not betoken a friendly feeling.

"No," answered Lewey, "we have no desire to fight against the United States. We shall remain here."

"I think not. You will go with us," was the stern reply.

"Do you dare to force a Frenchman and an American into your army?" Lewey asked, forgetting that we had registered.

"We dare to take any one who has signed a matriculador. You are subjects of Mexico, having thrown off your allegiance to France and the United States. You were allowed a month's notice before being drafted in the army. That month has nearly passed. Tonight you go with us, and tomorrow you will be on the way to Monterey. You have baffled me once or twice, but now my time has come. I coaxed the mother of the girls to let them visit this fandango, for I knew you were near here, and would probably attend. Fools, did you think that I was asleep, or had forgotten the indignities heaped upon me? There was only one thing I feared, and that was you might be induced to ship on board of some vessel as you have been advised to do. Then I might have lost you and my revenge. But love drove you here. I had prepared the way for your arrival. The reception was a warm one, was it not? I should like to have witnessed it. You gringo dogs, my hour of triumph has arrived. Every one in this room might escape, but you I shall hold on to."

"You will believe us," Engracia cried, as she clung to Lewey, "that we had no hand in this plot. We did not know that you were to be here, and were surprised when our madre told us we might venture to the dance. This is the man who visited our mother, and poisoned her mind, and that of the good priest. To him are we indebted for all of our misfortunes, for all of the unhappiness that has befallen us. Spy of the devil, we hope you will be punished some day for your crimes."

The man bowed, as if complimented. If we had been armed we might have defied him, but our pistols and rifles were at the ranche, and we were powerless to do our will on the dark-faced scoundrel.

"Shame on a government that employs such men," cried a voice, but the other rancheros present were cowed, and did not dare to express their minds. Each wanted to escape military duty if possible regardless of the others.

"Once more, will you sign for service?" demanded Sanchos.

"No, we 'll see you blanked first," shouted Lewey, and took a step toward our persecutor, Engracia clinging to him.

The pimp and spy raised one of his hands as a signal, and through the open door flew a reata. It encircled the French lad's head and arms, and in an instant he was prostrate on the floor, struggling and powerless. But, oh, the profusion of words he uttered in his native tongue, Spanish, and English, was enough to shock the sensibilities of an old salt, had he been present to have heard them.

I broke from the embrace of Anita, who strove to hold me back, and rushed to my friend's assistance, and as I did so I heard a number of voices shout, —

"Quedo," or "take care," but paid no attention to them. I saw that Lewey was a prisoner, and knew that I should do what I could to release him, or share his fate.

Before I could gain his side another lariat flew through the air, dropped over my head, and I was jerked to the floor, a prisoner, pinioned so securely that I could not move my arms, although my feet were free, and I kicked at Sanchos' shins, and did him some damage, I hope, for he stooped down and rubbed them, and blanked me in choice Spanish for the pain I caused him.

Anita and Engracia knelt by our sides, and tried to tear the reatas from our persons, but they made no progress in the undertaking, while Don Sanchos smiled at the girls for their devotion. The Mexican military gentleman lighted a cigarette, and looked as though rather amused at the sight before him. It was something novel, to say the least, or perhaps reminded him of the method of impressing the Indians when wanted for some drudgery, such as clearing the roads, or pulling guns through the mud.

"Listen to me," said Sanchos, as soon as the confusion had subsided. "As sospechosos I can doom you to an instant death. I have that power. But I want you, for my own purposes, to serve against the United States. That shall complete my revenge, and benefit Mexico at the same time. Will you do so?"

"See you blanked first," was our ready answer. "Do your worst, you black-faced son of a sea-cook."

He understood English enough to know that we had refused his offer. He motioned with his hand, and a greaser entered the room, bearing a reata made from the tails and manes of horses. It was rough and strong. A knot was formed, and thrown over my neck. Another Mexican stepped forward with a similar rope, and placed it around my friend's windpipe, and then the blood of the French lad showed its fiery heat.

"Ladrones and perros," he said, "do you know that this rope feels uncomfortable? That a woman's arm is to be preferred to a reata? Unbind my limbs and I will agree to fight any three of you greasers all at once, or first one and then the other."

He spoke in Spanish so that all could understand him. The Mexican officer smiled, and lighted a fresh cigarette. He was taking matters coolly, at all events.

"Tighten the ropes," said Sanchos, and, by Jove, they did, and the feeling was not comfortable, for the rough reatas cut into our flesh, and breathing became difficult. Anita and Engracia were on their knees beside us, uttering the most doleful of cries, and wringing their hands.

"Will you sign?" shouted Sanchos, watching the strain of the reatas.

We were nearly insensible, and made a movement of assent.

"Loosen the ropes," was the order, and we felt them taken from our necks. We were some minutes in recovering our respiration, and then Lewey said in English, —

"Country is all vell enough, I s'pose, but I is too young to die vid many sins on my head, and some day ve skall get a crack at dat greaser, and, on, von't ve make him jump if ve does. Ve vill sign, and don't you be afeared. Ve skall not hurt de Americans by all de fightin' dat ve does. You jist be governed by me in dis ding, and ve comes out all right. Besides, vot kind of husbands vould two cold dead mens make? No girls have us vould. Dey like live husbands, and blame them not I. Yes, ve vill sign anyding dat dey vants us to, and I vish I vas on board de old ship vonce more."

"Are you satisfied?" asked Sanchos, as soon as we were able to look around.

"Yes, we are satisfied that you can strangle us. What more do you want?" we demanded.

"Your signatures to this paper. I know that you can write. Sign," and he ordered our arms to be released, and thrust a pen into our hands.

We did not stop to read the whole document. We saw that it was an enrollment in the service of the State of California for the space of five years, unless sooner discharged, subject to all the pains of military discipline. That was enough for us. We signed, and the instant we had done so the

Mexican officer stepped forward, and told us to hold up our right hands. There was nothing to do but comply. He mumbled over some words, and then we were soldiers of Mexico, and the next instant Anita and Engracia were in our arms.

"Tear the fools apart," yelled Don Antonio. "The Mexican soldier has other business beside love-making."

Two men started to comply with the order. Then the Mexican officer came forward, sabre in his hand.

"Let the lovers alone," he said. "It is but a short time they will have for such trifling. They surely can enjoy themselves while they have the chance."

"But I order them to be separated," Sanchos thundered, "and my word is law here."

"Not quite," was the answer. "The men are now soldiers of Mexico, and as such they will obey me, not you. Your power ceased when they passed from civil life to that of a military career. Now the men are under my charge. Interfere with them at your peril."

Don Sanchos turned on the young officer as if to assault him, but the military man raised his sabre, and it would have fallen on the head of the scoundrel if he had advanced a step.

"I shall report you to General Castro," Sanchos muttered. "He will see that you are punished for daring to defy me."

"Caramba, you must suit yourself in that respect. I know my duty and you do not. I am no enganchador, or pimp, like you," and the young fellow showed the contempt that he felt for the man who had caused him such disagreeable duty. Then he turned to us, and said, —

"I recognize both of you young men. I was in Monterey the night you gave the exhibition. Diablo, how much I did laugh. I was told that you were matriculadors, and liable to serve in the army. Had I known all I would have remained away, and let you enjoy the company of the girls until you tired of them. Don Sanchos seems to have some spite against you. The best way to defeat it, and set him at defiance, is to go with me. I am a captain in the army, and you shall serve in my company. I promise you kind treatment, and plenty of work. Had you not signed that confounded matriculador I would let you go free. But it is too late. You must make the best of it, and be faithful to Mexico. Long life to the republic, and confusion to its enemies."

No one took up the cry and repeated it. The captain said that his name was Fernando, and that he was endeavoring to fill up his company, and should repair to Monterey as soon as possible to meet an expected attack by Fremont, his trappers and Indians.

"I know you have been sailors," the captain said, while Sanchos stood glowering at us, "for I have seen you on ship board many times while on the coast. You can ride quite fairly, but before you have been in the cavalry a year you will sit your horses like real rancheros. I noticed you in Santa Barbara the other day. You were well mounted, and looked like brave young fellows. I hope you will prove so. Serve the State faithfully, and when the war is over come here and marry the girls, and with them you can receive a grant of land that it will take you all day to ride over."

"Can we marry before we are forced to march?" I demanded.

"No. I want no new bridegrooms in my company. All thoughts of love must be thrown aside until the war is over."

The girls uttered a loud, wailing cry as they heard the command, and saw that their anticipated happiness was to be postponed to some indefinite period.

"I knows lots of girls in Monterey," Lewey whispered. "It von't be so bad as it seems. As soldiers of Mexico dey vill smile on us much more den eber."

No misfortune dampened that boy's courage or anticipations. He was always looking forward to something bright and pleasant, and did not propose to die with a broken heart, if he could help it. The girls would not have felt flattered had they understood my friend's comments on the situation, but luckily he spoke in English, so they were ignorant of his meaning.

"It is useless to keep up that howling," the captain remarked, as the girls stopped their cries to take breath, and then began again. "Go outdoors and do your spooning there. We have some serious work to do here yet."

"Are you not afraid to trust us so far away from your presence?" I asked.

"No, for the place is surrounded by my men, and any attempt to escape would be disastrous to you. Give me your word that you will report here tomorrow morning, with your horses and equipments, and you may see the girls home, and take a long farewell of them."

We looked at Don Sanchos and his brother Carlos, and the captain understood the meaning of the glances.

"You need not fear the enganchadors," the officer said, in a careless tone. "I shall keep them with me. The person who dares to raise a hand against a regular Mexican soldier would have but a few days to live. Do you promise?"

"Yes, senor, we promise," was our ready answer, for we saw that Don Antonio did not approve of the project, and we wanted to annoy him.

"Sergeant, pass these men and the girls outside of the line. Let them go where they please, and see that they are not annoyed," was the captain's command, but just as we were leaving the room our friend Alberto rushed forward.

"You will release me, senor captain?" he cried. "To serve in the army might ruin me. My cattle would go astray and my ranche overrun during my absence. Please let me return to my home, and I will donate twenty horses for the use of the government."

"The proposition is accepted," Don Sanchos cried. "As the agent of the State I have the power to grant release of services for a consideration. You can go," and Alberto left the room with us, and, confound him, he did not, or would not, take a hint, but walked all the way home with us and the girls, and stood staring like a born idiot while we talked, and kissed the young ladies. We told him to return to his ranche, and that we would join him in the course of an hour, but he said that fears for our safety prompted him to remain near us. We had a strong desire to strangle the young man, but finally concluded to let him live, then kissed the girls a sad farewell, and left them, promising to return as soon as possible.

"This is the end of all our hopes and ambitions, Lewey," I said, as we retraced our steps toward the ranche. "It is the saddest blow we have yet received."

"Don't you be cast down," my friend remarked. "De United States vill knock de Mexicans higher dan a kite in a leetle vile. Ve shall not hab much fightin' to do, and ven it is all ober den ve vill be married in earnest. I sees much fun in de life of a sojer. And, arter all, it is not good for a man to tie himself down ven he is young, and not seen much of de vorld. S'pose ve should meet some von ve liked better dan de girls ven it vas too late? By gar, dat vould be bad for us. All is for de best. I shall shed no tears. Ah, here comes de cavalry. Let us step into de chapparel, and vait for 'em to pass, for dey might make a mistake, and fire at de wrong parties."

We dodged out of the road, hid in the long grass, and counted forty horsemen, and eight impressed rancheros, who were on foot, and uttering doleful complaints because they had no money or personal property to bribe Don Sanchos and his brother.

After the cavalcade had passed we resumed our course, and soon arrived at the ranche. We did not feel like sleeping with the prospect before us, so made a fire, and prepared a pot of coffee, and then sat and smoked for an hour or more, not too well pleased with our evening's entertainment, for, although we had been to a fandango, we had danced to very discordant music.

At last, tired with speculations on the future, we went to sleep, and when we awoke the Indian woman had prepared a nice breakfast in honor of our departure. We brought in our horses, rubbed them down, and made all preparations for going to the rendezvous agreed upon. Alberto was sorry for us, and regretted that we must part, but was too glad at his own escape from military duties to shed many tears over our fate. He rounded in his mustangs in the corral, selected the poorest lot that he owned, and was all ready to drive them to the house where the fandango had occurred, as soon as we were prepared to leave.

At first we did not know what to do about Jack. He would be in the way if we took him, and might break his heart with grief should I leave him behind. The poor animal sat and looked at us while the discussion was going on, and I believe that he understood every word that we said, for all at once he threw back his head, and uttered a prolonged howl, and tears poured out of his eyes like those of a human being who has suffered some great disaster.

"By gar, ve vill take him," Lewey cried. "Jack can look arter himself as vell as ve can. He knows more dan a greaser, I dink," and the dog showed his appreciation of the words by attempting to kiss our faces.

At nine o'clock we slung our rifles over our shoulders, said good-by to the cook, mounted our horses, and helped Alberto drive his mustangs to the rendezvous. We found Captain Fernando and his men waiting to receive us, and the military gentleman said with a laugh that Don Sanchos was so much occupied at Ranche Refugio he could not be present to watch our departure. We knew that the scoundrel was determined the girls should not see us again, and was the means of their being housed until we were many miles on our course.

Our captain was not a bad-hearted fellow, and I have no doubt would willingly have consented to our discharge had he not feared the evil influence of the spy at head-quarters. He was quite civil, and appointed us corporals on the spot, our badge of office being a strip of yellow cotton cloth pinned on the left arm of our jackets. I think we were thus promoted on account of our carrying rifles and pistols, which appeared to produce a profound impression on the minds of our companions, for they evidently took us for desperate warriors, and when we shot a turkey buzzard at a distance of fifty yards even the commander of the company said that we were wonders, and would kill a lot of gringos before the war was ended, and these greasers, who could handle a knife but not a gun, were ready to obey us in all things.

We had not the slightest knowledge of cavalry movements, and did not need any on the march. The captain was to ride in advance, and all were ordered not to crowd too closely on him. Then came the two trumpeters, and the rest of us as we pleased. Lewey and I took our places somewhere near the rear of the horsemen, so that Jack could see us, and thereby rejoice. The captain had given his consent to the arrangement, and said that he did not care if there were fifty perros so long as they did not bother him.

The impressed men were mounted on Alberto's horses, and shed tears of regret at the idea of leaving places where they had been living idle lives for so many years. In fact, Lewey and I were so rejoiced to see other people suffering more than ourselves that we actually brightened up, and when the captain rode to the rear, to see that his troop of fifty men were all right, and looked warlike, my friend asked, —

"Senor Capitan, how much per month is the pay of a first-class cavalryman like myself?"

"Eight dollars and found," was the answer.

"Where shall we find the eight dollars when it is due?" Lewey demanded.

"Quien sabe," was the answer and a suggestive shrug of the shoulders. "The saints are kind, but they will not tell us that much. You may have to take your pay in land. It is very cheap, and there is enough of it. By my patron saint, I believe that I have the best company in the State. Adelante," and we commenced our journey to Monterey, and all the girls of Ranche Refugio, except Anita and Engracia, turned out to see us off, and would have waved their handkerchiefs for our benefit if they had owned any. As they did not, a shake of their skirts was the next best thing. Even the two pretty sisters came near us, and Lewey raised his sombrero, and seemed to feel a little proud that he was a soldier, as the young ladies smiled on him, and called him a defender of the honor of Mexico, and the French lad winked at me as he heard the words.

"I should n't vonder," my friend remarked, as he replaced the hat on his head, "dat if I should come back here a hofficer von of dem girls vould be glad to jump at me as a husband, and it vould n't be a bad match. You take von and I de udder."

"Adelante, muy presto," was the command, and we rode away from the fascinating faces, and in a little while my friend had forgotten the pretty sisters, and was thinking of other matters, probably where he should find senoritas capable of holding his attention for a week at least.

We followed the trail that led to San Luis Obispo, but when the afternoon's sun was hot we halted near a ranche, unsaddled and piquetted our horses, and then there were orders to capture a bullock, and kill it. The owner of the property came toward us, and called the men all the vile names he could think of, but our captain only laughed at him, and smoked cigarettes in his face. The ranchero went over a hill at a dashing pace as if to summon help, and Lewey and I walked toward the adobe house to see if there were any terrified females who needed assurances of protection from the officers of the Mexican army. We supposed there were ladies at home, but they had shut and bolted the doors, and we could not get a view of them. They seemed to fear us, I judged from appearances, and I did not wonder at it.

While searching one of the out-buildings we came across a barrel that attracted our attention. We knocked out the bung, smelled of the contents, and it seemed to us to be aguardiente. We inserted a straw, and tasted. It was rum, and no mistake, and old at that. We saw a fine chance for refreshing and cheering our comrades. One of them was near us, seeking what he could steal and carry away. We pointed to the barrel, and mentioned the word aguardiente. It was enough. In an instant the greaser was on his knees, and filling himself with the fiery liquor. We left him at his work, and strolled back to the camp, and there encountered a little rat-eyed sergeant, the only man who knew anything of military duty in the command, aside from the captain.

"Sergeant," I said, "one of our men is filling himself with rum at the house. There is a barrel of it, old and good."

"Holy Virgin, do you mean it?" the old fellow asked, and made a straight course for the house.

We hinted the same information to the rest of the men, and in ten minutes there was no one in camp but the captain and ourselves. The former was smoking cigarettes, as usual, and reclining under a tree, his head on a saddle.

"Cabo de esquadra?" asked our commander, "where have all the men gone?"

"Senor Capitan," Lewey answered, "I think they have found something worth stealing at the house. They are inclined that way."

"All right," was the careless answer. "But be sure and not let them load down the horses," and then the young fellow took his usual siesta, and he must have slept half an hour when he was awakened by a noise that proved the rum was operating.

With howls and yells the gallant soldiers issued from the building, some rolling the barrel, and others struggling to stop its progress, so that more drink could be obtained. At one moment half a dozen of the greasers would be piled up on top of each other, and the person who was nearest the bung-hole dragged away to give place to another man, perhaps a trifle more drunk than the rest.

"Caramba," cried the captain, "what is the meaning of all this, corporal?"

"It looks to me as though the gallant heroes were drunk," Lewey remarked.

"I think you are right," our superior said. "Keep the dogs away from me, and when they get sober we will boot and saddle."

One of the wild-eyed warriors came toward us with a calabash of aguardiente in his hand.

"Drink to the success of Mexico, and confusion to her enemies," he said, and, just as he was handing the liquor to us, stepped on Jack's tail. The indignant dog responded by a grab at the seat of the greaser's trousers, and tore out a mouthful of cloth, such as it was, while the man uttered several emphatic oaths, whirled around rapidly, tumbled to the ground, spilling the rum, and immediately went to sleep.

"I must stop this debauch," Captain Fernando remarked, as he arose, and buckled on his sabre. "Take your rifles, and come with me, corporals."

It was a job we did not care for, but, as the young fellow was full of pluck, we could do no less than follow him, and see how he would subdue the noisy brawlers.

The captain marched up to the barrel, pushed aside the men who were struggling to get at its contents, and said, —

"Turn that barrel so the rum will run out. We have had drinking enough for one day."

"Let the aguardiente alone," one ferocious Mexican said. "It is ours and no one shall deprive us of it."

The young officer raised his sabre, and dealt the speaker a blow with the flat of the blade, full on his dark, ugly face. He was one of the rancheros who was impressed the night before, and did not quite comprehend military duty and respect to a superior.

The greaser was hot-tempered and quick. Like a flash he drew his long, sharp knife, and made a bound for the captain. He was drunk, but not so intoxicated as to prevent his hand being firm. The blow would have struck the young officer full upon the breast, if we had not noted the act, and raised the butt of our rifles. With a crash we let the breach of our guns fall upon the Mexican's arm, and it fell to his side, and the cuchillo dropped to the ground.

"You did well," the officer remarked in a cool, unconcerned manner, as he noticed our act. "I won't forget this, be assured."

The regular soldiers appeared frightened at what had occurred, while the would-be assassin moaned with pain. Some of the men began to move away, as though they had partaken of all the fun they desired.

"Sergeant," said the captain, lighting a cigarette, "find a reata, and bring it here."

He spoke to the fierce little Mexican, the only person who seemed to know much about military duties, except his superior and one or two others.

The fellow with the broken arm turned as if to move away.

"Halt," thundered the captain. "Remain as you were. Move a step, and I'll cut you down like a dog."

The greaser obeyed. The sergeant came toward us with a lariat, saluted, and awaited orders.

"Put that reata around the dog's neck, and hang him to the nearest tree," the captain said.

The sergeant coolly proceeded to do the bidding, but when the criminal struggled and resisted, the captain turned to Lewey and myself.

"Corporals, aid the sergeant," he said, "in hanging that scoundrel."

"Captain," we both exclaimed, "we do not relish that kind of work. Will you please detail some one else to do it? A hangman's position is one not to be desired by young men of our class."

"Oh, yes. No need of making excuses. Here, you two, come and help hang this man," speaking to some of his regulars.

The fellows did not hesitate. They fell upon the wretch, who no longer struggled, put the reata around his neck, and dragged him to a tree. No one dared to remonstrate, even if all were drunk, or under the influence of liquor, as half of the men were asleep, and knew not what was going on.

The captain lighted a fresh cigarette, and appeared the most unconcerned man in the camp.

"Captain," I said, "is there no mercy for the greaser?"

"No. Why do you ask?" was the short answer.

"To see if there was any hope of pardon. His crime is great, but his punishment is terrible."

"He dies," was all the answer the young fellow made, and turned his back on us, returned to the tree and resumed his horizontal position, caring no more for the life of his countryman than that of a sick dog, if quite as much.

"Lewey," I said, as we avoided looking at the scene of the hanging, "the next time we find a barrel of aguardiente we will spill the contents on the ground. Our joke has not been a success thus far."

And the French lad crossed himself, like a good Catholic, and muttered a prayer for the dead, as, when he ventured to steal a look at the tree, dangling from a limb was the lifeless body of the greaser.

I do not know if the execution was an example of Mexican military severity, and legal or illegal. At any rate, the young officer took upon himself the responsibility of hanging a man for an attempted murder. There was no court-martial held, and no one asked for an explanation at Monterey, when we arrived there. This may have been Mexican law, but, if it was, some changes were needed, it seemed to me at the time.

At four o'clock the trumpets sounded to saddle, and the men, with aching heads, were awakened, kicked and cuffed into motion, and at last got in line for inspection. The body of the dead still dangled from the tree, no orders having been issued to cut it down.

"Soldiers," said the young captain, "you have witnessed a slight example of punishment for military insubordination. Let it be a warning to you in the future. The good and brave will be rewarded. The cowardly punished. Corporals Thom and Lewey are promoted to the rank of sergeants for saving my life. Hereafter they will ride near me, at the head of the troop, as my body-guard. Long live Mexico and the republic. Death to her enemies."

"Vell, dis is a go," whispered Lewey. "All dings is for de best, artei all. Ve keeps on, and soon ve skall be ginerals, and den vot von knows but ve can marry de pretty sisters."

"And forget Anita and Engracia?" I asked, in tones of reproach.

"As ginerals ve should hah to look higher. Our stations in life vould be so different dat ve vould be fools to gib our hands unless dar vas some nomer comin' to us by de operation. You leaves all to me, for I knows de ways and de proples better much dan you do."

Somehow I could not help wishing that the French lad was a little more firm in his love affairs, and not so worldly in hopes and aspirations. The last pretty face was sufficient to set him wild, and make him forget all past vows and protestations. The only thing in which he was constant was his friendship for me. That never wavered or grew cold, and he was ready to fight for me, or die for me, if necessary. But with women it was so different. I could only sigh and hope he would improve with age and experience. At the same time there was much sense in the lad's suggestion. The sisters were pretty, and had money, two desirable things in a woman.

There was no cheering when the announcement was made of our promotion, not that the men were envious, for all knew the manner in which we had been impressed, but because their heads were dazed by the debauch of the day. We wheeled in sections of fours, and went on our way, to the great relief of the women of the ranche, it is probable, and the indignation of the owner. He must have been surprised when he returned to see what kind of fruit one of his trees bore, for we left the Mexican where he had been hanged.

We camped at San Luis Obispo the next morning, and went through the town like a flock of hungry wolves. Nothing was safe from the hands of the soldiers. Chickens and pigs were taken wherever found, and for a while Lewey and I seemed to catch the infection, and were half disposed to plunder all whom we encountered. For a time we were separated. I had ridden up to a large adobe house, where I thought a good breakfast could be obtained, dismounted, pushed open the door, and went in. Lewey had thought food looked more promising in another direction.

"What do you want?" demanded an elderly lady, and she was one, I could tell that by the first glance at her face and gray hair.

"Breakfast," I answered. "I have traveled all night, and am famished," and off came my hat, and I made a low bow to the only inmate of the room.

"Are you a Mexican soldier?" she demanded in a haughty tone. "You do not speak like one."

"I am not a Mexican, but at present a soldier. A poor one, I am sorry to say. We have marched all night, and the men are looking for rations. If I disturb you pray let me retire, and find that which I seek in some other place," and, bowing, would have left the premises, but she stopped me with a gesture.

"Remain," she said. "You shall be served with the best the house affords."

Just at this moment four of our men opened the door of the casa, and dashed into the room. They had seen my horse in the corral, and supposed that I had struck a bonanza in the shape of feed.

The old lady looked the indignation she felt.

"Leave the house, you unmannerly ruffians," she said to the newcomers.

"Go to the devil," was the curt answer of the cavalrymen. "We want to eat, and mean to pillage the house."

At this moment a door opened, and a pretty little woman entered, leading a child by the hand. She looked some of the fear she felt, for the lady trembled, and the little one was whimpering, and clinging to its mother's skirts.

"Here goes for the first kiss," cried one of my men, and he jumped toward the prize, and threw his arms around her. She uttered a shrill scream of terror, and her child repeated the cry, and covered its face with the mother's dress.

"I want only a dozen warm ones," a second man said, and he too made a bound for a share of the kisses.

I clubbed my rifle, and let it fall upon the fellow's head, — the one who had first proposed the kissing game. He dropped to the floor half stunned, and then I hit the second scoundrel a blow that laid him low.

"Go," I cried, and pointed to the door.

The two uninjured greasers hesitated for a moment, and their eyes looked knife'sh, but just then Lewey entered the room, in search of me, and to say that he had found lushings of feed.

"Vot is de row?" he asked.

"Some of our men have insulted these ladies," I answered.

"Vot? Insult de ladies? No Frenchman stand by and see dat. Ve vill love dem, and ve vill die for dem, but, by gar, no von skall insult dem vhile I has de strength to strike a blow. Get out of dis, you black-hearted scoundrels, vot don't know enough a kiss to vin by fair means," and he raised his foot and kicked the two greasers from the room, and by this time the injured soldiers had gained their feet and slunk out of the way, with not a word of remonstrance, for they did not dare to face us, knowing that we were non-commissioned officers, and therefore had a little more power than the privates.

"Senors," said the elderly lady, "we owe you thanks for what you have done. Your good action shall not go unrewarded. My husband, General Castro, shall be informed of this at an early day, and he too will be pleased to compliment you."

This was a surprise to us, but we could only bow, and bless our stars that we had behaved in a decent manner, and not like ruffians. But there was greater astonishment yet in store for us.

"This caballero appears to have forgotten me," said the pretty little mother, as soon as she had quieted her child, and, as she came forward, placed a small hand in mine. "I fear that I am not so attractive as before my marriage, if a boy forgets me thus quickly."

She was the nice little girl who one day had given me a kiss at Monterey, just out of fun and a spirit of mischief, and the lady who had promised me a dozen of the same kind at the time she supposed the town was attacked by wild Indians, and then refused to complete the bargain, saying that I was a fool not to take them when I had a chance. I never thought that she treated me well, on that account, but now that she stood before me, a pretty little wife, with a child by her side, I forgave all, and would have kissed her willingly, if I supposed she cared about it.

"How handsome you are," I remarked, wanting to say something light and graceful, that would prove acceptable, and not too abrupt, — kind of a delicate compliment.

"Do you think so?" she asked, and smiled.

"I am certain that I never saw any one so beautiful as you," was my response, and I heard Lewey groan, as though he doubted the truth of the statement.

"You always was a good boy, and I now think you a nice young man," the little wife exclaimed, and then Lewey acted as though he was sick. I wanted to kick him he was so rude. "You may take one kiss for this morning's kindness," the pretty little woman said, and put up her lips.

"It sick makes me to see so much slobberin' goin' on," my friend remarked with a groan.

He wanted a chance himself, but the mother knew goodness when she saw it, and kept the French lad at a distance.

The Senora Castro did not even frown as I bent down and saluted the red lips and small mouth held up for the kiss. I had just finished the agreeable duty when the door opened, and in walked our captain, looking very much astonished at seeing his two sergeants present, and talking to the ladies in a very free yet courteous manner.

"H'l'o," he said, "what the devil are you doing here?" and then, to our surprise, the pretty little wife threw herself into his arms, and kissed the officer a dozen times, which made Lewey so discontented that he wanted to kick Jack, but thought better of it, and only muttered about being aggravated when so many good things were thrown away on the undeserving.

"O! Fernando," cried the little wife, as soon as she could take breath, "how surprised and delighted I am to see you. I did not know you were near me. I supposed you were still at Santa Barbara, recruiting for your company."

"My company is nearly full, and I am on my way to Monterey. We arrived here this morning, and march tonight," the captain answered.

"For the sake of the saints go sooner," Senora Castro exclaimed. "I think, from what I have seen, that your men must be the worst in California. They have grossly insulted us already."

"In what way?" Captain Fernando demanded, and put his hand on his sabre, and gave us a look that did not speak well for our future promotion.

"Four of your men attempted to kiss me," the young wife said, "and were otherwise violent," and here she sobbed, but did not say a word about the salute she had given me.

"You blanked ladrones," howled the captain, and would have fully drawn his sabre, but the young wife held him so tightly in her arms that he could not move until an explanation had been made.

"Be quiet, Fernando," the elderly lady remarked. "You misjudge these caballeros. They are gentlemen, if they are common soldiers. To them are we indebted for protection. They drove off the bad ladrones who would have assaulted us, and at some risk to their own lives."

"Yes, yes," the young wife cried eagerly, "your men would have kissed and maltreated me had not these young gentlemen knocked two of them down, and kicked the others out of the house. They are heroes, Fernando."

The young officer's face lost its flush of anger. He released his hold of the sabre, and held out his hand for us to shake, and forgive him.

"Pardon me," he said. "I should have known that the men who saved my life would not insult unprotected ladies. This is my sister, the Senora Costello, and this lady is the Senora Castro, the wife of the governor, the commander-in-chief of the California army, and my uncle," and, as he introduced us the ladies bowed, and we assured them that we were delighted to make their acquaintance, as is customary in polite society, and it does not matter if you do utter a falsehood at the time the assertion is made. It is only a white lie.

"Aunt," the young captain said, "these young men were impressed into my company through the machinations of that scoundrel, Don Antonio Sanchos, whom uncle will keep in the pay of the State, as a spy and enganchador. They were green enough to matriculador, and so we claimed them for military duty, as we had a right to. The foolish young fellows were in love, and wanted to marry two girls at Ranche Refugio."

"A very laudable desire," both ladies remarked. "It was a mean act to take them away from those they admire. We are sure they would make excellent and faithful husbands."

"Yes, senoras, we should, be assured of that," the unblushing Lewey remarked, and from that moment my French friend grew in favor with the ladies.

"Now, I have a plan that requires your help, my good aunt," the captain said. "I owe the young men a debt of gratitude as well as yourself. Write a letter to the general, detailing all the circumstances of this morning's outrage. Paint glowingly the service the senors have rendered you and Sister Costello. The army is no place for them. Before they have been in it a month they will be murdered by their companions, just as sure as they are now alive. To save them I shall not even ask the names of the ladrones who assailed you, for, if the scoundrels were pointed out and properly punished, their comrades would avenge the act on the first dark night, by the thrust of a knife. I could let them desert, and welcome, but Sanchos would set his hounds on their trail, run them down, and then shoot them. There would be a volley, and two dead matriculadors. The best plan is for General Castro to grant a formal discharge from the army, with a promise on the lads' part not to serve against California or Mexico. How would this suit you, senors?" the young captain asked, turning to us.

I expressed my joy at the prospect of a speedy release, but Lewey did not respond so readily. The fact of it was the French lad had really begun to like the life we were leading. There was excitement and activity in it, and some fun. He could order the greasers about, and began to feel all the delights of one who is in authority, and can show his power. Besides, had not our men stolen everything that they could lay their hands on, or else destroyed what they could not carry away? There is something fascinating in a predatory life after all, especially when you have no property of your own, so that retaliation can be made by the sufferers, and this was our case.

"Before I answer the question, let me ask one, capitan," Lewey said.

"Is there any chance for us to become generals or colonels in the army?"

"Not the slightest, amigo," was the ready answer. "We have more officers than soldiers and more generals than companies. You can hope to rise no higher, for jealousy of foreigners would be a bar to your promotion."

"Then," said Lewey with a sigh, "I am ready to be mustered out. It seems as though fate, or the saints, was against us all the time. We can neither get married nor stay in the army. All doors are closed on us."

The Mexican laughed, and then the ladies caused an excellent breakfast to be prepared for us, and the captain did not hesitate to invite us to sit at the table and eat with him.

While the meal was being got ready Lewey and I went in search of some of the male peons of the estate, swore at them in true trooper style, to impress upon their simple minds that we were men not to be trifled with, made them remove our saddles, groom our horses, and the one the captain rode, feed the animals with barley, and give them plenty of water, and, while this was being done, heaven only knows where the rest of our men were, or what they were doing. We could hear a yell once in a while, and a shrill scream, as though some Indian woman was being kissed against her will, but, as we were not responsible for the morals of the greasers, we did not rush around, knocking on the head the disorderly ones, for our lives were of some value to us, and worth all the Mexicans in the country.

Sometimes a straggler would roam near the house, where the captain was taking his ease, but we had only to point in a different direction, and off the fellow would go, and leave us in peace.

After breakfast we lay down under the shade of a tree, and went to sleep, Jack keeping watch over our persons. We slept until four o'clock, and were then awakened by the loud blasts of our trumpets, calling in the stragglers, and as a signal to get ready to march.

We were rolling up our blankets, and strapping them, when Captain Fernando called us into the house.

"Sergeants," he said, "I shall leave you two here tonight, and tomorrow you will start, and act as escort to my sister and aunt. They go to Monterey. They have had enough of San Luis Obispo, and prefer the former and death to life and this place. Their husbands have sent for them, and they are willing enough to start. Do you think you can look after their welfare on the route? They will ride in a rough volante, drawn by two mules, the same that brought them here a few weeks since. A peon will act as postilion, and you must protect the ladies from insults, if any are offered. The senoras prefer you to their own countrymen, which is a great compliment."

We said that we should like the job very much, and I thought of the pleasant little chats I could have with the young wife while on the way.

"Then that is settled. To tell you the truth, I fear some of my men may not like broken heads from gringos. Now here is a paper requiring all the people on your route to grant you protection, shelter, and assistance, under pains and penalties of martial law. Do not hurry over the country, for it is rough, and be careful in descending the mountains, and crossing the rivers and streams. See that no harm happens to the senoras or the muchacho. On this duty will depend, in a measure, your discharge. And now adios. I must get my ladrones in line, and march."

He sprang into the saddle, threw a kiss to his sister and aunt, and dashed down to the plaza, where the men were mustering to the shrill blasts of the trumpets, and the fierce carambas of the orderly sergeant.

All the cavalry men reported for duty, and we stood near the road, and saw the heroes depart, and, as they filed by, they hurled questions at our heads as to our absence from the ranks, and swore that there was not a thing left in all San Luis Obispo worth stealing.

We said that we were ordered on a scouting expedition over the mountains, to look after Fremont and his men, and then the greasers crossed themselves, and closed up their ranks, as if fearful of an attack. The two ruffians, whose heads I had injured in the morning, did not look pleased at the thought of our being left behind, and I imagined that I read murder in their eyes as they passed us.

We had a delightful evening at the house. Senora Costello and her aunt played on guitars and sang for us, just as though we were on an equality. As soon as they learned we had some education, could read and write, had attended schools in our own countries, they dropped all reserve, and acted like friends more than distinguished ladies of rank, with rich fathers and husbands.

That night we slept in the house, with our rifles beside us, and Jack on the watch, for we feared some of the bold soldier boys might return in an unexpected manner, and not only put us out of the way but injure the ladies. But nothing happened to disturb us, and early in the morning we mounted our horses, and rode to the house where we had danced with Anita and Engracia the night we were sent on shore to watch hides at the Cave. Then we pushed on, went to the landing, and the stream of fresh water, where we stopped, and had a most delicious bath, with plenty of California hard white soap to start the dust and perspiration, the accumulation of weeks of travel.

The Cave had not changed. The surf beat lightly on the shoal shore, and not a vessel was at anchor in the open roadstead. We laughed as we thought of the stolen hides, the dead coyote, and the bear story, and then rode back to the house, refreshed and clean, even if we were a little ragged. The ladies assured us that we would be ill from exposure to the cold water, but we pacified and tried to convince them that there was no danger. They did not believe in such rude attempts at cleanliness, and, when we stated that our countrywomen were extravagantly fond of bathing, our Mexican friends held up their hands in speechless horror, and thought they must be very untidy to require so much washing.

As soon as breakfast was finished the volante was brought to the door, our horses were saddled, and in nice condition for a start, the ladies were helped into the vehicle, with a good supply of provisions for the journey, the pretty little wife smiled on me as I covered her feet and child with a serape, to keep off the keen morning air, and my face glowed with pride and pleasure as the handsome lady said, —

" To the saints and to you we commit ourselves. Do not disappoint our anticipations, and when we arrive at Monterey, if you are real good, you shall be rewarded by a kiss."

" For such a prize I would do and dare anything," was my gallant response, and Lewey asked in English, in a sneering tone, —

" How many vomen de same has you said dat to?" just as though I was accustomed to flatter the fair sex, imitating his free-love ways.

The postilion cracked his whip, we slung our loaded rifles over our shoulders, whistled to Jack, who was creating a disturbance with a neighboring cat, and did not like to leave until he had worried her a little more, threw ourselves into the saddles, and were off, following the trail that led along the base of the mountains, and over which a carriage could journey, if the driver was careful, and avoided the rocks and ruts, for the government had paid some attention to the road, a chain gang being engaged in clearing it for many years, and yet did not make such marked improvement as one would naturally expect.

The morning was so bright, the air so pure and bracing, our condition was so changed from the experiences of the day before, that we actually felt quite content with our lot, and Lewey hummed a French love song, and wanted me to join in the chorus, and when I refused said that I was spoons on some one, and I did n't know what he meant at first, until he nodded toward the volante, and smiled, while I blushed, and repudiated the idea.

We rode ahead of the vehicle, the better to observe the best portion of the trail, and, when the hour of noon arrived, thinking the women were tired, we haited on the borders of a little stream that descended from the mountains, assisted the ladies to dismount, and, while Lewey and the peon looked after the animals, turning them loose for feed on the rich grass, I took my fish line, and caught a nice lot of trout, and baked them on some coals, and while we were eating our dinners, the meal was interrupted by the sudden appearance of four evil-looking rancheros descending the mountain, and advancing toward us on a lope.

CHAPTER IX.

A BRUSH WITH LADRONES. — A YOUNG LADY'S MODE OF EXPRESSING THANKS. — THE PEON'S MURDER. — A LONG CONFESSION. — ON THE MOUNTAIN SIDE. — THE TRAPPERS. — MONTEREY ONCE MORE. — DON SANCHOS RECEIVES A BLOW. — THE AMERICAN CONSUL EXPRESSES AN OPINION. — AGREEABLE QUARTERS. — AN EARTHQUAKE, AND A TUMULT. — AN INTERVIEW WITH GENERAL CASTRO. — ANTONIO AND CARLOS SANCHOS ARE SNUBBED. — A DANGEROUS MISSION TO CAPTAIN FREMONT.

WE were eating our dinners of baked trout and cold chicken, and rather stale frijoles as an adjunct, the ladies were expressing the pleasure they derived from the journey, and the happiness they anticipated in soon seeing their husbands, when the four horsemen appeared in sight, having crept down the mountain side in such a stealthy manner that we should not have noticed them until they were close upon us had not Jack uttered a significant growl, and thus caused us to look up, just as the strangers began to lope their horses toward us.

"Ladrones," suddenly exclaimed the peon, and made a backward leap, and landed in some bushes, out of sight.

The rancheros did look like thieves, and we were suspicious that they were of that grade of humanity, for the fellows had their long lariats in their hands all ready for a throw. In a few minutes more we should have been entangled in their coils had not the dog given us warning. The ladies uttered subdued exclamations, and then repeated the first prayer they could think of, and it sounded in Spanish something like our English version of "Now I lay me down to sleep."

"Que quiere usted?" Lewey challenged.

"Amigos," was the ready response, but we doubted their being friends, for their movements were far from being friendly in that wild, deserted part of the country.

"Keep off," my comrade cried. "Do not advance. We want none of your company."

"You will like us better after a short acquaintance," the rancheros responded. "We are poor men, and mean no injury."

"In the name of the Virgin do not let the ladrones harm us," Senora Costello cried, as she clasped her child in her arms, and her face, so beautiful and pure, showed the fear she experienced, while Senora Castro, like the wife of a warrior, looked the courage she felt, and regarded the newcomers with haughty defiance.

"Senors," I said, as soon as the little wife had made her appeal, and it was not a vain one, for I resolved to defend her with my life, "this lady is the wife of General Castro, the governor of the State. We desire that she shall not be annoyed. Your presence troubles her. Will you, like gallant men, retire and no longer give her anxiety?"

The fellows whispered together for a moment, and we thought they would comply with our request, but instead of galloping off they drew nearer, and one of them said,—

"We are poor men, our ranches have been despoiled by the forces of the government, and we own not a peso. Give us all the money you have, your guns and powder, and we will let you pass without further molestation. What say you, is it a bargain?"

"Give them nothing," was the stern command of the elderly lady. "They would not spare us if you did."

As we supposed she understood the nature of her countrymen better than we did, her words inspired us to show fight and save those committed to our charge. We did not fear the ladrones if we could keep them at a distance, and our necks from the encircling influence of the terrible lariats. If they threw them, and we were caught, death was certain, for they would gallop over the plain, and drag us at their horses' heels until life was extinct.

"Ladies," I said, "the safest place for you is the volante. Go to it quietly, but as speedily as possible, and leave us to deal with these men. We will not desert you, but fight to the last."

The senoras arose and obeyed us without a word. As the rancheros saw the movement, and understood its significance, they prepared for a charge. Now they never would have thought of such an act if they had understood the power of rifles. They supposed that we were armed with the old-fashioned Mexican musket, that did not carry a ball within three fathoms of the point aimed at, and a regiment of soldiers, equipped with that weapon, have been known to fire all day in a pitched battle, and not kill more than fifty men, and wound but a few additional enemies.

"Let us to them gib it," Lewey muttered, as the ladrones dashed toward us.

We waited until the fellows were within fifty feet and then aimed at the two foremost ones, those who were a little in advance of the others. With the crack of our rifles the men singled out reeled in their saddles, and then leaned forward and clutched their horses' manes. They did not seem to take much interest in the rest of the fight, for their animals, frightened at the report of the guns, dashed across the plain toward the mountains, and disappeared in the thick chapparel, the riders having no control over them.

As we discharged our guns we ran as fast as possible to the shelter of the volante, and threw ourselves flat upon the ground, with arms extended, and it was well that we did so, for two lariats flew through the air, alighted on our persons, and, as they touched our heads, we raised our hands and pitched them some distance from us, and so saved our lives by that simple manœuvre.

The rancheros dashed on, baffled but not defeated. They knew that we could not have time to re-load our rifles, so supposed that we were sure to be captured at the next charge. With a light touch of the heavy curb they threw their horses on their haunches, wheeled them like a well-drilled soldier, and once more came toward us, determined to ride us down if the lariats failed.

"De pistols to dem gib," whispered Lewey, who always spoke bad English when excited.

We rolled over, close to the wheels of the volante, where the women were praying for our success, drew our pistols, which the ladrones did not suspect we had on our persons, and, when the Mexicans were close upon us, fired, just as the lariats were thrown. The mustangs swerved in their course, and thus disconcerted the aim of the men. The reatas flew wide of their mark, grazed one of the wheels of the volante, slipped to the ground, and, as the horsemen passed us, we gave them a second broadside from the other pistols, and had the satisfaction of hearing one fellow utter a yell of pain, and then both mustangs pitched to the ground, and the Mexicans went with them, one with a broken leg, and the other with a bullet in his shoulder.

"Don't mind 'em, cried Lewey. "Let de blanked scoundrels suffer as much as dey can. Load de guns and de pistols. Dar may be udders of 'em not far off."

The advice was too good to be rejected. We let the injured ladrones lie on the ground, one of them with a leg under the wounded mustang, and grinding the fellow's flesh into the saddle and earth at every movement of the animal.

"Bueno," cried the two ladies, as they clapped their hands. "Brave men. A thousand thanks. Kill the ladrones."

When a Mexican woman has her blood up she does not stand for trifles. She can be as cruel as one of the male members of her race. The senoras smelled blood, and there was no mercy in their hearts.

We did not feel that way. We had conquered in the fight, and were satisfied with what we had done. We did not propose to despatch our prisoners, but let them get well the best way they could. While we were re-loading our rifles and pistols, however, the black, savage peon, who had run away at the first sign of danger, glided out of the chapparel, and went toward the injured men. We did not note his movements very closely, thinking that curiosity alone drew him to the spot. But suddenly we heard a yell for mercy, and then a sickening crunch, and, on running to the spot, saw that the cowardly savage had killed both ladrones where they lay on the ground with well-directed blows of his machete, or heavy knife, sharp and thick.

"Dog," we asked, "why did you do this?"

"So that they will no longer trouble honest people," was the prompt reply. "They have gone to the devil who created them."

"Do not scold the peon," cried the ladies. "He did right. The ladrones would have maltreated us. They missed their game, and had to suffer the consequences."

We were not so hardened as that, but were guiltless of the murders, thank God. We should have spared the injured rancheros, and let them escape. But what could we say or do? The peon was not under our command, and did as he pleased regardless of our wishes. The ladies gave him orders, and he obeyed. If we had pleaded for mercy a smile of contempt from the savage would have been all the reply he might vouchsafe. So we held our tongues, and left the fellow to pillage the bodies, and secure such articles as he thought valuable.

"Now we will finish our dinners and coffee," the elderly lady said, as we assisted her to alight from the carriage.

Lewey and I.

"By gar," cried Lewey, when he heard the words, "this is cool. Some nerve has I, but de ladies beat it all out of sight."

"And I," said the little wife "will now reward my gallant preserver with as many kisses as he will take. My life, my honor, my child has he saved. May the saints bless him."

I could not refuse the polite invitation, so saluted the fair lady with two kisses, but somehow there was not that vim and sweetness in them that I experienced at Monterey previous to her marriage, or before the time of the tragedy that had been enacted before our eyes. We look for gentleness and tenderness, mercy and forgiveness in women, and when we do not find them masculine admiration does not become an instinct, and so it was in my case. The beautiful woman was before me, but she had shown no pity toward the vanquished, and I did not think she was so pretty as when I saw her the day before, asking for protection from the rude assaults of the soldiers.

"Vare does my share of de kissin' come in?" asked the envious Lewey.

The Senora Castro must have divined the question, for she held out her hand, a very well formed one even if it was a little dark.

'You," she said, "for your bravery on this occasion shall be permitted to kiss my hand."

"I vill do it," cried Lewey, "but I is not hungry for such dings," and he pressed his lips very respectfully on the lady's fingers, and then he winked at me.

As he spoke in English the senora's feelings were not hurt, as she could not understand a word he uttered. He looked eagerly at the thin lips of the young wife, but she did not take the hint, although both ladies praised us in no stinted manner for the part we had performed.

We made a fresh pot of coffee, smoked a few cigarettes, in which the ladies did not disdain to join us, and at two o'clock were once more on our way, leaving the dead men and injured horses where they had fallen, food for the coyotes and mountain lions, unless there were companions to look after the remains.

We passed through a beautiful section of the country, with the high coast range of mountains on our right hand and the seashore on our left. Sometimes, from our elevated position, we could catch a glimpse of the ocean, solitary and deserted, with no sail in sight to break the monotony. We could not travel fast, as the trail was rugged, so were not sorry to catch sight of the adobe walls of a ranche house just as the sun was sinking, and the chill air of the coming night swept through the valley, fresh from the waters and snow-crowned mountains of the northern sierras.

The owner of the ranche, an aged Mexican, and a priest, came out to meet us and make us welcome. Captain Fernando had passed that way the day before, and stated who would follow him, so that there was no surprise expressed as we drove up. The holy father belonged to the Mission Carmel, four miles from Monterey, was on a tour of confession and christening, and ready to marry such as desired to enter the holy bands of matrimony.

"Welcome, daughters, to such as the house affords," the padre said, as he came forward and assisted the women to alight, while the aged Mexican stood uncovered, out of respect to the rank of the ladies. "We could have wished," the priest continued, "that your reception and entertainment were more regal, but the government troops were here last night, and they did not leave much of any value behind," and here the good man smiled, and glanced at the sister of the captain of the cavalry company, but the Senora Costello did not seem to think that any apology was needed for the conduct of the men, for she simply said, —

"Holy father, I suppose soldiers must live the same as priests."

"Yes, child, but they need not steal what they can't eat. But God be with you, daughters. Enter the house, and supper shall be served immediately."

As we were not invited we piquetted our horses, found them a mess of barley, and made preparations for spending the night. As we knew that we should not be permitted to sleep in the house we cleared out a place in the out-building, and then waited for such portion of supper as the ladies might be disposed to send us, and I am glad to state, for the honor of the sex, that we were not forgotten, as we had a bountiful supply of frijoles and tortillas, and some coffee, the latter none too good, as the cook had not settled it, in his haste to serve the distinguished visitors.

While we were disposing of the food the priest came toward us, and raised his hands over our heads. We saw what was coming, arose, and stood uncovered before him.

"Soldiers," he said, "the ladies have told me of your bravery. Although you are foreigners and heretics take an old man's blessing. It never yet harmed any one."

"Holy father," said Lewey, "I am a Catholic, but not a good one."

Here I nodded an assent, and my friend continued, —

"I do not make love to every pretty face that I see, like some gringos I could mention, yet I have not confessed for many months. Will it please you to hear me if you have the time and patience?"

"Holy father," I remarked, "if he makes a full confession you will have no sleep tonight. Better take him by installments. Two or three hours this evening, and the rest early in the morning."

The good priest did not smile at the words. He simply said, —

"As a servant of the church I will give your friend all the time he requires," and the two walked to a secluded spot, and Lewey must have had a long catalogue of sins to answer for, as he was gone an hour or more, and when he returned said that he was all right for a year at least.

The ladies came out in the court yard and sat for a while, their shoulders covered with serapes to keep off the heavy dew and cold night air. They were very pleasant, and spoke more than once of the service we had rendered them, and how grateful they felt for our exertions in their behalf. Then Senora Costello complained of fatigue, and gave me her hand as she bade me a quiet good-night, and a hope that I might sleep well.

We were not disturbed by the cries of the coyotes, and got up and washed long before the ladies were dressed and ready to show themselves. We fed our horses, had breakfast, and by eight o'clock once more resumed our way, and nothing happened of interest until we were ten miles from the Carmel Mission, then, while climbing a mountain, at a snail's pace, for the trail was rugged, four men stepped from the bushes, rifles in hand, huge knives in their belts, and pepper-pot revolvers on their hips.

"The saints preserve us," the ladies exclaimed, "here are more ladrones, and no retreat."

We could not turn the volante, and if we had it would have been of no use, for the strangers might shoot the mules from where they stood, and not half try.

I knew from the dress and appearance of the men that we had not fallen in with another party of Mexican ladrones, but four Americ.. tramprs, and what they could want of us was a mystery.

"Put up your rifle, Lewey," I said, as my friend began to unsling the weapon from his back. "Here we will find better marksmen than ourselves, and before we could fire they would riddle our bodies with bullets. Let me deal with these people, for fighting is of no use with such odds against us. If they are Americans I can manage better with them than you."

"Senors," cried the two ladies, thrusting their heads out of the side of the volante, and looking a little alarmed, while Senora Costelo clasped her child close to her breast, "we hope there is no danger to you and us"

"I trust not, ladies," I answered, "but we must hope for the best. Remain calm and quiet while I go forward to meet the strangers, and question them."

Followed by Jack I rode slowly forward, the trappers still remaining near the centre of the trail, their rifles carelessly thrown across the bend of their arms, and right hands on the locks of their guns. They looked at me with as much curiosity as I manifested, and, when I was within a few paces of the men, they motioned for me to halt, and I obeyed the mandate without delay. They were tall, brawny, muscular fellows, wearing red shirts and slouched hats, and on their feet they had Indian moccasins, trimmed with beads and porcupine quills. Their eyes were bright and very alert, and seemed ever watchful, as though expecting an enemy to appear near them at any moment.

"Tip the greaser a little Mexican lingo, Bill," one of the trappers said to a comrade, who was supposed to be the linguist of the party, and, thus urged, the man who was addressed as Bill took a step forward, and said, —

"Buenos days, saynor?"

I laughed as I answered, —

"I think we had better palaver in English, gentlemen. We shall understand each other better."

"Blank me, the fellow a'n't no greaser," Bill remarked. "Mexicans don't speak like that 'ere."

"No, gentlemen, I am an American like yourselves," I said.

"Then what is yer doin' on here?" was the next question. "Ride up and let 's take a squint at yer close to."

I rode near the men, and they looked me all over, and seemed a little puzzled at my Mexican costume.

"Whar did yer come from, pard?" one of the trappers asked.

"Santa Barbara."

"Will, jist tumble off that 'ere hoss for a minute. We wants to talk with yer for a while," and I obeyed the request, as I knew it would not do me any good to refuse the polite command.

"Sot yerself down on that stump, stranger," one of the men said, the person who seemed to be the leader of the party.

I obeyed, pulled out my pipe, lighted it, and smoked with apparent unconcern. The men imitated my example in the pipe line.

"Keep yer eyes peeled for the greasers, Bill," the leader said. "There may be some scoutin' round here, although I think not. We don't want

to be took by surprise nohow, jist at this time," and then the man turned to me and resumed his questioning.

" Who is you anyway, stranger ? " he asked.

" I have told you. I am an American, formerly a sailor, but left my ship at the end of the voyage for the purpose of marrying and living in the country."

As I mentioned the word "marrying" all of the men laughed, but in a subdued manner, as though they were not accustomed to make any noise when giving expression to their mirth.

" What ship was you on, stranger?" demanded the leader.

" The Admittance, of Boston," was my prompt answer.

One of the men gave me a sharp look, and asked, —

" What was the name of the skipper of that 'ere ship ? "

" Captain Peterson."

" Korrect," was the ejaculation. " Now one thing more. That 'ere ship was at Santa Barbara one time, and a party of trappers was aboard of her. Now, stranger, what did them 'ere men do while they was thar ? "

" In the first place," I said " they all had a tot of aguardiente, and then fired at champagne bottles hung from the yard-arm."

" Korrect to a hair," was the complacent expression of the questioner.

" I was thar, mate, and knowed all about it."

" You bet, especially the rum part," one of the trappers cried, and a subdued chuckle passed around the group.

I did not remember the man, but had no doubt he was on board the Admittance at the time, as we were often visited by trappers for the purpose of buying powder and lead.

" Now one thing more, pard," the questioner asked. " What else did we do ? "

" You desired to borrow one of our boats so that you could hunt otter in the kelp," I said. " The captain refused to let you have the gig as he feared trouble from the greasers."

" That 's gospel truth. Yer was thar, stranger, as sure as yer are alive. There 's no make up in that yarn. Yer Yankee fast enough."

" That 's all very well," the leader remarked, " but we wants some other things jist now. Whar is yer goin'? and who has yer with yer ? "

" I am on my way to Monterey, and my shipmate and myself are escorting two ladies to that town to join their husbands," was my prompt reply.

" Who is the women ? "

"I have told you, — ladies."

"Well, all women is ladies, a'n't they?"

"Not in every case. These are real ladies under our protection, and we mean to see them safely to their homes."

"That is all right, stranger," was the gruff reply. "We don't object to that by any means. What we want to know is this, — has yer seen anything of the greaser soldiers about here?"

"We heard that a troop of cavalry was just ahead of us," I answered, for I thought the men would realize the fact as well as ourselves if they were out on a scout.

"That's the truth. Now yer know that the United States and Mexico is at war, don't yer?" the leader asked.

"I have heard so."

"Well, it's a fact. Now which side does you take in the fight?"

"Can you doubt?" I asked, and the answer seemed to satisfy the man, for he said, —

"That's all right. Now we wants you to go with us and see the cap'en."

"What captain?"

"Fremont. He's not far from here, and might like to question yer on some pints we has neglected to call up."

"You must excuse me this time," I said. "I hope to see him hereafter."

"Could n't we persuade yer to go?" the leader asked with a smile, a very significant one.

"Certainly, for you are in force, and we are weak, but I trust American trappers will respect the ladies and their escort."

"What's the use, Jim?" the man who had been on board the Admittance remarked. "The Yank is all right. Let him and the women folks go."

Most of the men nodded an assent.

"I a'n't no objections. You can travel, and mind yer don't mention havin' met us on the trail," and the leader motioned for me to continue my journey with the volante and ladies.

"By the way," I asked, as I mounted my horse, and prepared to join my anxious friends, "is Captain Fremont encamped near here?"

"Never yer mind whether he is or not," was the short answer.

"How many men has he under his command?" I asked.

"None of yer business."

"Is he on the war path?" I ventured to question.

"Will yer git, yer everlastin' poll parrot?" the trapper remarked, and threw up his rifle in an ominous manner, and I feared he meant business. I touched my hat, and galloped back to the ladies. When I reached them I glanced along the trail, but not a single person except our party was in sight. The scouts had vanished as suddenly as they appeared, and left no sign of the direction in which they had gone, yet I had no doubt they were watching our movements from the midst of some thicket, and hearing all of our conversation.

"Who were the men?" asked Senora Castro, as soon as I was within speaking distance.

"Some trappers who were uncertain about visiting Monterey, fearing the trouble would cause them to be held as prisoners. They will soon cross the mountains, and go back to their hunting grounds."

The ladies were satisfied with the explanation, and Senora Costello flashed me a warm look of thanks from her bright eyes, and make a motion with her lips as though she owed me a kiss.

"Dat is von big lie," Lewey said in English, as we resumed our snail-like pace up the side of the mountain. "Dem men vas scouts, and you knows it. Vas it a tight squeeze to git us by dem?"

"You had better believe it was. Captain Fremont is encamped near here I think, and that means bad luck for the greasers. Those trappers are some of his scouts, and are keeping a sharp watch over the trails. If they had suspected that one of our ladies was the wife of General Castro they might have held her as a hostage, although our countrymen do not make war on women. Remember, Lewey, we know nothing of the object of these men. They were only trappers, you recollect."

"All right," was the cheery answer, for my French friend took the hint without delay.

When we had crawled to the top of the mountain a magnificent sight met our view. The mules were so tired we concluded to remain where we were and eat our luncheon, having no fear of further molestation, as the town of Monterey was in sight, although at some distance, yet it seemed to be almost beneath our feet. The bright blue waters of the bay were rippling and dancing under a gentle southwest wind, and all along the extensive, crescent-shaped beach the white surf was rolling and tumbling, reminding us of hide-droghing days, when we were wet from morning until night, yet happy and careless of the future. Across the bay we could see the sand hills of Santa Cruz, and nearer, the black rocks of the Point of

Pines, and the dark, sombre trees in their rear. Close by was the Mission Carmel, the walls falling to decay, and affording shelter for but few priests, the owners of not many cattle, as the Mexican government had seized on all that was valuable, and converted them into money for the benefit of administradors and other speculators.

The ladies were delighted with the view. Even husbands were forgotten for a moment, as the senoras sat on a rock and looked off toward the town and bay. There was but one vessel in the roadstead, and that we supposed was the war-like schooner California, Captain Cooper, and I shuddered at the fate of our national ships, should any enter the harbor and engage the terror in battle, with its crew of kanakas, and old Queen Anne muskets for cannon.

We found a spring of sparkling water, but had nothing to eat except a few hard-boiled eggs. I was about to take my rifle to try and find a deer when a strange-looking Indian appeared on the scene, with a hind-quarter of venison on his shoulder.

He did not resemble the California native in feature or color, dress or appearance. He carried a light rifle in his hand, and showed no fear, as he approached us quite boldly, with a firm step and upright form, and eyes of fire.

I spoke to him in Spanish, but the Indian shook his head as though he did not understand.

"You speak English?" I said, and the stranger nodded.

"Will you give us a portion of your meat?" I asked.

"Yes; take what you want."

He threw the venison on the stones, and Lewey cut off what we needed for broiling on the coals.

"Who are you?" I asked, as I gave the man a piece of tobacco in payment for the meat.

"Me Delaware Indian," was the proud response.

"Who is with you?"

"Fremont."

"Where is he?" I asked.

"How should I know?" was the guarded reply. "He here today, tomorrow he gone. Who knows where he goes? The wind will not tell the secret. Delaware Indian no talk too much. No good."

He rose up and took his venison, disappearing in the forest, and that was the last we saw of him. He was one of Fremont's celebrated Indian scouts, and followed his commander from the Missouri clear across the continent suffering hunger and thirst, danger and almost death for the sake of being on a trail, or hunting expedition.

I was not sorry when the Indian disappeared from sight, for I did n't know but he might be on the war path. He had been scouting through the country, killed a deer during his wanderings, and was now returning to camp, wherever it was located.

The ladies asked about the Delaware, and I told them he belonged to the trappers we had met, and they were satisfied, but Lewey put a finger to his head, and drew an imaginary knife around his brow, as though he thought the Indian was after scalps, but I think my friend was wrong.

As soon as we had finished our plain repast we once more resumed our journey. Then we had to lock the wheels of the volante, for our course was down the steep side of the mountain, and the mules were to slide as well as hold back. I thought the danger so great that I begged Senora Costello to ride my horse and let me lead him, and Lewey made the same proffer to Senora Castro. Both ladies were wise enough to accept the offer, and, with the child resting in its mother's lap and arms, my gallant mustang carefully picked his way down the mountain, as though proud of the beauty on his back, and rather liked the change of riders.

We reached the base of the mountains in safety, even the carriage suffering no damage, and then once more the ladies resumed their proper places in the vehicle, and we dashed past the old mission toward the town.

As we drew near the village we heard the braying of trumpets, and saw our gallant companions-in-arms on the plaza, undergoing review by richly-dressed officers. The scamps did not present a very military aspect, and the line was not as straight as some mathematical demonstrations. Captain Fernando was at the head of his corps, and the fierce little sergeant was awful in his profanity as he damned every one who did not sit his horse and act like a cavalryman.

Our arrival attracted much attention, for it was not often that a volante was seen in the streets of Monterey. General Castro saw his wife, dismissed the inspection in all haste, and galloped toward us. There was an affectionate embrace, and then the husband of the pretty little wife came forward, and I envied him the kisses he received, for she did not seem to remember those which had been bestowed on me during the journey.

Captain Fernando left his fiery sergeant to get his men back to the barracks, and then exchanged a few words with his sister. She must have told him how boldly we had acted, for he thanked us, and then turned to the general

"These are the men I spoke about to your excellency," the young captain said. "They have added another chain of gratitude by repulsing a party of ladrones who made an attack on them. Your wife will give you the particulars at her leisure."

"I can relate some of them now," the lady said. "To these gallant young men are we indebted for our lives and honor. General, you must do something for them. Discharge both from the army, and let them return and marry the girls they love."

Of course Castro laughed. We expected he would do so, and were not disappointed.

"Any request that you make, my dear, I shall comply with," was the satisfactory answer, but just at that moment a familiar voice was heard near us, and, turning, we saw the sardonic face of Don Antonio Sanchos. The scoundrel had pressed forward, and listened to the conversation. Then he put in his oar, just as we expected he would.

"I trust that your excellency will give me a hearing before you comply with the lady's request," he said. "I can show you good evidence that the gringos are dangerous sospechosos, and have been acting as spies for the Americanos."

"You are a lying dog," cried the fiery Captain Fernando. "You mean enganchador, how dare you come near ladies and gentlemen when they are conversing?"

He raised his right hand, and struck Sanchos a ringing blow on the face, a blow so severe that the villain staggered back, and blood flowed from his nose.

Don Sanchos' first impulse was to put his hand on the hilt of his long knife. Then he thought better of it, for the young officer said, in a tone of scorn, —

"Oh, draw your cuchillo if you desire to, but the instant you raise a hand I'll run my sword through your body. General, it is a disgrace to keep such scoundrels in the service of the State. Instead of being a benefit he is an injury. I have some of his doings to report to you at the first convenient opportunity."

"I wish," cried Senora Costello, clapping her little hands, "that you would hit the scamp one more good blow for me, O brother mine. I should like it so much if you would."

But Don Sanchos had slunk away in the crowd, and the perplexed general, who was distracted with the thoughts of Fremont, the war, and the return of his wife, said that he would do justice, and ordered the volante to move on to his official residence, where the governors usually resided, near the hall where Lewey and I gave our celebrated exhibition of legerdemain.

"I have quartered you and your friend at my sister's residence," Captain Fernando said, as the carriage rolled away. "She will make you comfortable, and be sure that you protect her, and look after her welfare in case some rambling soldier invades the premises. You will have no other duty for the present. And now listen to me for a moment. Keep in the house nigh's. Sanchos has not forgotten or forgiven you. He carries a sharp knife, and knows how to use it."

"Do you not fear him?" I asked.

"No. The villain is a coward, and dare not strike at me. If he did his fate would be no uncertain one. It is people like you who feel his rage. But go to the house and rest. I must look after my men, for they are inclined to steal here as well as at San Luis Obispo."

We rode through the crowded streets, for there were some five hundred soldiers in town, getting ready to make an attack on Captain Fremont and his men, and, as we passed the house of the American consul, Mr. Thomas O. Larkin, we saw the gentleman sitting on the veranda of his residence, talking with his half-brother, Captain Cooper, the commander of the schooner California, the only Mexican man-of-war on the coast, and she carried but four men and an old musket.

Neither of the gentlemen recollected us until I dismounted, went toward them, and spoke. Then they were astonished, for they supposed we were at home.

"What in heaven's name possessed you to leave your vessel at such a time as this?" asked Mr. Larkin, his right hand to his ear, so that he could hear my reply, as he pretended to be a little deaf at times, or perhaps he was hard of hearing.

"We were in love, and wanted to get married," I answered, and knew what would follow, for of course both laughed, and Captain Cooper made a savage bite at his maimed hand, and kindly said, —

"What blanked fools."

"What are you doing here?" Mr. Larkin asked, as soon as he could recover his composure.

"We have just arrived as the escort of Senoras Castro and Costello. The fact of it is we were impressed in the Mexican army at Ranche Rufugio just as we were about to be married, and forced to march or die. We preferred the former."

"Good for the Mexicans," Captain Cooper cried. "You will live to bless them some day for doing you a service."

"I will soon set you free from the army," the American consul remarked. "Tomorrow I will speak to General Castro on the subject. They have no right to impress an American or a Frenchman. Perhaps I can make the government pay you damages."

"But we are matriculadors," I said.

"The devil you are! That alters the case. What fools boys do make of themselves. But I'll get you discharged just the same, or know the reason why," and the representative of American honor scowled at a greaser soldier who passed just at that moment, and shouted,—

"Down with the Americano gringos and their representative," meaning that the warrior wanted to share in the sacking of the consul's house, and steal a few of the dollars he had on the premises. The fellow paid no attention to us, for he supposed we were Mexicans, being dressed in the national costume.

"Just wait a little while, you miserable dog," Mr. Larkin muttered, and then in a whisper, speaking to me, "In a few weeks the frigates Congress, Independence, and Cumberland will be in the harbor, and then we will see who can talk the loudest. But keep this to yourself for the present, for it is not generally known that the ships are on their way to this port."

"If this is the case perhaps it would be advisable to move the schooner California to safer quarters," I said, addressing Captain Cooper, the commander, but the old salt took a ferocious nip at his hand, and declared that he would fight the whole Yankee fleet, and sink it in the bay if it dared to venture near him.

As we did not believe the captain was in earnest we laughed at him and his threat, and moved off to find the house of Senora Costello, where we were to be quartered. We knew the place very well. It was a pretentious adobe building, a little off the main street, yet near the plaza. Attached to the premises was a corral for horses, and a shed for the storing of rubbish, saddles and the Indian servants.

I entered the house, and announced to the mistress of the place that we were detailed to protect herself and family, and she did not seem in the least surprised. In fact, I think the arrangement was one she had made with her brother, as she put more confidence in us than in her countrymen, just at that time, when so much lawlessness prevailed all over the State. Her husband was at the government house, being an officer of some kind, so was not at home to welcome us in proper shape, but as the lady was the smarter of the two it did not matter much. She told us what to do. We were to turn our horses loose in the corral, we could find some barley in the shed, our saddles might be stowed away anywhere, and we were to sleep in the house, on our own blankets, and eat when we got a chance, which was quite satisfactory, as we were accustomed to Mexican irregularities on the food question.

The peons looked on in wondering surprise, and did not seem disposed to regard us with favor, but Senora Costello told them we were the most wonderful killers of Apache Indians ever known, and then they changed their tone, and seemed disposed to do all they could to keep us in good humor, fearing for their scalps.

As soon as our traps were disposed of we fed our horses, and then went in search of some new or clean clothes, for those we had on were not as fresh as they might have been, having worn them all the way from San Diego without a change, and I regret to say that our trousers were decidedly dilapidated on seats and legs, and a little off color, through dust and perspiration.

We passed along, and saw Cook sitting in the door of his pulperia, his nose a little redder than usual, and a general air of dejection seeming to pervade the man and his place. He did not recollect us at first, and, when he did recall our faces, sighed deeply as he thought of flush times when men-of-war were in port, and sailors buying aguardiente at a real a glass, and getting fighting drunk before sundown.

"Ah, but these are awful times," the old fellow sighed. "There's a crowd of people here in the streets, but not one has a real in his pockets. They are the poorest lot of greasers ever known in the town. Why, I could sell a barrel of rum a day, at two reals a glass, if I wanted to give credit. But come in and have a drop of somethin' for the sake of old times."

We declined his invitation to drink, as we were not in want of stimulants, but did enter the old shanty, close to the custom house, a well-known landmark for many years to those familiar with the coast.

We saw a lot of shirts and clothes piled up on his shelves, which he had taken for rum from man-of-wars' men and Mexicans. We looked the stock over, found it was new and in good order, and just what we needed for wear.

Now if we had said we wanted to buy the goods, the old fellow would have put on a fictitious price, and made a big profit, but, as we did not speak of purchasing, he thought a sale could be effected by a little plain talk.

"Fit yourselves out with a suit," he said. "I'll sell dog cheap. There are some Mexican costumes I bought of a tailor. He got drunk and pawned them. All good cloth and nice bell buttons, imitation of silver. The blue shirts came from a man-of-war, just out of the slop-chest. Take two for a dollar each. It's less than they cost me in the way of trade. Say a whole suit for five dollars. You won't? Well, take it for four, and not a medio less, if I starve."

As the price was low we bought two complete suits, returned to the house, found some soap and water, had a good wash, and donned our new garments, feeling all the better for being clean once more, even forcing Senora Costello to utter a few words of commendation on our changed appearance.

When the husband came home he was profuse in his thanks for the care we had taken of his wife, and said that the house was ours, which we knew did not mean anything, for we had heard the same thing many times before. However, he gave us some supper, and then we remained under cover all the evening, as we remembered the warning Captain Fernando had given us.

We slept in the room that was usually reserved for the reception of guests, and for taking such hasty meals as were provided by the cooks when they felt like it. I do not know what hour of the night I was awakened from a heavy sleep by the movement of the house, which was rolling and pitching like a ship in a light sea, and for a moment thought that I was on board the old Admittance. Lewey was snoring by my side, and not disturbed by the tumult.

I started up, and listened, and then from the plaza heard the loud clanging of the church bells, the yells of people in the streets, as though something extraordinary had occurred.

"Lewey," I said, giving my French friend a kick, "there's a tornado or a new revolution, I do not know which, but if we remain here we'll be buried alive."

"Let her rip," was the half-awakened reply, and, turning over, he was about to compose himself to sleep again, for the young man was tired as well as myself.

"El torremoto! el torremoto!" I heard half a dozen voices yell in the court-yard, and then far off in the distance the same cry was repeated, and the church bells clanged louder than ever, as though to awaken the faithful, and bid them come to the ark of safety if they desired to live until morning.

"Lewey," I said, as soon as I could collect my scattered senses, "there's a devil of an earthquake raging."

"Shoot it," was the drowsy reply, and then some one pounded on the swaying door of the house, and yelled loudly, —

"El torremoto! el torremoto!"

"Save me," cried Senor Costello, and made a bound from the room where he slept, forgetting for the time being that he was a married man and a father. "The earthquake will be the death of us. The saints have me in their keeping. I am going to the church to pray," and out of the trembling, shaking house he went at a bound, regardless of his costume, which was light and airy for that time of the year, and not quite suited for church services, especially if ladies were present.

"Vell," muttered Lewey, as he sat up on the floor, and pulled on his trousers, "if I has to die here I'll cover up my booful legs," an act I was not slow to imitate.

For a moment there was a cessation of the rocking and trembling of the house and the earth, and the cries ceased in the streets. The first shock had lasted a minute, I judged, but I could not be sure, for time passes slowly when you are expecting a building to fall on you every second. If it had not been of adobe, and the walls very thick and elastic, we should have been buried the first few seconds of the shock. As it was the tiles fell from the roof, and crashed to the ground, and the dogs uttered loud howls, and seemed frantic with terror. But Jack showed more courage, although the poor brute trembled, and uttered a low whine, as though he realized the danger, and feared that more trouble was to come.

Again the earth moved, and the building swayed. I had just buckled my pistols and knife around my waist, and, as I did so, staggered like a drunken man, and even felt sick at my stomach, and a strong inclination to vomit, so greatly was I affected, and Lewey, who was similarly afflicted, said,—

"Dis is russer dan a glass of old Cook's aguardiente, and a bottle of native vine on top of it."

"Save me, O amigo, and mi muchacho," I heard Senora Costello moan, and then suddenly recollected that her husband had run for his life at the first shock.

"Look to the child, Lewey," I cried, and ran as fast as possible to the room where the lady had been sleeping.

She was still in bed, not daring to rise, and in dishabille, but women do not stand on ceremony when an earthquake is raging, and the roof is likely to fall at any moment. A lamp was burning in her apartment, and from its feeble flame I could see the look of terror on the handsome face of the young wife, while the boy was sleeping by the side of her bed, and had not even awakened during all of the tumult.

"Where is my husband?" demanded the lady, as soon as she could speak, for terror had for a moment made her dumb.

"He has gone for help," I answered, wishing to excuse his absence as well as I could, for I did not want to make the man contemptible in such bright eyes as the lady possessed.

"It is a lie," she retorted. "He has fled to save his own worthless life, and left me and the child to die."

"No, no, not to die," I answered. "I will take you in my arms, and carry you to a place of safety," ignoring the word lie for the time being.

Even as I spoke the building rocked wildly, the church bells resumed their clamor, the people in the streets howled in terror, called on the saints and Virgin to save them, and vowed they would lead better lives in the future if the request was complied with. Of course this was forgotten in less than twenty-four hours after all danger was passed, but the scare showed that the Mexicans were a deeply religious people in periods of earthquakes and other calamities, and could do more promising in a given time than any men on the face of the earth, except the Spaniards.

"If stand here you do all de night, and talk and talk, de shanty vill our heads fall on. Grab de voman and get out of dis, and I vill take de boy. But you allers did go for de best dings, and leave me de vusser. S'pose I take de vife, and you de young von, and see how dat do?"

Lewey could do some hard grumbling when, occasionally, I crossed his path, but I knew his disposition too well to pay marked attention to it. I covered the petite form of the wife with several blankets, raised her in my arms, and, just as I thought we should be buried in the ruins of the house, passed out of the door, Lewey near me bearing the still sleeping child, and Jack following at our heels, subdued, and not disposed to fight the meanest cur that was near the building yelping with terror.

For a moment I stopped near the corral where our horses were snorting with fear, disposed to leap the walls, and break away for the high lands. But they recognized our voices, and came toward us, trembling in every limb, and reeking with perspiration. We petted and soothed them, and, as the earth continued to show signs of mutinous conduct, we did not believe that we could find a safer place for the depositing of our burdens than the open space at the rear of the house, in the corral where the horses were confined.

The streets were full of people, the soldiers praying at one moment and plundering the next, or as soon as there was a cessation of shocks. We saw a crowd of our cavalry company rush toward Cook's pulperia, and we calculated that his stock of aguardiente would suffer to some extent, with no money paid in by the customers.

High over our heads the turkey buzzards flew, and croaked like ill-omened spirits, and once in a while the fierce cry of eagles, as if protesting against being disturbed in the night. Cattle were bellowing and charging through the town, seeking the companionship of man for protection, and above the clamoring, discordant bells could be heard the mournful booming of the surf as it dashed on the shore with unusual spitefulness, covering the sandy beach with feathery white foam, and, strangest of all, a huge black bear came near us, growling and grumbling, yet not daring to attack any one that crossed its path, man or dog. It had come down from the mountains in the hope of finding less of a tumult than fallen trees and rocks torn from the sides of the hills where it made its home. We could have killed the wild beast from where we stood, but had no desire to make an attack on such a night, when death threatened us on all sides.

As soon as our horses were quieted I deposited my fair burden in a corner of the corral, and laid her sleeping boy by her side. We covered both with blankets to protect them from the cool, damp air, and then Senora Costello put one of her well-formed arms around my neck, drew my head toward her face, and kissed me.

"You will not leave me?" she asked.

"No, I shall remain by your side until all danger is passed. Do not fear. I think you are safe here."

"If you had been my husband would you have left me on such a night as this?" she asked.

"No, I would have remained, and lived or died with you," was my answer, and I meant every word I uttered.

She sighed, and then encircled her boy in her arms, and closed her large, black, glorious eyes. I hoped she would ask for another kiss, but there was no such luck. Then Lewey returned to the house and secured our rifles, for we did not know but the demoralized soldiers might visit the place, and offer violence to the lady. The peons had fled at the first shock, and did not return home until long after daylight, and some of them looked and acted as though they had tasted Cook's aguardiente, or some other strong drink.

The rumblings of the earthquake grew fainter and fainter, and at last entirely ceased. We could hear the priest in the church offering up prayers for the safety of his flock, and then the sudden blasts of trumpets showed that the officers of the soldiers had recovered their senses, and were calling in their men from pillage.

In the course of an hour Senor Costello returned to look after his wife and child. He did not seem to think that he had been derelict in his duty, but said that he had prayed for the safety of his dear ones, and was glad the saints had listened to his prayers, which was very kind on their part, all things considered.

Then Captain Fernando made his sister a visit, and, when he had heard all the particulars of the night, paid Lewey and me a compliment, and gave his brother-in-law a few words of condemnation which he did not fail to understand.

We removed to the house as soon as all danger was passed, and once more the wife returned to her bed, and the boy to his crib, the little fellow not even awakening through all the noise and tumult. Squads of infantry were in the streets, with fixed bayonets and loaded muskets, looking for those who did not respond to the trumpet's call, and with orders to shoot all who had not ceased pillaging the better class of houses.

As it was not yet daylight I laid down on my blankets by the side of Lewey in the hope of getting a little sleep, and the last thing I heard was the complaint of my friend, as he said, —

"I is tired of dis sort of ding. I does de hard vork and you gets all de kisses. By gar, I no stand it much longer," but in the morning the French lad had forgotten his growling, and was as happy and careless as ever.

The sun came up warm and clear, with a gentle south wind. The air was no longer impregnated with the smell of sulphur, the fumes of which came from the rents in the earth. The cattle were quietly feeding, and had forgotten the perils of the night. The bear had waddled back to his quarters in the mountains, and probably was dreaming of the commotion that had sent him to the village in such a hurry. Cook was sitting on an empty barrel damning all kinds of greasers, high and low, counting up his losses, and calculating how much he would have to water his next stock of rum to make the account good.

The soldiers were sleeping off the fatigues of the night, and not until seven o'clock did the blasts of the trumpets awaken them to activity and a short drill before breakfast. Householders were taking an account of stock, and wondering if the articles stolen from their premises would ever be recovered, while the alcalda issued a proclamation recommending a day of feasting for the miraculous escape of the people from death, and, as all danger was passed, it met the approval of the church and the citizens at large. A bull-fight was proposed, but as no one dared to scour the country in search of a fierce toro, on account of Fremont and his men being near, the plan was given up, and a magnificent cock-fight substituted late in the afternoon, and those who lost their money said that they preferred an earthquake to such wicked sports.

About eleven o'clock Captain Fernando, in full uniform, came to see us, and stated that General Castro would receive and hear us immediately in regard to our enlistment. When we were ready to go to the government house Senora Costello threw a dark mantilla over her pretty head, and stated her intention of accompanying us to the presence of the general. Her brother remonstrated, but the lady was firm.

"The young gentlemen," she said, "aided me last night when I was deserted by my husband. I was in danger, and they stayed by my side. I am grateful, and if I can do them any good by my presence they shall see that kindness is not thrown away on me. I can go and tell uncle all the particulars, and he must have a hard heart to refuse my prayers."

Captain Fernando made no further opposition. We walked across the plaza to the residence of the general, the sentry presented arms as his superior passed him, and crossing a hall entered a room where Castro was seated, smoking cigarettes, and dictating despatches to a secretary.

"General," said Captain Fernando, "these are the two young men I spoke to you about. They saved the lives of your wife and my sister while escorting them from San Luis Obispo to this place. Last night they devoted themselves to Senora Costello while the earthquake was raging and her husband visiting the church to pray, instead of helping first and praying afterward."

"Prayer is good for all of us," said a mild, gentle voice, and a priest entered the room. "It is seemly at all times, but still I think it is better to return thanks after your wife and child are in a safe place than trust them entirely to the saints, for the latter can't look after all during an earthquake. I will bless the young men for saving so good a daughter as Senora Costello."

He raised his hands, and we bowed our heads, and when I again looked up saw that the padre was the one I had met at Santa Cruz so many times, and who had let me feast on the strawberry beds of the old Mission, when a sailor boy on the Admittance. He recognized me at once, and a smile passed over his calm face as he said, —

"I am glad to see you once more, my son. I did not expect to meet you here. I supposed you were home long since."

"Do you know the young man, holy father?" asked Castro.

"Oh, yes, and a good boy he is. I will answer for him," and the padre patted me on the cheek, in his old familiar manner.

"Can't you vouch for me also, holy father?" asked Lewey. "I am a Catholic, and my friend here is only a Protestant. According to our creed I should be much better than he."

"My lad," smiled the good priest, "religion does not stamp a man so that he can pass current as a Christian. But I will take the risk, and say that I think you are no worse than hundreds of others whom I meet in my daily life. The Senora Castro has given me excellent accounts of both of you, and now my daughter here is fully as enthusiastic in your praise."

"But that is only faint commendation for me, holy father," remarked Lewey, with his usual impudence.

"Let it suffice until we can learn more of your worth which you seem to think is not suspected. Remember, I have not met you as many times as I have your friend, therefore must be a little cautious in my remarks," and just then the general's wife entered the room, and the priest gave Lewey a smile that showed he could appreciate a joke as well as the French lad.

I placed a chair for the lady near her husband, and then drew back and resumed my position by the side of Lewey, for we were not requested to sit down in the presence of so much dignity, not being on an equality with those present.

"We were speaking of these young men," the padre said, as soon as Senora Castro had taken a seat, and given us a smile of welcome. "After all that I have heard I do not see how the general can refuse to grant them a discharge. Had they been Mexican soldiers they could not have done more to protect the ladies."

"They were worth a dozen Mexicans when the ladrones attacked us," remarked the pretty little wife, and her eyes flashed as she spoke; but the general did not like the speech, as he put great faith in his country's soldiery.

"The question is this," the general's wife cried, in a tone that proved she could make her presence felt when desired, and I noticed that all were hushed while she was speaking, "are the young men to be discharged from the army or not?"

"Certainly, my dear," the general cried, in a tone that showed he wanted to conciliate her.

"Will you please to give me a chance to speak without being interrupted?" the wife asked impatiently.

"Certainly, dear. Go on. We are listening to you with much eagerness I am sure. I told you last night that I would do just as you wished in regard to these men," and the general rubbed his hands, and looked at the priest as if asking his protection.

"General," Mrs. Castro remarked, with a withering smile, "if you could fight as hard as you talk Fremont and his band of ladrones would all be dead long before this."

"Yes, my dear," the warrior muttered, and then yielded the floor to the lady. It was evident she meant to have her own way and the last word at the same time.

"The young men have been tricked and deceived," Senora Castro said. "They were persuaded to matriculador, and did not understand the meaning of the word. They wanted to get married, and they did n't get married."

Here the general sighed. He did not seem to think that was a great calamity, as near as I could judge by his face. In fact, I rather thought he wanted to congratulate us on our lucky escape.

"The reason the young men were not married was because one of your agents stepped in and spoiled the matter, and then threatened to hang the senors if they did not enlist. Is that the way to build up the State, and increase the population?" Senora Castro asked with a frown, and her lord scratched his head, and said that he was satisfied such a plan would result in a dead failure to build up any State.

"I am glad to hear you admit so much," the lady exclaimed. "Now I have taken the liberty to summon to your presence the State agents, Antonio and Carlos Sanchos. The youngest brother, Edwardo, is wounded. He was shot in the mountains of Sierra Monica, and may die, as he deserves, for he attempted to murder the young men present, as they were crossing from Los Angeles to Santa Barbara. The scoundrel was injured, and is still in a bad way. I have learned this morning, through a companion of your agents, that Antonio had some grudge against the young men, and took this means to obtain revenge. You must investigate, and then revoke the commissions of the ladrones. You second me in this, do you not, holy father?"

The padre bowed as he replied in his gentle way, with a smile at the domestic scene.

"If the men are unworthy the general can't do better than to dismiss them from his service. California is too noble a State to harbor villains for officials."

"Let me say one word," Captain Fernando said, as soon as the padre had concluded. "If I had known all I would never have enlisted the young men under the circumstances. I was told that they were matriculadors and sospechosos, and that it would be a good thing to keep them under our eyes. The first day from Ranche Refugio they saved my life from the attack of a drunken soldier. I hanged the fellow on the limb of a tree."

General Castro nodded as though he rather approved of such summary treatment. One drunken Mexican was of little account in his estimation.

"At San Luis Obispo these same young men saved your wife and my sister from insult, and would not inform on the parties who committed the assault, for fear I would hang the guilty scoundrels."

"Do give me a chance to utter a thought," the Senora Castro said, and Lewey winked at me as much as to say, "Dis is berry funny." "I have said but a word since I entered the room."

The general sighed, and seemed to wish that he was far away, on the trail of Fremont and his men, or traveling through the country.

"When I tell you, general, that these young men have killed Apache warriors you will be surprised," Mrs. Castro cried, and her husband, supposing that he must show astonishment, ejaculated.—

"The saints preserve us! You don't mean it?" and then lighted a cigarette.

"Senor Larkin," a servant cried, and threw open the door, and the American consul entered the room, and seemed a little astonished at the number of people present.

"I have called, your excellency," Mr. Larkin cried, "to demand the discharge of these two young men."

"The Senors Antonia and Carlos Sanchos," the servant roared, and the two agents of the State entered the apartment, and were more surprised than Mr. Larkin on seeing the company.

"Look here," the general cried, "you two scoundrels have persecuted these young men. My wife would be angry if she was n't an angel," (he was not emphatic when he said this) "the holy father is indignant, and the American consul is about to threaten us with the vengeance of the United States, but that we do not fear. Mexico can take care of herself, and against a hundred foes, but Mr. Larkin is a good man, and we like to oblige him. Captain Fernando and his sister are not feeling as though the sailers were well treated, and I think the former struck you last evening in consequence. Speak up, and give me an explanation of your doings."

"The blow of the captain is still seen on my face,' Antonio said, his voice showing some of his hatred for Lewey and myself, and the young captain. "I have labored for the welfare of California, and thought that I had done good service. I was told to arrest all sospechosos, and impress matriculadors for the army. My orders state this in positive terms. I met the young men at San Diego. I suspected them of giving information to the enemy. In fact, they were left behind for that purpose."

"That is a lie," responded Mr. Larkin. "The boys were discharged ill with the smallpox. I have the certificates of the captain of the ship, and also of the agent, to that effect. Here they are."

Don Antonio looked a little abashed at this information, for he had not expected such testimony from the American consul, and before any one could speak I stepped forward.

"Senora Castro," I said, speaking to the wife, for I knew that if I enlisted her aid I should have that of her husband, "let me explain the cause of this man's enmity. One day in San Francisco he insulted the daughter of General Vallejo, and my friend and I punished him for his cowardly act. He drew a knife to cut us, and in the struggle I jabbed the back of his hand with a boat-hook. You can see the scar if the fellow will hold up his arm."

Antonio did not seem disposed to do this, so I continued, —

"When the man found that we were left on shore, through our unfortunate sickness" (here Lewey winked with both eyes), "he determined to persecute us, and has continued to do so until we were fortunate enough to be placed as escort to two ladies, and they were so kind to us that it was a pleasure to defend them from the attacks of ladrones, or any one else. They owe us nothing. We owe them everything for their kindness."

"I couldn't do better mineself," Lewey said in English, in a half whisper, so low that even Mr. Larkin could not catch the words, as he was a little deaf. "By gar, but you did rub it on ; and dat voman vill swaler every vord of it', and believe all dat you say. De Yanks beat de French at de blarney."

"Did you ever hear a more manly little marinero muchacho?" asked Senora Castro of her husband, and the general said that he thought I stood away up to the head, as far as he could see, and Senora Costello murmured some words that sounded very sweet, and I thought she compared me to an angel.

"Now," said the wife of the governor, "do an act of justice. You have heard both sides. Issue the order for the young men's discharge, and withdraw their matriculadors, so that they will no longer owe allegiance to Mexico and California."

"It shall be done. Make out the papers immediately," the general said to his secretary. "Revoke the matriculadors, and give the young men documents allowing them to remain and travel in the State, where they please and when they please. All that I require of them is that they will swear not to take up arms against us or Mexico."

"We will do it," the impulsive Lewey exclaimed. "We love the people too well to raise our arms against them," and that seemed to satisfy all parties except the captain.

"I ask, general, that you will now revoke the commissions of these two enganchadors," pointing to Antonio and Carlos. "They are not such men as you need for the work. Dishonorably discharge them, and without delay."

"One moment," cried Antonio. "Let me say a word."

"How dare you speak without permission?" asked the general's wife.

"Yes, how dare you open your mouth until I have given consent?" thundered the general.

"He 's dished," muttered Lewey in English. "Nothin' can save him now. Ve has de vind aft all de time."

"Give up your commissions this moment," shouted the general, "and leave the town without delay, or I 'll have you shot before sundown."

"My own dear husband," cried Senora Castro, and threw her arms around the general's neck, and kissed him on the nose, the most convenient place.

"My own kind uncle," Senora Costello exclaimed, and around his neck went her arms.

Antonio and Carlos drew their commissions from their breasts, and laid them on the table, by the side of the secretary, and then bowing, left the room, glad to escape without further injury.

"How can we thank your excellency for this kindness?" I said.

The general, as soon as he could escape from the embraces of the women, seemed to think the matter over, and finally said, —

"You speak good English, do you not?"

"Yes, general. It is my native tongue."

"Then repay my kindness by doing me a favor. I want to send a messenger to Captain Fremont's camp. Will you take a letter to him from me?"

Mr. Larkin motioned with his lips to say "yes," for some reason or other, and I stated that I would go provided I could be accompanied by Lewey.

"I have no objections," the general remarked. "In fact, I will give you an escort of ten mounted men if you desire it."

"I do not require it," was my answer. "I think that if I am to hunt for Captain Fremont in the mountains it would be much better to go unattended. Of course you do not wish me to play the part of spy on his movements? That I will not consent to do."

"No," was the reply, in a hesitating tone. "I should like to know the strength of his force and what he means to do, but you need not play the part of a spy. None of my scouts seem able to get information, and all have returned to the town baffled, afraid of this American and his trappers."

"On those conditions I will undertake the task," I said. "When do you require us to start?"

"Tomorrow morning. By that time I will have your instructions all ready. You must return as soon as possible," and the general bowed to show that the interview was terminated.

As I left the governor's residence Mr. Larkin walked along the plaza by my side.

"Tonight," the consul said, "I will send you a sealed package by a trusty messenger. Do not let any one see it, or allow the fact to be known. The paper you must place in Captain Fremont's own hand, and bring to me his reply in an equally careful manner. I have been endeavoring to communicate with him for a week or more, but failed time and time again through the fear of my couriers. Your appointment as messenger by General Castro is a wonderful piece of good luck for the United States government and myself. Be careful and discreet, and when you return report not more than half what you see. Be faithful and you shall reap a rich reward. Ask your French friend to keep a close mouth. You can trust him, I suppose?"

"With my life," was the fervent answer.

"That is well. Still, do not tell him more of my business than you can help. We are surrounded by spies, and even now men are watching us. We must be seen together no longer. Do not come near me again, or speak to me if we should meet. I will see that a paper is slipped into your hand this evening, and that the letter you bring me from Captain Fremont is asked for outside the limits of the town. It may be an Indian woman who will give you my despatch and take the one you bring. If such is the case she will meet you on the trail, near the Mission Carmel, hold out her hand, and utter but one word, and that one will be 'papel.' It will be of no use to question her, for she will not respond. As soon as you hand her the paper she will plunge into the chapparel and disappear, and you will see her no more. If any one should be near pretend that she asked for charity, but drop the letter in the bushes. She will see your action, and secure the document. Do you understand all this quite plainly?"

"Yes, sir."

"Then good-by, and success to your mission," and the American consul walked off, and left me to the pleasing reflection that I was involved in a delicate piece of business, and might meet with trouble before I ended, for it looked to me as though I had got to serve two masters, and I might fail in pleasing them both.

Lewey, when I joined him, was delighted with the thought of undertaking the excursion. There was just enough danger in it to suit him. He wanted to be stirring, and meeting with adventures, and dreaded a life that was not full of excitement.

I did not think it advisable to go to the mountains in the costume of a Mexican ranchero, for I feared some of the trappers might make a mistake and pick me off by accident, or on purpose, so once more paid a visit to Cook and his sacked pulperia. The old man was disconsolate over the events of the past night, and had drunk more of his remaining stock of aguardiente than was good for his health, or his understanding. We told him that we now required complete outfits of sailor's costumes, and he had just what we wanted, — hats, trousers, and blue flannel shirts. The only change required being the removal of the word "Ceynne" from the bands on the sinnet sombreros, the men who had pawned them for rum not taking the trouble to conceal the name of the national ship from which they had come.

Our new additional suits did not cost us more than three dollars, and, as we paid cash for the articles, Cook was so much moved by the trade that he offered to treat us to a glass of liquor, and when we declined the tots said that he would drink them himself, and did so. Luckily, they were well watered so not much harm was done.

We passed the day in looking over the town, and in calling on our comrades of the cavalry. They professed great joy in seeing us, and learning that we were discharged from the service. Two ordinary greasers had been appointed sergeants in our place, and very proud they were of their new positions. I am sorry to state that Lewey and I never received a cent for the time we were in the Mexican army, and, in fact, we were so glad to be discharged that we did not think it prudent to put in a claim for pay, but if ever the Mexican government rewards its veterans for services rendered I shall ask for a grant of land, as I did as much duty for California as some of our soldiers who are on the United-States pension list, and in the same war, but under the American flag.

We remained on the plaza and saw our company drill in the afternoon. The horsemanship was magnificent, but the evolutions were wonderful to contemplate, and yet in less than six months that same body of men, under Captain Fernando, lent its aid in giving our people a severe thrashing, while on the march from San Pedro to Los Angeles, composed as the Americans were of good sailors and steady marines, five hundred of them in all, and not as many Mexicans, but the latter had a field-piece, and that decided the day against us, for the United-States forces were in such a hurry that they left their ships without artillery. It was supposed that an advance was equivalent to a victory, but it was not so in this case. The lesson was a dear one for our naval officers and it was not forgotten while on the coast, as when Commodore Stockton started his expedition from San Diego for the Pueblo Los Angeles, with five hundred men and sixty United-States dragoons, he took six pieces of artillery, and won a big victory at San Gabriel, entered the city of orange-trees and grapes in triumph, and held it during the remainder of the war.

In our rambles during the day we did not encounter Antonio or Carlos Sanchos, and were told that they had left town for San Francisco. We hoped that such was the case, but afterward learned that the scoundrels had gone in another direction, and we were destined to again meet them in an unexpected manner.

We went to the beach, and sat down on the veranda of the old custom house, and looked off on the quiet bay, and recalled the circumstances of our early days, and thought how quickly the years had fled. All of our hardships on board the vessel were forgotten, and our duckings in the surf were things to be smiled at, and not commented on in an unfavorable manner. We saw some of the crew of the schooner California, the first lieutenant, or mate, Mr. Willard, of Salem, Mass., and his tattooed kanakas, but the war did not seem to trouble them any, and they ate and slept as much as ever, when they could draw rations from the government. They did not think that any of our national ships would venture to attack the schooner, and in this we agreed with them, for who would venture near that old Queen Anne musket, backed by a kanaka?

We wondered where the Admittance was, and our shipmates, and thought how surprised they would be to see us, and learn about the adventures we had passed through since we separated,

Donna Costello was as pleased as ourselves at our release from the Mexican service, and for the first time insisted that we should sit and dine at her own table. As her husband ventured to offer an objection she asked him why he disappeared so suddenly the night before when the earthquake was raging. That silenced the man, and he made no more remonstrance.

During the evening, while Lewey and I sat in the front yard, smoking and talking over the business of the next day, an Indian woman staggered toward us, and, as she neared me, fell almost in my lap. I uttered an emphatic exclamation, and was about to push her from me, when I felt a paper thrust into my hand. Recollecting Mr. Larkin's instructions I put the document in the bosom of my shirt, and the woman regained her feet, and wandered off, staggering and muttering drunken curses on all mankind, and the white race in particular. Lewey did not notice the act, and I said nothing to enlighten him on the subject.

The night passed off without disturbance of any serious kind. The soldiers yelled themselves hoarse, but we were accustomed to the noise and paid no attention to it, sleeping until sunrise. Then we had a good wash, and donned our sailor suits, fed our horses with a measure of barley, ate our breakfast, and waited for the orders and letter from General Castro. Captain Fernando brought both at eight o'clock, and in a few minutes we had saddled our horses, taken leave of Donna Costello, who looked a little sad as she bade us good-by, whistled to the delighted Jack, and dashed out of town toward the Mission Carmel.

We did not meet even a ranchero on the road, or trail, and as we ascended the mountains made as much noise as possible, and even Lewey sang a French song in a shrill tone, as if desirous of attracting some attention.

When on the summit of the range, and near the place where we had met the scouts a few days before, one long, agonizing note from Lewey appeared to have the desired effect of awakening life in that vast solitude, for two rough, well-armed men stepped from a thicket of bushes in front of us, and looking back we saw others in our rear, with rifles all ready for use.

"Halt," was the order, and we obeyed.

"Who are yer?" was the next question, and we saw that two of the men were the same persons we had encountered once before on the mountains.

"I am an American," I said, "as I told you day before yesterday."

"Well, what do yer want here?" was the stern question.

"To see Captain Fremont. We have despatches for him from General Castro."

"Why did n't the gineral come with them himself?" asked the leader of the scouts.

"He is particularly engaged in counting his money and drilling his men," I answered.

"How much money has he, and how many men?" was the gruff question.

"That we do not know. He would not trust us with his plata, and we were not interested in the greasers under his command. We agreed to carry a letter to Captain Fremont, and expect to be paid for it. Show us your leader, and our duty is ended."

"Yes, and yer lives too, if you play any of yer monkey shines on us. Give me the letter, and I will see that the captain gits it," and the scout held out his hand.

"Gently, my friend," I remarked. "I must see the captain in person. I have a duty to perform or I get no pay, and you would n't take the bread out of the mouths of two hard-working sailors, would you?"

"Blast yer, were n't yer in greasers' costume the other day?"

"Yes, and today we are in our national dress, such as we delighted to wear under the stars and stripes."

The men consulted together, and then the leader said, —

"Come along with me. I 'll take yer to the camp, and if yer prove traitors we 'll put some bullets in yer carcasses so quick yer won't know what hurted yer."

The leader of the party and another man motioned for us to follow them. We left the trail, and they led us to a clearing where fire had raged sometime. Near the place were half a dozen horses hitched to trees. The men mounted, and rode through the chapparel and bushes for an hour or two, and when we were near Hawk's Peak, some thirty miles from Monterey, a halt was called for rest and consultation, and we imagined that we were near Fremont's quarters, and should soon see the explorer and his command.

CHAPTER X.

CAPTAIN FREMONT'S CAMP. — THE MESSAGES AND DESPATCHES. — A NIGHT SCENE AROUND A FIRE. — THE COYOTES' CALL. — THE LETTERS FOR GENERAL CASTRO AND MR. LARKIN. — INSTRUCTIONS. — ON THE TRAIL. — THE INDIAN WOMAN. — THE CAVALRY SQUAD. — THE SEARCH FOR LETTERS. — GENERAL CASTRO IS SURPRISED. — LEWEY TELLS SOME STORIES. — STORMING THE CAMP. — FISHING IN A FOG. — THE AMERICAN FRIGATE. — SPIES ON ALL SIDES. — A FRIENDLY WARNING. — A NIGHT OF TERROR. — A GLAD SIGHT.

AS soon as our guides called a halt on the summit of the mountain, a place that some people call San Juan and others, Hawk's Peak, although I think the latter name is the recognized authority, we knew that we were near the camp of the invader.

"Strangers," said the trapper, "yer can't go no further on this trail until yer is blindfolded. Yer may be all right, and I hope yer is, but we is used to Injun ways, and don't trust no one till he is proved honest. We 'll just slip a serape over yer heads, and then lead the hosses, and yer won't know much of our place arter yer leaves it. Now hold still, and keep quiet. We won't be rough unless yer is."

"Go ahead," we said. "Only don't fool with the dog as he is dangerous to strangers. Let him see all that he can, and we 'll go it blind."

"Them 'ere is good poker words, stranger," was the grim rejoinder, although we were not aware of it at the time. "Now hold still. I reckon yer won't see much, and if yer comes near smotherin' jist sing out and we 'll give yer a little air to save yer lives."

As the blankets were put over our heads one of the scouts uttered a cry like the bark of a coyote, and after a moment's silence the sound was reposted far off in the distance, but in what direction we could not tell, owing to our heads being muffled in such a disagreeable manner.

"All right, come along," the scouts said. "The trail is clear."

They seized our horses' bridles, and led them over rocky places, through groves of trees, up hill and down, for half an hour or more. Then the animals were halted, we heard voices expressing surprise at our appearance, the blankets were pulled from our heads, and we found ourselves surrounded by forty or fifty rough and tough looking trappers, dressed in various kinds of hunting costume, and armed with rifles, revolvers, and knives. We looked at the men as earnestly as they regarded us, and then one person asked, —

"Is them 'ere Castro's scouts? They seem fitted more for salt water than land service."

"Hold yer yop," our guide said. "Let the lads get their wind afore yer talks to 'em. Where is the cap'en? The young fellers has some papers for him. I 'spect Castro has sent us an invitation to dinner, and I a'n't got no biled shirt to put on to meet the Mexican senoras."

"You is handsome enough without," was the response, and then his companions laughed, and while the rough jokes were cracked fast and furious, Lewey and I dismounted, secured our horses, and waited for the appearance of the commander of the forces, a man we had heard of but never seen all the time we were on the coast.

"Why don't yer go and speak to the cap'en?" our guide asked, while we were looking around the camp, puzzled at all we saw, and bewildered by the remarks that met us on every hand, some of them none too polite.

"Where is he?" I demanded.

"Over thar, settin' on a stump. He 's waitin' for yer."

Now we had expected to see a man of commanding presence, with glittering uniform, and sword by his side, plumes in his hat, and a general air of daintiness and neatness, but the person pointed out as Captain Fremont was not up to our expectations, as far as show was concerned. He was slight in figure, wore a hunting shirt of dressed deer-skin, leggings and moccasins, and around his temples was a common cotton handkerchief, with bright colors, forming a singular-looking head gear, but such as the poorer class of Mexicans sometimes wore beneath their broad sombreros. The ends of the panuelo hung down the wearer's back, and were knotted as if containing small pieces of silver, the safest place to carry and have them convenient for use. There was no sword, no knife, not even a pistol in the captain's belt. He was the last person in the camp we should have selected for an important command, as, if the truth must be told, he was dressed a little worse than his companions, and perhaps a trifle dirtier. But his face and eyes were attractive, and showed power and endurance, and when he spoke there was something in his tones that denoted will and courage.

We were so astonished at the appearance of the man that we could only stare at him for a few minutes, unable to speak. Perhaps Fremont realized the feelings he inspired, and let us gaze without interrupting our meditations, but, after he supposed we had looked him over long enough, suddenly said, —

"Well, lads, who are you and what do you want?"

He did not speak in an impatient tone, or as though he was angry, but just as a business man does when he tells one of his clerks to fill an order and waste no time about it if he knows what is good for himself.

"Is you de celebrated Captain Fremont?" asked Lewey, who was anxious to make a good impression, "and does you speak de French?"

"I am Captain Fremont, but never mind about the French as long as you speak English," was the reply, and a cold, chilly smile accompanied the words, as if the speaker did not care for joking.

"Captain," I said, "this young man is a native of France, and I am an American. We were formerly sailors in the same ship, but were discharged on account of sickness. We thought of marrying, and settling down in the country, but have been disappointed."

At this stage of the story the captain grinned, as I supposed he would. Our pathetic love story always made both thoughtless and serious laugh, just as though two boys could not be stricken with the tender passion, and desire to wed.

"Come to the point," the captain remarked, as soon as the smile disappeared. "You wish to join my force since there is no chance for matrimony. Is that the case?"

"No, sir, far from it. We have had all the soldiering we desire for the balance of our lives," and I rapidly related our experience in the cavalry.

He was kind enough to listen without a word of comment, and when I had concluded asked abruptly, —

"How many men are there in that company of cavalry, and who commands it?"

If he expected to get any information from us he was mistaken, even if he did take us by surprise in asking the question.

"Pardon me, captain," I said, "we are not here as spies or tale-bearers, so please ask us no questions that would not be honorable in us to answer. We came here as messengers for General Castro simply because we were available, and can speak English. He discharged us from the Mexican service, recalled our matriculadors, and is to give us a pass to reside or travel in any part of the State. We perform this duty as a debt of gratitude to him, and with the understanding that we should not be required to state what we saw here, or heard, your strength or intentions. The general's despatches will tell you all that you require to know about his business."

He looked at us calmly, seemed to weigh each word that I uttered, as if to determine my sincerity, and, while the captain and I were thus occupied, Lewey put in his oar.

"Ve has been unfortunate in not bein' married, but at de same time ve is bery honest young men," just as though that was going to help us.

As Lewey uttered the words the captain looked at him, and so steadily that my friend dropped his eyes, for the first time a little abashed at his temerity in speaking.

"You need say nothing about the forces under General Castro," Captain Fremont said, after a pause, "if you think such a course compromises you in the least. I know as well as you do how many men he can muster, infantry and cavalry, and that the latter are not of much account just at present. I saw some of them pass over the mountains the other day, and the sight was not inspiring to a warrior. Give me the letter from the general. I will read it, and send an answer tomorrow. It is too late today for you to return to town. We shall have to keep you in camp all night. The passes are difficult, and my scouts might tumble on you in the canyons, or on the trails, and make a mistake, perhaps a fatal one. We will do all that we can to see that you are comfortable, and do not get hungry."

He nodded to a Delaware Indian, exchanged a few words with him in a low tone, and then said, —

"This man will look after your horses, and see that they are piquetted and fed. They will be safe in the morning, never fear, although both are nice-looking animals, and the temp'ation to steal them is great on the part of my men. The Delaware will watch over and guard the mustangs as if they were his own, or what is more, as if they had become my property."

I approached and put General Castro's letter in the commander's hand, and as I did so gave him Mr. Larkin's document at the same time.

"One is from the American consul," I said. "He is anxious to communicate with you for some reason best known to himself. I will take your answer, and see that he gets it safely. I do this for the honor of my country and not for gain. I act as messenger for General Castro, and not Mr. Larkin, but the latter will keep the matter to himself, and I hope you will also. My safety depends upon it."

He nodded, drew aside his hunting dress, and put the papers in his bosom, and as he did so I saw that instead of wearing white linen next to his skin he had a red flannel shirt like the rest of his men, and not a particle cleaner, as far as I could judge by a hasty glance.

I never fully knew the contents of either despatch, but I surmised that the Mexican general stated to Captain Fremont his firm intention of kicking him out of the State in short order unless he took his departure in a given time. Mr. Larkin's letter, I was afterward partially informed, contained the important announcement that the Columbus, Independence, and Congress were near the coast, and might be expected in Monterey harbor at any time. Fremont was advised to risk no general engagement, as the Mexicans were in strong force, and if they conquered the result would be disastrous for American interests. This was sound and good advice, and I have always taken credit to myself for carrying such valuable information to one who was hemmed in by mountains and an unfriendly and revengeful people. If the United States government is disposed to grant me a pension for my services on the occasion, dating from 1846, I shall not refuse it, for money is always valuable to people who write books for a living. But, as republics are ungrateful, I fear the government will never do justice, and vote me the money.

The commander of the forces retired to the shade of a tree to read his despatches, while Lewey and I wandered around the enclosure, which the men had fortified by felling trees, forming a complete abatis, the branches extending outward, making the storming of the place one of extreme difficulty, especially when the inner circle was defended by sixty-five men who were accustomed to the use of rifles all their lives, and dead shots at one hundred yards or more.

When dinner was ready we were requested to take our share with the men. The food consisted of venison, and not much else, but as there was enough of it no one went hungry. Every hour a trapper would drop in, and make a report, and another one depart for some secret service. It was evident that nothing went on outside of the lines that the commander did not know, and a surprise by the Mexicans was out of the question.

We were treated very kindly by the trappers. They saw that Captain Fremont had received us without suspicion, and while they asked us for news they did not insist upon knowing too much of what was going on in

town. One of them inquired if we were shaken up by the earthquake, and asked how Cook felt at the loss of his aguardiente? Then some of the men laughed, and one brawny fellow said, —

"I should like to have been thar, and got a whack at that rum. It seems to me, Jim, yer could have made away with a bottle or two outside of yer skin, darn yer eyes," and Jim responded by saying in a significant tone, —

"I had somethin' else to think of jist at that time, with a hundred frightened greasers around me, and any one of 'em ready to cut my wizzen at the first sign I give of bein' a Yank."

This was proof to me that one of the trappers had visited Monterey on the night of the earthquake, in disguise, and seen all that transpired, and taken note of the Mexican forces and surroundings. The mission was a dangerous one, and if he had been discovered his life would have paid the penalty of his rashness. But as Jim spoke some Spanish he probably moved through the crowd unnoticed and undetected.

That evening we sat around the camp-fire, smoked our pipes, and listened to the tough yarns of the trappers and guides. They told of bold encounters with Indians, grisly bears, and other animals, and seemed as careless of the future as school boys. They did not know the plans of their commander, and appeared regardless what they were, as long as he led them, confident that he would cut his way through all obstacles, though the Mexicans numbered ten to one. They had come from the banks of the Sacramento River, marched by easy stages to their present camp, and would leave when they got ready, and not before. I think that they were the most indifferent, careless set of men that I ever saw in an enemy's country, considering their number, and with no hope for relief in case they were cut off in their line of retreat.

The commander rolled himself up in his blankets under a tree, a saddle for a pillow, and went to sleep, six Delaware Indians — his devoted body guard — lying on the ground near him, ready to start into life and activity at a moment's notice, with rifles at their sides, and long knives ready to grasp.

It was a strange and weird scene, that night in camp, as we sat near the fire, with stout bearded men all around us, the wind sighing through the trees, the stars shining brightly overhead, and the mysterious noises of the forests coming up from the valleys and sides of the mountain. Once in a while the sharp bark of a coyote was heard, and then the trappers listened very attentively, and after the noise was repeated would mutter, —

"That 's a real brute arter a supper," or else some one growled out, —

"What's the matter with Jake that he's makin' all that fuss?" showing that these men of the wilderness could tell the false from the true, although to my ears both yelps sounded alike, and I could not distinguish the human imitation from the real snapping and snarling of the brutes.

One by one the hunters dropped off to sleep, and then Lewey and I and Jack rolled ourselves up in our blankets, and with saddles for pillows went to sleep, and we heard no more noise until daylight, when the men got up, yawned and stretched themselves, and some prepared breakfast, while others shouldered their rifles, and departed upon secret service, uttering no word, and receiving no orders.

"The cap'en wants yer lads," growled the trapper who had led us into camp, soon after breakfast, and we removed the pipes from our mouths, and went to the commander, who had resumed his seat on the stump of a tree, and looked just as he did the day before, handkerchief and all, calm and contented, apparently without a thought of what the day would bring forth.

"Have you eaten your breakfast?" Captain Fremont asked as we stood before him.

"Yes, sir."

"Then you can return to town immediately I suppose?"

"Yes, sir, if you desire us to go," was our prompt answer.

"I do," and then turning to a Delaware who stood near, ever watchful, for fear of treachery, Captain Fremont said, —

"Saddle these young men's animals immediately, so that they can depart."

The Delaware went on his mission, and then the commander took two documents from his pocket, and handed them to me.

"One of these," he said, "is for Mr. Larkin and the other for General Castro. You will see that both safely reach their destination. I have requested permission of the governor to make my way to Santa Barbara by land. He has refused compliance, and now I shall have to go without consulting him, and in defiance of his army."

"The task is a dangerous one, captain," I could not resist saying. "Twice your number of men could not accomplish it."

A faint smile passed over the bronzed face that looked so hard and stern, and then the great explorer remarked, —

"I know all the dangers of the route, young man, as well as you, perhaps a little better. But impress upon General Castro's mind, if he should question you, that my mind is made up, and go I will."

"I shall give him no information on that point," I cried hastily. " I did not come here as a spy, and refuse to act the part of one."

'Young man," the captain said in a stern tone, and with a look on his face that showed he was weighing his words very carefully, "I want you to benefit your country and me at the same time. You must volunteer to guide General Castro and his army to this camp."

"Never," I said very emphatically, and looked the indignation that I felt at the suggestion.

"Nebber," muttered Lewey. "Ve is not mouchers, by von blanked eight."

The explorer waited until our indignation had subsided, and then spoke quite as calmly as before, as though he did not feel discouraged by our refusal.

"Understand me, young men. No harm can happen to my command if you do as I request. I have a motive in making it. Listen to me attentively, and I speak thus plainly because I think you honest and trustworthy. If you were not I should withhold my confidence. General Castro must be led here, and given the impression that I am weak in point of numbers and intrenchment. I want him to charge the camp, and capture it."

"That would involve the shedding of much blood, and our own lives would be sacrificed by the defeated Mexicans. No, captain, you must think of some other scheme. We will not take part in the one you propose," I said.

"You silly boys," was the reply, "did I not say the camp was to be captured by the Mexicans?"

"Then you and the men will lose your lives. The Mexicans are prejudiced against you, and will spare not if they succeed in getting you in their power. Better fight and fall, than be captured and shot by the enraged greasers."

"Very wise counsel, young man," was the calm reply, "but I do not propose to be captured or shot if I can prevent it. All that I ask for is time, and time I must have. Listen to me, and pay particular attention to what I have to say, for it is important, and I will trust you. We have but ten rounds of ammunition for each man, and that is not enough for a siege. The sloop-of-war Portsmouth, I have just learned by a courier, is at San Francisco, and from her we can get all the powder and lead we desire. I expected some here, but my agents have been cut off. I thought I should find the frigate Congress in Monterey harbor, or at Santa Barbara, but she has not arrived at either place. General Castro is preparing to throw a force between me and the latter port. He has a regiment of cavalry at Santa Cruz to cut off my retreat to Yerba Buena. Tomorrow five companies will occupy the canyons between here and Santa Barbara. I could whip either force if I had plenty of ammunition. But as I have not I must do the best I can, and avoid giving or accepting battle. If Castro will withdraw his men from Santa Cruz, and concentrate them in front of me, under the impression that I am determined to go to Santa Barbara, all would be well. You can manage this by reporting that I am fierce for a forward movement, and will make one at all hazards, say by the day after tomorrow. Do you understand me?"

"Yes, sir. When the camp is charged on there will be no one here to capture," I remarked.

"That is about the whole story," was the careless reply, with a faint smile.

"I can do it," Lewey said. "If my friend no vant to speak on account of his country me do it for him. I does not vant to tell a lie, but I vill for vonce. Dat is, I let fall de hint."

The captain nodded, and waved his hand to intimate that the interview was terminated, and also for the Delaware to bring up the horses all saddled.

"You will not be blindfolded in returning to town," Captain Fremont said, as we mounted our mustangs and called the dog. "Keep your eyes open, and note the trails and canyons. You may want to find your way back in case of necessity," and, just as we were about to bid the explorer adieu, who should enter the camp, in charge of two scouts, but Antonio and Carlos Sanchos.

We could not divine their errand, for it was evident they were willing captives, and then it suddenly struck me that the greasers were Fremont's spies, and in his pay, or else were desirous of selling their services to him in revenge for their treatment by General Castro.

"Captain," I cried, as the Mexicans moved toward him, their dark faces showing some of the hate they felt for us, yet surprised at the meeting in an enemy's camp, "these two ruffians are the worst scoundrels in California. They will sell you for an ounce of gold. Do not put any faith in them. They will lie and steal from all parties."

"I know them," was the quiet response.

"And, cap'en," cried the irrepressible Lewey, "please keep de throat-cutters in de camp till ve is clear of de trails and de canyons. Ve does not care to meet sich peoples in de vilderness unless ve has de fust shot. Au revoir."

We touched the horses, and passed out of the only entrance that was clear of fallen trees, and as we did so saw the two Mexican greasers gazing after us, hate stamped on their ugly faces, yet baffled because they did not understand a word we had uttered, not comprehending our English, yet suspecting we had given Fremont a hint.

The rude trappers joked us as we passed them, and intimated that they would soon see us again.

"We shall be in Monterey in a little while," they said. "Tell old Cook to get in a fresh stock of rum, and not to water it. We want ours strong."

Outside of the abatis a Delaware Indian on foot joined us, and said that he was to act as guide to the main trail.

"Follow me, and keep still and close," he said, and then moved along the mountain side, down the valley, through a narrow gorge, and finally back the main trail that led to Monterey.

"You go dat way," the Indian said, and pointed in the direction of the town, and without another word he turned and plunged into the forest, and was lost to sight, and we could not even hear his footsteps over the dry leaves and fagots so careful was the red man in picking his way back to camp. We noticed that he did not return the same route that he followed when acting as our escort.

We had seen no one since leaving Hawk's Peak, and yet I had no doubt but that watchful eyes noted our movements, and kept the run of our course, and was the more convinced of this because, as we turned toward the town, we heard far up the side of the mountain the hoarse cawing of a crow, yet not a bird of that species was in sight. Then further along there was another "caw," "caw," and suddenly the wild scream of an eagle, and then all was quiet, and the forest seemed deprived of life, for not so much as a deer bounded across the trail as we loped along on our way to Monterey.

Just before we got to the Mission Carmel we noticed an Indian woman picking berries by the side of the road. She was so much occupied that she did not even look toward us, but continued her work, with head bent down and busy fingers.

"What luck, old lady?" asked Lewey, as we walked our horses past her.

She did not glance at us, but simply uttered one single word, and that was, —

"Papel."

Remembering Mr. Larkin's instructions, I dropped the letter which I had received for him from Captain Fremont into a clump of bushes, and passed on, but as I glanced back the Indian woman was working her way toward the place where the missive was concealed, and when we turned a bend in the trail, and took one more look, she had disappeared from sight, and I saw no more of her, but it was lucky she met us just as she did, for as we turned we ran plump into a squad of Mexican cavalry, who were drawn across the road, on the watch for stragglers and foreign scouts, and rather careless in the handling of their carbines, for four or five were pointed at us, all of them loaded and cocked, and the sergeant of the force yelled out in a fierce tone, —

"Parada."

Of course we stopped. It is always best to obey orders when you can't help yourself, and to have green soldiers fooling with loaded guns in your presence is not suggestive of a long and happy life.

"Who are you?" the sergeant demanded, as he rode up to take a look at us. The fellow knew us very well, but pretended that he did not, for some reason we could not divine.

"We are couriers in the employ of General Castro," Lewey answered. "We have despatches for his excellency."

"Let me see them," was the next order.

The paper was shown to him, but as he could not read it did not help matters much.

"Dismount, and let me search you," the petty officer commanded.

"What for?" demanded Lewey. "We do not wish to waste time. We have no papers on our persons except this one from Captain Fremont to the governor."

"You have seen the robber, have you?" asked the non-commissioned officer, and his men listened with eager looks.

"We left Captain Fremont only a few hours ago," was our cautious reply.

"How many men has he under his command?" the soldier asked.

"Pardon me," I cried, "these are matters for the general, and not for you. If we are detained much longer it is probable you will hear of it in some forcible manner. His excellency is not a patient man when he is waiting for news."

"He must wait this time," was the answer, "for I am going to search both of you. Such are my orders, I am sorry to say."

"Do you not recollect us?" I asked. "You must have seen us yesterday morning when we departed from Monterey."

"Yes, and when you came with the volante, as escort for the general's wife and Captain Fernando's sister. We know you quite well, but fo. all that we must search you. It is orders."

The cunning Castro, or some one else, had feared and suspected we would have a package for Mr. Larkin, and if that was obtained the true condition of Captain Fremont and his force would be known. The American consul knew the peculiarities of Mexican character, however, and had posted the Indian woman where she would be apt to encounter us before the soldiers were stumbled upon. The latter never thought the industrious berry-picker was waiting for a paper that the Mexican government was anxious to get hold of, and so she passed on her way, and the document was duly received that same evening by Mr. Larkin, and I may as well state hat we were awarded the sum of twenty dollars for our services, more than enough to pay for our sailor suits. I trust the United States reimbursed the consul for the outlay, but fear not.

We dismounted, and the sergeant went through our clothing like an expert pick-pocket. He found nothing, however, but was a little curious over our money belts, where our doubloons were secreted. Lewey told the man that they were charms for keeping off evil spirits, and so our gold was not disturbed, as we feared it would be, for there was enough to tempt a whole company of cavalry to commit murder.

"Go on," said the sergeant, as soon as the examination was concluded. "You are all right. We are satisfied that you have told the truth. Now ride fast, for General Castro is expecting you, and anxious for your appearance."

We did not waste any time, but remounted our horses, and dashed toward the town, arriving about three o'clock in the afternoon. We went directly to the government house, but the general was taking a hort siesta, and could not be disturbed, so waited an hour before he awoke and received us.

"Well, senors," he asked, as we were ushered into his presence, "how did you find Captain Fremont and his band of plunderers?"

"The captain is well, general, and sends you this despatch for your information," and I handed the governor the letter I had received from the explorer.

The general opened it, looked at the writing, and then said, in a tone of scorn,—

"It is in English. I do not read that language. Translate for me, and let us hear what he says."

I took the document, and by Lewey's aid made out that the captain was defiant, and intended to march to Santa Barbara at all hazards, and at an early day. He declared that his intentions were peaceable, but he should use force against force if necessary, and kill all who opposed his progress.

The governor was indignant, as he had a right to be. He swore a little in choice Spanish, and then turned to us and asked, —

"How many men has this Fremont under his command?"

"General," I said, "you know you promised we should not be used as spies. Please spare us the pain of refusing your request for information."

The general frowned, and Lewey saw that the answer was not agreeable. He tried to blunt the point of my speech by shoving in an oar in his usual impressive manner.

"My friend," he said, "is an American, and proud of his country. He thinks that it would be treason to give reports that might damage his nation. But I am a Frenchman, and can do as I please. Question me, general, and I will answer like a truthful man."

I gave Lewey a look that should have made him quiver, but he did not appear to notice it. He seemed hardened, and lost to all shame.

"Well, my friend," asked Castro, "how many men has Fremont under his command?"

"Two hundred," was the prompt response. "I counted them all, and know Every hunter is a dead shot with his rifle, and say that they can march all over the country, and no one dare to dispute their way."

I looked at the lad with admiration. He could lie magnificently when he was disposed to let himself out, and it was evident he was going to do justice to his reputation during the interview.

"I thought," cried the surprised governor, "that there were not more than one hundred los Americanos."

"A mistake, I assure your excellency. The captain is so strong that he thinks of sending part of his force to Santa Cruz, and capturing the regiment that is there. I heard the plan discussed," the wicked boy exclaimed.

"Diablo, is that so? We must look to it at once. My men have no idea of such an intention. I will send an aid to recall all the cavalry this very night. The saints preserve me, but what a lucky escape. Ah, you are a wonderful boy. You have your eyes open all the time."

The modest Lewey blushed at the compliment, and bowed very profoundly, while I gazed at my friend in wonder.

"Did you hear," insinuated the general, "at what time the Americans intended to take up their line of march for Santa Barbara?"

"The time was not definitely fixed," replied the youth, "but I suspect that they will move about the day after tomorrow."

"Then we will be ready for them. Not a man shall escape us," and the general rubbed his hands, as he thought of the surprise in store for Captain Fremont.

He nodded his head that the interview was ended, and we retired from the presence of the general, Lewey well satisfied with the part he had played, and grinning from ear to ear.

"How could you lie so outrageously?" I asked my friend, as we mounted our horses to ride to the house of Donna Costello.

"Dat is all right," the lad replied. "He vill lie to us to suit his pleasure, and ve must meet cheat vid cheat. I is a Frenchman, and vas born for de diplomacy. Had I de chance a future great vould be before me. Even de magnificent Napoleon could tell some hard yarns ven him it suited, and vy should not I follar his example?"

There was no use replying to such an argument, so I remained silent, but as we walked our horses across the plaza hundreds of people turned out to see us pass, for the rumor had gone forth that we had been on a mission to Captain Fremont, and returned alive, a wonder to every one.

We saw Mr. Larkin sitting on his veranda, but he paid no more attention to us than if we had been greasers of the lower order. He did not bow, or seem to care if he never saw us again, and yet the consul was devoured with anxiety to learn all the particulars of our trip, and if a certain letter would be placed in his hands before many hours, so that he could be informed of coming events. There were many watchful eyes on us, however, and on Mr. Larkin, and the least sign would be reported to headquarters, and luckily we were aware of the fact. And so we passed the old gentleman in pretended ignorance of his presence, and when we were at Donna Costello's house the lady received us with much affection, as though we had been her brothers, returning from a journey of several months' duration.

We turned our horses into the corral, gave them a feed of barley, and then listened to the questions of our sweet hostess, who was as full of interrogations as a school-girl. She supposed that Captain Fremont and his men were nearly akin to Apache Indians, black, with long hair, and half naked, savage and untamable, feasting on raw meat, drinking blood as a simple tonic, and murdering all who crossed their path or fell into their hands.

It was useless to reason with the lady, or convince her that she had formed erroneous impressions of my countrymen. She had been told by her people the most extravagant stories, and really credited them. In the year 1846 such yarns were generally believed, and women of superior education, far above that which most received in the country, declared they should prefer death to falling into Fremont's hands. The most absurd canards were reported by the government officials for the sake of firing the hearts of the people, and destroying the explorer and his men. I do not mean to intimate that the latter were angels when on a scout, or foraging expedition, but they were not near so bad as the Mexicans in their treatment of men and women at lonely ranches.

So Donna Costello, in defiance of her regard for me, would not be convinced, and I gave up the attempt, and let Captain Fremont take care of his own reputation, as I supposed he was capable of doing without any assistance on my part.

Captain Fernando called to see his sister in the evening, and had a long talk with us. From hints which he dropped we knew that General Castro was massing his troops for an attack in the course of a day or two. We told the young officer that we had seen Antonio and Carlos Sanchos in the camp of Fremont, and that it looked to us as though they had gone there willingly, and for the purpose of selling the secrets of the government to an enemy. He was much surprised at the news, and immediately repaired to the governor to impart the information, and the next day we had the pleasure of reading a proclamation in which all three of the brothers were declared enemies of the republic, and therefore outlaws, and a price set on their heads, dead or alive. This was something of a change from being the unscrupulous secret agents of the State, and we rejoiced that we had aided in their downfall, for they had persecuted us, and nearly wrecked our lives by their plots.

The next day being Friday, and having nothing to do, we borrowed the schooner California's boat, and went off the Point of Pines fishing, and great success rewarded our undertaking. We caught over a hundred pounds of red fish, and some other varieties, in the course of a few hours, and then distributed the catch among such families as our little hostess designated, the governor being made happy by the present of about twenty pounds, and Donna Augusta coming in for a share. This suggested to us a new field of industry and pleasure combined, for, with the bay full of fish, there was not a fisherman in the town, or a spare boat to navigate the waters. Sometime afterward Lewey and I made a profitable living in supplying the market with such fish as we caught, and sold to the people who had funds to buy. Quite a number would state in quiet and polite tones, when picking out a fish, that the money would be forthcoming some other day, or manana. I suppose the principal and interest of sums owed us in Monterey would pay for several months' board at the best hotel in the place, at the present time and present rates.

That evening Captain Fernando paid his accustomed visit to his sister, and, while we sat smoking, intimated that a movement would be made on Captain Fremont the next day, and asked if we would like to go with him, and see the fun. I did not know how to answer the question, and required time to think it over, while Lewey said that he would go at any rate. While the young captain was urging me to accept the invitation an Indian woman staggered along the court-yard, and fell nearly in my lap, but as she struggled to her feet I felt a little piece of paper pushed into my hand, and understood the meaning quite plainly, so said not a word, but concealed the slip in my pocket until I should be alone, and have time to look at it by the aid of a lamp.

"Get out of this, you drunken old hag," roared our friend, but the woman uttered some words in her native dialect, and staggered off, disappearing in the crowd.

I made an excuse that I wanted to fill my pipe, entered the kitchen, where a few coals were still alive in the little circle that answered for stove and range, lighted a sliver, and read on the paper the single word, — "Go."

Then I burned the scrap of writing, for I knew where it came from, and rejoined the young captain and his sister.

"You will accompany my brother, will you not?" Donna Costello asked. "I should feel so much easier in my mind if you and your friend were near him in the hour of battle. He is so rash, and the Americans are so deadly with their rifles. Say that you will go."

Of course I could not withstand such special pleading just after I had received almost a direct command from the consul, so said that I would do so, but that I must not be required to take part in any skirmish or fight against my countrymen. This was readily agreed to, and the same provision was made regarding Lewey.

"General Castro is to take command," the young captain said, "so we may expect hot and bloody work," and for the life of me I did not know if the officer was sarcastic or serious in his remark.

"The bugles will sound at five o'clock," Fernando said, as he prepared to leave us. "By six o'clock we shall be in the saddle. Better put on your Mexican costumes to prevent mistakes on the part of our men."

He kissed his sister good-by, and in a few minutes the house was quiet, and we slept until the loud notes of the bugles awakened us in the morning. We looked out, and saw men forming on the plaza, and heard the rumbling of three pieces of light artillery, as it made its way out of town, followed by a squad of cavalry, and then half a dozen companies of infantry trotted along, looking none too satisfied with the job before them.

We fed our horses, tied Jack up, as he was not wanted on such an expedition, had a cup ot coffee and breakfast of tortillas and frijoles, the cooks and servants looking at us with wonderment, thinking we were heroes, and then, in defiance of all military rules, lighted our pipes, and rode over to where Captain Fernando was hard at work getting his men in line, preparatory to acting as escort for General Castro.

As we took our places at the head of the column, special aids to the young captain, I looked across the plaza, and saw Mr. Larkin, as usual seated on the veranda of his house, and apparently quite indifferent to all that was going on around him. He did not even salute Lewey and myself, and appeared not to see us.

Our old comrades grinned when they saw us, and uttered joking remarks about our desire to smell gunpowder, and then there was a hush along the line as General Castro and a brilliant staff rode by and trotted out of the town.

"By fours," shouted Captain Fernando, and the men obeyed the order, and we were off at a lope, the women waving their hands, the boys cheering, and the Indians looking on in sullen apathy, not caring who licked, or if we never returned.

Just as we got about a mile from the town, and had settled down to a walk, having overtaken the advance, who should heave in sight but old Cook, mounted on a horse that he had picked up somewhere. We wondered to see him, as he was not a fighting man, but his errand was soon made known. Out of the fullness of his heart he had brought two large flasks of aguardiente, and gave them to Lewey and myself, on the ground that we had shown him many acts of kindness in the past, and bought all of our clothes from his store.

"It is for snake bites," the old fellow said, with a wink of his watery eyes. " Lots of rattlers in the woods, and one might nip you. Don't be too bold for the sake of the greaser. He 'd let you do all the fighting if you wanted to," and Cook returned to the town, reopened his shop, and hoped for the time when ships-of-war would enter the harbor, sailors crave rum, and have the cash to pay for it.

We marched until late in the afternoon, and then camped for the night, strong squads of infantry and cavalry being thrown out in all directions to s e if a foe lurked near. But no one of a suspicious nature was met, so we cooked our suppers, and ate them in peace, yet all that night, when awake, I could hear the fierce barks of coyotes on the sides of the mountains, and the solemn hoots of owls, or the shrill screams of eagles, and I wondered if Fremont's men were engaged signaling to their leader our position and numbers, or if the noises were natural ones.

At daylight we were under way again, and in the advance. We saw no sign of scouts, and not a shot was fired all day. The artillery was dragged over some rough places, and finally placed in position just at sundown, and the men cooked their suppers within sight of Fremont's camp-fires, and looked glum as they thought of the next day.

"Lewey," I said, after we had eaten a portion of Captain Fernando's rations, and lighted our pipes, " let us give the young fellow a lift, and a reputation for dash and courage."

"How?" the French lad asked. " I is reddy for anydin'."

"You know as well as I do," I continued, "that Fremont and his men are not in their camp at the present time. Their fires are burning but they have gone toward San Francisco, and will travel all night, and in the morning pursuit will be useless on the part of the Mexicans."

" Vell, vot of dat ? "

" Only this. Suppose we pursuade Captain Fernando to lead a charge at daybreak. He will dash toward the deserted camp, capture it, and his name will be mentioned for gallantry, and then promotion is sure."

"I do it," my friend exclaimed, and the next moment he was deeply engaged in an earnest conversation with the young captain, and the result was a hasty visit to the headquarters of General Castro, and when the officer returned he said that his request had been granted, and wanted to know if we would accompany him in the charge, and as there was no danger we agreed to do so.

The men were informed of their honorable position, but did not seem particularly pleased at the prospect before them. There was no retreat however, and just as the sky showed signs of light in the morning the dismounted cavalry was formed in line, a few hasty orders issued, and then came the word, —

"Adelante," or "forward."

We dashed over rocks and fallen trees, not a shot being fired, and with a cheer charged over the abatis, and the camp was in possession of the Mexicans. Not a single defender was in sight. All had vanished during the night, and left their fires burning, the embers still smoking. All the property had been removed except some old saddles and blankets not worth taking away. But the stronghold was captured, and Fremont had retreated. That was glory enough, and for a while the air was vocal with cheers and congratulations. Captain Fernando shook hands with us, and declared that his fortune was now made.

The cheers reassured General Castro. Up the mountain side he came on the run, his horse jumping over trees and stones, and when he was within the circle of the camp, and saw that the victory was complete, his joy knew no bounds.

"Glory to the saints," he cried. "Long live Mexico and the republic. The victory is ours. Give me a piece of paper."

Captain Fernando handed the governor a slip of paper, and then the general wrote a despatch for the people of Monterey. Instead of ink he used gunpowder, dissolved in a little water.

"On the field of battle," he wrote, "I pen this despatch. Our troops have achieved a great victory. The daring robber and his men have been driven at every point, and are in rapid flight. I shall pursue, and not leave a man alive to pollute our soil. To the saints belong the glory of this great triumph. I shall send all the spoil captured to Monterey. Let the bells ring, and the people rejoice. I proclaim a day of feasting for this success."

"Colonel," the governor said, turning to our young friend.

"Captain, your excellency," young Fernando responded, in a modest tone.

"No, sir, colonel, from this time forth. You have won the title, and shall wear it. For your bravery on this trying occasion take this despatch to Monterey, and lose not a moment. I will push on, and overtake the robbers."

It was with much difficulty that Lewey could prevent a shout of laughter escaping from his throat, and thus incurring the deadly enmity of the governor. He gave me a look, but did not dare glance at the newly-made colonel. The effort would have been too much for both of them. Fernando had won promotion and renown by our advice, and I hoped would prove grateful.

"General," said the young colonel, "I will hasten to the town, and carry the glad news, and if you have no objections these two young men shall accompany me."

"Take them if you wish. They have behaved as gallantly as Mexican soldiers, and I should like to promote them if they were in the army."

We were not sorry to leave the general and his enthusiastic followers. Descending the mountain we found our horses, mounted, and galloped toward Monterey, where the good news was received with shouts of rejoicing. The alcalda called a meeting of the inhabitants, and it was resolved to entertain the governor when he returned with a bull and bear fight, such as had never been witnessed in the village. The programme was carried out to the letter, for in a few days the troops made a triumphant entrance, Fremont having escaped all pursuit, as we knew he would.

First came General Castro and his staff, then the trumpeters, and following them were two pack-horses with the captured materials, consisting of old saddles and cloths, and a blouse which some one had forgotten. As it had United States buttons the soldiers swore that it was Fremont's uniform, and for several weeks it was on exhibition at the government house, among the trophies, and created the wildest enthusiasm. A Te Deum was celebrated in the church, and the bull-fight was a great success, only one Indian being killed, and four horses injured.

Colonel Fernando assumed the duties of his high position, and drilled his men until they were very proficient in their evolutions. He and his sister were so grateful to Lewey and myself that we were invited to continue to make Donna Costello's house our home, as a protection to her and the child. We accepted, after some faint urging, and then turned our attention to fishing in the bay, for the sake of passing away the time, and making a little money. We were free to do as we pleased, and could have gone to Ranche Refugio at any moment, had it not been so dangerous to travel by land, the whole country being infested with ladrones and wandering bands of rancheros, determined to steal, and kill all who opposed them. So we waited until a cavalry escort was ready, and in the meantime built a red-cedar flat-boat, large enough to hold four or five persons, and several hundred-weight of fish. In this we went to the Point of Pines every morning, caught all that we could before dinner, and sold what we did not give away. Our expenses were light, for Donna Costello would not accept any remureration for board, so we kept her table supplied with fish, and such friends as she designated. We were thus enabled to save a few dollars each week, and were very pleasantly situated. My evenings I devoted to teaching the pretty little wife English, and while she did not make much progress, the gratitude she expressed was more than enough to recompense me for my trouble.

One morning, in the early part of July, 1846, we were fishing off the Point of Pines, anchored near the black rocks, in a dense fog, with a light southerly breeze. The sport was good, and we were rapidly completing our fare, when suddenly we heard the flapping of sails, and rattling of blocks, and then the shrill notes of a boatswain's whistle, at the same time the monotonous tones of a leadsman, as he chanted,—

"By the deep nine," showing the ship was in nine fathoms of water.

"By gar," said Lewey, " von man-of-war near us. Hear dat quartermaster in de chains takin' de soundin's."

"By the mark eight," we heard from the ship, and we supposed she was feeling her way into port, but was too near the rocks, we judged, to be safe and prudent, if she would escape disaster, as there was a sunken ledge that run some distance from the shore. The fog was so thick we could not see the vessel, but we imagined her to be a man-of-war by the sound of the pipes of the boatswain's mates, and the regular chants of the leadsmen, one on each side of the craft, calling the depth of water every half minute.

"Ship ahoy," I hailed.

"Well, what is it?" responded a stern voice from the unknown vessel.

"Better starboard your helm a little, and keep off a point or two. You are near a reef."

We heard the order given to starboard, for the sailing-master must have known that the advice was good, and then we were hailed in return.

"Boat ahoy," came in ringing tones from the ship, as she fanned her way along, under the light breeze, just enough for steerage way.

"Well," was our answer.

"Who are you?" was demanded from the ship.

"Fishermen of Monterey," and Lewey grinned as I answered.

"Please come alongside," was the next command.

"Thank you," I replied, "we are very comfortable where we are."

"If you do not drop alongside we will send a shot in your direction," was the next threat.

"And waste your powder and lead. You could not hit a barn-door in this fog," and then the French boy laughed so heartily that he fell on the bottom of the boat, and nearly crushed the life out of our dog, who uttered a yelp, and then barked defiance at the strangers.

"Marine, give those impudent fellows a shot from the starboard gangway," we heard some one from the quarter deck exclaim, and, hung me, if the man did n't think the order was a serious one, for the report of a musket was heard, and a ball struck the water not more than three fathoms from our boat, and Lewey uttered a yell as though he had been hit, and groaned in the most pitiful manner, while Jack howled in sympathy.

"Boat ahoy," cried some officer from the ship-of-war.

"We have n't life enough left to answer you," I replied.

"Are you badly hurt, poor fellows?" and there was a tone of pity in the officer's voice, at the same time we heard a cutter lowered by the run.

"Hurt?" echoed Lewey. "Ve tells you dat you could not hit de side of de barn of de door, and now ve knows it."

"You impudent vagabonds. If we only lay hands on you we will show what we can do," came in threatening tones across the water, and I had no doubt the speaker was sincere in what he said.

"Keep quiet," I whispered to Lewey. "One of the cutters is in the water, and pulling in search of us."

We jumped to our anchor, and run it up, but just at that moment Jack commenced barking, and before we could quiet him our position was revealed. A boat dashed alongside, a midshipman and ten men looked us all over, and appeared much astonished at what they saw.

"Who in the devil's name are you?" the officer asked.

"No entender," we answered in Spanish, meaning that we did not understand him.

"Oh, belay all that," was the midshipman's comment. "You are no Mexicans, I know."

"Parlez vous Francais?" asked Lewey, with an innocent smile.

"I'll break your heads with a stretcher, if you don't stow all that," was the next threat, and then I looked at the young officer a second time, and saw that he was an old schoolmate, the same one I had met when he was attached to the Ceynne, and on the coast years before.

"Why, Bob, old fellow, how goes it?" I asked, as I recognized the midshipman, now grown to be a manly youngster, with a little down on his upper lip and chin.

He stared in amazement at my impertinence, and the next instant we were shaking hands, like good friends as we were.

"Why, Thom, old boy, who in the deuse would have thought of seeing you here?" he demanded. "So you are the one who has been playing pranks on the old frigate Cumberland and Commodore Sloat? Won't he dress you down when he sees you? Oh, no, I guess not."

"Let us slip out of this, Bob?" I pleaded.

"Can't do it. You must go on board and face the music. Out with the oars, men, and take the boat in tow. Well, well, to think we should meet here, in this dense fog, is one of the marvels of the age."

"Bob," I asked, "are you very anxious for the safety of your sturdy ship?"

"Yes, she is a staunch old craft, my home, and I love her like a mother."

"Then you had better hail, and tell the skipper to come to anchor, or he will be in trouble with this flood tide and light wind."

The midshipman looked horrified at the idea of my calling his captain a "skipper," but he waited until the leadsman called out, —

"Quarter less seven, and then hailed, —

"Cumberland ahoy."

"Cutter ahoy," came back in ringing tones from the frigate.

"The fishermen are Americans, and recommend that you anchor until the fog clears up. They know the harbor well, and think the tide is setting the ship too far in shore, and it is not safe to find the anchorage until the weather is clear."

"Ay, ay. Bring the fellows on board, and let us have a look at them," came from the frigate.

"Fellers," muttered Lewey. "Your skipper has de politeness not much. Ve is gentlemen of de leisure, and fish for de fun of de ding, and vot plata ve gits."

There was the piping of boatswains' whistles, — It was clew up and clew down, — and then a stern voice called out, —

"Stand by the anchor."

"Put your helm hard to larboard," was the next command. (If nautical men are inclined to find fault with the term "larboard," they will please to recollect that the word "port" was not officially introduced into the navy until Bancroft was secretary, when it was used to prevent confusion. This was about 1847, when Polk was president of the United States.)

"Let go the anchor," was the next order, and the huge piece of iron plunged to the bottom, and the chain rattled out, and the people on shore knew that a ship had arrived near the town, while Mr. Larkin sat on his veranda, and wondered if the naval vessels had come at last, and if it was his turn to laugh and become defiant?

"For gracious sake, Thom," cried the midshipman, "what prompted you to remain in this country?"

He asked the question while the cutter was towing our boat alongside, and after the frigate had anchored.

"Well, you see my French friend here and myself thought of marrying and settling down," and of course the midshipman had to laugh, as a matter of course, and the man-of-war's men all grinned, as though I had uttered a joke.

"You always was singular in your tastes," the midshipman muttered, "and I suppose you desired to be plural in your habits," but that remark was so profound no one smiled, as it was not understood, consequently my friend, Mr. Bob, hurled an adjective at the head of the midship oarsman, and told him to keep stroke, and mind his eye.

The huge proportions of the frigate loomed up through the fog, and, as we shot alongside, I saw that she carried two tiers of guns, in all about sixty, some of them very heavy ones for those days, and her complement of men was six hundred, as the middy informed us.

"Now your fun commences," whispered the officer. "Commodore Sloat will give you a dose of peppery remarks, you see if he does not. Keep cool, and be civil. A commodore is a great man in these waters, although he does not amount to much at home. Here we go. In bow. Way enough."

We slipped alongside, and many wondering eyes were on us as Lewey and I passed over the steps, the French lad with an expression on his face that seemed to say, "I ennui with all this attention, good people."

"Pass aft. The commodore desires to see you," a midshipman said, and then Satan seemed to possess that friend of mine, for he ran back to the gangway, looked down at our boat, and yelled out to the midshipman who had brought us on board, —

"De poisson! Do not if you please de men let steal him. Ve vork hard to catch, an I no afford to lose. Ve sell all for four cents de pound, cash, and no trust, vid de big von for de commodore at half price, for trade allowin' us to do."

There was horror depicted on the faces of the officers of the quarter-deck, and I feared that my French friend would be put under arrest, and fed on bread and water for a week. But he looked so simple and innocent, just as though he had no idea of offending, and cared for no one, that he was only pulled away from the rail by gentle pressure, and told in a hoarse whisper to stop his noise, and go aft.

"Ah, cap'en," the enthusiastic French lad cried to a third lieutenant, who blushed at being so saluted, "you vill our fish vatch ober for us, and if you sell him you vill de moneys all gib to me, and I skall be so much obliged as eber vas, for I is a poor boy, and far avay from mine native land."

"Will you go aft, you blanked fool?" whispered one of the lieutenants, "and if you do not stop talking until you are spoken to we 'll pitch you overboard with a round shot tied to your feet."

"Qu'est ce que vous voulez?" demanded the unblushing Lewey, but the lieutenant only shook his head, and pushed the French lad toward the commodore, who was all swelled up with offended dignity, having been kept waiting two or three minutes, owing to Lewey's desire for fun and frolic at the expense of the United States naval officers.

"Take off your hats," some one whispered, but my friend pretended not to hear, so his sombrero was removed from his head by an officer, and just as the commodore was about to open his mouth that wild boy went off on another tack.

"O capitan," he cried, "mine dog in de boat is. Vill you tells de mens not to steal him, as much value he is."

"Well, I 'm blanked," muttered the commodore. "Who in the devil's name are you? and where do you come from?"

"Me poor French boy," was the reply. "Me leaves home for de fortune to seek. Speak you de booful French, capitan?"

There was a negative shake of the head from the commodore.

"Ah, you like him so much. Skall I speak some for you?"

"Take this parrot away," roared the commodore. "He will drive me crazy with his lingo. Come here, you other boy. Let me see if you can answer questions in a ship-shape manner."

I stood before the commodore, not in awe, for I had seen bigger men, but determined to no longer provoke the officer, for his patience had been already tried quite severely.

"Who are you, sir?" asked the autocrat of the quarter-deck.

"I am an American, and at present a fisherman of Monterey, sir."

"That is to say a beach-comber," was the retort.

"I did not state so, sir, and fear that I am not up to the standard of a person who passes his time on the beach, in search of a ship and a job, and hopes never to find either," I said,

"Well how came you here, if you are an American?" demanded the commodore.

"I was honorably discharged from my ship, and expected to marry and grow up with the country," was my candid answer.

Of course I knew that all the officers would laugh. They saw the commodore smile, and followed suit. It was the usual custom.

"You are a fool," were the next blunt words, just because I had stated my intention of being married.

"Perhaps I am, sir, but a fool would not have asked you to anchor when you had six fathoms of water under your bows, and shoaling every moment, with a dense fog all around you."

"Are you the one who hailed the frigate for that purpose?" growled the commodore.

"Yes, sir."

"Why did you insult us and provoke a shot?"

"My French friend is a little loco, and not responsible for his words. He does not know what he is doing half the time."

"Blank me if I did n't think so," was the exclamation. "I can always tell a crazy man. He is as mad as a march hare," and the officers nodded confirmation of the words.

"Now," said the commodore, and he looked profound and serious, "what do you know of affairs on shore? In what part of the country is Captain Fremont?"

"He was near Monterey a few weeks since, but left for San Francisco when he found that an attack was to be made on his position, which he was not strong enough to resist."

"What is the force of the Mexicans on shore?"

"That is something I cannot answer you, commodore. We are neutrals, and must remain such, or violate an oath."

"Nonsense. I will give both of you positions on the ship, so there is no danger. Tell all you know. How many guns does the presidio command?"

"Not many, but you will have to find out by an attack. General Castro and the American consul have been expecting you for weeks, and perhaps are prepared for your reception."

"Can you take a note on shore for Mr. Larkin from me?" the officer asked.

"Yes, sir, but it would not be prudent on our part. We should lose the number of our mess if we did so."

"My guns can protect you," was the assured statement.

"They could not keep the point of a sharp knife out of our ribs the first dark night," I answered.

"Perhaps not, but we could avenge your deaths."

"That would do us no good. We prefer life to revenge, sir."

"May be you are right, but it seems to me that an American should aid his country in every way possible."

"What aid can a boy afford to a large frigate like this, full of men, and capable of reducing every fort on the coast? No, sir, we have promised to remain neutral, and we desire to keep our words. Even now, if it was known we had boarded your vessel, we should be looked upon as sospechosos, and treated badly. Let us go on shore, please, before the fog lifts, so we shall be safe and undiscovered."

"You can go," the officer said, and waved his hand. "But if Mr. Larkin should learn the Cumberland is near we should not feel ungrateful. Do you understand?"

"Yes, sir. He will hear of the event, it is quite probable, before sunset," and touching my hat I left the quarter-deck, and joined Lewey.

The French lad had negotiated the sale of all of our fish to the purser for the ward-room officers, and received four dollars for the catch. We took the bearings by the compass, entered our boat, and pushed off for the Point of Pines, and guided by the roaring of the surf made our way to the usual landing. As we hauled up our boat we saw Mr. Larkin sitting on a rock, near the gully by the presidio, and apparently quite content to wait until the fog had lifted and revealed the beauties of the bay.

"Well, boys, what luck?" he asked, as he came toward us and looked into the empty boat.

"Not much today, sir. The fish did not bite very lively," we answered.

"Perhaps the ship that recently anchored in the bay scared them away," the American consul remarked, as he examined the boat, and saw the debris of a good catch.

"Should n't wonder if such was the case, sir," and we turned the boat over, and washed all evidence of fish from the bottom and thwarts.

"Look here, boys," the consul said, in a low, confidential tone, so that no lurking spy could overhear his words, "what ship is that which recently anchored off the Point of Pines and is still obscured by the fog?"

We glanced around. No one was near us except a soldier of the presidio, who was on duty, and watching the fog and our proceedings at the same time.

"It is the frigate Cumberland, sir, Commodore Sloat."

"And you have been on board of her?"

"Yes, sir. We were requested to do so, and the polite command was backed by a cutter and eleven men."

"And von musket shot dat came near us," interrupted the irrepressible Lewey.

"Under the circumstances we went on board," I continued.

"And ve sells all our fish for four dollar," my friend remarked.

"A good price," Mr. Larkin said. "I am glad that you did so well. Now tell me, lads, did you not bring on shore a letter from the commodore?"

"No, sir, we did not dare to, for fear of suspicion. But you will hear from the ship in the morning, or as soon as the fog lifts."

"It is quite probable," was the short answer, and Mr. Larkin walked toward his house, near the plaza, and once more took his accustomed seat on the veranda, and looked off toward the bay and the fog, and even hummed a tune of a light and jolly character, when no one was near him.

The sentinel shouldered his gun, and resumed his monotonous rounds, as the consul disappeared, and two Mexicans came out from a little sand cave near the beach, and moved toward the custom house, on the rocky bluff. They had seen no exchange of packages, and therefore were a little disappointed. We had noticed the men when we landed, and knew they were spying on our actions, but they did not make much by the operation.

We had no fish for our regular customers that day, and some of them were a little disappointed, as it was the Lenten season, and meat was forbidden by the priests for the time being. We pleaded that the finny tribe were driven off by the fog and a shark, and the answer satisfied them. However, we promised an abundance for the next day.

When we reached our home for the time being, and inquired of Donna Costello the whereabouts of her brother, the colonel, we regretted to learn that he had ridden over to Santa Cruz to review some cavalry, and would not be back until the next day. We wanted to do the officer a good turn, get him out of harm's way, and perhaps capture, for we knew the town would have to surrender as soon as the Cumberland anchored near the presidio, and brought her guns to bear on the place. There was no force to stand before the ship, as the cannon of the fort did not amount to much, except in the way of ornament. But one thing remained for us to do if we would repay all the colonel's acts of kindness, and that was to give him warning at once to keep away from Monterey, or move his men out of harm's way.

We had not ridden our mustangs for several days. They were in the corral, and impatient for a run. Telling the pretty little wife we were going for a gallop along the beach, and should not return until late at night, we saddled our horses, slung our rifles over our shoulders, and started for Santa Cruz.

As we struck the hard, white sand the tide was fast ebbing, and there was a clear course after passing the remnants of a wreck about a mile from the custom house. We halted for a moment near the landing, and looked off upon the water, still covered with a dense fog. There was no sign of the Cumberland, and not even the creaking of blocks or spars, or the pipes of the boatswain's whistles were heard. All was silent, and no one would have suspected that a ship with six hundred men was so near us. This quietness was maintained through the strict discipline of the crew. The order had passed for repose, and it was obeyed to the letter. Even the sails were not furled, as they might be needed as soon as a little air should come along, and blow the fog away. A surprise was intended for General Castro and his troops, and it would have been successful had we not favored a friend, and the latter saved his countrymen from shot and shell, and a surrender.

"Alons," said Lewey, and just as we were ready to start our horses into a long and untiring lope four cavalrymen broke through the fog, and rode toward us, lariats in their hands.

"Parada," they said, and we halted on the instant, for we had no occasion to run away, and there was no show for us with those reatas ready to be thrown with deadly precision.

"What is wanted, amigos?" we asked as the men came toward us and looked us over.

"The general is anxious to know where you are going," one of the men said. "He noticed today you caught no fish, that you had a long conversation on the beach with Mr. Larkin, and he does not understand your movements. He dislikes to think that you are sospechosos, for he has a high opinion of your good qualities and bravery. But these are troublesome times, and we must be guarded."

"Tell the general — and may he live a thousand years, and enjoy the best of health — that we are taking a ride to Santa Cruz, just to see our friend Colonel Fernando, and to exercise our horses."

"You are sure, amigos?" asked the non-commissioned officer of the squad.

"Quite sure, comrade," was our positive answer.

"Then you will have no objections to company, O friends of my childhood, and bravest of marineros?" the officer asked.

"No; will you and your associates go with us?" we demanded, and we knew they would at any rate, as they had been sent to watch our movements, and spy out what we intended to do.

"With much pleasure shall we join you. We have nothing else for duty, and a long gallop will do us good. Vamos, senors."

They put up their lariats, coiling them on the pommels of their saddles, and away we went over the hard sand as fast as we dared to in the fog, although it was not so dense at the edge of the water as in the bay.

Our horses were so much superior to the cavalrymen's that we could have run away from them, but did not care to do so. We had no desire to pass as sospechosos, for our lives might have been endangered, and we had no place to fly to where we would have been safe, just at that time. So we did not hurry the pace, and therefore were two hours in reaching Santa Cruz. As we passed the old mission I saw my friend the padre, and stopped to exchange a few words with him and the housekeeper, the latter giving me a grin of delight at the meeting.

The priest told us where we could find Colonel Fernando, and on riding to the spot indicated found him inspecting a company of raw recruits. He was much surprised to see us, and also to find that we had an escort.

"Colonel," we said, " we have ridden this way to see you personally, but these gentlemen did not believe us, so came along to note if we spoke the truth."

As the men belonged to the colonel's regiment they did not hesitate when he said in a stern tone, —

"These senors are my friends. I will be responsible for them and their actions. Return immediately to Monterey, and report to General Castro my words."

The soldiers saluted, wheeled their horses, and were off, not even looking back to see if we were noting their movements.

"Now, senors, what is the news?" asked the colonel. "Something of importance has happened, or you would not seek me here. Is it my welfare or that of my sister which you have at heart?"

"Colonel," I said, "it is for your good that we have come. But what we communicate must be a secret between us. This you will promise?"

"Yes, quite readily."

"Look off upon the bay, colonel, and you will see a dense fog."

He glanced toward the ocean, and nodded his head.

"Under that fog, colonel, and near the Point of Pines, is a huge Yankee frigate. As soon as the mist rises she will be in position to threaten the town, and compel its surrender. We want to save you and your dear sister. There is no time to lose if we would do so."

"Diablo, I should think not. Our presidio will not stand a broadside, and my regiment might be made prisoners-of-war; and just as I had got it in good order, and feel my position and importance. Senors, you must return with me to Monterey. My soldiers will march tonight. To you can be entrusted the care of Donna Costello. Her husband does not know enough to have charge of a pretty wife in such doubtful times as these. I shall go into camp near the Mission Carmel. Your Yankee friends will not dare to follow me there. I only wish they would. I'd cut them off root and branch. There, don't be angry at my words. Our nations are at war but we are not. Let not the sound of strife destroy our friendship," and the gallant young man held out his hand. "And you came all this distance to give me warning, did you?" the colonel asked, "and General Castro suspected you of some treasonable design? He would doubt his own mother in war time. A little impulsive is the general, but he means well, and can fight hard with pronunciamentos. In fact, he can flog the whole of your nation with a dozen. But let the horses have a breathing spell, and we will return to town."

We went to the mission and had a bit of bread and an olia, fed our horses with a little barley and at four o'clock were on the road to Monterey, the good padre blessing us as we rode away from his house. I never saw him again.

The fog still hung about the bay, but no sound was heard from the frigate as we dashed along the beach. The colonel was to go immediately to headquarters, and as he turned to do so I said in a warning tone, —

"You will not mention the source of your information, amigo? Remember I am an Americano."

"Rest assured of me. I shall set you right in the general's estimation. He must not remain under the impression that you are a sospechoso. You have been good friends to me, and I shall prove so to you."

We went to our quarters prepared to pass an uneasy night, but did not tell Donna Costello that a foe was near. At nine o'clock there was a movement of the troops, and we saw the young colonel at the head of his regiment, marching out of the town, without sound of drum or trumpets, and with him went General Castro and the government officials. Old Cook rubbed his eyes, and wondered what the matter was, and Mr. Larkin sat on his veranda and looked across the bay as far as the fog would permit, and hoped the mist would rise.

As Senor Costello went with the governor the protection of the wife and child devolved upon us, and the duties were willingly assumed, for we had no doubt but that we should look after her in a satisfactory manner, and she had implicit trust in our ability and courage to defend her against outrage. The peons and Indians were more to be dreaded than the American sailors, as we had no doubt the captors of the town would respect all those who did not bear arms, and offer to fight for the glory of Mexico.

At ten o'clock it was known to the worst class of the community that the soldiers and officials had gone, and left the place defenceless. Then stores were entered, and liquor sought in all directions. Old Cook hastily concealed what he had, and shut up shop. Mr. Larkin disappeared from the veranda of his house, and no longer looked across the bay. Lewey and I loaded our pistols and rifles, and sat near the door of Donna Costello's house, in the dark, and heard the howls of the drunken brutes and the screams of women, and waited for dawn, but before that came we had to shed blood to save from outrage the pretty little wife who had been left in our charge, and the life of her only child, the sweetest boy in the State. It was the most anxious night we had ever passed, and we thanked God when light came, and the fog was gone, and out in the harbor rode two large frigates at anchor, the Cumberland and Independence, with the American flags at their peaks, and the rising sun kissing the stars and stripes as they floated in the light northerly breeze. And Mr. Larkin once more sat on the veranda of his house and looked across the bay, and hummed a tune all to himself, for no one was near him except an Indian woman, who had the reputation of being a drunkard. But we had to meet rough work before the sun rose, and the flags were seen to gladden our hearts and grant us safety.

CHAPTER XI.

THE ATTACK ON THE HOUSE AND ITS REPULSE. — EDWARDO SANCHOS MEETS A JUST FATE. — THE RESCUING PARTY FROM THE FRIGATE CUMBERLAND. — A WINDFALL OF GOLD. — THE BREAKFAST. — A PREDICTION. — HOISTING THE AMERICAN FLAG AT MONTEREY. — A LAST VIEW OF THE TOWN. — ON THE MARCH. — TERRIBLE DEATH OF TWO WOMEN AND A SPEEDY EXECUTION. — A NIGHT SCENE ON THE BEACH. — A SURPRISE, AND AN ESCAPE. — STRAY SHOTS.

IT was fully ten o'clock before pandemonium in its worst form broke out in the little town of Monterey. Then the native rum began to exert its full force, and the peons and half-breed Mexicans rushed through the streets in search of plunder and outrage. All of Donna Costello's servants had fled from the premises, and no one but Lewey and I were left to protect the house and its precious inmates. We closed and barred the door, put out the lights, and sat near the entrance, with our firearms all ready for use, dreading an attack, yet not disposed to shirk one should an assault be made. At one time we were inclined to put the lady on a horse, and escape to the mountains, but the sight of the crowd of drunken wretches, as they yelled and howled around us, showed that it was not feasible, and we determined to remain, and do the best we could, the little wife half the time on her knees praying to the saints for protection, and begging we would not leave herself and child to a shocking fate.

Luckily the boy slept through the tumult, and did not realize his danger, while I consoled the senora the best way that I could, and promised no harm should come to her if I could prevent it. A dozen times did the lady put her arms around my neck in the dark, when the noise was the loudest, and press her cheek to my face, tremble, and shed tears of terror, but she thought no more of the act than if I had been her brother, and I did not even strive to kiss away the moisture that flowed from her dark, glorious eyes. I imagined it would be sacrilege to do aught but comfort her, and hope for the best.

It was near twelve o'clock, we judged, when a crowd of drunken peons stopped in front of the house, shouting and yelling, while some of them entered the patio in search of plunder. They went through the cook-house like a tornado, but found nothing of value, as we had removed all the property that was worth anything to safer quarters. The scoundrels manifested their displeasure by a series of groans, and then some one, who seemed to be in authority, or the leader of the gang, came to the door, and pounded on it in a threatening manner.

"Cobardes, Americanos," he yelled, "come out of the house, so that we can see your white faces, and feel of your throats. We want you for a particular purpose."

Jack uttered an angry growl, as though he scented danger, but we quieted him with a word, and attempted to reassure the frightened lady, who was now certain that outrage was near. We made no reply to the demand, and it was repeated in more emphatic tones, and still we remained silent.

"Will you show your white faces?" the fellow said, "or must we break in the door?"

We hoped the gang would suppose we had made our escape to the mountains, so declined to answer, but the fellows evidently knew we were in the house, for the speaker again cried out, —

"Bring a piece of timber. We will batter down the door, and hang the Americanos, and then do what we please with the woman."

I could feel Senora Costello shudder at the words, and she clung still closer to my neck, but I removed her arms, and whispered, —

"Go into your room, and be with the child. You must not hamper me with tears and entreaties just now. There is to be a struggle, and a deadly one, but we hope it will result in our favor. Be bold, and pray for our success."

She kissed my hand, and left me. Then we heard fresh shouts in the patio, and knew that a piece of timber had been found, large enough to batter down the door.

"De Lord help de fust von vot enters dis room," muttered Lewey, and I heard the ominous click of the lock of his rifle, the re-arrangement of his pistols and long knife, as though he meant every shot to tell.

"Will you come out?" asked the leader of the peons, as soon as he had the piece of timber all ready to use as a battering-ram.

"Listen to us for a moment," my French friend said, in a determined tone. "We are well armed, and the first one who attempts to enter this room will die like a dog. Go away and leave us, or the worse for you. We shall defend the premises with our lives."

"You will find it different here from shooting unarmed men on the summit of the Sierra Santa Monica," the leader said, and then we knew whom we had to deal with.

"It is Edwardo Sanchos, the younger brother of Antonio, and the scamp who attempted to ambush us when we crossed the mountains, on our journey from Los Angeles to Santa Barbara," I whispered. "You remember, I hit him on the hand or shoulder with a rifle bullet, when he was attempting to throw his knife. Now he thinks his time has come to punish us."

"It has if he crosses de threshold of de door," Lewey muttered in a resolute tone.

"Do you yield?" asked Sanchos, after a moment's cessation of hostilities.

"No, we will die first," was our defiant answer.

"Down with the puerta," was the command, and the timber was raised, and dashed against the portal.

The slight door was torn from its hinges, but we stepped aside, and escaped the crash, and the next instant a dozen men sprang forward to enter the apartment.

"Gib dem de debil," roared Lewey, and bang went both of our rifles, and two peons staggered back, and fell into the arms of those who were just behind them, and we held the ruffians in check for a moment, and but for a moment.

"Adelante," yelled Sanchos, "the battle is won."

As the crowd surged forward, in obedience to orders, Jack seemed to recognize the voice and presence of a bitter foe, and sprang full at the throat of the speaker, for we could see the ladrones standing between us and the light, while they did not note us very well with our backs to the adobe wall.

It would have been short work with our dog, for Sanchos could have cut his heart out easily if we had not interfered. I raised a pistol and aimed at the greaser's head, and let drive. The ball struck the fellow near the right eye, and he tumbled over backward, and hardly moved afterward, while Jack, satisfied that there was no more fight in his late antagonist, deserted him and went for the seat of a half-breed's trousers, and tore out whole mouthfuls of cloth and flesh, and the fellow's yells were as fearful as the

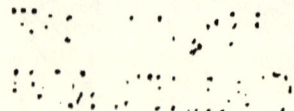

screams of the peons in the patio, who were furious for vengeance now that they smelled blood.

"Here goes for anuder von," cried Lewey, and as he fired there was a fall and a howl of agony. Then we poured in our two remaining shots, clubbed our rifles, dashed at the heads of the nearest enemy, and crushed the skulls of all who were close to us. There was much hot work for a few minutes, and the result would have been fatal for us, overpowered by numbers as we were, and confronted with greasers inspired with artificial courage, crazed with rum and a desire to be revenged on us for the death of friends, and also the thought that Donna Costello had money and jewels in the house.

One fellow made a hack at us with his heavy machete, but missed his aim, as we could see his motions, and he did not observe ours on account of facing the light. The next instant the stocks of our rifles descended on the Mexican's right arm, the terrible weapon was dropped, and a yell of agony told that the limb was broken near the hand.

We could not retreat. Our backs were to the wall, and half a hundred enraged scoundrels were confronting us in the room and the patio, and just as we were almost ready to despair of beating back the crowd of fiends, we heard a loud cheer in the street, and then the shout of, —

"Away, boarders, away. Give the greasers a touch of steel, boys. Down with the blanked scoundrels. Let 'em have hail Columbia."

We answered that sailor-like command with a yell of delight, put in a few fresh blows with our rifle-stocks, and then there was a rush from the patio, the greasers tumbled out of the house in headlong haste, only to be struck down with boarding-pikes and cutlasses, and in ten minutes after the first cheer from the relief party there was no one present in the court-yard except the dead and wounded, and half a hundred blue-jackets making merry and cracking jokes over the expeditious manner in which they had scattered the blood-thirsty mob, and not lost a man in return.

We struck a glim as soon as possible, and then spoke to the officer in command, who proved to be my old schoolmate Bob, a midshipman of the frigate Cumberland.

"Well, old fellow," he asked, "was it a tight squeeze this time?"

"The stiffest little breeze we ever saw," I answered. "A few minutes more and we should have been finished for good. Never did we hear a more joyful cry than 'Away, boarders,' in the English lingo."

"I thought that would fetch 'em," chuckled the officer. "If I had said charge' the boys would not have understood me. Stand still, you rascals.

Don't leave the ranks and hunt for aguardiente. There is none in the town." This was addressed to the sailors, who were getting restless for further adventures.

"Tell that to the marines," some blue-jacket cried.

"Who said that?" demanded the middy, but no one responded to the polite interrogation for reasons of his own.

"How did you happen to be on shore at this time of night?" I asked the middy.

"The simplest thing in the world. About six bells Mr. Larkin, the American consul, sent a despatch on board stating that the town was given up to pillage, and asking the commodore to land a party, and restore order if possible. There are two hundred of us scattered about the village, and we have kept the greasers on the run ever since we touched the beach. All the soldiers marched off at dark we had been given to understand, so there was not much of a chance for a fight after all, and perhaps it is just as well. Stand steady, you villains, or I'll break your necks as sure as you live. There is not a drop of rum in the place I tell you."

"We is anxious for water, Mr. Bob," a veteran said. "We is parched for a drink."

"Yes, of fire-water, but you won't get it, now I tell you. Stand still until the marines come up, and show 'em how steady you are on land."

"The sojers be blanked," was growled out, and then I whispered to the midshipman, —

"We have a few bottles of aguardiente in the house. Let one of your best men deal it out in gentle tots to the lads."

"All right. Here, Williams, you act as purser's clerk, and serve out a tot of grog to each man, and mind your eye while you are about it. No double splices if you please. I shall look after you, be assured."

The cheer that followed this announcement could have been heard on board the frigate, and away up the mountains.

We furnished a lot of tin pots, the liquor, and a light. The men were refreshed after their fight, and then wanted another scrimmage, in hope of getting more rum.

"By the way," asked Bob. "what are you doing here? Is this your home?"

"Yes, for the present. We were trying to save from outrage a lady who has been very kind to us."

"Is she pretty?"

"Very."

"Let me get a glimpse of her. I have not seen a petticoat for months, and long for the sight of a sweet face."

"Not tonight. There are too many dead bodies lying around loose to be agreeable to a young woman. Come in the morning, and you shall have an introduction, if the lady does not object to seeing a Yankee officer."

"She ought not to, after all of our efforts to save the place. But, by George, there goes the bugles. We are signaled to form on the plaza. Will call on you as soon as possible. Come, muster in line, men, and prepare to repel boarders. Away you go to the starboard. Stamp along lively. Keep a good lookout for breakers, and the greasers at the same time. Show the marines that you know how to march as well as the best of 'em," and away went the jolly blue-jackets, joking and roaring with laughter, as they pricked some drunken half-breed with their boarding-pikes, or an Indian who was a little too obtrusive.

As soon as the sailors had departed I pushed open the door and entered the room where Donna Costello and her child were concealed. The lady was on her knees, praising the saints in thanksgiving for her escape from death and outrage, and the little boy was sleeping quietly, not having awakened during the night, through all the tumult of the fight and riot.

"Senora," I said, " all danger has passed. The Yankees, whom you profess to despise so much, came to our assistance just in time, and put the ladrones to flight."

She arose and put her hands in mine, and then asked, —

"How should I have fared if you and your friend had not defended the house before they came?"

"We did the best we could, dear lady, until relief arrived," and as I spoke she put up her lips and kissed me, so great was her gratitude.

I begged her to lie down and sleep, and she promised to comply with my request. Then I left her, and joined Lewey, who, with the aid of a lamp, was examining the bodies of the dead.

"Dis blanked villain vill nebber harm us more," he said, as he showed me the dark face of Edwardo Sanchos, a pistol ball having passed through his temple, and ended his career of crime.

He moved the body as he spoke, and a clink of gold was heard. Lewey knelt down and tore open the breast of the dead man's shirt. A belt was revealed that passed completely around the body. With a cut of his knife the lad severed the buckskin, and when it was loosened a number of Spanish doubloons dropped to the floor.

"Dis vill us pay for dis night's vork," the French boy remarked, and counting the coin we found that there were just one hundred gold pieces, representing a value of about seventeen hundred dollars. This was a great surprise.

"Him heirs vill see dis not," Lewey said. "Ve vill keep it to remember de dead," and then we put the money out of sight, thrust the bodies of the peons and Mexicans into the patio, rigged up the broken door, spread our blankets, and lay down for a little rest before daylight, as the town was now quiet, and the sailors and marines had full possession of the place, the peons and ladrones having fled to the mountains, following in the wake of the army.

It was not a refreshing slumber that we courted, but we did get a few winks of sleep before sunrise. When we arose and looked out on the plaza we saw the sailors and marines lying down on blankets, and sentinels pacing back and forth, and a boat-gun in the centre of the parade, all ready for execution, while on the veranda of his house sat Mr. Larkin, looking across the bay at the frigates Cumberland and Independence, the latter having arrived during the night, and at the peaks of both ships floated the American flags, and at the main of the first-named vessel was the broad pennant of a commodore.

I fancied that I could hear the American consul, as he welcomed the sight so dear to his heart, hum a light and agreeable song, and thank God that the days of anxiety were passed, never to return as far as Monterey was concerned.

We hunted up several peons, and compelled them to remove and bury the dead, then found one of Donna Costello's cooks, and made him prepare breakfast, the best that could be obtained, and when all was ready I went in search of my midshipman friend, and invited him and several officers to come to the house, and satisfy their hunger and thirst with an olla and a cup of coffee. Very glad were they to accept the offer, but Donna Costello would not meet them, as she was too patriotic to break bread with the enemies of her country, even if they had saved her life the night before. She was a true descendant of the Spanish race, and could neither forgive nor forget when all danger was passed.

The naval officers were very polite, and made no unpleasant remarks about the lady's absence. They asked us to give their regards, and say how pleased they should have been to meet so beautiful a woman, and treated Lewey and myself as equals, for my friend Bob, the middy, had enlightened his messmates as to the French lad's position, and my own, and they looked upon us as two cracked-brained young men, who were seeing life, and finding adventures which others more sensible would have avoided.

The town was now quiet enough. A guard was placed near the residence of the American consul, but no further disturbance was anticipated, and at nine o'clock the sailors and marines were withdrawn from the plaza, and returned to the Cumberland, and from the quarter-deck of the frigate was heard the sound of martial music, and the stirring notes of the "Star Spangled Banner," attracting hundreds of people to the beach and custom house. But the better class of Mexicans did not show themselves, and the pretty senoritas kept within doors, and seemed to care nothing for the band or the officers.

During the day Senora Costello received notes from her brother and husband. They had heard of the tumult in the town the night before, and considered the place no longer safe for a young, unprotected woman. They advised her to join them at or near the Mission Carmel as soon as possible, and our friend the colonel made a personal request that Lewey and I would take charge of her, and see that she reached the lines of the Mexican army in safety. We could not refuse compliance with such a delicate demand, and passed the day in getting ready for the journey. We hunted all through the town for a carriage, but not one was to be obtained. The volante had been taken by Senora Castro the night before, when her husband made his escape, and was miles away, so the only thing we could suggest was to place the lady on horseback, and thus travel to the mountains, for one so gentle could not walk over the rough roads with a child in her arms, or by her side.

Our sweet friend did not object to the arrangement, but as there was no side saddle in the country it was a little doubtful how we could manage, especially as the lady declined to adopt man's usual style of occupying a position on a horse. We talked the whole thing over, and at last found a pack saddle, broad and strong, which Mr. Larkin let us have as a gift, when he learned our purpose. We covered it with some cheap cloth, rigged a stirrup for the lady's foot, found a bridle that was strong and serviceable, put a strap on the forward part of the saddle for a pommel, and thought the thing would answer the purpose very well. and when we exhibited our work to Senora Costello she was so pleased with the whole arrangement that she had no misgivings as to her ability to cling on while ascending or descending the mountains.

Then we hunted around and found a stately, sure-footed old mule, one that would not be likely to play any unruly pranks, and could walk all day without a bray of discontent. As we did not know who owned the borrico we confiscated him in the name of the government, and were never prosecuted for mule stealing, as General Castro and Colonel Fernando gave us immediate absolution, as soon as they learned all the circumstances of the case. Thus prepared we looked after our horses the night before we were to start, and at sundown wandered to the beach, sat on the rocks near the custom house, heard the bands on the frigates play national airs until nine o'clock, and, as I listened to the music stealing across the waters of the bay, a feeling of homesickness came over me, which my friend was not slow to perceive, for he said,—

"Come, let us back go, and sleep good for de night. All de best fun of our lives is soon afore us to be. Ve skall see Anita and Engracia, and tell dem vot ve has passed through for dere sakes, and dey vill pity us and love us de more."

"Do you know, Lewey," I cried, as we rose to go, "I begin to think that fate is against us, and that we shall never marry those half-breed Mexican girls."

"Darn if I care it ve don't," the fickle-minded French lad replied. "I begins to dink dat dey is not our equals in de life."

"And you would break your pledged word?" I demanded, quite sternly.

"Vy not? Dey vould do dame dings us for."

"Never," I answered. "They love us too well for that. They would remain true for years for our sakes."

"How little know you vomen about," Lewey said. "Dey throw ober us for better and richer men in von minute and a half. Do dink you, mon ami, dat ve has much moneys now. Ve has two dousand dollars, all in de gold, and dat is not bad for two young men to life commence vith. Besides, vot does ve vant of vives anyvay? Ve is free now, and goes vare ve pleases, and stays as long as ve vants to, and vot more does vant you?"

"At least you will go to the girls, and tell them that you have changed your mind?" I inquired.

"Oh, I don't know vot I vill do. Dare is time enough for all dat ven ve comes to it. Don't trouble let us borror. Alons, ve has a big future afore us," and just then we came across Captain Cooper, of the schooner California.

"I see that the Yankees have captured your war-vessel, captain," I remarked. "The crew did not make a vigorous defence I am afraid."

"The odds were too great against us," was the reply, with a vicious bite of his maimed hand. "Man to man we could have licked them, but the big guns did the business. However, the vessel is private property. I seized her several days since for debt. She will be restored to me, I think," and she was, by the commodore's orders.

The old salt passed on, grumbling, and we returned home, and slept for the last time in the house that had sheltered us for so many weeks, and where we had passed some very happy hours, and many anxious ones.

We were up bright and early, got breakfast for Senora Costello and her child, and also for ourselves, packed what clothes the lady needed, made her put on a broad brimmed straw sombrero to protect her head from the hot sun, fastened up the house by the aid of hammers and nails, and at nine o'clock were ready for our journey, then ambled out across the plaza, passed the house of the American consul, where Mr. Larkin was seated on his veranda, as usual, gazing off across the bay, and at the two heavy frigates, and as we bade him good-morning the old gentleman asked,—

"Boys, do you think of coming back to Monterey?"

"It is impossible to tell, sir. We do not know where we shall go, or what we may do."

"The Mexicans owe you a debt of gratitude for your heroic services the other night. I have sent a note to General Castro, and detailed them among other things. The American government is also indebted to you for what you have done, but I fear that the reward will be light."

This verbal testimony is all I have to offer the United States for the part Lewey and I performed in those trying times, and if a pension is offered me on the strength of it, I wish there would be no delay about its being made available in dollars and cents, or else the government should order twenty thousand copies of this book, and pay for them, as a slight recompense for my sufferings during the war in California.

We thanked the consul for his kind wishes, and were about to move off, as a crowd was collecting to see the novel picture of a lady with a straw sombrero on her head, riding a led mule, and with a child in her arms. It was a wonderful spectacle, and caused Senora Costello to blush at her awkward position.

"One moment, boys," Mr. Larkin said, and we held up to hear his words. "Do you know what day of the month it is?"

"No, sir. We have lost the run of such things."

"The seventh day of July, 1846. Remember it, for it will live in history for many years."

"Why so, sir?"

"Because in a few hours Commodore Sloat will hoist the American flag near the custom house, and take formal possession of California, and after the flag is raised this State is lost forever to Mexico. The stars and stripes will not be succeeded by the buzzard, and if you live long enough you may see this great territory teeming with life and industry, with wealth and contentment, prosperity and happiness, and so it will grow until people wonder at the enterprise and intelligence of its inhabitants, and from all parts of the world will commerce come to us, our harbors teem with life, and grain grow on every hill and in all the rich valleys. Then will California be blessed, and may I live long enough to see it."

"He is crazy," muttered Lewey, as we resumed our way, but I thought there was method in his madness, and his prophecy came true sooner than he anticipated, but he lived long enough to realize some of his predictions, if not all, for he did not dream of the great railroad and steamship lines in those days, or the overland cars, and immense hotels, where all was once wild and desolate.

As we turned from the plaza, and struck the trail that led to the Mission Carmel, I glanced back and saw the old gentleman still on his veranda, looking across the bay and dreaming of the prosperous days to come. I never saw him again, but if his remains are buried near Monterey I hope to have the melancholy satisfaction of placing a garland of flowers on his tomb some day in the near future.

"What was he talking about?" asked Senora Costello, as we left the village, much to the delight of Jack, who commenced sniffing game in every bush, and was glad to be once more in the woods and among the chapparel.

"Of the future of California, lady," I answered.

"There's no future for the State," she said, as a tear dropped from her bright eyes. "Under the rule of Americans life will not be worth much to the Mexican people," and she expressed the sentiments of all the better class of her race, and perhaps even years have not removed the impression that the Yankees are intruders upon the soil.

As we gained the elevation near where now stands the Hotel del Monte, we heard a gun fired from one of the frigates. We checked our animals, and looked over the village at our feet. There were barges being rowed to the shore, and in the boats were glittering uniforms and many men. We saw a crowd of people assemble near the cus'om house, a band played some national airs, the American flag was raised high above the heads of the spectators, and then the war-ships thundered forth a salute, and the State of California was annexed to the Union in deed if not in act, for our people had been striving to get possession too many years to give up the prize after peace was declared, and it is worth some of the sacrifices of the Mexican war, for its future will be as great as its past has been wonderful.

"I hate the Americans," said Senora Costello as she watched the scene, and the tears fell from her eyes.

"And I am an American, lady," I remarked with a smile.

"But I do not hate you," was the response, and she extended her hand, and I pressed it reverentially to my lips.

We turned away from the sight as the last gun was fired, and I saw Monterey no more, although we heard from the place quite often while we remained on the coast.

We pushed our way over the trail, the sun shining hot upon our heads, and before we were two miles from the village stumbled upon some outlying pickets, who challenged us, and then rode forward to ask the news. Most of the soldiers knew who we were, and did not express surprise at seeing us, for they expected their colonel's sister would not remain in Monterey, and run the risk of being insulted by the conquerers. They did not think that a lady was safer under the protection of American officers than the Mexicans of the lower order.

We were hurried forward to headquarters, and then conducted to the presence of General Castro, while Senora Costello was taken possession of by her husband and brother, and made comfortable in the hut of the latter.

The Mexican governor was anxious to learn if there was a chance for an attack on the town, and beating the Yankees, but when I told him that the frigates would interfere with his plans he gave up all idea of reconquering Monterey, and determined to turn his steps to the southern part of the State. He was in no haste to go, as the Americans were not disposed to attack him, and so we remained near the Mission for several days, and then marched for Santa Barbara.

In the meantime Colonel Fernando and the husband had learned of our valuable services, and we were thanked in a sincere manner. The former gave us quarters near his own, and made us honorary members of his staff, with very light duties and still lighter pay, for we got not a dollar for all that we did for the people, but had one advantage,—could steal all we desired of other men's property, and no one dared to say that we were unjust, as we were clothed with full authority to take horses and cattle when needed.

Our position enabled us to perform a kind action for some friends of ours, however, when we were encamped near the Salines River. One morning while we were riding about the country, we noticed a commotion in a clump of trees on the banks of the stream, and heard loud curses in the English tongue, and hearty carambas in Spanish. When we rode up to the place we were much surprised to find our former supercargo, Mr. H. F. Teschemacher, and Messrs. William Wolfskill and William Howard, gentlemen well known on the coast, engaged in an angry and exciting discussion with some of our cavalrymen, the latter having seized the former's horses, and were about to lead them off, all animals being confiscated by the order of General Castro. We soon put a stop to the hot words, and ordered the Mexicans to release the animals and restore them to their owners. Very reluctantly they obeyed, and then we escorted the gentlemen past the camp by a blind trail, and saw them safely on their way to Monterey. They thanked us for the service rendered, but we saw them no more while in the country. No doubt Mr. Teschemacher will remember the incident even at this late day, the only witness I have to prove my claim for a pension from both countries. I hope he will live until I get it, and if he does the oldest man spoken of in the Bible will be a mere infant in arms in comparison to the age of my friend when he dies.

We moved in short marches to Santa Barbara. No one was in a hurry, for there was nothing to be gained by haste. A report reached us at San Luis Obispo that some kind of a Bear Party, composed of foreigners, had met near San Francisco, and elected Captain Fremont governor of the State, but Castro laughed at the idea, and so did all the Mexicans, and it was soon forgotten.

Every day that we traveled I showed Senora Costello some polite attention, and looked after all her wants. She found the mule and saddle so much more comfortable than a volante or ox-cart that she clung to the conveyance until Santa Barbara was reached, where she remained during the war.

We passed the ranches we had stopped at on our way to Monterey, and to the indignation of the rancheros levied on their stock to feed the men. When at San Luis Obispo we once more visited the fresh water creek near the Cave, and had a most glorious wash, the first for some weeks, owing to the want of time and facilities. We went to the house where we had seen the fandango during our sailor boys' career, and laughed as we thought of the fun we had enjoyed that night.

On the eighth day after leaving Monterey we reached Santa Barbara, and the people turned out and gave us a reception. As we rode by the house of Don Noriego I saw his daughter on the veranda waving a scarf as a welcome to the gallant soldiers. As I was just in the rear of Colonel Fernando, and at the head of the column, I did not deem it out of place to take some part of the enthusiasm to myself, and when the handsome young lady smiled and bowed to us I raised my hat, and did all that I could to attract her attention, and she seemed amused at my persistency for there was a glow on her face, and Lewey growled out, —

"I s'pose you dink dat is for you, but it is n't. She is lookin' right at me all de time," which was a lie, as it was no such thing, but my French friend always was jealous of the lady for some reason or other, fearing perhaps that she would have the first place in my mind instead of himself.

As there were no ships-of-war in the harbor, and none had made their appearance thus far, it was proposed to remain several days at Santa Barbara, to recruit the men, and see what was best to be done, and where to go in case fighting was called for. We saw Mr. Robinson, and spoke with him for a few minutes, and very much astonished he was at the importance we had attained in so short a time, for Senora Costello did not hesitate to express her opinion as to our conduct, and praise us more than we deserved. Her brother also was very particular in his commendations, and thus, in the course of a day or two, I was formally presented to the Senorita Noriego, but she never knew me as the sailor boy who had admired her so much when he was connected with the Admittance, and in fact she acted just as though she had never seen my face before, which was a great triumph for Lewey, as he said, —

"I tells you so. No voman look at you twice ven I is near."

He did not mean to be personal, for he was as proud of my success as I was of his, only he was a little jealous that I would like some one he disapproved of.

The third day after our arrival at Santa Barbara, and when we had found very good quarters, we thought it about time to visit Ranche Refugio, and take a look at the girls we had left under such distressing circumstances. We did not exchange a word with each other about marriage, avoiding the topic by mutual consent, for somehow, as we mixed with the people, and saw ladies and gentlemen of good position, we thought it was best to reflect on what we were going to do before it was too late.

"Colonel," we said one morning, "we should like leave of absence for a day or two, if you think you can run the regiment without us."

He smiled as he said, —

"You are going to Ranche Refugio to see the girls?"

" Yes, colonel, such is our intention."

" You will not obtain leave of absence from me unless you promise one thing," our superior said.

" Oh, we agree to it," Lewey remarked, thinking that it was some trifling request.

" Very well. Then promise me you will not marry those half-breed girls until you have thought the matter all over, and consulted my sister and myself."

" We promise," Lewey cried, with remarkable promptness, and then we were told to take our rifles and go, but to be very particular to avoid all bands of wandering ladrones, as some of them were known to be in the neighborhood, and might attempt to injure us.

We directed our peon servant to prepare our horses, and about nine o'clock, during one of the most beautiful days of July, rode down to the beach, saw the old familiar surf, and then shaped our course for the Ranche, from which we were forcibly taken only a few months before. Somehow we were not so eager to reach the place as lovers usually are, and we loitered on the trail, to the great delight of Jack, so that it was near twelve o'clock when we stopped at the residence of the two pretty sisters, and begged for a cup of water. They did not recognize the smartly-dressed boys as their old friends, and we had to explain matters before we could make them comprehend who we were, and what fortunes we had met with since we saw them last. We claimed to be officers in the army, and were, in fact, but the positions were merely honorary, and given just to afford us protection while in the country.

We were invited ro remain and dine, but pleaded want of time, left the young ladies, and went toward the residence of Anita and Engracia. It would be unjust to say that we were not a little agitated as we drew near the poor adobe house we had visited so many times. We smiled as we thought of our previous reception by the mother of the girls, when we were eager for an interview, and how she had abused us for calling. We wondered if such a torrent of words would again fall upon our ears, and the question appeared to be promptly answered, for before a scant fire, but under the hot sun, sat the very old woman we had been thinking of, the mother of Anita and Engracia, and she was engaged in preparing an olia for her midday meal.

The woman looked up as we checked our horses, and seeing two caballeros before her uttered some rude words of welcome, but we declined to dismount until we had some assurances as to the whereabouts of the girls, and the pacific disposition of the mother.

"Where are your daughters, senora?" asked Lewey, in a bland and mild tone.

"With their husbands to be sure," was the blunt reply, and at the words we both uttered exclamations of surprise, and put our hands to our heads to endeavor to collect our scattered senses, for the shock was a great one.

"Vell, I 'm blanked," the French lad said, in a dazed sort of manner, and then he looked at me, and a sickly smile passed over his face, as he did not know what to say next.

"This is woman's constancy," I moaned, and yet to tell the truth neither of us felt like raving wildly over the matter.

"How long have the girls been married?" Lewey asked, after a moment's pause.

"Just a month," was the prompt answer.

"And whom did they marry?" I managed to inquire.

"Antonio and Carlos Sanchos," was the reply, and then we were indignant, for our fiancées had united their fortunes to the men who had persecuted us during our residence in California, and completed our humiliation by taking as husbands two of the worst scamps in the country. This was not flattering to us, and Lewey ground his teeth together as he thought of the disgrace of being superseded by a couple of dark-faced, elderly ruffians, old enough to be the fathers of their wives.

"Are you sure the girls are married?" I ventured to inquire.

"What does this look like?" the woman asked, as she dropped the sleeve of her chemise, and showed some terrible looking bruises on her poor old wrinkled bosom. "And what do you call this?" bending her head forward, and revealing a cut an inch and a half long on the back of her neck, looking angry and swollen.

"It seems as though some one had ill-treated you, you poor old thing," Lewey said in a tone of pity, all his former resentment gone at the sight of the injuries.

"It looks as though my daughters were married, does it not?" the woman asked in a sarcastic manner. "These blows were inflicted by my sons-in-law."

"The saints preserve me," muttered Lewey, "but the Sanchos have more courage than I supposed. How did they dare to attack her in such a reckless manner?"

"You see that not much was made in driving us away from your house," I said, and then the old woman glanced up, brushed the coarse hair from her face, and looked at us.

"The saints forgive me, but are you the two nice young gringos who wanted to marry the girls some time last spring?"

"We are the same persons," was our prompt reply.

"And I spoke a little hastily, did I not?"

"Well, we should think you did. You called us hard names in profusion."

"Ah, how sorry I am that I wronged you. Had you married my daughters I should have ruled your households. Now, curses on the ladrones, they rule me, and pound me if the food is not ready. How little did I know what was good for myself. I had better have let the souls take care of themselves, and looked after the bodies. But come in the house, and I will tell you all about it."

We entered the building, and prepared to listen to the old woman's story. It was to the effect that Don Antonio Sanchos had visited her one day, — before we had put in an appearance, or while we were journeying from San Diego to Santa Barbara, — and made such preposterous statements regarding us, as heretics and ladrones, that the woman got frightened. Then Sanchos played upon the feelings of the priest, and he put a veto on the match, not knowing us or our condition, and it was not until the priest of Santa Cruz wrote to the padre of Ranche Refugio that matters were explained. It was then too late. The girls had been married through the urging of their mother and father confessor, under the supposition that the candidates for matrimony had plenty of money, and a high official position, when, in fact, they were outlaws, and after being dismissed by General Castro, instead of going to San Francisco, hurried to the Ranche in the hope of further injuring us by taking away our intended wives.

"De saints be praised, it am all for de best," muttered Lewey as the story was finished. "Dings vork in de most mysterious vay, as some von has said. I know not von. Ve has preserved de honor of our names, and it am all right," and just as he spoke Anita and Engracia entered the room to see who had arrived.

They uttered wild shrieks when they saw us, and threw up their hands.

"Do not come near us. Keep at a distance, for we dare not speak or touch you," they cried, and then, woman-like, rushed toward us, put their arms around our necks, and kissed us as in days of old.

"Oh, why did you come here when you know that we are married? Leave us at once before our husbands find you in the house, and kill you, as they will do," both girls exclaimed.

We were not so much afraid of the husbands as the girls seemed to think, although we did put our old loves aside, and unwound their arms from our necks.

"You have been untrue to us," we said, "but we forgive you. Your punishment will be great. You had an opportunity to marry two of the most promising young men in California. That chance you have thrown away in a cool and deliberate manner. You can recall it to mind when you hear of our fame in years to come."

This was not modest, but we wanted a slight revenge for our humiliation.

The young girls, or wives, were awe stricken at our words. We had impressed upon their minds that we were a little above their grade in life, and that generally causes a woman to submit to all sorts of indignities for the sake of position, but even while we were thus engaged we heard the sound of horses' feet, and the next moment Antonio and Carlos Sanchos burst into the room, and the first thing the former did was to knock down the old woman, as a slight relief for his over-charged feelings, and when she was lying on the floor the curses she uttered against her amiable son-in-law were the most wonderful specimens of the Spanish tongue that it was ever my misfortune to hear.

"What are you doing with our wives?" the outlaws asked, as they laid their hands on their knives, and drew them.

"These are old friends of ours," the ladies said in a pleading tone. "They have only called for a visit, and will soon go."

"We spoke to the ladrones, the mean gringos," was the reply. "Let them answer us."

"We have no answer to make to your insolent demands," Lewey cried. "We know both of you scoundrels. There is a price set on your heads, so beware of capture. If the soldiers get on your trail there will be blood spilled, and you the victims."

"We will commence right here if there is blood to be shed," the men answered, and raised their knives to throw them at us, but the girls covered our bodies with their own, and when the weapons whizzed through the air we did not have a chance to draw our pistols, or use our rifles in self-defence, or even push the women aside, and save them at the expense of our own lives. Anita and Engracia clung to us, and when the knives sped on their way they struck the girls near their shoulder-blades, the steel penetrating to the lungs, and the poor things fell to the floor of the cabin, the blood flowing in torrents from their wounds.

"Dogs of Mexicans, you have murdered your wives," we shouted, while the old woman made the house ring with her yells of horror and anguish at the scene before her.

The brutes appeared dazed at the sight of the innocent blood that met their view. They made a rush toward us, but we struck them on the sides of their heads with the barrels of our pistols, and down they tumbled, and as we were about to follow up the victory in a sure manner, we heard the loud blast of a trumpet, and stayed our hands, and the shots that would have ended the career of two noted villains were not fired, for in the doorway we saw the form of Colonel Fernando, and back of him six of his men.

"What is the trouble here?" asked the young officer. "Two women bleeding to death, and the Sanchos brothers on the ground with broken heads, and my friends uninjured. Well, this is a lucky day even if it is Friday. The saints be praised, I am just in time to take an active part in this tragedy. Stop your howling, old woman. It will not prevent the flow of blood. Send the sergeant here. He knows something of knife wounds, for he has hacked people and been hacked more times than he has years over his head. Let him look at the girls' injuries. Secure those ladrones, and take them outside. They have just fifteen minutes to live, so one of you had better go for the priest. The girls will want some of his consolation before a great while, or I am no judge of the near approach of death."

We could not realize that the colonel was in earnest, but some of the cavalry commenced binding the limbs of the Sanchos brothers with reatas, and in the meantime we bent over the bodies of the dying girls, certain that they could live but a short time, as a change had already taken place in their faces, the sure precursor of death.

"You forgive us for our unfaithfulness?" whispered Anita. "We meant to be true and good, but were persuaded to marry against our wishes. We thought that we should never see you again. Every one said you were bad and heretics. But it won't matter in the next world, will it, what religion we profess? We shall be near each other in spite of ties on earth, and no one will part us. It is better as it is. You would have been ashamed of your dark-skinned wife, and wished her dead, or might have left her to mourn for your lost love. You will kiss me, and say that you forgive me for the past, and if you live long think of the many pleasant hours we had together, before there were troubles in the country, and men did not persecute you?"

I kissed her dark face. She closed her eyes, and seemed to sail down the river very fast, for she did not again look at me or speak. Her breath grew shorter and shorter, and then a shudder passed through her slight form, and she was gone to the great unknown world, and when she d'ed her sister's spirit also fled at the same moment, so that in death as in life they were not divided.

We covered the faces of the dead, and went out-of-doors, and as we crossed the threshold of the building the priest was just entering to administer the last rites of the church. He went to the bodies, knelt down and prayed long and earnestly for the repose of the souls of the young girls, and when he came out of the house Colonel Fernando was seated on a log, smoking cigarettes, as calm as the summer day overhead.

"Holy father," the officer said, "administer the last sacrament to those two men. As soon as you have finished they die."

"You will not dare to commit such an outrage," the padre cried. "They have had no trial, and are not yet proved guilty."

"Do your duty, holy father. In ten minutes they die, law or no law," was the stern command.

The priest bowed his head, and made no further remonstrance. He knew what military duties were, and how despotic commanders sometimes acted during martial law.

"Would it be of any use for me to plead for the ladrones?" asked Lewey.

"Not the slightest," and the colonel lighted a fresh cigarette.

"I have no intention of asking for the lives of the scoundrels," Lewey said. "I only spoke for information," and the colonel smiled, and puffed out volumes of smoke through his nostrils, and playfully blew rings in the air from his lips.

The padre went to the condemned and knelt by their sides, for they were lying on the ground securely bound, the hot July sun beating down upon their dark, swarthy faces, and with every expression of terror in their treacherous eyes.

"Colonel," the priest said, after he had heard the last confession the fellows were ever to make, "the poor men have a favor to ask of you. It is not a great one, and should be granted it seems to me."

"Name it," and the young officer scanned the heavens to see how low the sun was, and to judge of the time of day, and how much light he would have to get back to Santa Barbara. He was the most unconcerned person present, for Lewey and I and the soldiers were more agitated than he.

"These men who are about to die," the priest said, "desire to be spared so that they can have time to attend the funerals of their dear departed wives, whose deaths were so sudden and unexpected."

"Diablo," laughed the colonel, "but I must tell this to General Castro when I see him. He is just the kind of man to enjoy such a joke. Here are two ladrones, who steal away these gentlemen's intended wives by falsehood and deception (I will admit that I am glad of it), and at last murder them in cold blood, and now wish to attend the funeral of their victims. Well, this is a good specimen of impudence. It is the coolest thing I ever heard of. Sergeant, place the scoundrels in position against yonder trees, and give a volley to each. I have no more time to waste on them."

The condemned uttered a howl of terror, and the cries of the men, the wailing of the mother and other women, were enough to unnerve us, but the cavalry leader did not lose his composure for a moment. He smoked cigarettes in numberless quantities, and paid no attention to the shrieks that were going on around him.

The fierce little sergeant pounced upon the men, as though he rather liked the job he had undertaken. He dragged the ladrones to the trees indicated, lashed them in an upright position, for the fellows did not seem capable of standing without help, so weak were they in their knees, tore away the dark shirts and jackets, exposing the hairy breasts, then stepped back and surveyed his work with great satisfaction, just as though he was looking at a picture he much admired, yet did not quite approve of the shading.

"Pull his head up a little," the petty officer said to one of his subordinates. "He droops somewhat, and I fear the men's aim will be destroyed. Ah, that is better. Now slue him around so that he will show a fair front. Punch him in the ribs if he don't move fast enough. Well that. It could not be better for a sharp volley. Don't howl that way, you loco. It looks to me as though you had no confidence in the saints or a blissful hereafter. In the city of Mexico I have seen ten men shot before breakfast, and all of them put together did not make as much of a row as you are doing. Confound you, shut up that groaning and lamenting. It is enough to make me sick. You don't seem to appreciate the honor of being shot by some of the best cavalrymen in California. What do you say? Tell us all to go to the next place. Why, you ungrateful scoundrels, now I don't care if my men do mangle you. Five of you form in line, and take the fellow on the right, and five of you hit the one on the left. Now then, are you pretty comfortable? You a'n't? Well, whose fault is it?"

For the life of me I could not keep my eyes off the execution, although I dreaded to see it, and at the same time was amused at the coolness and composure of the sergeant, who seemed to be enjoying himself at the expense of others. The colonel still sat on a stump, smoked cigarettes, and did not betray any impatience at the delay. The scene reminded me of the time when Fernando was simply a captain, and hanged a man on the route from San Luis Obispo to Monterey for attempted murder.

"All ready, colonel," said the fierce little sergeant, turning and saluting his commander, with an eager look on his face.

"Go on with your execution," remarked the young officer, and lighted a fresh cigarette.

The sergeant threw a piece of blanket over the condemned men's heads, stepped one side, removed his hat, and said, —

"When I drop my sombrero fire, and don't throw away a shot like a gringo."

I turned my head, and looked at the priest, who was on his knees praying for those who were dead and about to die.

There was an irregular volley, for the crack cavalrymen could not fire with precision and regularity, some terrible groans, and then all was still. The good padre prayed silently for the dead, and the enemies of the dead, while the women fainted, and tumbled down in all directions, and Jack, our dog, sat on his haunches, lifted up his head, and howled as though mourning for the flight of two evil spirits to the gates of eternity, to trouble us no more.

Lewey watched the scene to the last. It seemed to have a strange fascination for him, and the last time I saw him, just after the Prussian war, he recalled the circumstances of the military execution at Ranche Refugio, and said that while some communists in Paris were being shot, his thoughts went back to his early days, and strangely enough the deaths of the two Mexicans were uppermost in his mind, for some of the victims of his loyal sailors were swarthy as Spaniards, and resembled the two Sanchos in features and height and vindictiveness of disposition.

"Dead, colonel," reported the little black sergeant, with a wave of his hand, as though he had done a good thing, and was proud of it.

"All right. Dig two graves and bundle them in. Or stay. One hole will be enough for both. Senors, let us mount, and ride down to pay a visit to some pretty young ladies who live near here. Our escort can join us there. I am tired of hearing these women yell and scream so loud," and the colonel motioned to his orderly to bring up the horses.

"Holy father," I said, as the colonel rode away, while Lewey and I lingered behind to take a farewell look at the faces of the dead girls, "if we had known each other better all this might have been avoided, and the women would now be alive and happy."

"It is the will of God, my son, and destined to happen. We cannot escape the fixed rules of the universe, strive as we may. I am sorry, my son, for the past. Let us be more wise in the future. I wish that I had known you better. I should have been less prejudiced against you, I think, from what I have this day seen. Take my blessing and go."

He raised his hands over us, and then was about to turn away, but I detained him for a moment.

"Father," I said, "the mother of the girls is poor, is she not?"

"She is poverty itself, my son."

"Then take these two golden ounces, see that the women are decently interred, pay for a mass for the repose of their souls, and donate the balance of the money to the parent. If you will do this we shall feel as though we had made some atonement for the past."

"The atonement for the past is in God's own hands, my son, and to him must all application for pardon be made. You and your friend should pray for forgiveness, confess, and strive to be better in the future. Go, my son, and thank the saints it is no worse. I may not speak of things which the confessional holds as sacred, but of this be assured, the poor children loved both of you devotedly, and it was wrong on your part to win their affections."

"But we were honorable in our intended marriage, holy father."

"Perhaps you were, but the poor girls would soon have suffered from your neglect. Desertion follows incompatability. The wise and the ignorant should not mate. You can read and write. The girls who are now lying dead could do neither. They knew not the meaning of a single letter, and had no accomplishments except that of the dance."

"But we could have taught them, holy father, as much as we know ourselves."

"Vain delusion, my son. Such things are not to be in this world. As lovers you are devoted, and exercise all due patience with each other. As husband and wife the teaching becomes a bore, and there are sharp answers instead of explanations for the purpose of unfolding the mind. If a lover is to be a teacher he must be kept in the position of a lover, and not a favored one at that. All interest ceases at marriage, and blessed is the woman who can retain the heart and devotion of a man six months after a union. The laws of my church forbid a priest to wed. The provision is a wise one, for if we had family matters to look after there would not be much time for parochial affairs. But we see with open eyes all the domestic relations of life, and so judge as we look, regretting, yet unable to apply any remedies except the best of advice, and that is rarely taken by either party. Yes, it was a cruel thing for two young senors like you to win the love of those g'rls. But go, and God go with you."

He again extended his arms, and we uncovered our heads, and were blessed, and then mounting our patient horses rode toward the house of the pretty sisters, and as we passed on our way saw a number of peons throwing dirt into a shallow grave, and the fierce little sergeant was sitting under the shade of an apple-tree damning them in no measured terms, and smoking cigarettes. We looked back and saw the good priest watching our departure, and when he saw us turn in our saddles waved his hand in token of farewell, and that was the last we ever saw of the padre or of Ranche Refugio.

We found our colonel enjoying himself in the company of the two pretty sisters. One of the latter was thumbing a guitar, and singing a love song, while their military visitor did not seem in the least dismayed by the tragedies he had witnessed during the afternoon.

"Come in, caballeros," he said when we stopped opposite the door, and as we entered the commodious adobe house were formally presented to the young ladies, and very gracious they were to us. We did not allude to the murders back of the vineyards, so there was no occasion for a cloud to cover the handsome faces of the girls. The colonel seemed to have forgotten all about the circumstance, if we could judge by the laughter he indulged in.

The young ladies put some bottles of cheap native wine on the table, a lot of dark bread, and nice fruit, and after we had partaken of the refreshments the colonel waltzed with one of the girls, and the other played on a guitar. The young officer was a very good dancer, and entered into the spirit of the movements with a zest that did him credit, but we were not inclined to be lively, and so declined the invitation to once more hold the girls in our arms as of yore. We thought it was a little too soon to throw our grief to the winds, and forget the deaths of poor Anita and Engracia, who might have been our wives if circumstances had been favorable for the union.

Presently the tramp of horses' feet and the clanging of sabres showed that our escort was at the door. We drank a glass of wine to the health and happiness of the pretty sisters, kissed their hands in gallant style, mounted our horses, and left the place, and as we filed out of the ravine the ladies stood at the door of their house, waved their scarfs, and smiled a sweet smile at the colonel, whose handsome face had touched their hearts, I have no doubt, for he married one of the girls some months later, when peace was declared, and had a bride that any man could be proud of. What became of the elder sister I never knew. I hoped she fared as well. We never saw them or the place again.

"Colonel," I said, as we gained the mesa land, "how did you happen to be present just as we needed you most?"

"Senors," he replied, with a blush and a laugh, "you are not the only persons in California who have had love affairs on their hands. Soon after you left Santa Barbara this morning I learned from one of our spies that the Sanchos brothers were here, and had married your girls. I feared that you would meet with trouble at their hands, so determined to kill two birds with one stone. do a little love-making on my own account, and bring to justice the most notorious scoundrels in the country. General Castro authorized me to seize the fellows wherever found, and shoot them on sight. I have attended to my duty, and now go back to camp with the thought that justice has been done."

"And your conscience does not reproach you for the shooting?" I asked.

The colonel smiled.

"Senors, a soldier should be destitute of such a thing. He must obey orders no matter what they are. Vamos," and striking his horse with his heavy spurs we dashed forward along the road that wound about the beach, and drew rein just at sundown, and as we dismounted Senora Costello came toward us.

"You have returned unmarried?" she asked, as she smiled on us.

"Our intended brides are dead," Lewey remarked in a low, sad tone.

"I am glad to hear it," was the careless comment, and as the lady spoke she laid a hand on my arm, and said, —

"Did you love her very much, my friend?"

"I thought so," was my response.

"And now?"

"Perhaps I have seen one whom I love better," and I sighed as the hand was withdrawn, and the sigh was re-echoed as the lady gathered her dark mantilla around face and shoulders, and entered the house, and I saw her no more that night.

"In de name of de saints," Lewey exclaimed, "do not make de love to dat lady. She is a married voman, and our admiration bring de ruin and disaster on all dat ve meet. Let but de sign be seen dat you is sweet on her and de life you has von't be vorth much. Serve her if you vill, but keep de varmth for some von else. Imitate me, and be cold and distant."

I looked at the young man with admiration for his impudence, and then without a word of explanation we gave our mustangs to a peon servant, for Colonel Fernando had detailed an Indian to look after our horses, and just as we entered the house where we were quartered the trumpets rang out a blast for evening parade, and the young ladies of the town hastened to the plaza, to get a glimpse of the graceful commander of the cavalry, and to strive to attract his attention by many a fan flirtation and flash of dark eyes.

We ate our suppers in silence, then wrapped serapes around our shoulders, lighted pipes, and strolled down to the beach. Jack started to go with us, then thought of the long run that he had during the day, gave us an appealing glance, hesitated for a moment, and returned to the house, curled himself up on the horse-blankets, and went to sleep. We did not blame him for refusing to accompany us, but it was the first time such a thing had occurred.

We halted opposite Don Noriego's house, where many of the officers were congregated, enjoying the usual evening's tête-à-tête and music, and then pushed on, for we did not care to join the company, our thoughts were too sorrowful for useless chatter, and when we reached the beach sat down on the damp sand and looked off upon the bay and the rolling surf, and our minds once more went back to our hide-droghing days and boating duty. Neither of us spoke, and I have no doubt that Lewey's thoughts were like my own with the past, and all the strange, wild life we had witnessed since we left our ship.

From this reverie we were aroused by rough hands being placed upon our necks and arms, and then the cold muzzles of pistols were pointed at our heads, and a stern-voiced man said in poor Spanish, —

"If you make the least noise I'll blow your brains out. Answer me a few questions, and ou shall not be harmed."

"My friend," I said, in the coolest tone I could assume, and glancing around saw that we were surrounded by half a dozen Yankee man-of-war sailors, and that an officer was holding one of the pistols in close proximity to my head, and a middy was paying the same attention to Lewey, who, in spite of the surprise, was still puffing away at his pipe in cool contempt of all danger, "do you not think that it would be better to converse in English. We should understand each other a little better."

"The devil," the officer said, and lowered his pistol, "do you speak English?"

"Well, sir, it comes more convenient than Spanish, as a general thing, for we make awful botches of the latter tongue sometimes, unless it is all plain sailing."

"I thought you were greasers," the commander of the squad said. "You are dressed in Mexican costume."

"That proves nothing. We supposed the navy was officered by gentlemen, and that they were not inclined to offer rudeness to people minding their own business. We were both mistaken, that is all."

"Don't be impudent," the officer remarked. "We must take life and prisoners as we find them. We want your company for a few hours on board our vessel."

"Indeed, and for what purpose?"

"Information which I think you can give. I suspect that you are an American," the officer said.

"You have not mis-stayed this time. I am an American, and this gentleman, my friend, is French. Now what do you desire to know? We do not intend to leave the shore tonight to visit any vessel."

"Do not be too sure of that, my friend," the officer said with a laugh. "We are strong enough to take you, and shall."

"You are over-confident, sir. One word from us and you could not move two fathoms from the beach without being surrounded by cavalry. Even now you are hemmed in on all sides except the water, and cannot escape unless you have the countersign. You can shoot us as we sit here, but that is not customary among civilized nations. Murder it would be called before a court-martial."

"But we can knock you on the head, and then take you," was the sullen rejoinder, "and I am not sure but we shall do it if you continue to give me any more lip."

"De lip is not all on von side, sir," Lewey remarked, speaking for the first time, although he had manifested a strong desire to break in for some minutes past. "Ve is gentlemen, and in no vay liable to answer questions. I am, sir, de French consul for California, and dis is de American consul, Mr. Larkin."

I was speechless with amazement at the audacity of the lad. The night was dark, and the naval officer could not well see our youthful faces, hidden as they were by the serapes, so the story was liable to be believed.

"Say not a word," Lewey whispered in French. "Let me manage this for you. Impudence must tell here, or we will be on board of a frigate in less than an hour, and then the saints only know what will become of us."

"Pardon me, gentlemen," the naval officer said, as he stepped back, raised his cap, and replaced his pistol in a belt. "I did not know your official positions or I should have spoken in a different tone. But in the first place I thought that Mr. Larkin, our consul, was at Monterey, his usual station."

"So i was, sir, but a few days since. Official business called me here, and the French consul, Monsieur Lewey, who has just been landed from a line-of-battle ship, wanted to see the country, so came to this place in my company."

The mention of a line-of-battle ship has a great influence on a naval officer. The stranger bowed lower than ever, as he said, —

"I have heard of Mr. Larkin, but this is the first time I was ever notified of a French consul being stationed on the coast. I suppose it is on account of our war with Mexico."

"Yes, on dat account entirely," hastily remarked Lewey. "My king tell me so hisself."

This was pretty strong, and I wondered the officer did not discover the lie, but he might not have been up in court etiquette. Perhaps he really thought King Louis Philippe of France held personal interviews with his foreign representatives, and gave them instructions.

"Now, sir," I said, as the officer recovered his composure, "you will please tell me what you are doing ashore at this time of night, and in a hostile country? Do you know that if discovered your life would not be worth a medio?"

"We have taken the chances, sir," was the answer. "My men are well armed, and will sell their lives very dearly, or would resist capture to the last. Our commodore is desirous of learning a little about the present state of affairs here, and so sent us on shore after dark. Our boat is anchored just outside of the rollers, off Point Arena, and will wait there until we return with what information we can pick up. Had you been greasers we should have taken you to the frigate, and obtained all the news we desired by the aid of money and judicious squeezing. Now we hope you will enlighten us as soon as possible."

"What is the name of your frigate, and who is your commodore?" I asked.

"The frigate Congress, Commodore Stockton, who is ordered to the supreme command of the squadron and the country," was the answer. "The ship is lying about four miles from shore, bound to Monterey. We entered the canal this afternoon, and hope to be well on our way at daylight."

"And may I ask your official position, sir?" I demanded, with a careless indifference that I by no means felt, for if the man discovered the imposition he would have made it lively for us.

"I am the third lieutenant of the Congress, sir," was the answer, "and this is Mr. Hapgood, one of our midshipmen."

We bowed to the middy, and then I said, —

"Give Mr. Larkin's regards to the commodore, and say how pleased he will be to meet him at Monterey when he returns. Report that the frigates Cumberland and Independence are in port, and that California has been formally taken possession of by Commodore Sloat. You can also mention the fact that Captain Fremont is in the North, and that there will not be much fighting on the land, and none at sea. That is all the information we can impart with the exception that General Castro is here in Santa Barbara, and has some good men under his command. Now get back to your boat as soon as possible, for if the patrol should find you here it would be bad for us and you also."

Just as I finished speaking we could hear the loud, ringing blasts of trumpets, and through the darkness saw a party of horsemen coming along the beach from the direction of Buenaventura.

"Run for your lives," Lewey and I whispered. "Here comes the patrol. If they see you there will be a devil of a row and no mistake."

The naval officer and his men did not stop for further advice. They ran along the shore toward Point Arena, while Lewey and I darted for the town, then threw ourselves in the tall, salt grass that fringed the beach, and remained concealed until the cavalry passed by. We heard some words of challenge, a few shots, a shrill yell, as if some one was wounded, and then left the shelter of the chapparel, and ran in the direction of the mission on the hill, so that people would not suspect we came from the usual landing-place if we met any one before gaining the town.

Just as we came to a post where some of our men were quartered the long roll was beaten, half a dozen trumpets sounded to arms, and then off Point Arena, more than three miles from land, we saw a blue light burned, and into the air leaped a rocket, which exploded, and revealed red white and blue stars. It was a signal of recall for the boat and crew, but we feared that some of the latter would never reach the ship if the Mexicans were aroused and cut off their retreat. We had not cared to remain and help the sailors, for if we had been discovered holding communication with an enemy a short prayer and a sharp volley would have settled our part of the programme at daylight the next morning. General Castro did not allow any trifling with the Americans by his friends.

Just as we gained our quarters the colonel was mounting his horse to get the men in line.

"I wish you two would go to the beach and see what the trouble is all about," the colonel said. "I can't trust some of these fellows. They report that a thousand men have landed on the shore, and are marching toward the town. Take as many men as you desire, and scout all along the beach, and let me know what is up."

We thought that here was a chance to distinguish ourselves, as no parties were better qualified for the expedition than Lewey and I, as we knew just what to expect, where to look for a foe, and how strong it was. We promised compliance with the request, and no one in the ranks suspected for a moment that we had been holding a conference with the enemy.

We mounted our horses, called for a dozen men, and then galloped toward the beach. As we passed through the town men and women were already on their way to the mountains so as to escape all danger from a blood thirsty enemy. There was hasty packing of jewels and good clothing for transportation to some safe place where the Yankees could not find and appropriate them as their own. Once or twice I heard the name of Fremont, as if he and his trappers had made a descent on the village, but this was not generally believed, for our men stood firm, and did not strike for the mountains, as they might have done had the report been true.

We dashed to the usual landing-place, where we knew we should find no one, and then hearing a commotion near Point Arena went there, and saw that the Americans were just embarking in their boat through the surf, and the Mexicans were making it warm for them by firing volleys from their carbines. As the horses were a little unsteady, owing to the discharge of fire-arms, no good aim could be taken, consequently my countrymen were not much injured. But there was danger of the cutter being capsized in the surf, and if such was the case all hands would be captured, and dealt with in a severe manner,

"Amigos," I said as I rode up, "let us not waste our time here with this one boat when there are so many others about to land and capture the town. Besides, if the ship should fire one of her heavy guns in our direction many of us might be killed, as this point is an exposed place."

Luck was on my side just then, for the Congress let drive a shot at the land, where the scene was lighted up by the flash of carbines, and a ball passed over our heads, so close that we were nearly knocked down by the windage, and our hats flew in all directions, so great was the current.

The attention of the officers of the frigate had been attracted by the firing on shore, and fearing the crew of the cutter were in danger a chance shot was hurled toward the land, with an elevation sufficient to clear the water, and not injure the sailors. It came just right, and at the proper time.

"Down to the beach," Lewey and I shouted. "The next shot may be a shell, and kill the whole of us. Let these men go while we look after the others."

There was a general compliance with the order, and no grumbling. As we turned to leave the seaman to get through the surf the best way they could another solid shot was discharged, struck the sand-hill, and threw more than a cart-load of gravel all over us, some of it lodging in the men's eyes, causing much needless profanity.

We did not wait for a third discharge, but got off that high bluff as soon as possible, and rode along the beach, and as we did so the Yankees in the boat gave three cheers, and then had the impudence to yell out, —

"Come on, you bloody greasers. We can lick a million of you," and with the words they went through the surf, and were out of harm's way in a short time, for how could we accept the challenge to "come on" when we had no boat, and could not walk the water?

For a mile along the beach we went looking for imaginary enemies, but found none, as a matter of course, and then, after seeing the frigate burn a blue light to show her position to the cutter's crew, we went back to town, and reported to the colonel that our men had beaten off a large number of enemies, and performed such feats of valor that Homer would have delighted to record them had he been alive at the time, and capable of grasping the situation.

Of course this pleased all who were engaged in the attack, officers and men, and General Castro issued an order thanking us for the energy and bravery we had displayed, and the young girls smiled on us, and sang their most fascinating songs for our entertainment. One crazy-headed, long-haired poet wrote some lines for the cavalry on the strength of the night's doings, and I remember it was very popular at the time. A translation reads something like this, —

> "See the heroes crushing, rushing,
> See their swords for blood are thirsting.
> Now the gringos they must run,
> For the Mexican with his gun
> Shoots all who on our soil do land,
> And for Yankees care not a —— caramba."

This is as near as I can come to the original. The poet is not alive at the present day, but some of his descendants are, and flourish not only in this part of the world but in California. The race never dies out, more is the pity.

The next day Pedro, our old friend the correo, arrived with important despatches from Los Angeles, and then came an order for the cavalry to move immediately on the town, take possession, and hold the place against all comers.

Colonel Fernando was detailed to go, and General Flores was to assume supreme command of all the forces assembled. We were invited to move with the rest of the valiant warriors, and as we had nothing better to do consented to march with our young friend, and look after his welfare. But before we started I had a short interview with Senora Costello, and a painful one it was on both sides, something never to be forgotten on my part, and remembered for many years by the lady I suppose, although I never heard from her or her secret thoughts after I left the coast. But if she is alive I should like to meet her once more, and talk over old times and old adventures. It would be worth a trip to California to speak with her but for a moment.

CHAPTER XII.

I BID SENORA COSTELLO FAREWELL, AND HAVE NO COMMENTS TO MAKE. — THE MARCH TO LOS ANGELES. — THE BATTLE AND ITS RESULTS. — ON THE ROUTE TO SAN DIEGO. — A LUCKY FIND OF GOLD. — A DISAPPOINTMENT ALL ROUND. — SAN DIEGO. — SCOTCH JACK GIVES US A RECEPTION. — A UNITED STATES FLEET. — OFF FOR MAZATLAND. — HOME AT LAST. — LEWEY'S BEAUTIFUL SISTER. — A HAPPY LIFE AND A DARK CLOUD. — THE END.

IT was Colonel Fernando who informed me that his pretty little sister, Senora Costello, desired to see me before we left Santa Barbara for Los Angeles, and although I had no wish for the interview, and would have avoided it, there was no reason why I should act impolitely and decline the invitation to call and exchange a few parting words with one who had always treated me with so much respect and consideration for several months. I did not dare to analyze my feelings toward the lady, for she was a married woman, a devoted mother, and her relatives were high in the confidence of the government, rich and influential, proud and despotic.

"Now," said Lewey, as I started on the way, "do not a fool you make of yernself. Be like me, cold and distant, and remember dat ve has de reputation to keep up."

I took no notice of the impudent young man, but went to the house where the lady was residing with her husband. She received me in a cordial manner, invited me to take a seat by her side, as she was all alone, and said, —

"Do you leave today with the regiment?"

"Yes, senora, in a few hours we shall be on our way."

"And when do you expect to return to Santa Barbara?"

"Perhaps never. We think of going to San Diego, and from there take t' : first vessel for home. Our life in this country has been one series of disappointments. We are tired of fighting against fate and without hope."

"I am glad you are going, and trust you will never return. Today we see each other for the last time on earth, I sincerely hope. I speak plainly, do I not?"

"Yes, senora," but I trembled, and felt hurt at her words. I knew not why.

"You have been like a brother to me," the lady whispered, as she raised her dark eyes and gave me a glance I did not dare to meet. "Have you always thought of me as a sister?"

"Yes, lady, as a very dear sister."

"Cou'd you at all times trust yourself with me as a relative?" she asked, a little nervously I thought.

"Yes, senora, as a man of honor I should never fail to treat you as your high position requires."

"Do you realize that I am married and love my husband?" the lady demanded imperiously.

"Yes, senora, I comprehend all that."

"And if I was single, what then?"

"I should hope, and remain in the country, lady."

"What do you mean by those words?"

"They express my feelings, and are very plain."

"Good-by," she said, and held out her little hand.

I bent down and kissed it, and turned to leave her with a stifling sensation in my throat, and eyes that were dim with moisture.

"Stay," she said in an impetuous manner. "One word more, senor."

I remained to listen, with head bowed low, not daring to raise it to look at her handsome, glowing face, and flashing eyes.

"Do you remember," the lady cried, "the night we supposed the Indians were to attack Monterey, some years ago?"

"Yes, senora."

"And you carried me in your arms to the boat, and were mean enough to demand kisses for your labor?"

"It was no labor, lady. It was a pleasure to serve you. I would have done much more to aid you had I the power at the time."

"And do you dare to deny from that night you loved me?"

I did not answer her, but watched the flickering sunlight as it entered the windows and danced around the room, tinging with gold the dress and form of the majestic little woman before me, who was playing with her victim like a tigeress with a stricken animal, too weak to make its escape, and too timid to die willingly.

"Why do you not deny my words?" Senora Costello asked, and stamped her little, well-formed foot, the toes of which were enclosed by a slipper without sides.

"There is no occasion for words from me, senora. I am but a humble young man, poor, and dependent upon favor for fortune. If I was a gentleman I could have spoken some years ago. Now it is too late. Let me go I entreat you. This interview is very painful to me, and can do you no good."

"Do you remember," she asked in a more gentle tone, "how you saved me from insult at San Luis Obispo?"

"Yes, lady."

"And defended me from ladrones on the journey to Monterey?"

"I remember all, lady. The earthquake and uprising after the troops had left the town. I would gladly do the same again and again for your sake, and think that I was repaid for my trouble if your safety was secured."

"How dare you talk to me, a married lady, in such a manner? Do you know your position and mine? Do you realize who you are and what you are? Do you recollect that a few months ago you gladly herded with girls of the peon class, and felt honored at their notice, and would have married one if she had not tired of waiting for you, and chose another more to her taste?"

"Why do you remind me of all this?" I asked, with a weary sigh, as I raised my head and looked at the flashing eyes of the lady.

"To show you the difference in our positions. I am of a rich family and the daughter of a gentleman," she said with the haughty pride of the Spanish race.

"What constitutes a gentleman, lady?" I asked.

"Wealth, sir," was the answer.

"Then I can lay no claim to gentility. Let me go. I shall never see you more after today," and moved toward the door as I spoke.

"Remain where you are, sir, for the present," Senora Costello said, as though I was her peon and slave, "and answer me a few questions. You can read and write, and have an education, a better one than I ever could hope for. There is not a caballero in Santa Barbara who can speak English, Spanish and French, and write those languages. There is not one who has traveled so extensively as you have. who is so bold and devoted, and yet with all these wonderful qualities I hate you, scorn and loathe you, and would kill you if I dared."

"For what reason, lady?" I asked, astonished at this burst of uncalled for rage from the pretty little woman.

"Wretch," she cried, as though she would like to fall afoul of me, and tear my hair out in great handfuls, "did you not kneel by the side of that dying peon girl, and kiss her lips, and shed tears, as though you mourned for her justly-deserved death?"

"I admit the accusation, lady."

She seemed inclined to make a spring at me, and scratch my face, and I wondered what the deuse was the matter with one usually so gentle and kind.

"Go," she said. "Your presence here polutes the air. You are dead to shame and all noble feeling. You are the meanest young man I ever met in my life."

I bowed in silence, and turned away. I thought she was a little out of her head, and had no idea why she should treat me in such a curt manner. Surely I had been very polite to her all through our acquaintance, and never spoke a rude, impatient word, or cherished an improper thought. If I had kissed her it was as a brother and not as a lover, and now that she was driving me from her presence with a scornful gesture and bitter words I bowed my head, and with tears in my eyes passed out of the room, and did not even look back to see if she waved me a farewell.

But as I reached the veranda a little hand was laid on my shoulder very lightly, and a soft voice whispered,—

"You will not leave me in anger, will you?"

"No, in sorrow more than anger, sweet lady."

"Forget all the harsh things that I have uttered, senor," the lady said. "In your departure remember me as one who could have loved if she had had the chance, and fates were propitious. But do not speak to me, or I shall again hate you, as I think of that dead peon girl, and you bending over her. There was another who should have been shot beside the Sanchos. Here, take this ring. Wear it sometimes for my sake, and then think of me as kindly as you can. But do not return to Santa Barbara, or remain in the country, for you might sometime marry, and then I should kill you and your wife. I know I could not help doing so."

"For what reason, senora?" I asked in innocent surprise.

"You are a bobo," was the sharp reply, and when I look back to that y terview I think that I must have been what she called me,—a fool,—for I did not suspect for a moment why she hated all whom I loved.

She thrust a ring into my hand, and re-entered the house, and I walked slowly along the hot, dusty streets. As I did so I glanced at the trinket, and saw that it was a valuable diamond, a large, brilliant stone, of a delicate straw color, yet flashing in the sunlight like a star on a winter night in high latitudes.

I own that valuable gem at the present time, set in a rich masonic jewel, and when I wear it my thoughts go back to Senora Costello, and I wonder if she is still alive, and remembers her boy lover, and his modest diffidence and misunderstanding of a woman's heart and whims.

The trumpets were sounding cheerfully as I regained my quarters, and found the horses saddled, and waiting my return to join the head of the regiment, which was drawn up for the march over the mountains.

Lewey was sitting on the door-step, smoking his pipe, all equipped for the journey. He looked at me long and earnestly, and then said,—

"Before I my hand gives to you tell me dat as a man of honor has you acted."

"As a man of honor, my friend, I assure you."

"Den I takes you to mine heart. I knew dat trust you I could. Alons, let us go, or de trumpeters vill deir heads blow off. I is glad to see dat my example is good for von foolish boy like you. Imitate me, and all vill be veil."

I could not give the French lad a piece of my mind, for I was in no condition for badinage. We whistled for Jack, mounted our horses, and rode to the head of the column just as the order was given for "fours right," and with a shrill blast from the trumpets we filed through the streets, and were admired by the ladies as usual. Senora Costello was on the veranda of her house, and although she threw a greeting to her brother, never looked at me, or noticed my profound bow, and so we passed out of sight, and I never saw the pretty little mother again, but I did not forget her, and shall not as long as I live.

We toiled up the side of the mountain, and on the crest I halted my horse, and looked at the sleepy, picturesque little town, the surf and beach, the old mission, and then turned and resumed my journey, and that was the last view I ever had of Santa Barbara, the scene of so many hours of pleasure and pain.

We swept through the district like a swarm of locusts, eating and destroying all that came in our way. Some of the rancheros were so unpatriotic as to declare that the Yankees were to be preferred to the Mexicans, but we always supposed they were a little prejudiced against the cavalry on account of its freedom and bravery in attacking herds of cattle, and running off such horses as we needed for our men, many of them breaking down a good animal in twenty-four hours, through racing and skylarking over rough ground.

We were three days on our tramp to Los Angeles, and then swept through the town like a whirlwind, and drove all the Americans out of the place, except those who had become naturalized Mexicans, and married into the influential families. Here we were able to repay some of the former kindness of Messrs. Stearns and Temple, for we had a guard placed over the store of the former, while Lewey and I took up our quarters at the house of the latter. In this way we were enabled to save both gentlemen much annoyance, and keep their property intact, something worth considering when one thinks that there were about eight hundred restless men in town, and many of them would not distinguish between right and wrong where plunder was concerned.

We should have been very pleasantly located at Los Angeles, as far as quarters were concerned, if Mr. Temple had not insisted upon our sitting up late at night and drinking strong punch and playing monte. We generally made an excuse and escaped all damage, but the temptation was strong, and we had much difficulty in getting away by pretending military and staff duties.

Lewey and I were quite popular in Los Angeles, our persecuters were well remembered, and the young ladies never tired of asking after the fate of the girls we were supposed to have desired to marry. The friendly manner in which Colonel Fernando and his officers treated us was another evidence that we were capable of obtaining anything we desired in the way of preferment had we been disposed to ask it. We were invited to some very nice houses, and had no duty to perform except at the dress parades, when it was desirable that the regiment should show as many men in line as possible. To be sure, for this arduous duty we received no pay, but were told that we could have all the land we desired, even ten leagues square if we would signify our wish for as much.

At one time we thought that we would take a grant, and settle down for life, but the feeling for home in Lewey's breast and my own grew stronger and stronger, and at last we concluded that we had seen enough of California, and a sight of our friends' faces would be desirable. We were not quite penniless, yet far from rich, and if we wished for wealth it was to show that four years of our lives had not been wasted in reckless adventures.

It was while we entertained such feelings that the rumors of war became more numerous. We learned that Fremont had been appointed by Commodore Stockton governor of the State, and also lieutenant-colonel of a mounted regiment of rifles, and that he was threatening the whole of Northern California, and had, in fact, subjected it to his control, and was marching toward Santa Barbara. Then came a despatch stating that five hundred marines and sailors were being disembarked at San Pedro from the frigates lying there, the Savannah being the principal vessel.

Our scouts learned enough to know that the force was intended for Los Angeles, and this set General Flores in motion, with about four hundred men (all well mounted, and under the command of Colonel Fernando), and one little light six-pounder, which the Mexicans picked up somewhere, and had prepared about twenty-five rounds of ammunition for the same. I never knew where the powder or shot came from. It was a mystery to most every one except Flores.

Lewey and I were invited to go and see the battle, and as we were mounted on fast horses had no objection, thinking we could keep out of the way of the American warriors should the attack become a serious one, which we did not anticipate for a moment, as we imagined our Mexican friends would stand one volley, and then retreat as soon as possible, gaining the tops of the neighboring mountains, and from thence carry on an irregular warfare for months to come, with safety to themselves and danger to the enemy.

It was a lovely morning when we galloped out of Los Angeles, and took the road for San Pedro, but as the sun got up the heat became intense on the mesa lands, as there was not a breath of air stirring. The little brass field-piece was drawn by two large mules, staid old beasts, that required much pounding to get into a run, and so keep up with the horsemen.

When about ten miles from the town we sighted the advance guard of the Americans, all on foot, sailors and marines, stretched along the road as though going to a picnic, and caring no more for us than if we had been so many women. In fact we were despised, and yet it is not good generalship to laugh at any force that may be sent against you, for fortune is a fickle jade, and sometimes deserts the best of generals, men who count on their stars and not on the resolution of a foe, like Napoleon at Waterloo.'

General Flores called a halt, and sent a few scouts forward to reconnoitre. The rancheros were superbly mounted, and some of the best horsemen in the country. It was a beautiful exhibition of dash and carefulness to see them hovering around the Americans, sometimes on the flank, rear, and in front, and yet out of musket shot all the time, for not a ball touched them. They irritated the invaders like vicious flies in the summer-time around bald-headed men, for occasionally we could see a dozen Jack-tars start off on the run to get a little nearer the fleet enemy, and then the Mexicans would laugh and make insulting gestures, in the hope of inducing the Yankees to continue the pursuit, and be cut off from the main body.

The rancheros were like sparrows on the wing, now here and there, and away on the run when there was a chance to distract the attention of the enemy, or throw a lariat around a sailor just out of bounds.

"Thom," said my friend Lewey, after we had sat and watched the enemy for half an hour or more, "your countryman like a fool acts. I see disaster to him unless he keeps in line and not fret ven de Mexican is near. Now at dat look."

I did look, and could only groan at the manner in which my friends were acting. They seemed to think that the Mexicans were a set of vagabonds and destitute of courage or skill, and that an American could walk away with a dozen of them on foot or horseback, forgetting for the moment that the rancheros were as expert riders as could be found in the world, and not devoid of a certain amount of desperate pluck, when well led by men in whom they had confidence.

Suddenly the sailors gave three cheers, and rushed toward us, not in the best of formation, but a rollicking sort of way, as though expecting us to scatter and run. There was a magnificent chance for a charge of cavalry, and I expected General Flores would give the order to move forward. Even Colonel Fernando drew his sabre, and, smiling, told me to get out of line unless I desired to ride over my own countrymen. If the dash had been made with boldness not a hundred Americans would have escaped. But the order was not given, for Flores had other plans, and was afraid of defeat, yet victory was certain if a little earnestness had been shown by the Mexicans.

Up to the front came the two mules with the field piece, and it was pointed at the invaders when they were not more than half a mile distant. There was a ringing discharge, and down fell a dozen or more sailors and marines, killed and wounded.

"Tocar a lar retirada," sounded the trumpets, and I was in hopes the Mexicans were about to fall back to the town, without more fighting, but the wounding of the Americans seemed to enrage the sailors, as they uttered a yell and came for us as fast as they could run.

"Fuego," shouted Flores with a smile on his face, as he saw the imbecility of his opponents.

The mules once more came to the front, there was a roaring discharge, and down tumbled many men who should have been spared such a cruel fate. The marines gave us a volley, but no one was injured, for their muskets, old-fashioned ones at that, did not carry a ball like the breach loader of modern days, when it is possible to kill at a distance of over a mile. Had our people been armed with such weapons at that time the Mexicans would have been defeated with great loss. But they were not, and so had to suffer.

As the Americans advanced the Mexicans retreated, slowly, yet fast enough to keep beyond the reach of the invaders, and when a chance presented, the field piece was brought into use, and at every discharge men fell. There were shouts of rage and pain from one party, and yells of triumph from the other, but at last it was reported that there was only one round of ammunition left for the brass gun, and I was glad to hear it, although I did not dare to express my joy at the news, for if I had my life would not have been worth a real. In fact but few in the regiment knew that I was an American, as it was not considered desirable to parade my nationality before every one, by the advice of Colonel Fernando, who was a good friend to us as long as we were with him.

The invaders did not pursue the Mexicans any further. They gathered up their dead and wounded and retired to their ships at San Pedro, sadder and wiser men, while the cavalry went back to Los Angeles flushed with triumph, and received an ovation so flattering no wonder the heads of all the officers were turned for the time being, and proclamations were as plentiful as oranges in modern days.

Americans became decidedly unpopular in the town, as the soldiers were clamorous to be again led against the Yankees, and while this feeling prevailed Colonel Fernando one day sent for Lewey and myself, and spoke to us very seriously and calmly.

"This is now no place for you," he said. "Our people are growing more excited every day against foreigners. At the present time you stand well, but still there are murmurs that you are Americans in disguise, and acting as spies for the United States. It is useless to state I do not believe a word that is whispered against you. Still I can't entirely shut the mouths of those who are clamorous for fame in the hope of obtaining an office and wealth. If we had not met with an accidental victory the other day matters would have been different, and you would remain secure. Better leave us and the country while there is time, and your lives are safe."

We believed that there was much wisdom in the advice, and agreed to accept it. We had noticed cold looks for several days, and the senoritas did not smile on us as formerly, for some reason which we did not comprehend.

"Go to San Diego," the colonel said, "and take refuge in your old hide-house. That is neutral ground, and you will not be disturbed there. I can get you passes all through the lower part of the State, so that no one will molest or detain you on the way, or at San Diego. I have already a document from General Castro in your behalf, and today I will obtain another from General Flores. It shall be reported in the town that you have gone on a scouting expedition over the mountains, and it is not likely you will meet with any one to interfere with your affairs. I dislike to part with such dear friends, but it is for the best. I am only studying your interests, believe me."

"Colonel," I asked, "what is the prospect of Mexico retaining possession of the State?"

"None," the officer answered with a sigh. "We shall ultimately be ground to powder, extinguished and exterminated. There is no hope for us. The United States have been endeavoring for years to get a foothold here, and there is not a stream, a pass, a canyon, or a trail that is not down on some of their maps. Exploring parties have been through the country under the guise of trappers and hunters, and noted everything of interest, and it will be turned to good advantage. Already Fremont has raised a regiment of mounted rifles, and who can stand before his men? General Kearney is headed for San Diego, on an overland trail, as we learn from couriers. Commodore Stockton and the general will join forces and march on Los Angeles in such strength that we shall be defeated if we offer battle. Hemmed in on all sides what hope is there for us, especially when you recollect that not one-tenth part of the male population has come forward and offered to assist us? We could keep up a guerrilla war for years by taking to the mountains, but what use would it be? Should we ultimately secure our Independence? No, a price would be placed on our heads, and the Indians might hunt for us like cattle, and one by one we should fall. I see the end, and it is not far off. Deserted by the national government, without guns, ammunition, or money, what can we hope for against a powerful nation? It commands our ports, and soon will occupy the land, fight as hard as we may to preserve it."

I saw tears in the gallant young man's eyes as he spoke. He turned to the window for a moment to hide his emotion, and then once again faced us.

"You, senors, have been to me like brothers for the past few months. You have saved my life, and that of my sister and her child on several occasions. Let me make some return for all your kindness before we part. Here are two bags. Each contains in doubloons the sum of one thousand dollars. Oblige me by accepting the same as some recompense for your interest in my behalf. The amount is small, and I wish that it was ten times larger, but it is all that I can afford just now."

"Colonel," I said, "we thank you for your many acts of kindness, and wish that we could remain with you until peace is declared. We have long felt that we occupied a peculiar position, and discussed the prospects of getting home. Your words have only hastened our action. We cannot serve against the United States, and we have taken an oath not to raise a hand in opposition to Mexico. What can we do but retire from the State, or else espouse one side or the other to prevent suspicion being attached to our actions. Keep your money, for we want none of it."

"You need it more than I do," the colonel said, "I can do nothing with so much gold at the present time, unless I bury it, and then if killed who is to benefit by it? My wealth is all in land and cattle. The cattle may disappear, but the land will remain and yield me a home some time or other I hope, even if it is under the stars and stripes. Don't be afraid of the money. I won it last night from Senor Temple on the turning of a card. He won't feel it, for he has plenty more somewhere. I made the stake in the hope of reaping a rich harvest so that I could be generous to you."

"And if you had lost, Senor Colonel?" I asked.

"I should have given him a township in the Valley of San Gabriel," was the answer. "I own half a county there I believe, although I have never seen much of it. With one hundred thousand acres on the Sacramento River, and one or two hundred thousand near Monterey, and what I have here, I am pretty well provided for. Take the gold, senors. Unless you do, I shall feel that you do not think the sum is enough."

Under the circumstances we did not again refuse the generous gift. We left the presence of the young officer feeling the highest respect for a man who would risk a principality for the purpose of winning a lot of gold for the use of his friends.

The same day we quietly commenced our preparations for departure. We did not intend it should be generally known that we were going, so confided the secret to Messrs. Temple and Stearns only. They approved of the step we were about to take, and thought it a judicious one. We determined to use our peon servant, as he was a smart, active fellow, and very trustworthy if rum was kept out of his way. He had looked after our horses for some months, knew our ways, and was eager to go on a scouting expedition, or anywhere else, provided he was paid a few dollars a month, which he was certain to lose at monte in less than two hours after receiving the money.

We told him to pick out two good, safe pack-mules from those belonging to the army, with saddles and reatas, also the mustang he was accustomed to ride on the march. This he did, and Colonel Fernando gave them to us without price. To be sure the animals did not cost the Mexican government a cent, as they were taken when needed, and from whomsoever happened to have a stock, no money being passed during the transaction.

We gathered a supply of tobacco, matches, dried beef, coffee and sugar, pilot bread, and a fresh lot of fishing lines and hooks, besides a coffee pot, and skillet to fry what we could not broil. Then we collected a lot of ammunition for our rifles and pistols, and while we were buying the latter Mr. Stearns made us a present of a spade, the last thing we should have thought of taking with us, but we were assured that it would be useful to dig worms when we went after trout. We did find it useful, but not for the purpose indicated.

As soon as all our purchases were collected, and stowed away in thick canvas bags, ready for packing on the mules, we went around and bade goodby to our most intimate friends, and the next morning long before daylight we had eaten our breakfast, and were in the saddle. Just before we started Colonel Fernando came to us and shook hands, wishing us all kinds of good luck, and then as the first streaks of daylight touched the faces of the rugged mountains, to the delight of Jack we filed out of town, halted every few minutes with the sharp cry of, —

" Que quiere usted? Parada."

"Amigos," was the answer, and then the password of "Castro" was next in order, and thus running the gauntlet of challenges we were soon outside the limits of the town, and near the Mission of San Gabriel, driving our mules before us, or, rather, our Indian did, in the usual style of rancheros, and just as we had passed the last sentinel Lewey checked his horse, and said, —

"De saints hab me in deir keepin', but I has forgotten von ding dat is important."

"And what is that?" a little startled at the thought that it might be our money.

"Vy, vot skall ve tell de daughters of de rancheros on de vay? To von — Florencia — I promised much. To de fadder of de udder you say many foolish dings. But de question now is vot skall ve do and libe? Ve can't ved."

"Do not let us borrow trouble until the time arrives for it," I remarked. "Perhaps the girls are married, and out of the way by this time, so all difficulty will be avoided."

"I dink not. Ven a girl say she love me it is for life. But, alons. We can swear dat ve is de bearer of despatches and has no time for de matrimony."

With this consoling thought we pushed on after Juan, the Indian peon, and at sunrise were on the spur of one of the mountains of the Sierra Madre, and looking off toward Los Angeles, the mission, and the lovely Valley of San Gabriel, while away to the west sparkled the blue waters of the Pacific Ocean, and the white Cataline Island, lying off the coast, rendered more distinct by the gleams of the sun, just starting on its daily course through a cloudless sky.

The scene was too beautiful to part from in a hurry. We called to Juan to unload the mules, and start a fire. Lewey and I prepared a pot of coffee, brought forth some bread and cold meat for an early breakfast, and while we ate and drank our animals fed on the dry grasses and wild oats of the district.

Jack was delighted with the change. He scented game in every copse, and through the bushes roamed in constant expectation of meeting something he could punish and worry. Juan was satisfied with our unlimited supply of cigarettes and tobacco, and the hope of earning a few dollars so that he could have the pleasure of losing the same at monte, just as soon as we struck the town of San Diego.

For an hour we sat on the mountain spur, smoking and looking at the beautiful scenery beneath us, enjoying every moment of the time, and thinking how we had rested in the same place but a few months before, on our journey toward Ranche Refugio, with high hopes of matrimony and love, only to be disappointed. And yet we could not bear to turn our backs on the place that had sheltered us for so many weeks, and where we found warm friends when we needed them.

"Load up, Juan," we said. "We will push through the canyons and camp on the other side of the mountains for the night."

The peon obeyed, and was soon hurrying his pack-mules over the trail, while we mounted our horses, took one last look at the surrounding country, and then resumed our journey, but we agreed that in all the world there could not be a more beautiful spot for a home, and since then thousands of people have come to the same conclusion, for the San Gabriel Valley is now teeming with life and industry, and vineyards and grain have taken the place of cattle ranches, and where the coyote once roamed in a wilderness now school children are seen on their way for instruction. The store-keeper has forced the ranchero from his stronghold, and left only a tradition of his former power, and expertness on horseback, and with the lariat in his dark, sinuous hands, that never knew the meaning or use of soap, even in a long and savory career of cattle tending. A new world has opened for the attraction of industrious men and women, but it has one great fault, for who would want to die when once comfortably settled in such a paradise?

We went through the canyon in a careful, leisurely manner, saw the same eagles overhead, the same hawks and buzzards, and at last came to the point where we had witnessed the exploits of the bear in pitching rocks into the stream beneath him, for the purpose of seeing the water splash upward, and, strange as it may seem, there was a bear at the very spot, and engaged in the same monotonous sport. It might have been the one we saw when we went through before, or a companion, but the circumstance was a singular one to say the least, and when we stopped and looked at the old fellow, and shouted to him across the ravine, he sat up on his haunches and actually beckoned us to come over, and have a close and confidential chat. Lewey vowed that he saw the brute wink one eye, but then the French lad was not inclined to always confine himself to facts, and wandered a little in his great desire to imagine things which really did not exist.

The brute was so cool and independent that we did not desire to disturb its happiness. We left it pitching down stones, and felt as though we had seen an old friend for the last time. Juan said that bears always hunted in couples when after fish. That one would take a position over a brook, and hurl bowlders into the water hoping to kill a few trout, while a confederate might be stationed down stream to secure all that floated along without life. The peon related the yarn with a grave face, as though it was true, and I give it for what it is worth, just as it was told to me many years ago.

I had no time verify the matter by actual experience. If the bears of California fished in that way it certainly denoted an amount of instinct and intelligence that they never had credit for. I should like to have investigated and found out how many stones had to be thrown to kill one fish, for although trout were very plentiful, it seemed to me that the noise of falling rocks must have frightened the finny tribe, but perhaps they were attracted and not repelled by the stones, no one ever fishing the streams in those days, so trout were not as timid as at the present time, when every one is anxious for a big string.

It was near three o'clock in the afternoon before we reached our old camping-ground, where we had shot the prowling mountain lion. Our horses recollected the spot as well as ourselves, for they snorted and sniffed, and were uneasy for some time, evidently looking for another attack.

We concluded to camp on the same spot as of old, and as Juan was picqueting the mules and horses where the grass was greenest, by the side of a small stream, Lewey and I took our fish lines, and wandered along the banks of the brook, and soon had a nice mess of handsome trout, and while we were thus engaged there occurred one of the greatest surprises that we had encountered in California. I had taken the spade along for the purpose of digging some worms for bait, and while I was replenishing my exhausted stock so that we could do a little fishing early in the morning my shovel struck a hard substance, and I threw it one side thinking it a stone, but the color attracted my attention, so I picked up what I thought was a peculiar piece of quartz, as large as a man's hand, and so heavy that I was astonished at the weight.

"Lewey," I said, calling to my friend who was some distance from me, "what kind of stone is this? It looks like gold."

The French lad ran toward me, and as I tossed him the nugget his eyes expressed the astonishment he felt. He looked it all over, balanced it in his hands, from one to the other, and then cried, —

"Mon dieu, man alive, dat is gold, and de best of its kind."

"Are you sure?" I asked, almost dazed at his words.

"Sure, vell I should dink I am sure. I vonce studied de mineralogy, and I knows about de dings of de earth. Vy, old ami, dat little piece of de precious stuff is vorth all of two dousand dollars. By gracious me, but ve has found a gold mine, and ve is rich for eber and eber. Gib me de spade. Let us see if dar is much like him round here."

He went to work with a vim, and threw the loose earth far from the place where I had dug for worms. In a few minutes he was rewarded for his labor, as another nugget came to light about as large as the first one, and then darkness put a stop to our operations for the night. We gathered up our gold and fish, and returned to camp, but considered it not expedient to inform Juan of our good fortune, as we did not know but he might be induced to murder us while we slept, as so much wealth was a great temptation to a poor peon. We concealed the treasure among our clothes in the bags, using the latter for pillows at night.

As one might suppose we were too excited to eat or sleep much that night, but we smoked many pipes of tobacco in the evening, talked over our plans, and how we would remain where we were until we had collected a fortune, if the gold held out. When we did slumber we started up at every unusual sound, and even the barking of the coyotes seemed threatening. But Juan slept on undisturbed, and dreamed of being at last lucky at monte.

At daylight we were again at work. One of us dug over the gravel down to a ledge, and the other fished, but no more nuggets were found, which we thought hard luck. Juan wanted to know why we used the spade so much, and we told him that we had come across some peculiar-looking quartz which we were anxious to take home as curiosities, showing him a lot of pebbles at the same time. He though it a simple kind of mania, and only laughed at our ideas of what was valuable. To get rid of him we let him take one of our rifles, and set out in search of deer, as soon as breakfast was over, while we went to work in earnest, and found several small nuggets of gold in the course of the forenoon, but they were not larger than English walnuts.

Juan came back in the afternoon with a small deer over his shoulder, and very proud of his exploit. We had venison for supper, and did not think we were likely to starve for the want of food as long as game and fish in abundance, and easily obtained, were close at hand.

For two weeks we worked our bonanza, and then seemed to have exhausted the pocket, although much fine, scale gold was obtained. We could only estimate the value of the prize, but thought that there could not be less than two hundred pounds in weight, all pure and free from quartz. But we continued to dig day after day in the hope of finding more wealth, and when we were disappointed packed up our traps and moved onward, happy in the thought that we were rich even beyond our dreams.

It was near four o'clock in the afternoon when we reached the ranche owned by the man who was anxious I should marry his daughter at the time we passed the night there, on our journey to Los Angeles. The place was unchanged, and we had the usual gauntlet of questions to answer, the same escopeta to dodge as of old. But when the Mexican and his son at last recognized us we were made welcome, and offered the best in the house. I saw the girl who was so anxious for a husband, and she gave me a pleasant smile of greeting, but did not rush to my arms, and call me blessed, as is the custom now-a-days. Besides, there was a strange ranchero there, a fellow we had never before seen, and he seemed a little familiar with the lady, more so than good taste would warrant, I thought. But then Lewey laughed at the idea, and said that I was jealous.

While Juan was looking to the mules and horses, and after we had carried our bags of treasure to the shed, the Mexican father said that he desired a few minutes' conversation with me.

"You know," he said, "I wished you to marry my daughter?"

"Yes, there was some talk on the subject," I answered meekly.

"And you have come all this way to carry out the plan?"

"I have thought of the matter many times since we parted," was my evasive reply.

The Mexican appeared a little embarassed, but at length freed his mind in this manner,—

"The fact of the matter is," he remarked, after a pause, "my daughter has done better than if she waited for you. She is already married, and that rancher is her husband. I am sorry for your disappointment, but you should have come sooner."

I tried to look the dejection that I did not feel, and said that it was unfortunate, but undoubtedly all for the best, and the man was glad I did not upbraid him for his bad faith.

I told Lewey of my narrow escape, and he said I might have expected as much. No women would care, he thought, to wait for me any length of time.

"You shall see how faithful my little Florencia is. She go not back on me, neber," and . said that I would wait and test his confidence in womanhood. It appeared to me that we were having hard times with our love affairs in California. All of our ventures were destined to end in disappointment and disaster.

The next morning we resumed our journey, crossed the low range of mountains, forded the San Felipe Creek, then camped in the very place where we had encountered the Apache chief and his warriors. There were no signs of savages in the vicinity, and the only troublesome guests we had were the coyotes, and they made unwelcome music all night, but did not venture near enough to steal from our larder, fearing the fire which we kept burning to keep bears at a distance.

The evening of the fourth day from our gold mine we galloped up to the lonely ranche, where we had stopped the first night from San Diego. The owner was sitting in his patio when we arrived, and near him were his handsome daughter and faded wife. The Mexican was much surprised to see us, and gave us a cordial welcome, but the girl, as soon as she saw Lewey, entered the house in a hurry, and did not again appear all the evening. The meeting with one who had professed to love her a few months before was evidently too much for the young lady's nerves and presence of mind. I could see that the reception nettled my friend, but I said not a word, and when supper was served, to which we contributed coffee and sugar, the father grew confidential to his visitors.

"Florencia," he said, "is a little modest about appearing before men just now. She was married a few months since to our neighboring ranchero, Tobias, the same one you met the first few hours out from San Diego. He is a brave man, and will make her a good husband. Better than either of you. She is home on a visit, or you might have missed seeing her. For some weeks after you were gone she could talk only of the brave gringos, but the sighs of the ranchero became warm, and the result was a wedding. They are very happy together. He bears the same name as myself, and for some months we have looked upon him as one of our family, as now he is in reality."

Lewey uttered a suppressed groan, and said that he cou'd not eat much supper, but smoked a good deal, and we went to bed early.

"Lewey," I said, as we rolled ourselves up in our blankets, "what was it you said about a certain girl being ever constant for your sake?"

"Oh, let me to sleep go," was the answer in a pettish tone. "You dink you is funny, don't you?"

"We have had hard luck with our loves, and perhaps it is just as well, old fellow. If we had married we should never have found a fortune with our wives as we have in mother earth," I remarked.

The only answer was a snore and a kick, and I let my French friend and his injured vanity rest for the night.

We were off at an early hour in the morning, even before the sun was up. As we rode out of the patio I caught a brief glimpse of Florencia in the doorway, and I wondered if she thought of her flirtation with my friend, and how I had interrupted it, the night before we fought the Indians and defeated them.

As we stood on the summit of the hill that overlooked the valley, and glanced at the lonely adobe ranche, Lewey relieved his pent-up feelings by asking, —

"I vonder if dar is von voman in all dis vorld dat true is to man?"

"There is still one more chance, my friend," I said. "You can now fall back on the jailor's daughter. If she has forgotten you then I am willing to believe all that your thoughts imply."

He uttered an exclamation of disgust, and we resumed our journey, and all that forenoon we galloped over the mesa lands, the arid sands, and at four o'clock sighted the sleepy little town of San Diego, just as the people were awakening from their usual siesta. The first person we saw whom we knew was Captain Fitch. He could hardly realize that the two bronzed boys in Mexican costume were the ones he had aided some months before, and had returned in safety, and able by their papers to pass all over the country without question, standing high in the estimation of General Castro and his officers, and also in the esteem of the Americans with whom we had been brought in contact.

He insisted that we should take up our residence at his house, free of all expense, until a vessel sailed from the port, but we had to decline the offer on account of Scotch Jack, whose feelings we feared would be hurt if we neglected him and his hide-house. But we promised to visit San Diego often, and then requested the captain to place in his safe for secure keeping the gold coin and nuggets we owned. If he was surprised before, the sight of so much wealth was a greater wonder to him. He was anxious to learn where the bonanza was located, but we preferred to keep the place a secret, as we thought that we could sell out our rights for a handsome sum, and we did, for Captain Fitch formed a company, and purchased our interest for ten thousand dollars in gold, and the organization prospered for some years after peace was declared. It is a singular fact that General Kearney and Commodore Stockton, with their combined forces, marched from San Diego to Los Angeles, and camped for a day at the foot of the mountains where we found the nuggets, yet never saw so much as the color of gold. One reason is they never looked for it, or supposed that the precious ore was in the earth beneath their feet.

We saw our treasure packed away in safety, took a receipt for the same, and then promising to call and dine the next day, mounted our horses to ride to the beach.

Just as we were moving off the jolly red face of Captain Fitch was lighted up with a smile as he shouted after us, —

"Boys, you need not be afraid to come up to the town at any time. The jailor's daughter is married, and out of the market."

"Anuder von," muttered Lewey. "Shall ve eber hear de end of 'em? O voman, voman, thy name is forgetfulness of all de holy feelin's of de nature," and then his head was bent for a moment upon his breast, and when he looked up there was a smile on his face as he said, —

"I is glad of it. The fate of hand is ever ober us. Vot is deir gain is our loss. Alons, ve vill do better in France."

It was about six o'clock when we reached the hide-house. The harbor was entirely clear of shipping, and the bay looked peaceful and sleepy under the summer's sun. There was no work going on ashore, and Scotch Jack sat on the doorstep of his hide-house smoking a black pipe, the same one he had used for a year or more. As we drew up, the old sailor merely glanced at us, and asked, —

"What in bloody thunder does you greasers want here?"

We asked him a question in Spanish, but he waved us off with majestic dignity.

"Go away from here," he said. "We can't gam together, and you knows it."

"Jack, old boy, don't you recollect our hail?" we asked, and then the ancient salt gave a yell that was heard all over the beach, and he came toward us with outstretched hands, his hard face lighted up with joy at our unexpected return.

For a few minutes he could not speak he was so excited, but as soon as we had dismounted and entered the old house his feelings found vent, and he went to the door and gave a yell that brought all the members of the beach gang to the door to see what the matter was.

"We will have a reception tonight, lads," Jack cried. "Here, you kanaka, take this dollar, and trot up to the town and get the money's worth of aguardiente. We 'll have a roarin' punch by and by, and every one shall get a fair share."

"But, Jack," we said, "we have returned poor, and can't repay the money."

"It makes no hodds, lads. I has some pesos, and you shall share with me to the last real. Here is your home, and here you is welcome. Blank that kanaka, why don't he move? And I wants a drink so bad."

There had been but few changes at the beach, and work was not very brisk. We were gladly welcomed back, and required to tell all the news, but after we had taken possession of our bunks, and stowed our traps away, secured and fed our horses, supper was prepared, and over our pipes we told to an admiring crowd all our adventures. I am sorry to state that the kanaka did not return with the rum that evening, as he sampled it on the way, and got very drunk, for which we should have rejoiced, as we were very tired, and needed rest more than a reception, had not Jack been so disappointed in his attempts at hospitality.

We found our chests and clothes undisturbed. Our shipmate had taken good care of them, even if he had not expected to see us again. The war had not troubled the people at the hide-house, and the few vessels on the coast, engaged in collecting queros, came and went undisturbed by the Mexican authorities. Some parties had spiked the guns in the little presidio at Ballast Point, and the damages had never been repaired, so there was clear sailing in and out of the handsome bay.

At breakfast Jack was very anxious to know if we were married, and when informed that our love venture had not been a success his gratification was great, and he begged us to remember the advice he had given some time before.

In the afternoon we mustered enough good clothes to dress in proper costume, and rode to town to dine with Captain Fitch. Here we met the old alcalda, submitted to him our papers from General Castro, and he was pleased to say that we had nothing to fear from any one. It was after dinner that we made a bargain with our host and some other Americans, whereby we sold our bonanza to them for the neat little sum of ten thousand dollars, all in gold doubloons, which added to the amount we had on hand, made quite a respectable fortune for us. Ours was the first prolific mine ever discovered in California, but the find was kept secret for years, for fear of robbery and violence. Only a few men worked the placer, and those at odd spells to escape observation. A large amount of gold, coarse and nuggets, was taken out, and Captain Fitch was made very rich by the mine, as well as those who joined him in the enterprise.

After dinner we walked to the calabozo, and looked over the place where we were imprisoned for a day or two. We saw the jailor's daughter, and although she was not overpowered with joy at the sight of our faces, she did manage to blush a little as she presented us to her husband. We gave her an ounce of gold, and the act won her thanks even if it did not her heart.

We kept Juan in our employ to look after the horses and wait upon us, and one day we disclosed to Jack that we were not as poor as we seemed, and the old salt was rejoiced at the information, but when we proposed to give a feast to all of our old friends on the beach, and made our shipmate president of the day, with orders to get up the best dinner that money could buy, Jack was in paradise. He calculated that half a barrel of aguardiente might fill the bill, and that very little meat and pilot bread would be sufficient for a regular blow-out, such as sailors enjoy. But we vowed that we would not have any drunken rioting going on, and Jack was forced to submit to cold punch, and not very strong at that.

The dinner was served in our hide-house, all the tables and tin ware on the beach being pressed into use for the occasion, and every cook volunteered his services. We bought all the luxuries we could at San Diego, fruit and fresh meats, and invited Captain Fitch, the alcalda, and all the foreign residents to come down and share in the feast. They accepted the invitation, and it was something worth seeing to notice Jack, with Lewey and I on his right and left, presiding. He made a speech, and it was a remarkable one. He hoped the greasers would get licked in the war, which was not in good taste, as Mexicans were present, but as they did not understand a word that was said it did not matter much. Lewey and I responded to the toasts complimentary to ourselves, and just as the fun grew fast and a little uproarious we heard the sound of a heavy gun off Point Loma, and rushing out to see what it was all about, beheld a fleet of United States ships entering the harbor, one of them flying the pennant of a commodore.

"Diablo," muttered the Mexicans, and mounting their horses rode for San Diego as fast as spurs could urge their steeds, while Scotch Jack loaded up the old muskets, and fired volley after volley as a welcome to the visitors. Then feeling tired with his exertions went back to the feast, and with the aid of companions finished the punch, stretched himself on a chest, fell asleep, and did not awaken until the next morning, so thirsty that there was fear of a water famine for a day or two.

The ships came to anchor in a grand and seaman-like manner, and then a cutter was sent on shore to learn the news. Lewey and I walked down to the beach, and encountered a lieutenant, and as we were dressed in civilian's clothes, and no longer wore the garb of sailors, we were treated very politely, and requested to go on board and submit to an interview on the part of Commodore Stockton, who was anxious to see us, or any one else, if information could be obtained.

We had no objection, and found the commodore a pleasant man, a little bit on his dignity, as one would naturally suppose. He was quite pleased when he learned that we had just arrived from Los Angeles, and was particular in his inquiries as to the route, and whether artillery could be transported through the canyons and gorges, over the mountains and sandy plains. We said that there were no very formidable obstacles to overcome, and then he hinted that he would give us commissions as acting midshipmen if we would join his vessel, and serve as guides over the trails to the Pueblo. But this we positively declined, on the ground that we had taken an oath of neutrality, and would not violate our vows, relating to the circumstances of our enlisting in the Mexican army. He listened very attentively to all we had to say, and of course smiled when we mentioned our hopes of marriage. However, we recommended Juan as a guide, and the peon was engaged at once, at a salary so large that he played monte for a week before his first month's wages were exhausted.

The commodore was here joined by General Kearne, and a company of United States dragoons, having marched overland. Then commenced the formation of a force that was destined to end the war in California. The navy furnished five hundred sailors and marines, and six pieces of artillery, for an advance on Los Angeles, and let me here state that the Americans met the Mexicans at the Rio San Gabriel, about one hundred and twenty miles from San Diego, on the 11th of January, 1847, won a battle, and entered the Pueblo in triumph. General Flores and his cavalry fled, fell into the hands of Colonel Fremont, near San Fernando, and that was the end of the struggle, but not of the controversy between the naval commodores, General Kearney and Colonel Fremont. There were constant quarrels, uncalled for and unseemly, but that is a matter of history on record, and does not concern my yarn, so I shall not espouse either side, for it would help no one at this late day.

While the expedition was fitting out there was such a demand for good horses that Commodore Stockton offered us three hundred dollars each for our animals and equipments. It cost us a bitter pang to part from two such noble mustangs, but we could not use them any longer, or carry them with us, so accepted the money, and Juan was continued in charge of the steeds until Los Angeles was reached.

While the preparations were going on the schooner California drifted into the harbor, on her way to Mazatland, with a few Mexicans who had obtained permission to leave the country, and stop at the latter port, then in possession of the Americans. Captain Cooper was flying the United States flag, and had a pass from the commodore to exempt his vessel from capture, in case some of our national ships might overhaul him on the ocean. We suggested to Captain Cooper that we should like to take passage with him, thinking that we could get home from Mazatland quicker than from California, as no vessel was ready to load for Boston, or any other port. The old gentleman bit his hand, and then said he should be delighted to have us for company, and would not charge us a real if we would stand his watch, for he was a hard sleeper, and could not keep awake nights. But he added that we would have to obtain a pass from Commodore Stockton, as he was running matters to suit himself in all things appertaining to California and the schooner. We waited on the naval officer, and stated what we desired, and he did not hesitate a moment to grant our request, at the same time did not fail to hint that we should do much better by remaining with him, and accepting positions that he thought the secretary of the navy would confirm upon his recommendations. But we once more declined the tempting offer, at the same time thanking the commodore for his kindness.

We had some small boxes made, marked them "minerals," and packed away all our nuggets, no one but Captain Fitch knowing their true value, for gold was almost unknown in its native state, except a little dust at Los Angeles, in those days. The boxes we shipped on board the schooner, put them in the run out of sight, and the day the armed expedition started the old California sailed for the lower part of the coast.

There were only six Mexican passengers, ladies and gentlemen, so that we were pleasantly located. We took a kind farewell of all our friends, left in Captain Fitch's hands the sum of one thousand dollars for the benefit of Scotch Jack, and when we told him what we had done the honest old tar shed tears, and swore that he would not take the money, but thought better of it after a while, accepted the present, and much good it did him in his old age, we hope, when he needed a shot in the locker.

As the California drifted out past Ballast Point Jack and some of the people on the beach fired muskets as a salute, and Lewey and I, and dear old faithful Jack, our dog, acknowledged the compliment by three cheers and a series of barks, and the last we saw of San Diego Bay the sailors and marines were on their march, the hide-house people were drinking our health in native wine, and the Scotchman was straining his eyes to get the last glance he ever had of his two young shipmates to whom he had acted a friendly part for so many months.

"Now, gentlemen," said Captain Cooper, as we cleared Point Loma and the thick kelp, with a strong northwest wind, "I did n't sleep well last night. Keep the old craft moving on about a southwest by south course; and I guess she 'll clear everything all right. If she don't, luff up a little until she does. I 'll turn in for a nap. Call me if there is anything strange and new, and not unless there is. There are some islands off the coast, and our course brings us near them. Keep your eyes peeled, and don't run over them, for there is room enough for all of us."

And the old gentleman tumbled into his berth, all standing, and did not wake up until the next forenoon, when he declared that he felt like a new man after twenty-four hours of solid sleep.

I do not think that in all California there was a kinder hearted man than Captain Cooper, the Mexicanized American. It was related of him that at one time he employed a greaser to look after one of his ranches, and the fellow sold most of the cattle, and put the money on the wrong card at monte. Captain Cooper had the Mexican arrested, he was tried and convicted, and sentenced to six months in a chain-gang. When his time expired he called upon his old employer and asked for aid, with all the assurance of a beggar.

"Not a real," roared the admiral.

"I am poor, and in need of clothes," pleaded the Mexican greaser, and if Cooper did n't take the rascal home, fit him out with a complete dress, gave him five silver dollars, and ended by once more putting the half-breed back on the farm,' where he again stole cattle, as a matter of course. This is but a sample of the generosity of the old salt, and yet I think he died quite well off in the State of his adoption some years since.

Lewey and I stood watch and watch, for there were no first or second officers on board, and the sailors obeyed our orders if they felt like it, and refused if they did not. However, we hit on a plan that secured respect and prompt obedience. There were several casks of aguardiente among the cargo, and we pumped out one or two buckets full a week, bottled it, and then promised the men liberal tots of grog at the end of the watch if they would keep a good lookout ahead, and make and take in sail quickly. The temptation was so great that we had no more trouble on the voyage, the fear of not getting the liquor prompting the sailors to be active and vigilant.

We kept dead reckoning all the way, yet once in a while the captain would take a noon observation, then eat his dinner, and have a siesta, again retiring quietly at eight bells in the evening, and although the wind might blow, and the vessel roll, and the sails slap, the old man never lost an hour's sleep, for there was no waking him up until morning.

In the meantime Lewey and I enjoyed ourselves with the lady and gentlemen passengers as soon as they got on their sea-legs. We would sit and hear them converse for an hour at a time, and while they were patriotic enough to dislike those who had overrun their country, they had the manliness to admit that California would be a great and flourishing State under American rule, and increase in population much faster than the Mexicans could hope for.

We were three weeks running down to Mazatland, and without a serious disaster. There were several of our national ships lying there, the town being in possession of the Americans. We were boarded before we dropped anchor, but the pass of Commodore Stockton was respected, so we entered the inner harbor, where we were secure from southwesters, and found ourselves close to the town, and the United States flag floating over all the public buildings and presidio.

The next day Lewey and I went on shore for a visit, but there were so many men-of-war's men and marines encountered, none too sober, that we did not care to remain but a short time. We learned that there was an English clipper bark, the Helena, of London, Captain Henry Thornton, lying in the outer harbor, all loaded, and ready to sail in a few days for England. By some means the vessel was permitted by the naval authorities to take in a cargo of logwood in spite of Mazatland being blockaded. How it was accomplished I never knew, but suppose through favor.

Just as we were ready to return to our vessel Captain Thornton, a large, fine-looking, gentlemanly person came to the landing, in company with the master of the schooner California. We were introduced, and requested the privilege of taking passage in the Helena for London, the most expeditious manner of returning home for Lewey and myself. Captain Thornton invited us to go on board with him, and see what accommodations he had, and whether they would suit us. We did so, Captain Cooper making one of the party. While being pulled to the vessel by four apprentices of the bark, Captain Cooper was pleased to say so many kind words in our behalf that Captain Thornton became quite affable, and stated we could certainly go with him if we were satisfied with such state rooms as he was able to place at our disposal, and even consented to take Jack, the dog, without extra charge, as he liked animals as well as ourselves.

The Helena was only about six hundred tons burden, and as handsome a model as the Admittance, but she carried more men, a crew of thorough sailors, and four apprentices, one of the latter being the only son of the owner of the vessel, yet he was treated just like the rest of the lads, no better and no worse, and did not presume to put on airs to his messmates on account of his parent's wealth.

We found that there were two large, vacant staterooms, much better than we hoped for, and while supping with Captain Thornton, agreed to his terms for passage, only two hundred dollars each, which was quite reasonable, and we thought ourselves lucky to secure such quarters. We had money enough to afford luxuries, and had no idea of doing seaman's duty while homeward bound.

The next day we transferred our luggage and boxes of minerals to the Helena, stowed everything out of sight so as not to excite comment, went on shore and paid our passage money to the consignees, purchased a supply of cigars, tobacco, and other luxuries that would prove acceptable, and the following day the Helena up anchor, and we stood to the southerd, with a fresh breeze from the northwest, and the best wishes of all the naval officers we had met. Captain Cooper remained on board until the last moment, and then bit his maimed hand, and bade us good-by. We never saw the gallant old gentleman again. He died in California some years ago, respected and loved by all who knew him.

I have not the space to relate many incidents of our voyage home. It was a lazy life Lewey and I led, with nothing to do, able to sleep at night, and not obliged to turn out to reef topsails or furl them. We had a good crew, nice mates, and a very dignified and jolly captain. That is, he was clever and kind, but knew his position and maintained it, except on Saturday nights, when he threw off his reserve, and over a bowl of punch told stories, sang songs, toasted sweethearts and wives, and poked fun at Lewey and myself because we were French and Yankee. We did not drink as much as suited his ideas of a jolly time, but the master could take our portion and never grumble, so we got along very well. On this vessel grog was served out to the men at eight bells (noon) every day, and a stiff tot was also given every time topsails were reefed. To keep from rusting once in a while Lewey and I would lend a hand in taking in sail off Cape Horn, and then insist that we were entitled to splice the mainbrace like the rest. The steward always allowed our claim, and we would pass the liquor over to some of the old men-of-war's men, much to their delight.

On the whole it was a pleasant passage. We had the usual amount of rough and cold weather off Cape Horn, but there was always a fire in the cabin, so we did not mind it much. Our vessel was fast, the winds favorable, and we soon left the Pacific Ocean, entered the Atlantic, and headed north, and on the first day of June we sighted Land's End, took a pilot, and arrived at the entrance gate of London Dock three days afterward.

Lewey and I found modest but convenient lodgings near Mile End, and as soon as we were settled sold our gold for just ten thousand five hundred pounds, and when we came to exchange all of our funds for English money we were worth about thirty-two thousand dollars each, not a bad fortune for two adventurous boys, who had started in life, with but little money they could call their own, at San Diego.

Then came up a serious question. We had tried not to think on that subject, and as just often as it disturbed our minds we had pushed the phantom one side. It was this — how soon before Lewey and I must part? We knew that we had got to separate, but each dreaded to allude to the matter, and so we would think of past adventures, sigh, and go and take a long walk, enjoying the sights of London, which we saw for the first time, and under favorable auspices, for Captain Thornton was our guide and councillor in all things, and it was by his advice that we deposited our money in a safe bank, so that we could not be deprived of it by robbery.

"Lewey," I asked one day, "when are you going home?"

"Ven you goes vid me, not afore," was the answer, and question him all that I might that was the only reply I received.

I reasoned with my friend, I talked to him earnestly, but go he would not unless I went with him, and so at last I consented to pay a visit to Havre-de-Grace, and see his father and mother. Then I wrote a long letter to my guardian and friends in Boston, the first for more than a year, and one morning Lewey and I took the steamer, and landed on French soil.

Lewey was not enthusiastic as he stepped on shore. He seemed a little dazed, dejected, and I think wished himself once more in California, careless and free. Sailors have such feelings, especially those who wander all over the face of the globe, and come home for a welcome, yet dread to meet it for some unaccountable reason, and the sense of isolation and dejection does not wear off for several days.

"Thom," said Lewey, as we walked up the dock toward a coffee-house, "if ve eber part dink of me as ve vere ven boys together, full of vigor and de true friendship vot skall neber die in mine heart. Remember de night at de foot of de mountains, ven you vas homesick and shed de tears, and I takes your votch, and hums de song to make you dink I vas happy, but I vas vusser den you, and now I is more like de crying den on dat dark night, and I vish ve vas back agin, and if you say de vord ve vill go, and mine friends vill know me no more."

We went into a café and called for some coffee and a bottle of vin ordinaire, and there I talked to my friend for an hour or more on the folly of returning to California, and by the time I had concluded we were both in tears, and Lewey had made up his mind to go and see his parents. They lived a short distance outside of the city, and calling a voiture he left me, promising to return as soon as possible.

I waited for him until nearly dark, passing the time the best way that I could, for it was dull work for me. Then he came in company with a tall, white-haired gentleman, who by his looks I knew was Lewey's father.

"I was a surprise," my friend said, "and nearly kill de mudder and de sister, sich a pretty girl, and vill do just for you, and if you vill fall in love and marry her, I happy can be."

"Speak French, Louis," said the father. "Remember I am not an English scholar like you and your companion."

I was glad the gentleman did not understand my friend, for his speech made me blush, it being the first intimation I had received from Lewey that he owned a sister. In fact she was so small when he left home for a wandering life that he had not considered her of the slightest consequence, but now, when he returned, and saw what a beautiful girl she was, he began to feel proud of her.

General Artenato, my friend's father, a soldier who commanded one of the forts of the city, gave me a cordial welcome, and an invitation to take up my residence at his chateau, three miles from the town, and on a bluff that overlooked the ocean and English Channel. As the request was not one of courtesy alone, but sincere in every respect, I complied. Jack and I entered the carriage, a porter looking after our luggage, and we were soon at the house, one of the most imposing and costly chateaus that I saw on the road.

General Artenato had so many questions to ask the son about his travels, that I did not interrupt their conversation. It was evident that the wandering sailor boy had been forgiven, and eccentricities forgotten. He had suffered enough hardships without now being taken to task for his folly. Lewey had spoken of me in terms of praise, I could see that by the deference with which his father treated me, and his desire that I should feel quite at my ease in his dignified presence; but when I was presented to the mother and daughter, and the former put her arms around my neck and kissed me, I knew that she was laboring under the impression that I had acted the part of guardian angel to her boy, and brought him home safe and good through my example. This was very flattering to me, and I did not deem it wise to undeceive her, since a very pretty little girl, just seventeen years of age, recently returned from a convent school, gave me her hand in the most confiding manner, and then blushed at her boldness, but still she did not fail to steal a timid look at my face to see what kind of man her brother's friend was like, and as she raised her dark eyes they met my glance of admiration, and then I flushed, and acted more like a school-boy, than a person who had seen so much of the world. This exhibition of modesty on my part so delighted Lewey that he laughed, and said, just to give me confidence, speaking to his relatives in French,—

"I have seen my American friend under all kinds of difficulties, as he danced with Mexican senoritas, when he pretended to save the lives of young girls, and demanded kisses in return for his trouble, but this is the first time that I ever knew him to blush," and then he laughed, and his mother chided him for his rudeness, while the young lady walked to the window and looked out upon the sea, and probably wondered why sailors were so careless of their reputations, and bold toward women. The general did not appear to think that a few kisses were of much account, for like a real Frenchman he asked,—

"Are the young ladies of California very beautiful?"

"Beautiful?" echoed Lewey. "They are the handsomest women in the world, always excepting my mother and sister. Why, we were near marrying two young ladies, whose eyes were black as midnight, and hair trailed on the ground when they walked, and they loved us very dearly too, but a wish to return home kept us free."

Lewey's sister appeared to have heard all that she desired, for she left the apartment, and I was glad of it, if my friend was to continue the conversation in the same strain.

I was shown to my room, made some changes in my dress, and while I was thus engaged Lewey joined me.

"Thom, old friend," he asked, "vot does you dink of dat sister of mine?"

He always spoke English to me when we were alone, because it was more convenient, and he really thought that his Anglo Saxon speech was better than his French.

"She is very handsome," I said, and that appeared to give him much pleasure.

"I dink dat she is good as she is booful. Now if you von't act like a great fool you can marry her, and den vot a nice time ve could hab here. No more vanderin's, no more sea life, and vid money enough to lib on, vot more could you desire?"

But just at this moment the dinner-bell rang, and we went down stairs, and I had the honor of escorting Mademoiselle Rose to the salle à manger;

and sat by her side all through the dinner. She was a little shy of me at first, but when she did find courage the questions came from her mouth quite as fast as I could answer them. I told her all about Lewey's friendship, how we had clung to each other for more than four years, our adventures in California, the persecutions we had endured at the hands of Antonio Sanchos and his brothers, the battles we had witnessed and participated in, the wild Indians we had killed, the ladies whose lives we had saved at the risk of our own, but not one word of the love-making or kissing her brother had alluded to.

In fact I became so eloquent under the influence of a single glass of champagne that I forgot there was any one present to listen to me except the young lady, and when I happened to look up, and saw that father, mother, son, and daughter were paying strict attention to what I said, broke down, and suddenly ceased speaking, too much embarrassed to finish my narrative in bad French, which no one had the impoliteness to laugh at.

"Please continue, monsieur," the young lady pleaded, but I had said enough for one night.

"You will relate some more adventures to me tomorrow?" mademoiselle asked, as we arose from the table, and she gave me a most fascinating smile.

"With great pleasure," I answered, "if your kind mother does not object."

"She will never refuse as long as you continue to praise my brother. He has always been her pet in spite of his wildness," and then we separated for the night, and I dreamed of Anita and Engracia, the Ranche Refugio, and the dead girls' faces appeared to reproach me for forgetting them so soon.

But the living and not the dead were in my mind the next morning when I awoke. For a long time after I had bathed and dressed I stood at the window of my chamber, and looked out upon the sea, and thought of the future, and asked myself a serious question, but the answer was not ready for some weeks. I struggled and fought against the ebb tide that was setting me toward a dangerous shoal, but the time came when I could no longer resist, and then the flood came, and drifted me into the harbor of happiness, to the entire satisfaction of Lewey, his parents, and dear little sister.

I do not know how it came about. Perhaps Rose loved me, like Desdemona, for the dangers through which I had passed, or because of the attachment of her brother, and his desire that I should be a brother in name as well as feeling. I only realized that one day she placed her hand in mine, and said that she was happy in the love of an honest man, and then there was a year of paradise, and such bliss as rarely falls to the lot of us poor mortals.

Then there came a black cloud, and I saw a pale, wan face, a faint smile, felt a little kiss on my lips, and knew no more for many weeks, for there was a blank in my life. When reason returned the first person I saw was Lewey, seated at my bedside, holding one of my hands, and showing the compassion he felt in his expressive eyes, while Jack was lying on the floor and regarding me with mute looks of pity, such as only a faithful dog can show for one it loves.

"Thom, my brudder," Lewey whispered, "you vill be a man now dat you is most vell?"

I could not reply, but turned my face to the wall, and tears fell from my eyes in torrents as my thoughts went back to the past.

"Do you remember de old times in California," Lewey said, very softly, "ven ve vas free from care, always in de mischief, and inclined to dink dat dings vas rough for us? Yet ve alvays come out on de top, because de good God directed all for de best. He has done so in dis case. It is hard for you, and de rest of us, but He ordered it, and ve must not repine."

Some weeks afterward I was enabled to leave my chamber, a prematurely old young man, bent and weak with grief. Every one was very patient with me and kind, but I could no longer remain where so many things reminded me of my lost wife and child. I returned to Boston, settled up affairs with my guardian, and for eight years traveled in every part of the globe. The wound healed at last, but the scar remains.

In one corner of the cemetery at Havre is a small, white marble monument, bearing the simple inscription, "ROSE AND HER SON." It tells its own story more eloquently than words. Kind hands on each anniversary of death place upon the cold marble a wreath of lilies, emblematical of the life of the dead when living. God must have been merciful to her, she was so good.

OPIE READ'S NOVELS

HANDSOME NEW EDITIONS
OF
Mr. Read's Famous Stories

It is perhaps because Opie Read writes *of* the people and *for* the people that his books are more and more in demand each year, and this popular-priced edition of his **Exclusive Copyright Works** will meet a want that has become almost a necessity.

"Turkey Egg" Griffin
The Harkriders   The Starbucks
The Carpetbagger (Dramatized)
The Jucklins (Dramatized)
Old Ebenezer
My Young Master
A Kentucky Colonel
Len Gansett
On the Suwanee River
The Wives of the Prophet
A Tennessee Judge
The Colossus
Emmett Bonlore

This new edition is full-size 12mo, printed on special stock, and substantially bound. These 14 titles embrace the cream of Mr. Read's writings, and will be a valuable acquisition to any library, for the appearance and genuine worth will give purchasers thorough satisfaction.

Bound uniformly in vellum de luxe cloth, each case stamped in two colors, per copy, ... **75c**

For sale everywhere, or sent, postpaid, on receipt of price, by
LAIRD & LEE, Publishers, 263-265 Wabash Ave., **CHICAGO**

UNIVERSITY OF CALIFORNIA LIBRARY
BERKELEY

8 Nov '45

Return to desk from which borrowed.
This book is DUE on the last date stamped below.

FEB 13 1980
FEB 4 1980

23 AUG '54 JD

REC. CIR. MAY 4 1981

MATH.-STAT.
LIBRARY

SEP 17 1954

REC'D LD
APR 28 '64 -4 PM

LD 21-100m-9,'48(B399s16)476

914660

THE UNIVERSITY OF CALIFORNIA LIBRARY

www.ingramcontent.com/pod-product-compliance
Lightning Source LLC
Chambersburg PA
CBHW020122020526
44111CB00049B/990